Nursing and the Law:
Trends and Issues

Kammie Monarch, RN, MS, JD

AMERICAN NURSES
ASSOCIATION

WASHINGTON, D.C.

Library of Congress Cataloging-in-Publication Data

Monarch, Kammie, 1961–
  Nursing and the law; trends and issues / Kammie Monarch
    p. Cm.
  Includes index.
  ISBN 1-55810-175-6
    1. Nursing—Law and legislation—United States.   I. Title.

KF2915.N8 M66 2002
344.73′0414—dc21

Published by
American Nurses Publishing
600 Maryland Avenue, SW
Suite 100 West
Washington, D.C. 20024-2571

ISBN 1-55810-175-6

NL22   1.5M   02/02

Acknowledgments

No project like this comes to fruition without the assistance, guidance, and support of many people. Had it not been for people who willingly shared their perspectives and insights this book would never have been written. Now that the first edition has been completed, I must extend my thanks to a number of friends and colleagues who helped me. Specifically, I offer my thanks and sincere appreciation to Lana Bolhouse, Michael H. Brady, Winifred Carson, Ann Cary, Christine deVries, Charles Green, Patrice Greenawalt, Carolyn Lewis, Linda Minich, Barry Nance, Stephanie Reed, Barbara Sapin, Jan Jones Schenk, Mary Smolenski, Margretta Madden Styles, Leslie Uriss, Marjorie Vanderbilt, Norma Wallace, Teresa Welch, Susan Wilburn, Susan Whittaker, and Rosanne O'Connor and the staff at the American Nurses Publishing Company for their contributions as these chapters were written and revised. This work is better and more complete because of the fingerprints left by each of you.

To my family: words cannot adequately express my thankfulness for each of you. In spite of your worries, and your hectic days you seem to always be there encouraging, and supporting me. Mom, your telephone calls and e-mails continue to reassure and motivate me to do my best work. Dad, your "I think I can" spirit has rubbed off and works to keep me focused.

Again, to each of you, "Thank you."

As well, I would like to acknowledge the considerable contributions and insights from the people who reviewed this material, either in its earliest form as a book proposal or all or parts of early manuscripts. They were: Leonore L. Boris, BSN, MS, RN, JD; Mary Bowen, RN, DNS, CNAA JD; Suzanne E. Collins, RN, MPH, PhD, JD; Gail Day, MSN, CS-P/MH, PhD; Diane Dubay, BS, MBA, RN; Karen L. Elberson, RN, PhD; Jo-Ann Kamenick , MBA, MSN, RN; Lolly Lockhart, RN, PhD; Bich Nguyen, JD; Deborah L. Phillips, RN, JD; Terri R. Roberts, RN, JD; Linda A. Simunek, RN, PhD, JD; Yolanda G. Smith, RN, MSN, CCRN; Angelic Winters, BSN, JD; and Karen Worthington, MS, RN, COHN-S.

§

To Levi

May your life's work be as fulfilling and gratifying as mine is proving to be.

§

Table of Contents

Introduction

Nurses spend their educational experiences learning how to care for individual patients, their significant others, and groups of patients in a variety of settings. Great care and attention is given to instilling the knowledge, skills, and abilities that are needed to practice safely. Throughout the educational process, students are reminded that the nursing profession is ever changing and that opportunities for profession-long learning need to be seized to ensure that one's knowledge base remains current and that patients receive care consistent with the prevailing standard of care. The same is true with regard to the legal aspects of nursing practice, and little time is spent familiarizing nurses with the U.S. legal system. Accordingly, this book seeks to introduce nurses and other interested readers to the wide variety of legal issues faced by nurses.

As health care professionals, nurses continue to refine the skills that they were introduced to as students, acquire new skills, and begin to broaden and deepen their knowledge base within their chosen specialty. Along the way, nurses learn that outcomes are not always positive for patients or for nurses themselves. At times, those adverse events carry with them legal ramifications. These ramifications can be career ending for nurses, and life ending for patients.

Because of the potential legal consequences associated with the care that nurses provide, it is imperative that nurses know what to expect from the civil and criminal justices systems. Nurses also need to have a basic understanding about the legal implications associated with their failure to act consistently with the standard of care.

The twelve chapters that comprise this book seek to provide nurses with that foundational information, and non-nurses with information about the interaction between nurses and the criminal and civil justice systems in the United States.

Chapter 1 introduces the reader to the U.S. judicial system. An overview of the federal and state judicial systems is given, as well as discussion about pursuing health care related claims in the United States.

Chapter 2 focuses on nursing as a regulated profession. The role and responsibilities of state boards of nursing and the National Council of State Boards of Nursing are identified. In addition, this chapter contains a detailed discussion about the model nurse practice acts proffered by the American Nurses Association and the National Council of State Boards of Nursing. Currently, this is the only publication that compares and contrasts the model practice acts to any significant degree. The detailed discussion about the model practice acts is included in an attempt to better inform nurses about the key features of the document that constitutes the contract that nurses make with their licensing jurisdictions. As the chapter unfolds, the author notes gaps, inconsistencies, and trends in nurse practice acts, and this information can be used by nurses to amend currently codified nurse practice acts so that they are more comprehensive and address contemporary practice issues.

Chapter 3 concentrates on the civil litigation process and the role of the nurse in that process. Doctrines and terms used in civil litigation are introduced. Actions and omissions on the part of the nurse giving rise to civil litigation are also discussed. One of the unique features about this chapter is that the author has organized the actions and omissions using the nursing process. The result is that alleged failures and omission on the part of the nurse are categorized as either assessment, planning, implementation, or evaluation failures. The framework illustrates that liability can be imposed for actions and omissions that occur throughout the entire nursing process.

Chapter 4 continues to focus on the nurse as defendant. However, the criminal, rather than civil, litigation process is the context within which the nurse as defendant concept is addressed. This chapter profiles the criminal litigation process, associated terminology, and crimes for which nurses may be charged. Now, more than ever, nurses are finding themselves the focus of criminal investigations. Accordingly, this material has been included so that nurses know what to expect from the criminal litigation process, and to encourage nurses to practice in a way that honors societal expectations.

Chapter 5 explores some of the legal issues faced by nurses practicing as employees. The chapter begins by addressing some of the contemporary clinical issues nurses are encountering: abandonment, employment status, mandatory overtime, needlestick and sharps injuries, staffing, and whistleblower protection. Following the contemporary clinical issues discussion, federal and state laws protecting employees are identified.

Chapter 6 delves into a number of legal issues confronted by nurses practicing as independent contractors. As new practice opportunities continue to emerge, more and more nurses will find themselves practicing as independent contractors rather than employees. In anticipation of that change in employment status, the material in this chapter provides nurses with the information they need to execute independent contractor agreements. The terms usually incorporated into independent contractor agreements are delineated, and cases focusing on the liability of independent contractors are presented. The cases used in this chapter concern the actions of independent contractor-physicians because the case law in this area is composed of physician-independent contractors. However, the principles articulated by the courts that heard these cases are applicable to nurse-independent contractors, and indicate how nurse-independent contractor issues will likely be addressed in U.S. courts.

Chapter 7 shifts the employment status focus of the last two chapters, and discusses the legal issues encountered by nurse-educators. Liability associated with catalogs, students with disabilities, dismissing students, providing students with a safe environment, warning third parties, clinical experiences, and the privacy of academic records is presented. One of the unique features of this publication is contained in this chapter, and that is discussion regarding the intellectual property issues nurse-educators, as well as nurses practicing in other settings, are encountering.

Chapter 8 explores the legal issues associated with the nurse's role as administrator. In this chapter, a number of doctrines that impact the nurse administrator are identified, including the captain of the ship doctrine; charitable, governmental, and sovereign immunity; corporate negligence; res ipsa loquitur; and vicarious liability. Following that, a number of causes of action are delineated: failure to protect patients, negligent supervision, wrongful termination, and right to privacy violations. The causes of action listed in this chapter have legal implications for nurse-administrators, and have the potential of subjecting nurse-administrators to disciplinary action.

Chapter 9 examines the legal issues associated with counseling patients. Most of the cases discussed in this chapter occurred in a psychiatric-mental health context, but the principles derived from these cases can be applied to other practice settings. In this chapter, breach of confidentiality is discussed, as well as the counselor's failure to warn third parties. In addition, sexual misconduct, improper hospitalization, failure to protect suicidal patients, improper medication administration, negligent patient supervision, negligent release and discharge, and third-party litigation are identified as possible sources of liability for those engaged in counseling activities.

Chapter 10 highlights the emerging sources of legal liability in managed care environments. Managed care has forever changed the way that most patients are treated and most health care professionals practice. The transition from a predominately fee-for-service payment system has been rocky; however, the escalating costs of providing health care services in the Unites States have slowed, and quality of care issues are being addressed. Along the way, managed care-related claims began to be filed. A number of those cases are included in this chapter to highlight some of the problems encountered with the implementation of managed care. The cases should also serve as a reminder to health care providers that courts continue to hold health care providers accountable for the care that is given and denied to patients.

Also included in Chapter 10 is a lengthy discussion regarding the work of registered nurses from around the United States, referred to as the Managed Care Working Group, convened by the American Nurses Association to address issues and concerns about managed care as a health services delivery mechanism. The Managed Care

Working Group met over a number of months, and made recommendations that were adopted by the ANA Board of Directors. However, the work of this group was never publicly disseminated. It is included here so that the wisdom and insight of the members of the Managed Care Working Group can be shared with others.

Chapter 11 explores the concept of credentialing. The multiple uses of the term credentialing are presented, as well as the purpose of credentialing mechanisms. In addition, credentialing activities engaged in by the nursing profession, and the credentialing activities engaged in by health care organizations, are identified. This chapter points out that as practice opportunities continue to expand, and as advanced practice nurses continue to provide primary care services to many individuals, the organizations in which they practice will continue to require that they submit evidence of competency. The process of gathering and reviewing the competency data is reviewed, and clinical privileging case law is discussed. The author notes that the clinical privileging case law has developed to a significant extent around the clinical privileging requests made by physicians. Therefore, some physician-focused cases are used to illustrate the way in which the judicial system handled the credentialing issue. Cases involving advanced practice nurses have also been included so that readers can see how courts have handled the clinical privileging requests made by nurses.

Chapter 12 points out that although nurses have an obligation to practice consistent with standard of care, they also have an obligation to practice ethically. The author acknowledges that an in-depth discussion regarding the ethical aspects of practice is beyond the scope of this manuscript, but outlines introductory information so that nurses have a framework within which they can deal with the ethical issues they encounter. To that end, the chapter compares and contrasts laws and ethics, identifies the *Code of Ethics for Nurses*, and discusses some of the ethical issues encountered by nurses practicing as employees, independent contractors, educators, administrators, counselors, case managers, and credentialed health care providers.

Every effort has been made to include contemporary issues and case law that illustrates how courts deal with the issues identified in this manuscript. Common themes, consistencies, and differences among jurisdictions have been identified. However, like nursing, the law continues to change, and variations exists from state to state. Consequently, nurses who are facing a specific legal issue need to seek the advice and guidance of a competent licensed attorney to ensure that the specific legal issues faced by that nurse are addressed according to that jurisdiction's statutory scheme and case law.

About the Author

Kammie Monarch is a master's prepared registered nurse and attorney. She is currently on staff at the American Nurses Association. She also maintains a private law practice in Oklahoma City, Oklahoma, and Washington, D.C., focusing on corporate, employment, administrative, and professional negligence matters.

As a nurse, Kammie practiced as a pediatric and neonatal intensive care nurse at Children's Hospital in Oklahoma City, Oklahoma. She later served as the Director for Nursing Development at Children's. After graduating from law school, Kammie joined the trial practice firm of Brady, Schaulat, and Falsetti, in Oklahoma City, Oklahoma, and continues to be associated with that firm.

In Washington, D.C., Kammie has created the Nightingale Foundation, a private, nonprofit, charitable organization dedicated to providing nurses with litigation-related resources. She plans to use a portion of the proceeds from the sale of this book to establish the Nightingale Fund. The Nightingale Fund will be used exclusively to assist nurses with personally incurred litigation expenses.

Table of Cases

Mercil v. Mathers, 517 N.W. 2d 328 (Mn. 1994).

Downey v. Mitchell, 835 S.W. 2d 554 (Mo. 1992).

Mathias v. St. Catherine's Hospital, Incorporated, 569 N.W. 2d 332 (Wi. 1997).

Vassey v. Burch, 262 S.E. 2d 865 (N.C. 1980).

Alvis v. Henderson, 592 N.E. 2d 678 (Il. 1992).

Bell v. Western Pennsylvania Hospital, 437 A. 2d 978 (Pa. 1982).

Anderson v. St. Francis-St. George Hospital, 671 N.E. 2d 225 (Oh. 1996).

Vidana v. Garfield Medical Center, Los Angeles County Superior Court No. GC011-608, August 16, 1995.

Adams v. Krueger, et al, 856 P. 2d 864 (Il. 1993).

Fein v. Permanente Medical Center, 695 P. 2d 674 (Ca. 1985).

Gold v. United Health Service, Incorporated, 98 LWUSA 51 (January 11, 1999).

Brookover v. Mary Hitchcock Memorial Hospital, 893 F. 3d 411 (1st Cir. 1990).

Gordon v. Willis Knighton Medical Center, 661 So. 2d 91 (La. 1997).

Pellerin v. Humedicenter, Incorporated, 696 So. 2d 590 (La. 1997).

Odom v. State Department of Health and Hospitals, 733 So. 2d 590 (La. 1999).

Chin v. Barnabus Medical Center, 734 A. 2d 778 (N.J. 1999).

Fieux v. Cardiovascular and Thoracic Clinic, et al, 978 P. 2d 429 (Or. 1999).

Miles v. Box Butte County, 489 N.W. 2d 829 (Ne. 1992).

Garcia v. United States, 697 F. Supp. 1570 (Co. 1988).

Borretti v. Wiscomb, 930 F. 2d 1150 (6th Cir. 1991).

Scribner v. Hillcrest Medical Center, 855 P. 2d 437 (Ok. 1992).

Haney v. Alexander, 323 S.E. 2d 430 (N.C. 1977).

Ahrens v. Katz, 575 F. Supp. 1108 (Ga. 1979).

Kenyon v. Hammer, 688 P. 2d 96 (Az. 1979).

Doe v. Ohio State University Hospital Clinics, 663 N.E. 2d 1369 (Oh. 1995).

NKC Hospitals, Inc. v. Anthony, 849 S.W. 564 2d (Ky 1993).

Deese v. Carol City County Hospital, 416 S.E. 2d 127 (Ga. 1992).

Sparks v. St. Lukes Regional Medical Center, 768 P. 2d 768 (Id. 1989).

Northern Trust Company v. Louis A. Weiss Memorial Hospital, 493 N.E. 2d 6 (Il. 1986).

Chiricosta v. Winthrop-Bren, 635 N.E. 2d 1019 (Il. 1994).

McClain v. Glenwood Regional Medical Center, 602 So. 2d 240 (La. 1992).

Koeniger v. Eckrich, 442 N.W. 2d 600 (S.D. 1988).

Parker v. Southwest Louisiana Hospital Association, 540 So. 2d 1270 (La. 1989).

McMullen v. Ohio State University Hospitals, 725 N.E. 2d 1117 (Oh. 2000).

Eversole v. Oklahoma Hospital Founders Association, 818 P. 2d 456 (Ok. 1991).

Lama v. Borras, 16 F. 3d 473 (1st Cir. 1994).

Candler General Hospital, Incorporated v. McNorrill, 354 S.E. 2d 872 (Ga. 1987).

Gould v. N.Y. City Health and Hospitals, 490 N.Y.S. 2d 87 (N.Y. 1985).

Griffin v. The Methodist Hospital, 948 S.W. 2d 72 (Tx. 1997).

Smith v. Cote, 513 A. 2d 341 (N.H. 1986).

Duplan v. Harper, 188 F. 3d 1195 (Ok. 1999).

Reynolds v. Swigert, 697 P. 2d 504 (N.M. 1979).

Manning v. Twin Falls Clinic and Hospitals, 830 P. 2d 1185 (Id. 1992).

Meuser v. Rocky Mountain Hospital, 685 P. 2d 776 (Co. 1984).

Bigtown Nursing Home v. Newman, 461 S.W. 2d 195 (Tx. Civ. App. 1970).

Mock v. Allen, Alabama, No. 1980985, June 30, 2000.

Martinmaas v. Engelmann, South Dakota, No. 2000, June 28, 2000.

Ferris v. County of Kennebec, 44 F. Supp. 2d 62 (Me. 1998).

Sandejar v. Alice Physicians and Surgeons Hospital, 555 S.W. 2d 879 (Tx. 1977).

Skar v. City of Lincoln, 599 F. 2d 253 (8th Cir. 1979).

Chapter 4, The Nurse as the Accused in Criminal Litigation

Miranda v. Arizona, 384 U.S. 436 (1966), *rehearing denied*, 385 U.S. 890 (1966).

State of New Jersey v. Laura Winter, 477 A.2d 323 (N.J. 1984).

Somera. In Creighton, H. 1986. *Law Every Nurse Should Know*, 5th ed. Philadelphia: W.B. Saunders; pp. 231–232.

Moore v. State, 64 Ga. 449 (1879).

Records v. Aetna, 294 N.J. Super. 463 (App. Div. 1996).

People of the State of New York v. Chaitin, 462 N.Y.S. 2d 61 (N.Y.S. Ct. App. Div. 1983).

State v. Lora, 515 P.2d 1086 (Ks. 1973).

Samuels v. Southern Baptist Hospital, 594 So. 2d 571 (La. 1992).

Chapter 5, The Nurse as Employee

Husher v. Commissioner of Education of the State of New York, 591 N.Y.S. 2d 99 (N.Y. 1992).

Hainer v. American Medical International, Inc., 492 S.E. 2d 103 (S.C. 1997).

Bosch v. Perry, 311 S.E. 2d 481 (Ga. 1983).

Czubinsky v. Doctor's Hospital, 139 Cal. App. 3d 361 (Ca. 1983).

Kirk v. Mercy Hospital Tri-County, 851 S.W. 2d 617 (Mo. 1993).

Hansen v. Caring Professionals, Inc., No. 1-95-2346 (Appeal from the Circuit Court of Cook County, February 20, 1997).

Rhoney v. Fele, No. COA98-1299 (N.C. Ct. App. August 17, 1999)

Burk v. Sage Products, 747 F. Supp. 285 (Pa. 1990)

Willits v. Superior Court of Santa Clara County and Health Dimensions, Inc., 24 Cal.Rptr. 2d 348 (1993).

Blythe v. Radiometer America, Inc., Community Medical Center and Michael Biggins, 866 P. wd 218 (Mt. 1993).

Vallery v. Southern Baptist Hospital, 630 So. 2d 861 (La. 1993).

Siemon v. Becton Dickinson and Company, 632 N.E. 2d 603 (Oh. 1993).

Doe v. Aliquippa Hospital Association, 1994 U.S. District Court, LEXIS 21284.

Doe v. Yale, 1994 Connecticut Superior Court, LEXIS 2621.

Gasper v. Bruton, 513 F. 2d 843 (10th Cir. 1975).

Carter v. Anderson Memorial Hospital, 325 S.E. 2d 78 (S.C. 1985).

Falvo v. Owasso Independent School District No. I-011, et al, 229 F. 3d 956 (10th Cir. 2000).

Chapter 8, The Nurse Practicing as Administrator

Ravi v. Williams, 536 So. 2d 1374 (Al. 1988).

Fanklin v. Gupta, 567 A. 2d 524 (Md. 1990).

President and Directors of Georgetown College v. Hughes, 130 F. 2d 810 (D.C. 1942).

Hyde v. University of Michigan Board of Regents, 393 N.W. 2d 847 (Mi. 1986).

Jones v. Baptist Memorial Hospital-Golden, 735 So. 2d 1099 (Ms. 1999).

Darling v. Charleston Community Memorial Hospital, 211 N.E. 2d 6 (Il. 1986).

St. John's Hospital and School of Nursing, Inc. v. Chapman, 434 P. 2d 160 (Ok. 1967).

Coleman v. Rice, No. 94-CT-00807-SCT.

Beeck v. Tuscon General Hospital, 500 P. 2d 1153 (Az. 1972).

Washington v. Washington Hospital Center, 579 A. 2d 177 (D.C. 1990).

Valentin v. La Societe Francaise De Bienfaaisance Mutuelle De Los Angeles, 172 P.2d 359 (Ca. 1946).

Stelkoff v. St. John's Mercy Health Systems, 218 F. 3d 858 (8th Cir. 2000).

Page v. Goodman-Wade Enterprises. In Willmann, J. 1998. *Annotated Guide to the Texas Nurse Practice Act,* 3rd ed. Austin, TX: Texas Nurses Association; pp. 16–17.

Haddle v. Garrison, No. 97-1472, December 14, 1998.

Trombley v. Southwestern Vermont Medical Center, No. 97-320 (Vt. July, 1999).

Union Pacific Railway v. Botsford, 141 U.S. 250 (1891).

Whalen v. Roe, 429 U.S. 589 (1977).

Tryon v. Colorado State Board of Nursing, 989 P. 2d 216 (Co. 1999).

Chapter 9, The Nurse as Counselor

Berger v. Sonneland, No. 18163-4-III, June 13, 2000.

Tarasoff v. The Regents of the University of California, 529 P.2d 334 (Ca. 1976).

McIntosh v. Milano, 403 A. 2d 500 (N.J. 1979).

Lipari v. Sears, Roebuck and Co., 497 F. Supp. 185 (Ne. 1980).

Hedlund v. Orange County, 194 Cal. Rptr. 805 (Ca. 1983).

Emerich, et al v. Philadelphia Center for Human Development, et al, No. J-253-96. November 25, 1998.

Brady et al v. Hopper, 570 F. Supp. 1333 (Co. 1983) and 751 F. 2d 329 (10th Cir. 1984).

Boynton v. Burglass, 590 So. 2d 446 (Fl. 1991).

Ermutlu v. McCorkle, et al, 416 S.E. 2d 792 (Ga. 1992).

Shaw v. Glickman, 415 A. 2d 625 (Md. 1980).

Thaper v. Zezulka, No. 97-1208. June 24, 1999.

Charleston v. Larson, 696 N.E. 793 (Il. 1998).

The U.S. Legal System 1

Introduction

Since the Constitutional Convention of 1787, the legal system of the United States has evolved. Congress and state legislatures continue to pass new laws and amend old ones. In addition, federal and state court judges continue to issue opinions that add to a growing body of U.S. law. This growing body of law is typically categorized as either state or federal law. State law is created by state legislatures, the state judiciary, and must be consistent with the constitution of each state. Federal law, on the other hand, is created by Congress, the federal judiciary, and must be consistent with the tenants of the U.S. Constitution. Some of the unique features of the U.S. Constitution, and federal and state law are discussed below.

The U.S. Constitution

Ratified in 1787, the U.S. Constitution delineates the powers of the executive, legislative, and judicial branches of government and is the supreme law of the United States. The U.S. Constitution grants exclusive authority to the federal government with regard to the postal system, citizenship, immigration, naturalization, interstate commerce, federal taxation, maintaining an army, and war. All state constitutions, statutes, regulations, and judicial decisions must be consistent with the principles contained in the U.S. Constitution.

Since adoption, the U.S. Constitution has been amended 26 times. The first 10 of these amendments are referred to as the Bill of Rights. The *Bill of Rights* limits the power of the government by guaranteeing that individuals have freedom of speech, freedom of the press, freedom of religion, freedom to assemble peaceably, freedom from self-incrimination and double jeopardy, freedom from search and seizure, the right to a speedy and public criminal trial, freedom from cruel and unusual punishment, the right to bear arms, and the right to petition the government.

For nurses, the constitutional principles of substantive and procedural due process, and equal protection must be complied with when disciplinary action is threatened or taken by the regulatory agency responsible for the practice of nursing—typically, the state board of nursing. Failure to adhere to constitutional mandates will work to nullify disciplinary action taken against the nurse.

Substantive due process guarantees that laws be reasonable, not arbitrary. Substantive due process issues are raised when a law limits the liberty of all persons engaged in some activity. For nurses, substantive due process questions can be raised when regulatory bodies governing the practice of nursing issue rules or regulations that allegedly arbitrarily limit some ability of all persons subject to the agency to engage in a particular activity. Where a regulatory agency's rule or regulation limits a fundamental right of the nurse, it will be upheld only if it is necessary to promote a compelling governmental interest. Fundamental rights include the right to travel, right to privacy, right to vote, the freedom of speech, freedom of the press, freedom to peaceably assemble, freedom of religion, and freedom of expression.

Nurses, like other U.S. citizens, possess not only substantive due process rights, but they also have procedural due process rights. Procedural due process is addressed in the fifth amendment of the U.S. Constitution and guarantees that the government will not take a person's life, liberty, or property without due process of law. Due process contemplates a fair procedure that provides the accused with an opportunity to present objections to any proposed action. For the nurse facing disciplinary action, procedural due process requires that the nurse be afforded a meaningful opportunity to present evidence in an effort to vindicate him- or herself.

In addition to the substantive and procedural due process right, nurses possess a right to equal protection. *Equal protection* guarantees that similarly situated individuals will be treated similarly. Where similarly situated individuals are not treated similarly because of race, national origin, or alienage, the action taken by the government will be readily invalidated. Where an agency action compromises an individual's fundamental rights, that action will be invalidated on equal protection grounds. For nurses, equal protection issues arise when governmental action typically, by the state board of nursing, has the effect of treating similarly situated registered individuals dis-similarly.

Equal protection issues also arise in schools of nursing. In *Mississippi University for Women v. Hogan*,[1] the Mississippi University for Women, a state nursing school, had a women-only admissions policy until the U.S. Supreme Court deemed the policy to be a violation of the equal protection clause of the U.S. Constitution. Prior to the ruling by the U.S. Supreme Court, male students could audit courses at the women's only school, but had to travel to a coeducational nursing school if they wanted to obtain credits for the courses they successfully completed. In reaching their decision, the Supreme Court Justices noted that similarly situated female students did not have to bear that kind of burden, and that the disparity violated the equal protection rights of the male students.

Federal Law

Article 1 of the United States Constitution vests all legislative powers in the United States Congress. Article 2 delineates the powers of the executive branch of government, and Article 3 outlines the powers of the judicial branch of government. According to Article 1, Congress has the power to take action in 24 areas. In addition to these Article 1 powers (listed in a sidebar), Congress has the power to propose amendments to the Constitution. Article 5 describes the process that must be used when proposing constitutional amendments.

Article 2 of the U.S. Constitution identifies the role and responsibilities of the U.S. President. According to Article 2, the President is the Commander-in-chief of the U.S. Army and Navy, and of the militia of the States. In addition, Presidential power extends to eight major areas (see sidebar).

U.S. Constitution, Article 1: Congressional Powers

- Lay and collect taxes, duties, imposts, and excises
- Pay U.S. debts
- Provide for the common defense and general welfare of the United States
- Borrow money on U.S. credit
- Regulate commerce with foreign nations, among the states, and with Indian tribes
- Establish uniform naturalization and bankruptcy rules
- Coin money
- Regulate the value of money
- Fix the standard of weights and measures
- Establish post offices and post roads
- Promote the progress of science and useful arts
- Constitute tribunals inferior to the Supreme Court
- Define and punish piracies and felonies committed on the high seas
- Define and punish offenses against the law of nations
- Declare war
- Grant letters of marque and reprisal
- Make rules concerning captures on land and water
- Raise and support armies
- Provide and maintain a navy
- Make rules for the government and regulation of naval land and forces
- Provide for the calling forth of the militia
- Provide for organizing, arming, and disciplining the militia
- Exercise exclusive legislation within the seat of the U.S. government
- Make all laws that shall be necessary and proper for carrying out legislative powers of the U.S. Constitution

---

U.S. Constitution, Article 2: Presidential Powers

▮ Grant reprieves and pardons
▮ Make treaties, provided two-thirds of the Senate concur
▮ Nominate and appoint ambassadors, other public ministers and consuls, Supreme Court Justices, and all other U.S. officers
▮ Fill Senate vacancies
▮ Give to Congress state of the union information
▮ Recommend to Congress necessary and expedient measures to be taken
▮ Receive ambassadors and other public ministers
▮ Commission all U.S. officers

Article 3 of the U.S. Constitution delineates the judicial powers vested in the U.S. Supreme Court and in inferior courts ordained and established by Congress. According to Article 3, the judicial branch of government has power to act in all cases arising in 11 general areas (see sidebar).

In keeping with its constitutional mandate, Congress created a federal court system. Currently, there are 94 districts in the United States. Every state has at least one federal district court; California and New York have four each. For appellate purposes, 13 circuits have been identified. The circuit courts are courts of appeal hearing cases that have previously been decided by one of the U.S. district courts, and by many federal administrative agencies. Figure 1–1 indicates which states and territories belong to each circuit court.

U.S. Constitution, Article 3: U.S. Supreme Court Powers

▮ Law and equity
▮ Under the U.S. Constitution
▮ Under the laws and treaties of the United States
▮ With ambassadors, other public ministers, and consuls
▮ In admiralty and maritime jurisdiction
▮ Between a party and the United States
▮ Between two or more States
▮ Between a state and a citizen of another state
▮ Between citizens of different states
▮ Between citizens of the same state claiming lands under grants of different states
▮ Between a state or a citizen of the state and foreign states, citizens, or subjects

The numbers beside each state or territory indicate to which circuit the state or territory belongs.

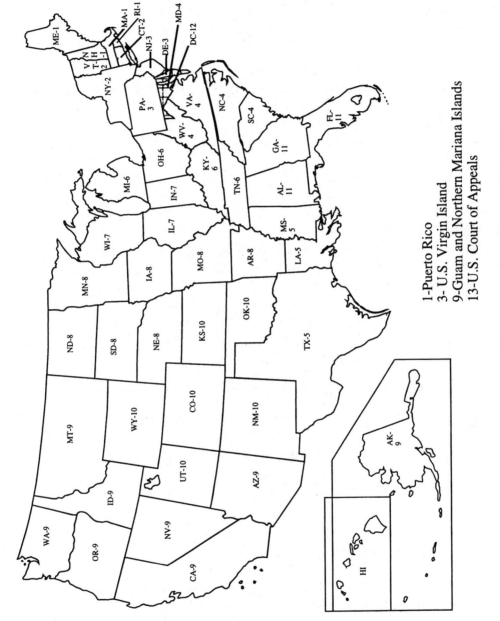

ME-1
MA-1
RI-1
CT-2
VT-2
NH-1
NY-2
NJ-3
DE-3
MD-4
DC-12
PA-3
WV-4
VA-4
NC-4
SC-4
FL-11
OH-6
KY-6
GA-11
MI-6
IN-7
TN-6
AL-11
WI-7
IL-7
MS-5
LA-5
AR-8
MN-8
IA-8
MO-8
OK-10
TX-5
ND-8
SD-8
NE-8
KS-10
CO-10
NM-10
MT-9
WY-10
UT-10
AZ-9
ID-9
NV-9
WA-9
OR-9
CA-9
AK-9
HI

1-Puerto Rico
3- U.S. Virgin Island
9-Guam and Northern Mariana Islands
13-U.S. Court of Appeals

F I G U R E   1 – 1   Thirteen Circuits by State and Territory

State Law

Every state has a state constitution that mirrors the U.S. Constitution. Typically, state constitutions grant the state legislature the authority to create and amend laws. Individuals elected to serve as state legislators do so for a specified period, and are elected by individuals who reside within specified geographic boundaries. State legislatures convene at regular but varying intervals, and work to pass laws that are needed within that particular state. Laws that are passed by both houses of the state legislature must be signed by that state's governor.

Administrative agencies, such as state boards of nursing, exist because the state legislature passed laws that created them and that charged the board with carrying out specific, agency-related legislative directives. Administrative agencies then promulgate rules and regulations that govern agency operations and individuals who are required to report to them.

Recently a Louisiana Court of Appeals, in *Aron D. Hemphill v. Louisiana State Board of Nursing*[2] determined that the class of individuals who are subject to the oversight of the State Board of Nursing is limited, and does not include nursing students. In *Hemphill*, Aron D. Hemphill was admitted to the School of Nursing at Southern University. Prior to commencing the clinical component of the curriculum, Aron was told that he needed to obtain approval from the State Board of Nursing. After a hearing, the Louisiana State Board of Nursing determined that, until he had achieved 2 years of continuous sobriety, and complied with the treatment regimen delineated by the Board, Aron could not begin or progress to the next clinical course, and that he could not request a hearing to progress to the next clinical course.

Approximately 2 months later, Aron filed a petition with the trial court seeking a review of the action taken by the Louisiana State Board of Nursing. The trial court affirmed the decision of the State Board of Nursing, and Aron appealed the trial court decision to a Louisiana Court of Appeals. Aron contended that the Louisiana State Board of Nursing was without authority to discipline because he was a student who had not applied for a license, nor did he already have a license issued by the Board of Nursing. The Court of Appeals agreed with Aron, and concluded that the Louisiana State Board of Nursing was without jurisdiction to take disciplinary action against him. As a result, the order issued by the Louisiana State Board of Nursing was deemed null and void.

Hemphill, as well as other cases, confirm that although most state laws are created by state legislators, there are laws that are created by state courts. State courts are established by a state, county, or city and are categorized as either trial courts, intermediate appellate courts, or final appellate courts. *Trial courts* are the setting in which most crimes are prosecuted and civil disputes are heard. Typically, issues such as broken contracts, family disputes, and other civil wrongs are heard in these settings, as are crimes like murder, robbery, kidnapping, and other felonious offenses. These courts are considered to be courts of general jurisdiction because a wide variety of cases are heard in these kinds of courts. Civil negligence and malpractice cases involving nurses are typically handled by trial courts with general jurisdiction. By contrast, there are trial courts with limited jurisdiction. These limited jurisdiction courts hear only traffic, juvenile, or small claims matters.

Cases decided by trial courts are usually contested by the losing party. In most states, an intermediate appellate court will hear the contested case. However, some contested matters may be appealed directly to that state's Supreme Court, without having to be heard by an intermediate appellate court. This may be the case for decisions made by administrative agencies that govern the professional practice of nursing in each state.

State Supreme Courts have the final say in matters involving state law and the state constitutions. Decisions issued by state Supreme Courts are not appealable to any other court, unless federal constitutional issues are involved. State Supreme Court decisions involving federal constitutional issues are appealable to the U.S. Supreme Court. Figure 1–2 illustrates the ways in which cases make their way to the U.S. Supreme Court.

Pursuing Health Care-Related Claims

Historically, patients have been required to pursue their medical malpractice or negligence causes of action in state courts rather than federal courts. However, in *Roberts v. Galen of Virginia, Inc.,* the U.S. Supreme Court recently determined that patients may sue under federal statute where a hospital transfers or discharges a patient too soon.[3] The federal law being reviewed by the Supreme Court Justices was the Emergency Medical Treatment and Active Labor Act (EMTALA).[4] Under EMTALA, a health care facility can be liable if it transfers or discharges an emergency room patient without first stabilizing the patient. The health care facility can also be liable if it fails to provide patients with appropriate medical screening to determine if an emergency condition exists.

In *Roberts*, a patient was transferred to another facility before the transferring hospital determined whether or not the woman's urinary tract infection responded to antibiotic therapy. Originally, the sixth circuit concluded that the patient could not sue unless she showed that the hospital had an improper motive in transferring her to another hospital. The U.S. Supreme Court disagreed with the sixth circuit, determining that EMTALA did not require an improper motive on the part of the health care facility.

The effect of *Roberts* is significant in that, in certain types of cases, it allows patients to avoid state law limitations on the amount of money that can be recovered in medical malpractice cases, and it works to hold hospitals liable for the actions of physicians and other providers who are not employees. In addition, EMTALA extends whistleblower protection to hospital employees who might have information that indicates that EMTALA violations have occurred.

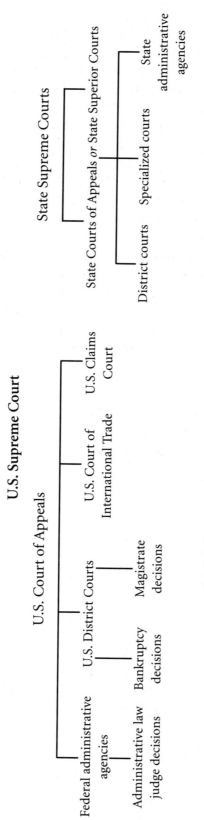

FIGURE 1–2 Pathways to the U.S. Supreme Court

Summary

The U.S. Constitution serves as the foundational document upon which the U.S. legal system is based. Although it has endured for more than 200 years, the U.S. legal system has continued to change. Consequently, it is important for nurses to be aware of current federal and state laws that affect their practice. Membership in a state nurses association may be the most effective means of keeping abreast of ongoing changes in state and federal laws. Federal legislative initiatives are tracked by the Government Affairs Department at the American Nurses Association, and the status of those initiatives are summarized in *Capital Update,* which is distributed to state nurses association members who subscribe to the newsletter. Subscription information is available at www.nursingworld.org.

Nurse Practice Acts, like other state laws, also change. These statutes delineate what nurses are permitted and prohibited from doing as licensed health care professionals. It is imperative that nurses understand the Nurse Practice Act under which he or she is practicing, and abide by the mandates incorporated in the Act. Failure to do so could result in the revocation of a nurse's license to practice nursing. Chapter 2 focuses on Nurse Practice Acts and their impact on nursing practice.

End Notes

1. 458 U.S. 718 (1982).
2. 713 So. 2d 1265 (La. 1998).
3. No. 97-53. January 13, 1999.
4. 42 U.S.C. 1395dd.

The Nurse as a Regulated Health Care Professional 2

Introduction

In each state, the District of Columbia, American Samoa, Guam, Northern Mariana Islands, Puerto Rico, and the Virgin Islands, the practice of nursing is regulated by a legislatively enacted Nurse Practice Act (NPA). Although each NPA is unique, most contain similar provisions. NPAs generally include a scope; a purpose; definitions; a description of the composition of the members of the Boards of Nursing (BON); powers and responsibilities of board members; requirements for initial licensure and licensure renewal; licensee responsibilities; protected terms, titles, and abbreviations; an approval process to be followed by nursing schools; a section identifying violations and penalties; a process and grounds for taking disciplinary action; a provision granting the BON the authority to seek emergency relief; sections identifying individuals and entities obligated to report practice act violations to the BON; exemptions, revenue, fees, and fines; a grandfathering and a severability clause; and a provision for repealing portions of the NPA.

NPAs, along with administrative rules, and the Administrative Procedures Act (APA) determine what nurses and other health care groups regulated by the BON (e.g., nurse aides and nursing schools) can and cannot do within that jurisdiction. Where members of the state board of nursing determine that the NPA has been violated, disciplinary action will be taken. Disciplinary action may consist of requiring a nurse to attend educational courses or may include the revocation of that nurse's license to practice. For nursing schools, violations may result in the closure of the offending school.

Every nurse needs to know what the NPA says about the practice of nursing in that jurisdiction. The American Nurses Association (ANA) and the National Council of State Boards of Nursing (NCSBN) recognized this several years ago and published Model Practice Acts (MPAs). These MPAs were written in an attempt to provide guidance in the midst of rapidly changing practice, legislative, and regulatory environments. Differences between these two MPAs will be discussed, and provisions that are or should be part of all practice acts will be identified. Following that, the APA and the disciplinary action process will be discussed. Finally, trends that will likely impact the practice of nursing from a regulatory perspective will be explored.

Nurse Practice Act

Purpose

NPAs are enacted to regulate the practice of nursing so that the health, safety, and welfare of citizens is promoted and protected. Usually, the *purpose* section of an NPA identifies the legislative intent behind NPA enactment, the licensee groups to be regulated, and the agency responsible for regulating licensees. The agency charged with regulating licensees is usually referred to as the Board of Nursing (BON). Most BONs are independent agencies; others are part of a larger health professions agency. For example, the Oklahoma Board of Nursing is an independent state agency, whereas the Board of Nursing for the Commonwealth of Virginia is part of the Department of Health Professions. Whatever the organizational structure, the charge to BONs is the same: to protect the public. To protect the public, BONs administer and implement the NPA enacted in that jurisdiction.

Definitions

This is the most important section in any NPA because it is here that parameters are delineated, and the meaning of key terms identified. Key terms usually defined in this section include: act, Advanced Practice Registered Nurse, assistive personnel, board, health care occupation, health care professional, Licensed Practical/Vocational Nurse, license, licensee, licensing authority, licensure, practice of nursing, and registered nurse. If these terms are not already part of the NPA in a particular state or territory, careful consideration should be given to adding these key terms. It is important for nurses to know how these terms are defined by the licensure board overseeing the practice of nursing in that jurisdiction. The following definitions are typical, but not reflective of specific definitions codified in every jurisdiction.

The term *act* ordinarily refers to the NPA; whereas *Advanced Practice Registered Nurse (APRN)* comprises nurse practitioners, nurse anesthetists, nurse-midwives, and clinical nurse specialists. To be designated as an APRN, it is required that the individual have a license as a registered nurse (RN), as well as graduate level education and national certification. The NCSBN suggests that the APRN definition include the skills APRNs are permitted to perform, and that the following be included in the APRN definition:

- assessing clients, synthesizing and analyzing data, and understanding and applying nursing principles at an advanced level;
- providing expert guidance and teaching;
- working effectively with clients, families and other members of the health care team;
- managing clients' physical and psychosocial health–illness status;
- using research skills;
- analyzing multiple sources of data identifying alternative possibilities as to the nature of a health care problem and selecting appropriate treatment;
- making independent decisions in solving complex client care problems;
- performing acts of diagnosing, prescribing, administering, and dispensing therapeutic measures, including legend drugs and controlled substances, within the scope of practice; and
- recognizing limits of knowledge and experience, planning for situations beyond expertise, and consulting with or referring clients to other health care providers as appropriate.[1]

In addition, NCSBN has issued proposed uniform licensure/authority to practice requirements for APRNs. These requirements address what is needed for initial APRN recognition, as well as for renewal and for the endorsement of APRN status. According to NCSBN, APRN licensure/authority to practice requirements need to contain three basic components: licensure, education, and certification. With regard to licensure, NCSBN recommends that APRN applicants possess an unencumbered RN license, and that APRNs seeking endorsement by a jurisdiction must also hold an unencumbered license or authority to practice as an APRN. Regarding the education component, APRNs must be graduates of a nationally accredited APRN program or must complete the requirements associated with the successful completion of an APRN certificate program by 2003. With the certification component, the NCSBN recommends that APRNs hold and maintain APRN specialty certification that is reflective of the APRNs educational focus, and that the specialty certification be obtained from a nationally recognized certification body. Where national certification is available in a specific specialty, the NCSBN recommends that the APRN be required to participate in a competence maintenance program. These requirements are outlined at Table 2–1.

T A B L E 2 - 1   APRN Licensure/Authority to Practice Requirements Issued by NCSBN

	Initial requirements[1]	Renewal requirements	Endorsement requirements
Licensure	Unencumbered RN license	Unencumbered RN license	Unencumbered RN license as well as unencumbered APRN authority in another jurisdiction
Education	By 2003, graduation from or successful completion of the requirements of a nationally accredited APRN school.	N/A– Will have addressed initially.	Same as the requirement for initial licensure or successful completion of an APRN certificate program by 2003.
Certification	APRN specialty certification that is reflective of educational program by a national certifying body. Where no appropriate certifying examination is available, BONs may develop alternative initial competence validation mechanisms.	Appropriate APRN specialty certification obtained through a nationally recognized certifying body must be maintained. Where no appropriate certifying examination is available, participation in a competence maintenance program is required.	Same as renewal requirements.

1. Graduates of U.S. APRN programs
Reprinted by permission of the National Council of State Boards of Nursing, Inc., Chicago, IL, from www.ncsbn.org.

Table 2–1 identifies only the initial requirements for APRN graduates of U.S. programs; the requirements for individuals educated in APRN programs outside the United States have also been identified. The requirements are the same, except that the APRN program from which the applicant graduated must meet accreditation criteria that is equivalent to a national accrediting body.

Assistive personnel is used to describe those who assist with the provision of nursing care. Commonly, these individuals are unlicensed.

Board refers to the BON in that state, territory, or District of Columbia. All 50 states, the District of Columbia, American Samoa, Guam, the Northern Mariana Islands, Puerto Rico, and the American Virgin Islands have at least one BON. California, Georgia, Louisiana, Texas, and West Virginia have two BONs each. In these five states, there is one board for registered nurses and a separate board for licensed practical/vocational nurses.

Health care occupation is the practice of delivering health care services through licensure, certification, registration, or other means. A *health care professional* is an individual who delivers health care services under the authority granted by the agency that regulates that health care profession. A *license* is a document or card issued by the BON to a qualified individual that permits an individual to practice nursing in that jurisdiction. *Licensee* refers to the individual who holds an active license, issued by a governmental agency, to practice in that jurisdiction in accordance with that jurisdiction's practice act.

Licensed Practical/Vocational Nurse (LPN/LVN) includes individuals who have graduated from an accredited practical/vocational program, and practice under the supervision of an RN, APRN, or licensed physician or dentist. According to the NCSBN, the NPA should indicate that the LPN/LVN

- contributes to the assessment of the health status of individuals and groups.
- participates in the development and modification of the plan of care.
- implements the appropriate aspects of the plan of care.
- maintains safe and effective nursing care rendered directly and indirectly.
- participates in the evaluation of responses to interventions.
- delegates nursing interventions to qualified others.[2]

Licensing authority in NPAs means the BON. According to the ANA MPA, this definition is necessary because of professional corporation laws that identify the kinds of organizations professionals can form. The ANA believes that nursing needs to be among those professions permitted to develop limited liability or professional corporations, and including this definition permits nurses to formulate their own corporations through which health care services are provided.[3]

Licensure refers to the process by which a state agency grants permission to an individual to engage in an occupation, after finding that the applicant has attained the essential degree of competency necessary to ensure that the public health, safety, and welfare will be reasonably well protected.[4]

Practice of nursing means assisting individuals or groups to maintain or attain optimal health, implementing a plan of care to accomplish defined goals/outcomes, and evaluating responses to care and treatment.[5] This definition encompasses the performance of acts that require substantial, or specialized or general knowledge, judgment and skill based upon principles of the biological, physical, behavioral and social sciences.[6]

Registered nurse (RN) denotes an individual who possesses the knowledge, skill, and ability necessary to practice the full scope of nursing practice. The NCSBN suggests that the full scope of nursing practice include but not be limited to

- assessing the health status of individuals and groups.
- establishing a nursing diagnosis.
- establishing goals to meet identified health care needs.
- planning a plan of care.
- prescribing nursing interventions to implement the plan of care.
- implementing the plan of care.
- delegating nursing interventions to qualified others as the NPA permits.

- providing for the maintenance of safe and effective nursing care rendered directly or indirectly.
- evaluating patient responses to interventions.
- teaching the theory and practice of nursing.
- collaborating with other health care professionals in the delivery of health care services.[7]

Board Composition

All practice acts describe the composition of the BON. Some practice acts simply say that the BON shall be composed of a certain number of members, with a majority of members being nurses, and one or two consumer members. Other practice acts go into more detail. If the number of RNs, LPNs/LVNs, and consumers is not clearly delineated, confusion and conflict may arise. To avoid that, most practice acts delineate the specific number of RNs, LPNs/LVNs, and consumer members who are to serve as board members. Some states and territories identify the number of APRNs who are to serve on the board, whereas others require that board members include representatives from specific specialty areas like nursing administration or nursing education. In addition, some NPAs require that board members be appointed from specific geographical regions within the state or territory.

The NCSBN recommends that practice acts require each RN, LPN/LVN, and APRN member be registered to vote in the state or territory, licensed in good standing, currently engaged in the practice of nursing, and have not less than 5 years of experience as a nurse, with at least 3 years of experience immediately preceding appointment to the board.[8]

With regard to consumer members, the NCSBN proposes that the consumer member be a registered voter who is knowledgeable about health matters. To ensure that independent judgment is exercised by consumer members, the NCSBN advises that consumer members neither be, nor ever have been, associated with the provision of health care services, or be enrolled in any health-related education program.[9] The ANA MPA goes one step further and recommends that practice acts prohibit the appointment of consumer members who own, operate, or who are employed in a business that has as its primary purpose the sale of goods or services to health care professionals or health care facilities.[10]

Term limits are placed on board members, and terms of service are typically staggered, so that continuity is preserved. Board members usually serve 5-year terms and are restricted to two consecutive full terms of office. Appointments to the board are made by the highest elected officer of the state or territory, usually the governor. Where the governor has the power to appoint board members, only the governor may remove board members. Grounds for removal include incompetence, misconduct, conflict of interest, unprofessional conduct, or neglect of duty. However, most NPAs do not delineate the specific conditions under which board members will be removed, nor do they describe the process to be used to remove a board member. The absence of clear removal provisions can prove to be problematic, and compromise board credibility when board members no longer practice nursing, use their position on the board to threaten other nurses, or fail to act in a manner that preserves the integrity of the profession.

The NPA in Colorado addresses removal issues in a way that every NPA should. The Colorado NPA requires that board members be engaged in the practice of nursing, and insists that nurse–board members be actively employed in specialty of nursing they were appointed to represent. Where nurse–board members no longer practice in the area for which they were appointed, the Governor of the state of Colorado has the authority to remove those nurse–board members.[11]

Board Powers and Responsibilities

BONs are vested with the power to enforce the NPA. To do that, BONs are authorized to create, revise, and enforce administrative rules and regulations that explain NPA provisions so that the profession is properly regulated and the public protected.

Many NPAs list the specific responsibilities of the board. In jurisdictions with NPAs that do not list board responsibilities, it may be difficult for the BON to show that it acted within its scope of authority when board. According to NCSBN, board responsibilities should be identified in NPAs. At a minimum, board responsibilities should include, but not be limited to

- developing and enforcing qualifications for licensure.
- developing and enforcing standards for nursing practice and nursing education.
- licensing qualified applicants by examination or endorsement, as well as renewing and reinstating licensees.
- developing standards for maintaining the competence of licensees continuing in or returning to practice.
- collecting and analyzing data regarding nursing education, nursing practice, and nursing resources.
- disciplining licensees as needed.
- regulating the manner in which nurses advertise their practice to the public.
- issuing special licenses where a modified scope of practice or accommodations are specified by the board.
- informing licensees about changes in the law and rules governing nursing practice.
- maintaining records of proceedings as required by law.
- providing consultation, conducting conferences, forums, studies, and research on nursing education and nursing practice.
- appointing and employing a qualified RN as executive director, and approving additional staff positions.
- maintaining membership in national organizations like NCSBN, which seek to improve the legal standards of nursing practice so that public health, safety, and welfare are protected.

- requiring surety bonds as necessary.
- determining and collecting reasonable fees.
- receiving and expending funds in the pursuit of the authorized objectives of the BON.
- adopting a seal that is in the care of the executive director and shall be affixed only as prescribed by the board.[12]

The ANA MPA lists other duties that should also be added to the list of board responsibilities. According to the ANA, responsibilities of the board should include:

- administering examinations, issuing licenses, and renewing licenses of qualified individuals.
- ascertaining and enforcing reasonable and uniform delegation standards.
- enforcing reasonable and uniform standards for all levels of nursing practice.
- issuing subpoenas, examining witnesses, and administering oaths.
- investigating complaints of alleged violations of the NPA.
- receiving and reviewing complaints alleging NPA violations.
- conducting hearings.
- invoking or requesting that disciplinary action be taken or invoked against a licensee or an unauthorized person practicing nursing.
- issuing nursing practice advisory opinions that interpret and reinforce the scope of nursing practice.
- determining nursing professional and related multidisciplinary group structure appropriate for independent nursing practice as professional or limited liability corporations.[13]

The authority of one BON was the issue in one case that was tried in Alabama. In *Alabama Board of Nursing v. Pearl Lee Lucas Herrick*,[14] the Alabama Board of Nursing adopted the findings of fact and the conclusions of law issued by a hearing officer. After finding that a nurse had been intoxicated while on duty, the hearing officer recommended that the nurse's license be suspended for 90 days. In spite of that recommendation by the hearing officer, the Alabama Board of Nursing decided to revoke the nurse's license. The matter was appealed, and the appellate court determined that the Alabama Board of Nursing had the authority to take disciplinary action they thought appropriate. As a result, the order of the Alabama Board of Nursing was considered reasonable, not arbitrary, and was affirmed.

Initial Licensure Requirements

Initially, a license to practice nursing is issued by the BON from which the applicant seeks licensure after an applicant proves that he or she is qualified, and successfully completes the national licensure examination, or it is issued by endorsement. Licensure by endorsement is permitted when an already licensed individual seeks to practice in a new jurisdiction. Typically, the licensure board that oversees the practice of that individual will validate that the individual holds a license in good standing in that jurisdiction, and licensure will subsequently be extended in the new jurisdiction without the applicant having to take the licensure exam again. Whether an applicant seeks licensure by examination or endorsement, eligibility criteria must be met.

Applicants seeking to be licensed as a nurse must be qualified to apply for licensure. To be qualified to apply for licensure, applicants must meet the eligibility criteria delineated in the NPA. In addition, the individual must prove that he or she is fit to practice nursing in that jurisdiction. Generally, a conviction that bears directly on the individual's fitness to practice nursing will result in that person being deemed unqualified and unable to receive a nursing license in that state. In addition, applicants must submit proof of graduation from an educational nursing program approved by the BON that is nationally accredited. In addition, graduates of foreign nursing programs must provide proof of eligibility and meet English proficiency requirements by passing the exam given by the Commission on Graduates of Foreign Nursing Schools (CGFNS). Finally, once an applicant is qualified to apply for licensure, the national nursing examination, the National Council Licensure Exam (NCLEX), must be successfully completed.

For those currently licensed individuals who seek to be licensed in a second state or who seek to transfer their license from one state to another, licensure by endorsement may be requested. However, where an individual has had their license revoked or suspended in another state, endorsement will generally not be granted. In addition, for a license by endorsement to be granted, standards for licensure must be substantially similar, verification of licensure must be submitted, and continuing competency requirements, if any, must be met.

In *John v. Department of Professional Regulation*,[15] standard comparability was contested by Aleyamma John, an RN in Florida. Nurse John applied for an RN license by endorsement in Illinois approximately 2½ years after she passed the NCLEX in Florida. Ms. John finally passed the NCLEX in Florida on her eighth attempt. In all, Ms. John took the NCLEX exam five times in Illinois and three times in Florida.

In December 1996, Ms. John, RN, filed a licensure by endorsement application with the Illinois Department of Professional Regulation. In March 1996, the Illinois agency denied her application citing that she must have been licensed under a statute that was substantially similar to the statute in force in Illinois on the date that she was licensed in another state. At that time, Illinois required applicants for licensure to pass the NCLEX within 3 years. Florida's NPA contained no time limitation. As a result, Ms. John could not receive an Illinois license by endorsement.

Nurse John appealed the denial, and the trial court decided that her licensure by endorsement application submitted by Ms. John, RN, should have been granted. The Illinois Department of Professional Regulation appealed that decision to the Illinois Court of Appeals. The Court of Appeals heard the matter, and rendered a decision in favor of the Illinois Department of Professional Regulation, concluding that the Florida and Illinois practice act provisions pertaining to this matter were not substantially similar. In reaching this decision, the court of appeals reasoned that it would be an anomaly for the state of Illinois to require applicants by examination to pass the NCLEX within 3 years, but permit those who fail to pass within 3 years to be issued a license by endorsement.

Licensure Renewal Requirements

Licensed individuals who fail to renew their license to practice nursing in accordance with the timeline identified by the BON are considered unlicensed, and subject to sanctions for practicing nursing without a license. Accordingly, it is important for licensees to be proactive about licensure renewal, and to promptly return all licensure renewal applications correctly and completely executed, accompanied by the requested information and renewal fees. Nine BONs renew licenses annually (Connecticut, Louisiana, Maryland, Montana, South Carolina, Washington, and West Virginia) or triennially (Iowa, New York); the majority of boards have a biennial renewal schedule. Some renewal schedules are on a calendar year, whereas others are on the agency fiscal year, and others are on a birth date or birth year schedule. Because of the wide ranging approaches to licensure renewal, it is important for licensees to know what the renewal period is in the jurisdictions within which each RN license is held.

Where renewal deadlines are missed by licensees, those licenses are considered lapsed, and the practice of nursing is prohibited. Most BONs allow individuals whose licenses have lapsed to apply for reinstatement. The reinstatement process must be strictly adhered to if the previously licensed individual is to be reinstated. The MPA published by ANA suggests that the BON not reinstate the license of a nurse who fails to apply for reinstatement within 5 years of the expiration date of the license.[16]

Licensee Responsibilities

Although most BONs do not list licensee responsibilities, the NCSBN recommends that licensee responsibilities be included in NPAs. According to the NCSBN, licensee responsibilities should include, but not be limited to

- providing personal, professional, or demographic information to the Board. NCSBN goes further by suggesting that failure to provide personal, professional, or demographic information may be grounds for licensure nonrenewal.
- requiring licensees to submit to physical or mental examinations. Failure to comply with an ordered examination constitutes an admission of any allegation that prompted the examination to be ordered.
- requiring all licensees to report to the BON acts or omissions that are violations of the NPA or that are grounds for disciplinary action.[17]

The ANA MPA also contains language that allows BONs to order that mental or physical examinations be done. However, mental and physical examinations can be ordered only if there is probable cause to believe that

- the nurse is abusing any narcotic or controlled substance.

- the nurse is providing or attempting to provide nursing services under the influence of alcohol, narcotic or controlled substance.
- the nurse is using any narcotic, controlled substance, or any other drug in excess of therapeutic amounts or without medical indication.

Moreover, mental and physical examinations may be ordered only where the nurse has neither requested nor received treatment for drug addiction or abuse.

Although many NPAs do not deal with licensee responsibilities to any significant degree, nurses do have a responsibility to maintain competence, because practice problems in one jurisdiction may result in a nurse's inability to obtain a license to practice in other jurisdictions. *Hazel Scott v. The Board of Nursing of the State of Nebraska*[18] provides an example. In this case, Hazel Scott was licensed in New York, but wanted to obtain a license to practice nursing in Nebraska. Her application was processed, and a temporary license was issued. However, the Nebraska Board of Nursing ultimately denied her application to practice nursing citing unprofessional conduct as the basis for denial. The BON decision was appealed to the district court where the decision was reversed. The BON appealed and the Supreme Court of Nebraka reversed the district court decision, upholding the denial decision issued by the Nebraska Board of Nursing.

Title, Term, and Abbreviation Protection

NPAs typically protect nursing-specific titles, terms, and abbreviations. Generally, the following titles, terms, and abbreviations are protected in NPAs: licensed practical/vocational nurse (LPN/LVN), registered nurse (RN), advanced practice registered nurse (APRN), nurse practitioner (NP), clinical nurse specialist (CNS), certified registered nurse anesthetist (CRNA), and nurse-midwife (NM).

The ANA MPA recommends that the following terms and phrases be protected: nurse, licensed professional nurse, licensed nurse, registered professional nurse, practical nurse, and vocational nurse.[19] Protecting these terms and phrases prohibits those who are not licensed by the BON from using those terms. For instance, without term protection, unlicensed assistants may be deemed dental nurses or office nurses by the health care professionals for whom these individuals are working, without being licensed by the BON.

The ANA takes the misuse of terms like nurse seriously. The ANA recommends that anyone who inappropriately holds him- or herself out as a nurse should be prohibited from continuing to practice, prohibited from continuing to represent him- or herself as a nurse, fined, and sanctioned by the state consumer protection and other applicable laws.[20]

Nursing School Approval Process

To fulfill its charge to protect the public, BONs approve nursing education programs. Provisions governing this approval process are usually outlined in the rules and regulations promulgated by the BON. Rules and regulations followed by the BON describe the procedures to be followed so that the NPA is adhered to.

According to the rules and regulations, standards regarding the administration and organization of the nursing education program, the resources, facilities, and services available to the nursing education program, students, faculty, curriculum, as well as program and student evaluations must be complied with prior to opening an approved nursing education program. Usually, provisional approval is extended to nursing education programs until licensure results are returned from the first graduating class. Once a nursing education program receives full approval, periodic evaluations are conducted to ensure that standards are continuing to be met. Typically, BONs evaluate nursing education programs every 3 to 5 years.

Where a BON determines that standards are not met, a conditional approval may be granted. If standards are not met by the expiration of the conditional approval, the BON may withdraw its approval of the nursing education program. Withdrawal of approval results in graduates of that program being ineligible to take the licensure examination.

Violations and Penalties

Many NPAs simply relegate the violations section of the practice act to one sentence declaring that violations of the practice constitute a misdemeanor, and are punishable by a nominal fine of not less than $100. However, rules and regulations enforced by the BON contain a more extensive list of penalties that can be invoked when disciplinary action is taken.

The NCSBN encourages its member boards to address NPA violations specifically, and in detail. In its MPA, the NCSBN asserts that no person shall

- engage in the practice of nursing without a valid, current license, except as otherwise permitted.
- practice nursing based on an illegally or fraudulently obtained diploma, license, or other record.
- practice nursing while his or her license is suspended, revoked, surrendered, inactive, or lapsed.
- in any way imply that he or she is a nurse unless he or she is duly licensed as an LPN/LVN, RN, or APRN.
- fraudulently get or supply someone else a license by or for money or anything of value.
- knowingly employ unlicensed persons to practice nursing.
- fail to report conduct that violates the NPA.
- open a nursing education program without first having the program approved by the BON.
- otherwise violate the NPA, or aid or abet anyone else to violate any provision of the NPA.[21]

Although the MPA published by the ANA does not contain a list of NPA violations, it does identify 10 sanctions that should be available to BONs:

1. Deny a license to an applicant.
2. Revoke or suspend the license of a licensee.
3. Revoke or suspend the privilege to practice nursing in that state.
4. Reprimand any nurse permitted to practice in the state.
5. Impose civil fines for each infraction.
6. Require attendance at remediation courses.
7. Place a licensee on probation.
8. Limit or restrict a licensee's license to practice nursing.
9. Enjoin or request injunctive relief so that an individual or entity, not otherwise subject to the NPA, can be required to discontinue doing something that is in violation of the NPA.
10. Issue cease and desist orders, as well as other emergency relief where there is cause to believe that anyone is violating the NPA, and the violation has caused, or may cause immediate and irreparable harm to the public.[22]

The MPA proposed by the ANA also suggests that violators of the NPA can be subject to civil and criminal prosecution. According to the ANA MPA, a civil cause of action and criminal prosecution may occur prior to, during, or after action taken by the BON.[23]

Ann Marie Rafferty v. Commonwealth of Pennsylvania, State Board of Nurse Examiners[24] illustrates the willingness of U.S. courts to affirm BON decisions to discipline nurses. In *Rafferty,* the license of Ann Marie Rafferty was revoked after the BON found that Rafferty disconnected the respirator on a comatose patient to perform an unauthorized evaluation of the patient's spontaneous respirations. Thereafter, she reportedly left the patient with no heartbeat, failed to provide cardiopulmonary resuscitation, and did not call a code. Subsequently, Rafferty failed to attach the cardiac monitoring strip to the patient's chart.

After hearing the evidence, the Pennsylvania State Board of Nurse Examiners revoked Rafferty's license. Rafferty appealed that decision to the commonwealth court where the revocation decision was reversed. The Pennsylvania State Board of Nurse Examiners appealed that decision to the Pennsylvania Supreme Court where the Board decision to revoke Rafferty's license was affirmed.

Grounds for Disciplinary Action

NPAs or their implementing rules and regulations contain a laundry list of things that may result in disciplinary action. Typically, these provisions grant the BON the authority to deny, revoke, or suspend the license of an individual who is found to have committed an offense that is grounds for disciplinary action. The rules governing disciplinary action in Oklahoma are illustrative. These rules are extensive, but are consistent with the rules and regulations followed by other BONs. The section begins with a list of definitions so that the meaning of key terms is clarified, and is followed by a list of offenses.

In Oklahoma, the rules and regulations pertaining to disciplinary action are as follows:

1. *The terms* fraud *or* deceit *shall include but not be limited to:*
   A. *false representation of facts in connection with an application for licensure, or certificate, or renewal of license; or application for recognition as an advanced practitioner; or*
   B. *false representation by having another person appear in her/his place for the licensing examination.*
2. *Negligence means the failure to possess and exercise that degree of knowledge, skill, care, and diligence that is possessed and exercised by nurses in the same field of practice who are practicing under similar circumstances.*
3. *Negligence of an advanced practitioner is the failure to possess and use that degree of learning and skill ordinarily possessed and used by other advanced practitioners in good standing in the same expanded role in the delivery of health care under similar circumstances.*
4. *Negligence of an advanced unlicensed assistive person is the failure to possess and use that degree of learning and skill ordinarily possessed and used by other advanced unlicensed assistive persons in good standing in the same role in the delivery of health care under similar circumstances.*
5. *The term* habitually intemperate *or* addicted *shall include but not be limited to the use of any drug, chemical, or substance that could result in behavior that interferes with the practice of practical nursing, registered nursing, advanced practice nursing, or advanced unlicensed assistive persons and the responsibilities of the licensee or certificate holder.*
6. Sufficient knowledge or reasonable skill *means adherence to minimal standards of acceptable practical nurse practice, registered nurse practice, advanced nurse practice, or advanced unlicensed assistive persons' practice generally prevailing in the State of Oklahoma.*
7. Unprofessional conduct *is nursing behavior (acts, knowledge, and practices) that fail to conform to the accepted standards of the nursing profession, or advanced unlicensed assistive persons' activities generally prevailing in the State of Oklahoma and that could jeopardize the health and welfare of the people, which shall include but not be limited to the following:*
   A. *inaccurate recording, falsifying or altering patient records; or*
   B. *verbally or physically abusing patients; or*
   C. *falsely manipulating drug supplies, narcotics, or patient records; or*
   D. *appropriating without authority medications, supplies, or personal items of the patient or agency; or*
   E. *falsifying documents submitted to the Board of Nursing; or*
   F. *leaving a nursing assignment or patient care assignment without properly advising appropriate personnel; or*

G. violating the confidentiality of information or knowledge concerning the patient; or

H. conduct detrimental to the public interest; or

I. discriminating in the rendering of nursing services or patient care assignment; or

J. aiding and abetting the practice of practical nursing, registered nursing, advanced practice nursing, or advanced unlicensed assistive persons by any person not licensed as a licensed practical nurse or a registered nurse or recognized as an advanced practitioner or not certified as an advanced unlicensed assistive person;

K. impersonating any applicant or acting as proxy for the applicant in any examination required for the issuance of a license or certificate; or

L. impersonating another licensed or certified practitioner, or permitting another person to use her/his license, certificate, or certificate of recognition for any purpose; or

M. aiding, abetting, or assisting any other person to violate or circumvent any law, rule, or regulation intended to guide the conduct of a nurse or advanced unlicensed assistive person; or

N. forging a prescription for medication/drugs; or

O. presenting a forged prescription; or

P. selling or attempting to sell a controlled dangerous substance or otherwise making such drugs available without authority to self, friends, or family members; or

Q. while caring for a patient, engaging in conduct with a patient that is sexual or may reasonably be interpreted as sexual, or in any verbal behavior that is seductive or sexually demeaning to a patient, or engaging in sexual exploitation of a patient; or

R. obtaining money, property, or services from a patient, other than reasonable fees for service provided to the patient, through the use of undue influence, harassment, duress, deception, or fraud; or

S. engaging in fraudulent billing practices, including violations of federal Medicare and Medicaid laws or state medical assistance laws.

8. Conduct that jeopardizes a patient's life, health, or safety shall include but not be limited to the following:

A. Failure of a licensed practical nurse, a registered nurse, or advanced practitioner to supervise adequately the performance of acts by any person working at the nurse's direction; or

B. Delegating or accepting the delegation of a nursing function or a prescribed health care function when the delegation or acceptance could reasonably be expected to result in unsafe or ineffective patient care; or

C. Unauthorized alterations of medications; or

D. Failure to utilize appropriate judgment in administering safe nursing practice *or patient care assignment based upon the level of nursing for which the individual is licensed or recognized; or*

E. *Failure to exercise technical competence in carrying out nursing care or patient care assignment; or*

F. *Performing new nursing techniques, procedures, or patient care activities without proper education and preparation; or*

G. *Failure to report through the proper channels the unsafe or illegal practice of any person who is providing nursing care or patient care.*[25]

Although this list seems exhaustive, there are additional grounds for disciplinary action recommended for inclusion in NPAs by the NCSBN. These additional grounds include

- failing to demonstrate the applicant for licensure satisfies the licensure requirements.
- conviction by a court or entry of a plea of nolo contendere (no contest) to a crime in any jurisdiction that adversely impacts on the practice of nursing or adversely reflects on the ability of an individual to practice nursing.
- having the license to practice nursing or another health care discipline denied, revoked, or suspended or otherwise restricted in any state.
- engaging in unethical conduct.
- practicing beyond the scope of practice for APRNs.[26]

Although the NCSBN NPA limits practicing beyond the scope of practice to APRNs, it should be applicable to every health care worker regulated by the BON. For example, staff nurses have begun to remove central venous lines and endotracheal tubes. These tasks have historically been undertaken by physicians. For nurses, it is important to know whether these and other tasks are within the scope of nursing practice. If particular tasks are deemed to be beyond the scope of practice, a nurse could be subjecting him- or herself to an allegation of practicing medicine without a license. As a result, NPAs that do not have a practicing beyond the scope provision should be amended to clarify which actions can lead to disciplinary action.

In addition to practicing beyond the scope of practice, grounds for imposing disciplinary action should be clearly and thoroughly discussed in NPAs. The Oklahoma NPA and the NCSBN MPA clearly and thoroughly delineate these grounds.

It is imperative for licensees to understand the numerous grounds for disciplinary action. Not knowing the grounds for disciplinary action could prove devastating to an individual licensee, because not knowing that an actionable offense has been committed is no defense to the imposition of disciplinary action. Memorizing the list may seem overwhelming, but taking time to have a working knowledge of offenses that will result in disciplinary action may prove to be well spent if BON disciplinary proceedings are to be avoided.

Disciplinary proceedings were not avoided in *The Matter of Suzanne Elizabeth Kring Cafiero, RN v. North Carolina Board of Nursing.*[27] In *Cafiero*, Suzanne Elizabeth Kring Cafiero found herself facing disciplinary action after an infant patient for whom she was caring was electrocuted. The patient was electrocuted because the cardiopulmonary monitor leads had been placed directly in the electrical cord rather than the patient cable. The patient had to be resuscitated, but survived, sustaining multiple burns. It was uncontested that Suzanne's clinical performance before and after this incident was exemplary. Subsequently, the North Carolina Board of Nursing issued a complaint against Suzanne and, after a hearing on the matter, suspended her license to practice as a registered nurse for 30 days. Suzanne appealed the decision contending that a single act alone cannot give rise to disciplinary action. The case was eventually heard by the North Carolina Court of Appeals. That court affirmed the disciplinary action taken by the North Carolina Board of Nursing saying that Suzanne engaged in conduct that endangered public health. In spite of their decision, the court agreed that a single act alone could not result in the nurse being negligent. In affirming the North Carolina Board of Nursing's decision, the court noted that two acts gave rise to disciplinary action. First, Suzanne failed to properly apply the cardiopulmonary monitor. Second, she proceeded to hook up the monitor without waiting for assistance.

Emergency Relief

Some NPAs contain provisions that expressly grant the BON the authority to temporarily suspend or revoke a license. The authority to temporarily suspend or revoke a license exists only where the continued practice of nursing presents an imminent and serious risk of harm to others. It is rarely used, but can be an important tool used to maximize public protection.

The procedure for taking emergency relief is usually spelled out in the state's APA, and that process must be adhered to. Temporarily suspending a license prior to a formal hearing raises serious and significant constitutional issues, but the interest of the BON in protecting the public warrants the temporary suspension of a nursing license where imminent and serious risk of harm to others exists. Temporarily suspending someone's license to practice nursing requires that hearings be promptly scheduled and conducted so that the licensee has an opportunity to be heard. The MPA proposed by the ANA urges that the time be short between the board's decision to temporarily suspend a license to practice nursing without a hearing and the hearing and decision on the matter. In the ANA MPA, the licensee whose license has been temporarily suspended without a hearing should have the right to request a hearing within 72 hours after his or her receipt of the notice of temporary suspension. In addition, the BON must hold a hearing on the matter within 72 hours of the timely request of the licensee, and issue a decision, in accordance with the state's APA, within 72 hours after the hearing.

Reporting Obligations

Most NPAs require that practice act violations be reported. Some require that the chain of command be used, whereas other require that violations be reported directly to the BON. Because reporting suspected NPA violations is required, the NCSBN recommends that immunity from civil causes of action be extended to anyone providing good faith information to the board, including witnesses, members of professional review committees, board members, and staff of the BON.[28]

In Texas, the NPA takes reporting obligations farther than other states by affording nurses protection when they refuse to engage in conduct that violates the NPA and for reporting what they perceive to be unsafe care.[29] Comparatively, most practice acts are silent when it comes to these issues.

Peer Review

Again, Texas leads the way when it comes to peer review. Whereas most NPAs do not address the issue of peer review, a comprehensive, employer-based peer review system is operational in Texas, and is part of the Texas NPA. Every jurisdiction without a comparable peer review provision should seriously consider adding it to the NPA.

In Texas, employers with 10 or more RNs are required to comply with peer review process. *Peer review* refers to "the process of evaluating nursing services, the qualifications of a nurse, the quality of patient care rendered by a nurse, the merit of complaints issued against nurses and the care provided."[30] When a peer review committee finds, after giving the nurse an opportunity to provide rebuttal evidence, that a nurse:

> . . . exposed or is likely to expose a patient or other person unnecessarily to a risk of harm, engaged in unprofessional conduct, failed to care adequately for a patient, or failed to conform to the minimum standards of acceptable professional nursing practice, or that a registered nurse's practice is or is likely to be impaired by chemical dependency shall report in a signed, written report to the Board the identity of the nurse and such additional information as the Board may require. The report shall include the corrective action taken against the nurse, and whether the committee recommends the Board take formal disciplinary action.[31]

Peer review findings are advisory only, when it comes to action an employer may take against the nurse. In addition, where chemical dependency is suspected or confirmed, and where mental illness is concerned, the nurse can be reported to the Texas Peer Assistance Program for Nurses, and not to the Texas Board of Nursing Examiners or the peer review committee.[32]

The Texas NPA recognizes that the peer review process is usually invoked involuntarily. However, it also recognizes that it can be invoked voluntarily. Voluntary peer review occurs where a nurse believes that he or she is being asked to do or not do something that violates the NPA. The nurse who believes that he or she has been asked to engage in conduct that violates the NPA may request that the peer review committee make a determination about the matter. After a peer review determination has been made, the nurse cannot be disciplined for the conduct that was the subject of the requested peer review. Where a nursing administrator, in good faith, believes that the decision of the peer review committee incorrectly determines a nurse's duty, the findings of the peer review committee are not binding.[33]

Chemical Dependence

The nursing profession, like other professions, has professionals within its ranks who are chemically dependent. The challenge has been to balance the interest nurses have in practicing as licensed professionals with the interest of patients who are the recipients of the care delivered by nurses. Because of its' charge to protect the safety and welfare of the public, NCSBN has outlined steps that can be taken when it comes to dealing with chemical dependency in nursing. An online NCSBN article published in 1987 entitled, *Regulatory Management of the Chemically Dependent Nurse*[34] compares and contrasts approaches to chemical dependency by BONs. According to the article, boards deal with chemical dependency in one of the following eight ways:

1. Statutory arm of the BON
2. Statutory disciplinary alternative under the BON with services contracted to an outside agency
3. Special BON committee
4. Consent order for suspension and probation
5. Special disciplinary provision for the voluntary surrender of a nursing license to the BON
6. Professional association peer assistance program that operates in collaboration with the BON
7. Professional association peer assistance program with no relationship to the BON Peer assistance or employee assistance program with no relationship to the BON[35]

Regardless of the organizational structure of the entity that oversees chemical dependency issues, the NCSBN asserts that all programs should be state-of-the-art sobriety and compliance with program mandates should be closely monitored, and nursing performance should be evaluated at frequent intervals.[36] Generally, these programs allow a nurse the opportunity to retain his or her privilege to practice nursing so long as the nurse complies with program mandates. When a nurse does not comply with program mandates, the nurse is removed from the peer assistance program, reported to the BON, and disciplinary is action taken. Typically, nurses are dismissed from peer assistance programs for resumption of substance use, failure to comply with drug testing protocol, failure to attend support group meetings, or failure to practice in accordance with the guidelines delineated by the peer assistance program. When the nurse completes all of the program requirements, the nurse is released from the program, and allowed to practice nursing without limitations or restrictions, and no disciplinary action is taken by the BON.

Chemical dependence issues involved in *Colorado Board of Nursing v. Colleen Crickenberger*[37] and *Hogan v. Mississippi Board of Nursing.*[38] Both cases demonstrate the willingness to set aside inappropriate orders issued by BONs, especially when chemical dependency issues are involved.

In *Crickenberger,* Colleen Crickenberger, a nurse who was never intoxicated or under the influence while at work, voluntarily began alcohol treatment. The director of nursing at the facility at which she was employed knew about Colleen's voluntary treatment. Approximately 2 months following Colleen's treatment, she called in sick. The director of nursing reportedly thought that the absence was relapse related. As a result, Colleen was terminated and a report was filed with the Colorado Board of Nursing. The hearing officer dismissed the complaint finding that Colleen had not consumed alcohol since she began treatment. The BON accepted the findings of fact submitted by the hearing officer, but concluded that alcohol dependence was proven and disciplinary action was imposed. The matter was appealed to a Colorado Court of Appeals. That court determined that the Colorado Board of Nursing exceeded its authority and abused its discretion in finding that Colleen was addicted to or dependent on alcohol and imposing discipline. As a result, the order issued by the Colorado Board of Nursing was set aside.

In *Hogan,* the Mississippi Supreme Court determined that the Mississippi Board of Nursing acted improperly when it revoked the license of a CRNA who failed to account for twenty-five 100-mg ampules of meperidine (Demerol). Hogan contended that the revocation was improper because there was no proof that the Demerol was converted to her own use. The Mississippi Supreme Court agreed, concluding that with narcotics-related allegations the evidentiary standard imposed on the BON was heightened, and that the board's finding that Hogan was guilty of failure to reasonably account for missing narcotics did not meet that standard.

Continuing Competency

Many NPAs do not address continuing competency. However, the ANA suggests that language be added to NPAs giving the BON authority to establish by regulation the continuing competency requirements necessary for licensure renewal.[39] Because continuing competency is not addressed in most NPAs, the issue will be discussed in more detail in the Trends section of this chapter.

Exemptions

NPAs only apply to specific individuals. Others are exempt and free from the requirements of the NPA, as well as the implementing rules and regulations. The ANA recommends that the following individuals be included among those exempt from the NPA:

- anyone who provides advice or administers treatment in an emergency.
- anyone employed in the state, Washington, D.C., or U.S. territory by the U.S. government while he or she is acting in an official capacity, so long as the individual maintains a current license in at least one jurisdiction.
- a nurse licensed to practice in another state who travels with a patient through a state
- anyone enrolled in an approved nursing education program.
- any person assisting in the care or peaceful death of a friend or family member, including the administration of remedies or medications, or care of the sick provided by family members, companions, or volunteers.

Revenue, Fees, and Fines

NPAs authorize BONs to collect fees and fines, thereby generating operational revenue. Generally, licensure fees are the primary source of revenue for BONs. However, BONs may generate additional revenue by charging for all of the services they provide. No single BON receives income from all of these potential revenue sources. In fact, the majority of boards receive income only from initial licensure and examination fees, licensure renewal fees, verification services, issuing duplicate licenses, reactivating and reinstating licenses, mailing labels, and charges for bad checks. Other sources of revenue should be explored by BONs so that operational costs are spread over numerous revenue sources, and so that licensure-related fees are not artificially inflated.

Grandfathering Provisions

Grandfathering provisions are those portions of the NPA that incorporate individuals who were licensed under previous versions of the NPA. These provisions are typically used when eligibility for licensure changes and when titles change. The ANA's MPA uses this kind of provision to address educational requirements for nurses. According to the grandfathering or grandparenting section of the ANA MPA

1. The board shall waive the educational requirements of licensure for any nurse in good standing who submits application for renewal prior to the expiration of the nurses' current license; and
2. For a period of 2 years following the date of the enactment of legislation that requires RNs to have a baccalaureate education, education requirements shall be waived for all RNs who fulfill all other requirements for licensure and who are in good standing within and outside of the state in which they are licensed, who apply for licensure as an RN.[40]

This language has not been codified in NPAs across the country. North Dakota is the only state to adopt the baccalaureate degree as the required educational level for individuals licensed as RNs. Although this specific language has not been adopted, it illustrates the use of grandfathering or grandparenting provisions.

Revenue Sources for Boards of Nursing

- Granting retired nurse status
- Registering nurses who reside in the state, but who are not currently licensed in the state
- Reactivating, reinstating, or inactivating licenses
- Issuing duplicate licenses and duplicate forms
- Processing applications for initial licensure
- Renewing licenses
- Endorsing licenses
- Issuing temporary permits to practice within the jurisdiction
- Maintaining a nurse aide registry
- Late fees for not adhering to all deadlines
- Making name and address changes
- Accessing information systems
- Approving nursing education programs
- Initial licensure application fees
- Continuing education approval
- Collecting practice privilege information
- Reviewing APRN credentials
- Disciplinary costs
- Registering nursing corporations
- Expanded role certification
- Registering individuals on an unlicensed assistive personnel registry
- Registration at board-sponsored educational programs
- Distribution of printed material
- Lists and mailing labels
- Checks that are returned for insufficient funds
- Participation in the peer assistance or alternative program

Severability Clause

Although the MPAs from NCSBN and ANA contain a severability clause, many NPAs do not. *Severability clauses* simply state that where any specific provision of an NPA is declared unconstitutional, illegal, or invalid, the remaining provisions remain constitutional, legal, and valid. Where a severability clause is not part of the NPA, the NPA should be amended to add one.

Repeal

Most NPAs contain a section at the end of the NPA that identifies which provisions have been changed, and thus, is a good place to find the history of the NPA. In addition, changes in the NPA can be reviewed to see whether a change was semantic, procedural, or substantive.

Contrasting the MPAs from ANA and NCSBN

Unique features can be found in the MPAs from the ANA and the NCSBN. First, unique provisions of the ANA MPA will be listed. Then, unique features of the NCSBN MPA will be identified.

The ANA MPA contains provisions that

- allow BONs to develop training and regulatory systems for all persons providing patient care services, including unlicensed assistive personnel.
- incorporate APRNs in the definition of nursing practice, and allows BONs to make distinctions with tasks and activities based on the level of nursing practice.
- delineate board responsibilities.
- allow flexibility in the appointment of board members. Designated seats have been removed so that flexibility and diversity are enhanced, and so that representatives from emerging nursing specialties have an opportunity to serve on the board.
- prohibit membership in any professional nursing organization from being used to decline to appoint a board member.
- address causes of action with delegation and APRN issues.
- prohibit discrimination and economic restraint against nurses where clinical privileging, reimbursement, and prescribing services are concerned.
- grant authority to the BON to determine the types of providers that may form limited liability companies.
- allow nurses to voluntarily surrender their license.
- address procedural aspects of disciplinary hearings.
- outline reinstatement requirements.
- recognize that an RN may declare death.
- propose alternative sanctions.
- permit the issuance of injunctions.
- allocate all money collected from fines from regulating nursing practice in the state, territory, or District of Columbia.
- outline licensure requirements for foreign-educated nurses.
- reflect adherence to federal antidiscrimination laws like the American with Disabilities Act.

The ANA MPA does not separate levels or scopes of practice for each level of nurse regulated by the BON, nor does the ANA MPA deal with the approval of nursing education programs. The ANA contends that nursing is the only health profession in which regulatory boards also certify schools, and suggests that approval of nursing education programs not be conducted by the BON.

Like the ANA MPA, the NCSBN MPA contains unique provisions. Unlike the ANA MPA, the NCSBN MPA

■ delineates the roles of the RN, LPN/LVN, and APRN.
■ provides reasonable compensation to the BON for performance of official duties.
■ addresses the issuance of temporary permits.
■ exempts nursing students in postbaccalaureate education programs, where the student is not currently licensed in the state in which he or she is a student in a postbaccalaureate education program.
■ allows reinstatement where nurses who have been out of the practice of nursing have taken nursing refresher courses.
■ permits fines collected by the BON to be used at the board's discretion for BON projects.
■ adopts the APA.
■ contains no definition of neglect of duty, incompetence, unprofessional, or dishonorable conduct where those terms are listed as grounds for removal from the board.

NPAs around the country should be reviewed in light of the recommendations made by ANA and the NCSBN to ensure that key issues are addressed, and that the NPA is comprehensive. Where the NPA is silent with regard to any of the issues addressed in this chapter, careful consideration should be given to amending the NPA.

Administrative Procedures Act

Whereas BONs enforce NPAs, the APA ensures that the procedures used at boards of nursing are fair. Typically, APAs have an articulated purpose, rulemaking process, as well as a delineated procedure to be followed in individual proceedings. In addition, APAs usually contain provisions requiring that meetings and records be open to the public.

Purpose

APAs are enacted so that state citizens can anticipate the procedures to be used when administrative agencies enact rules, and conduct disciplinary hearings. Not all state agencies have to comply with the APA. Typically, exemptions are identified. However, no state APA specifically exempts the BON from compliance. Accordingly, all BONs are required to comply with the provisions of the APA codified in that jurisdiction.

Rulemaking

Within each APA, rulemaking provisions exist that outline the process to be used to formulate a rule. Typically, rule changes, whether they be new rules, proposed amendments to existing rules, or rule deletions have to submitted to an agency responsible for collecting and compiling this information. In addition, rule changes must be published in an official publication, and public hearings on the rule changes must be held.

In some states, after rule changes have been adopted by the agency, the adopted rule must be submitted to the state legislative leaders, as well as the governor for review and approval. Once the governor and state legislative leaders have approved the rule change, the rule is considered finally adopted. In other states, legislative and governor approval is not required. In these states, proposed rule changes should be carefully followed so that the rule change impact is carefully considered.

Adjudication/Individual Proceedings

The APA requires that rules be formulated using a rulemaking process, and it delineates the process to be used when disciplinary matters are addressed. Basically, these provisions ensure that individual proceedings occur in a manner that respects an individual's constitutional due process rights.

Due process is honored when individuals who are the subject of individual proceedings are given an opportunity to be meaningfully heard. This standard is met when all parties involved in the disciplinary matter receive timely notification of the hearing time, place, and subject matter. BONs are also required to provide a statement of their legal authority to take action, if any. In addition, BONs are required to identify which sections of the NPA and its rules are involved in the matter, and are required to summarize the allegations in a short, plain statement.

Following a disciplinary proceeding, the BON will issue a Final Agency Order. This order must be in writing, and must contain findings of fact and conclusions of law. In a nutshell, this is the document describing the facts that led to the disciplinary proceedings, rules of law, and the action, if any, taken by the BON. Unless the matter is reversed on appeal or rehearing, the Final Agency Order concludes an individual proceeding. Final Agency Orders delineate disciplinary action that has been taken, if any. Disciplinary action can range from reprimand to the revocation of a nurse's license to practice nursing.

Final Agency Orders can be reviewed by state courts, and may ultimately be reviewed by State Supreme Courts. The opportunity to have a Final Agency Order reviewed by the judicial branch of government provides an important control on administrative agency action. Although district courts and State Supreme Courts are reluctant to overturn a BON decision, that option exists in a number of situations.

Barbara Woods v. D.C. Nurses' Examining Board[41] indicates that courts will reverse BON decisions where procedural protections are not extended to nurses. In this case, Barbara Woods had her D.C. license revoked after her Maryland license was revoked. She was later placed on probation for 1 year in Maryland. She then applied for reinstatement in D.C. That application was denied. Barbara appealed this decision. Her case was eventually heard by the D.C. Court of Appeals. The appellate court reversed the reinstatement denial decision by the D.C. Nurses' Examining Board

---

Grounds for Overturning a Board of Nursing Decision

A State Supreme Court can overturn a BON decision when

- constitutional provisions are violated.
- the BON acted beyond its statutory authority.
- the procedure used was unlawful.
- there was an error of law.
- the BON reached a clearly erroneous decision when reliable, material, probative, substantial, and competent evidence was presented.
- the BON made an arbitrary or capricious decision.
- findings of fact were not made by the BON.

---

because Barbara was not afforded the opportunity to have a hearing on the reinstatement denial decision, and was denied fair notice of the criteria governing reinstatement. The court considered these failures violations of Barbara's due process rights.

Open Meeting Act

APAs require that BON meetings be publicly announced and open to the public. This requirement is contained in a provision that is referred to as the *Open Meeting Act.* Regular meeting dates, times, and places must be announced, and agendas posted prior to the meeting being convened. Special and emergency meetings may also be convened, but public notice of these meetings must occur prior to the special or emergency meeting. Violations of this act constitute a misdemeanor, and subject violators to incarceration and a monetary fine.

Open Records Act

Closely related to the Open Meeting Act is the *Open Records Act,* which requires that the BON make certain records accessible to the public. Like the Open Meeting Act, the Open Records Act is maybe contained within the state APA, or it may be codified as a separate statute. Although some records are exempt from the Open Records Act, it does require that BONs and other administrative agencies maintain complete records of the receipt and expenditure of public funds. It also requires the BON to disclose other records to the public. For instance, BONs are required to post, in advance, the agenda for meetings. Although BONs must comply with disclosure requirements, the Open Records Act permits BONs to impose reasonable, direct costs of duplicating records on the person or entity requesting the information. Like the Open Meeting Act, violations of this act are considered misdemeanors, and violators are subject to incarceration and a monetary fine.

The Disciplinary Action Process

BONs have the responsibility to protect the public from nurses who pose a threat to the safety, welfare, and health of the citizens of that jurisdiction. To do that, disciplinary action is taken against thousands of nurses each year. This section outlines the disciplinary process so that those who find themselves the subject of a BON investigation can be more informed, and can anticipate what is likely to occur once a complaint is filed with the BON.

Investigation

The BON has an obligation to investigate all complaints filed with the agency. BONs typically hire nurse–investigators to conduct these investigations. These nurse–investigators come from a variety of practice settings, and may have completed a national investigation certification program in an effort to conduct legally defensible, thorough investigations.

During an investigation, medical records and other documentation are reviewed and analyzed. In addition, witnesses are interviewed, and witness statements collected. This may include patients, family and friends of patients, co-workers, and supervisory personnel.

Sometime during the investigation process, the BON will request to interview the nurse or nurses who are involved in the complaint that was filed with the BON. Nurses need to carefully and thoughtfully consider whether or not to voluntarily meet with the investigator. On one hand, it may work to exonerate the nurse who provides evidence that he or she should not be the target of an investigation. On the other hand, these matters are quasi-criminal, and anything said can and will be used against the nurse. Nurses who retain attorneys to represent them will find that their attorneys will probably advise against making voluntary statements where there is a possibility that the nurse giving the voluntary statement will be considered the target of an investigation.

When a BON investigator is unable to substantiate the claims made in the complaint filed with the BON, the investigation will be closed. The person or entity that filed the complaint with the BON will then be notified that the investigation was closed. When the BON investigator substantiates the claims made in the complaint, a formal complaint will be issued.

Complaint

A complaint, usually received via certified mail, is typically the first, formal notice that the nurse receives from the BON accusing the nurse of violating the NPA and its rules. As required by the APA, the complaint will identify the BON authority for issuing the complaint, as well as a general statement of the facts, alleged NPA violations, and a hearing date.

If the nurse has not already retained an attorney to represent him or her, it is important to consider taking this step. It will be expensive, from a financial perspective, but not retaining an attorney could prove to be more detrimental should the nurse decide to tread these adversarial waters alone. The financial burden associated with defending oneself can be minimized if malpractice insurance has been purchased that permits the nurse to have legal representation at administrative hearings.

Usually, acts or omissions will allegedly constitute negligence or unprofessional conduct. It is important for nurses to know how BONs determine that a nurse has embarked on negligent or unprofessional conduct.

Negligence is the "failure to possess and exercise that degree of knowledge, skill, care, and diligence that is possessed and exercised by nurses in the same field of practice who are practicing under similar circumstances."[42] Nurses need to be sure that BONs prove that negligence occurred as it is defined in the practice act. Often, negligence is asserted without asking if nurses in the same field of practice practicing under similar circumstances would have done anything differently. In addition, this definition of negligence focuses only on the degree of knowledge, skill, care, and diligence of the nurse. As a result, where the nurse can show that he or she exercised the requisite knowledge, skill, care, and diligence, negligence allegations must fail.

Just as what constitutes negligence can be one source of ongoing controversy in a disciplinary matter, what constitutes unprofessional conduct can be just as contentious. Courts have had to get involved. Most of the time, courts uphold a Final Agency Order that concludes that the facts constitute unprofessional conduct. However, *Tuma v. Board of Nursing of the State of Idaho,*[43] a frequently cited nursing case, illustrates the Idaho District Court's willingness to overturn the Idaho BON's decision to sanction Nurse Tuma for unprofessional conduct after she talked to a patient about alternative therapies available for the treatment of lymphoma. In *Tuma,* the court recognized that the right of nurses like Tuma to practice their profession was a valuable property right, and that the BON's conclusion that Nurse Tuma's conversation with a patient about alternative treatments for lymphoma was outside of the definition of unprofessional conduct in the Idaho NPA.

Answer

Once the nurse receives the complaint issued by the BON, he or she has an obligation to respond to facts and alleged allegations contained in the complaint. Typically, answers deny the allegations, and affirmative defenses, if any, are presented. After the answer is filed with the BON, there is time to collect additional information. This time period is referred to as the discovery period.

Discovery

Discovery is used to identify the time period within which information is exchanged between the BON and the nurse who is accused of violating the NPA. Medical record information is provided, as well as witness statements and other documentation supporting the BON's assertion that the NPA has been violated. Additionally, depositions may be taken.

Depositions are taken under oath, in the presence of all parties and a court reporter who records questions asked and answers given. Depositions are time consuming, but can yield valuable information.

Once discovery is completed, a hearing date is scheduled. It is on this date that the nurse confronts the BON members face to face.

Hearing

At the BON hearing, the BON investigator, through the BON attorney, will open the disciplinary proceeding by providing the BON with a historical picture of the nurse's licensure status, and presenting the evidence gathered during the investigation process. Witness statements, if any, as well as medical records and other documentation are usually introduced and discussed by the investigator. The ability to introduce a wide range of evidence through the investigator will usually mean that the BON will not present other witnesses.

Once the BON attorney has completed questioning the investigator, the nurse's attorney will have an opportunity to question the investigator further. Typically, questions focus on the investigator's clinical background and the investigation process, as well as the substantive information that was gathered during the investigation process, information not collected by the investigator, and information collected but not presented at the BON hearing.

Once the nurse's attorney concludes questioning the investigator, the BON has an opportunity to present corroborating evidence from other witnesses. After each of these witnesses testifies before the BON at the hearing, the nurse's attorney has the option to question each witness further.

After the BON attorney presents all of the witnesses and evidence for consideration, the nurse's attorney has an opportunity to present witnesses and evidence to exonerate the nurse. After each of the nurse's witnesses concludes their testimony, the BON attorney has an opportunity to question them further.

After the nurse's attorney presents all of the witnesses and evidence he or she wants the BON to consider, the BON and nurse's attorney have the privilege of making closing arguments. Closing arguments allow both sides to tie the evidence and witness statements together so that the BON renders a decision in their favor.

Once closing arguments are completed, the BON retires to confidentially discuss the matter and render a decision. Once a decision has been reached, BON members return to the hearing room to announce their decision. Board members will be individually polled to determine if disciplinary action, if any, will be imposed.

Decision

Should the BON decide not to impose disciplinary action, the matter will be closed. Should the BON decide to impose disciplinary action, several options are considered. Typically, NPA's give BONs the authority to reprimand, suspend, and revoke a nursing license. In addition, the BON may place a nurse on probation, and refer a nurse to the state's peer assistance program where chemical dependency issues are dealt with.

Once a decision is made to take formal disciplinary action, and a specific sanction is imposed, the BON is responsible for issuing a Final Agency Order delineating the findings of fact, conclusions of law, and the sanctions imposed. Unless the nurse contests the Final Agency Order within the statutory period of time, the matter is closed.

Appeal

Where a nurse objects to the Final Agency Order and files a timely appeal, the district courts, as well as the state Supreme Courts, generally have the authority to review the matter. Typically, agency orders are upheld. However, some decisions are reversed, so the decision to appeal should not be quickly ruled out. Such was the case in *Slagle v. Wyoming State Board of Nursing.*[44]

In *Slagle*, Lennea Slagle alleged that the Wyoming State Board of Nursing violated her right to due process when it suspended her license to practice as an advanced practice nurse for 1 month. The case was ultimately reviewed by the Wyoming Supreme Court. The Wyoming Supreme Court concluded that Lennea had a property interest in her license to practice as an advanced practice nurse, and that the board must give her notice of the alleged grounds upon which she may be disciplined. In this case, the Wyoming Supreme Court noted that Lennea was not given this kind of notice, and that her due process rights were violated because of the omission. As a result, the court reversed the board's suspension decision.

Trends

Multistate Licensure

The NCSBN estimates that approximately 8 to 12% of all practicing nurses practice in more than one state. Anticipating that number to grow, the NCSBN proposed that the licensure system for nurses be changed so that practice in more than one state is permitted. Five models were considered. The five models were reciprocity, fast endorsement, mutual recognition, federal law, and corporate credentialing.

Mutual recognition emerged as the preferred model. Mutual recognition was reportedly the simplest and most workable model.[45] This determination was made after evaluating the five models against specific criteria. Mutual recognition is a licensure system proposed by the NCSBN that allows a nurse to practice in every state that has adopted an interstate compact. An interstate compact is a legislatively enacted agreement between two or more states to coordinate activities associated with nurse licensure.

After evaluating the five models, the NCSBN concluded that mutual recognition best met the evaluative criteria. Some question the conclusions drawn by the NCSBN, contending that given the criteria, the current licensure system performs favorably.

Evaluative Criteria Used by the NCSBN

1. Anyone practicing nursing is accountable.
2. The source of legal authority for scope and location of practice is delineated.
3. Licensed nurses must have demonstrated knowledge, skill, and abilities to provide safe and effective nursing care.
4. Standards for education, licensure, and discipline are established.
5. An expeditious disciplinary process is promoted, while ensuring due process protection for all parties.
6. Effective monitoring of practitioners' competency and professional conduct is provided.
7. The protection of the public by dissemination of information about disciplinary action with and across jurisdictional boundaries is provided.
8. An open information exchange system is provided.
9. The criteria are compatible with state sovereignty.
10. Barriers to interstate practice are eliminated.
11. Interstate commerce is facilitated.
12. The administration is cost effective and cost conscious.
13. Revenue to support operations is generated.

National Council of State Boards of Nursing, Inc (NCSBN). *Model Nursing Practice Act*, 1994, National Council of State Boards of Nursing, Chicago, Illinois, pp. 7–8.

Currently, anyone practicing nursing must be accountable; there is a scope of legal authority for practice and discipline in every NPA. Nurses must demonstrate that they have the knowledge, skills, and abilities to provide safe and effective care because more and more NPAs contain continuing competency provisions. In addition, due process is ensured for nurses who face disciplinary action and practitioners are monitored for continuing competency and professional conduct. The public has access to information about and disciplinary action taken against nurses and state BONs already exchange information to ensure that disciplinary action is enforced across state lines. Also, state sovereignty is unquestioned, and interstate practice is permitted where the nurse holds a license in the jurisdiction in which he or she practices. Interstate commerce is also preserved, and cost efficiency and cost consciousness is practiced by BONs. Finally, sufficient revenue is already generated to meet current operational expenses incurred by many BONs, and opportunities to increase revenue potential continue to exist.

As a result, those skeptical about mutual recognition observe that when compared to the current licensure model, mutual recognition does not seem to meet the criteria any more effectively. In their view, mutual recognition actually falls short of meeting some evaluative criteria: state sovereignty is affected, barriers to practice are not necessarily eliminated, interstate commerce may not actually be facilitated, and revenue generation is expected to be adversely affected because the cost associated with implementing mutual recognition is anticipated to be significant, requiring BONs to generate substantially more revenue to cover the operational costs.

The ANA's House of Delegates expressed concern about mutual recognition, and an action report, sponsored by representatives of nine state nurses associations (Colorado, Hawaii, Kentucky, New Mexico, Nevada, Oklahoma, Oregon, Texas, and Washington) was passed in 1998 that directed that the ANA support the implementation of alternative approaches to state licensure, including, but not limited to, mutual recognition only if specific guidelines were followed. The guidelines issued by the ANA House of Delegates can be found in Appendix A.

Although this 1998 directive from the ANA House of Delegates outlines the concerns about the mutual recognition model proposed by NCSBN, ANA supports a licensure model that provides public protection, requires that anyone practicing nursing be accountable for complying with all laws of the area within which they practice, and facilitates interstate practice. In spite of the disagreement that exists regarding mutual recognition, by the end of 2000, nine states had enacted mutual recognition (Arkansas, Iowa, Maryland, Mississippi, Nebraska, North Carolina, South Dakota, Texas, and Utah). Similar legislation died in Idaho and Wisconsin.

As an alternative to imposing a system that created a new licensure scheme, ANA the proposed three models that could be used to strengthen the current licensure system for nurses, afford nurses the opportunity to practice across state lines physically or electronically, and ensure the public maximum protection. The first alternative was to ensure that every NPA contained a rapid endorsement provision. *Rapid endorsement* calls for the BON currently overseeing the practice of the nurse to expediently verify that the nurse is a practitioner in good standing in that state, and then for the BON to which the nurse is applying to permit that nurse to practice in that jurisdiction without having to take the licensure examination again. Second, the ANA suggested that NPAs should require that every nurse register in every state in which he or she practices nursing. Third, the ANA recommended that careful consideration be given to concluding that care is delivered at the site of the provider, rather than the site of the patient. This option was consistent with proposed regulations issued by the Health Care Financing Administration (HCFA).[46] In addition to these alternatives, at least one other alternative exists: enacting interstate compacts, but allowing nurses to opt into the compact. BONs are already going to have to use multiple record keeping systems, so the voluntary nature of the compact would not result in any increased record keeping. In addition, nurses who need or want the privilege to practice in the states that have enacted the interstate compact pay for that privilege.

How interstate practice issues will be handled in the future is unclear. For the ANA, the 1999 House of Delegates agreed to

1. Support the following approaches for regulating interstate/multistate practice:
   - Physical practice in any state requires licensure by that state. Such authorization might be achieved through a mutual recognition compact which meets the 14 criteria established by the 1998 ANA House of Delegates;
   - Rapid endorsement by state agencies that have jurisdiction over nursing licensure supports multistate practice and mobility.
   - Telenursing practice, in which the nurse is located in a state different from that of the recipient of care, is facilitated by conferring licensure jurisdiction to the regulatory agency of the state in which the nurse is located.
   - A state may choose to use a registry or telehealth permit to hold out-of-state nurses accountable to its licensing agency and its regulations.
2. Recognize that some state nurses associations (SNAs) have determined, or will determine, to participate in implementing a mutual recognition compact for multistate practice.
3. Monitor and evaluate activities including the development of administrative rules related to the initiation and implementation of the various approaches for regulating interstate practice for RNs and advanced practice nurses.
4. Request the ANA Board of Directors bring to the ANA House of Delegates in the year 2000 an evaluation of the 14 points on interstate practice with supporting information, data evaluation, and new environmental trends to support discussion on the matter.

Clearly, interstate practice is a priority for ANA, NCSBN, SNAs, and nurses who practice in more than one jurisdiction. Approaches to interstate practice are likely to be varied, and the implementation of the mutual recognition model may be slow because financial impact issues need to be addressed. Also, most attorney general opinions issued on the subject to date suggest that Constitutional problems exist with mutual recognition, such as the unconstitutional delegation of legislative authority and infringement on states' rights.

Telehealth

Telehealth is defined as the use of telecommunications equipment and networks to transfer health care information between participants at different locations.[47] Telehealth, in an ANA publication, is defined in more conceptual terms as the removal of time and distance barriers for the delivery of health care service or related health care activities.[48] Regardless of the definitions used, telehealth technologies eliminate the need for traditional face-to-face contact, and instead, rely on computers, telephones, video monitors, telecommunication networks, and other technologies to facilitate a health care-related interaction.

Recognizing the integral role that telehealth will play in the delivery of twenty-first century health care services, the ANA issued 12 telehealth principles that can be used to guide members of the nursing profession and other health care professions. the ANA's issuance of these telehealth principles is reflective of the organizations'

ANA Telehealth Principles

1. The basic standards of professional conduct governing each health care profession are not altered by the use of telehealth technologies to deliver health care, conduct research, or provide education. Developed by each profession, these standards focus in part on the practitioner's responsibility to provide ethical and high-quality care.

2. A health care system or health care practitioner cannot use telehealth as a vehicle for providing services that are not otherwise legally or professionally authorized.

3. Telehealth services must adhere to basic assurance of quality and professional health care in accordance with each health care discipline's clinical standards. Each health care discipline must examine how telehealth affects or changes its patterns of care delivery and what modifications to existing clinical standards may be required.

4. The use of telehealth technologies does not require additional licensure.

5. Each health care profession is responsible for developing its own processes for ensuring competencies in the delivery of health care through the use of telehealth technologies.

6. Practice and clinical guidelines in telehealth should be developed based on empirical evidence, when available, and on professional consensus among all involved health care disciplines. The development of these guidelines may include collaboration with government agencies.

7. The integrity and therapeutic value of the client–health care practitioner relationship should be maintained and not diminished by the use of telehealth technology.

8. Confidentiality of client visits, client health records, and the integrity of information in a health care information system are essential.

9. Telehealth documentation requirements must be developed that ensure documentation of each client encounter with recommendations and treatments, communication with other health care providers as appropriate, and adequate protections for client confidentiality.

10. All clients directly involved in a telehealth encounter must be informed about the process, the attendant risks and benefits, and their rights and responsibilities. Clients must provide adequate informed consent.

11. Client and practitioner safety must be ensured. Safe hardware and software, combined with demonstrated user competency, are essential components of safe telehealth practice.

12. A systematic and comprehensive research agenda must be developed and supported by government agencies and health care professions for ongoing telehealth assessment.

American Nurses Association. 1999. *Core Principles on Telehealth*. Washington, D.C.: American Nurses Publishing.

ANA Recommended Measures to Accompany Implementation of Telehealth Technologies

▮ Previously established confidentiality and privacy protections of health information should be maintained as well as scrutinized to establish if they are sufficient.

▮ Patients who are the recipients of telehealth interventions should be informed of potential risks and benefits.

▮ Dissemination of patient data or identifiable patient images should be controlled by explicit consent of the patient.

▮ Patients should be informed if other individuals outside the health care team are involved in the telehealth interaction.

▮ Individuals who violate established privacy, confidentiality, and security regulations and misuse information should be penalized.

Available at URL: http://www.nursingworld.org/readroom/tele2.html

belief that the strength and promise of telehealth lies in providing increased access to health care services by augmenting existing services, not replacing them.

With telehealth, access to health care services will not be limited by state or international boundaries. The possibilities are endless. The concern is that the proliferation of telehealth technologies will be used to replace the independent judgment and assessment of health care professionals. Additionally, concerns about privacy, confidentiality, and security are heightened. Because of these concerns, the ANA recommends that specific measures accompany the implementation of telehealth technologies in patient care situations.

The nursing profession is addressing telehealth issues by considering licensure models like the mutual recognition models proposed by the NCSBN. However, the medical profession is focusing on telehealth, not by considering sweeping licensure reform measures, but by passing legislation and administrative rules that regulate a physician's telehealth interactions. By September, 1998, 21 states had issued telehealth rulings requiring physicians to have full licensure where physicians practice using telehealth technologies in those states (see sidebars, next page).[49]

Colorado and Montana allow out-of-state physicians to obtain a limited telehealth license or certificate. The action taken in these two states is consistent with the model telehealth legislation proposed by the Federation of State Medical Boards. The model telehealth legislation proposes a limited license for physicians practice using telehealth technologies.[50] A limited license, certificate, permit, or registration might provide effective alternatives to facilitate telehealth practice by nurses.

States Enacting Telehealth Legislation Affecting Physicians

- Alabama
- Arizona
- Arkansas
- California
- Colorado
- Connecticut
- Florida
- Georgia
- Hawaii
- Illinois
- Indiana
- Maine
- Mississippi
- Missouri
- Nebraska
- North Carolina
- North Dakota
- Oklahoma
- South Dakota
- Tennessee
- Texas

Confidentiality

Facilitating telehealth practice raises closely related concerns about confidentiality, privacy, and security for patients, and providers. Roy L. Simpson, in a 1994 issue of *Nursing Management*, outlined intentional misuse, unauthorized access from browsing, and untrained users as the primary causes for breaches in confidentiality, privacy, and security of electronic medical record information.[51] Additionally, confidentiality, privacy, and security issues arise when electronic patient information is properly accessed but improperly used.

Concerns about confidentiality, privacy, and security led Congress to pass the Federal Privacy Act of 1974.[52] This act ensures that patient records held by the federal government and state governments will generally not be disclosed to third parties without their consent. However, records held by nongovernmental entities are not required to abide by the Federal Privacy Act of 1974, and state statutes (in spite of the Uniform Health-Care Information Act of 1988 proposed by the National Conference of Commissioners on Uniform State Laws) do not necessarily exist to protect these records. In fact, in 1994, federal or state statutorily enacted laws did not specifically protect the privacy of patient records.[53] Since that time, the Fair Health Information Protection Act of 1994, the Medical Records Confidentiality Act of 1995, as well as other federal and state health care privacy legislation have been proposed.

State Medical Boards Codifying Telehealth Provisions

- Arizona
- Florida
- Iowa
- Maine
- Massachusetts
- New Mexico
- New York
- Pennsylvania
- Rhode Island
- Virginia

Finally, on August 21, 1996, the Health Insurance Portability and Accountability Act (HIPAA) was signed into law by President Clinton. Among the acts' mandates was the directive to develop comprehensive privacy and confidentiality protections for patients and their medical record information. The intent of the privacy rules was to give patients greater control over the information in their medical records and impose stiff penalties for violations of the privacy rules. HIPAA is discussed in more detail in Chapter 8.

Federal laws are beginning to provide privacy protection for patients and their medical records, and so are the states. Georgia's statute allows anyone who is injured because the statute is violated to seek damages and recover the cost of filing suit. In part, the act says that anyone "who uses a computer or computer network with the intention of examining any employment, medical, salary, credit or other financial or personal data relating to any other person with knowledge that such examination is without authority shall be guilty of the crime of computer invasion of privacy."[54] This statute was allegedly violated when Thomas Boyer, MD, director of Digestive Disease at Emory School of Medicine, accessed Nurse Cynthia Ruocco's medical records without her permission. Nurse Ruocco sued Boyer, Emory University, Emory Clinic, and Dr. Michael W. Fried. Dr. Fried was reportedly Nurse Ruocco's immediate supervisor and allegedly fired her shortly after Nurse Ruocco learned that Boyer accessed her medical records. Not only did Nurse Ruocco sue for $20 million in damages, she has also asked that Boyer be criminally prosecuted for violating the computer invasion of privacy statute.[55] Criminal violations of this statute are considered felonies, and could cost Boyer his license to practice medicine, as well as his freedom.

Continuing Competency

Published position statements from the NCSBN on the issue of continuing competency date back to 1984. In 1984, the NCSBN recognized that continuing competency was an issue that was beginning to receive increased attention, and that passage of the licensure examination did not ensure that public health, safety, and welfare was protected throughout the career of the nurse.[56]

Since the publication of that initial position paper, the NCSBN has continued to focus on continuing competency. They have defined *competence* as the application of knowledge and the interpersonal, decision-making, and psychomotor skills expected for the nurse's practice role, within the context of public health, welfare, and safety.[57] They have also defined *continued competence* as the ongoing ability to render safe direct nursing care or the ongoing ability to make sound judgments upon which nursing care is based.[58] In addition, the NCSBN has identified mechanisms to evaluate continuing competency, offered a continuing competency conceptual framework, described the regulatory responsibility inherent with continuing competence by articulating a regulatory model for competence assurance, and created competence standards.

State BONs have also begun to address the issue. For example, in Kentucky, open forums were held to discuss continuing competency,[59] and in Oklahoma, professional portfolios have been identified as a mechanism that will likely to be used to ensure continuing competency. These portfolios can include self-evaluation forms, evidence of continuing education and other professional development activities, and certification materials. Sulinda Moffett, MS, RN, former executive director of the Oklahoma Board of Nursing, and Ann Ferguson, PhD, RN, former associate director for nursing education for the Oklahoma Board of Nursing published an article outlining the Oklahoma BON's portfolio approach to continuing competency.[60]

In spite of those efforts, the Pew Health Professions Commission released a report in 1998 that determined that existing state regulatory models were limited, and asserted that the ability of current regulatory bodies to remove egregiously incompetent providers had failed to keep pace with dramatic changes in health care. As a result, the Pew Health Professions Commission recommended that health care professionals be required to demonstrate competency throughout their professional careers.

The 1998 Pew Commission report recognizes that professional associations, like the ANA, established and continued to perfect standards, goals, and evaluation measurements to meet the demands for competence throughout a health care professional's career. The report goes on to suggest that these standards, goals, and evaluation mechanisms were good places to start to ensure continuing competency.[61] ANA agrees, and is working in collaboration with the NCSBN and other stakeholders to ensure that continuing competency of nurses is clearly conveyed to consumers. Numerous mechanisms are being considered.

NPAs outline the scope of practice for registered nurses and licensed practical nurses. They also identify the activities in which unlicensed assistive personnel and other identified health care workers may engage. Failure to act in accordance with the mandates of the NPA subjects a licensee to disciplinary action. Disciplinary action varies depending on the offense allegedly committed by the licensee and is imposed after a licensee is afforded an opportunity to be heard.

Continuing Competency Mechanisms

- Peer review
- Professional certification and recertification
- Testing and retesting
- Continuing education
- Self-assessment
- Chart audits
- Electronic and clinical simulations
- Combinations of mechanisms

The specific requirements of each NPA, APA, and case law vary from state to state. Nurses granted the authority to practice in a given state should be aware of the specific provisions of the NPA, and should work to ensure that the NPA addresses such contemporary issues as staffing, whistle blower protection, mandatory overtime, and abandonment. In so doing, the nurse ensures that he or she is practicing within the scope of practice of the NPA, and that the it provides guidance regarding the issues faced in the practice of nursing. Failure to act in accordance with the NPA could lead to disciplinary action, as well as to civil and/or criminal litigation. The 18 nurses at Boston's Dana-Farber Cancer Institute know first hand what can happen when an alleged failure to act in accordance with the NPA occurs. In 1994, two patients at Dana-Farber were given chemotherapy overdoses over a 4-day period. One patient died soon after the overdose, and another sustained severe heart damage and died 3 years later. The Massachusetts Board of Registration in Nursing investigated the matter and by March, 2000, more than 6 years after the alleged wrongdoing, completed the disciplinary proceedings. In the end, 16 of the 18 nurses involved in the overdose accepted reprimands. Two nurses were exonerated. They were Ilene Galinsky and Susan Coggeshall-Aikey. The Massachusetts Board of Registration in Nursing exonerated them because they only monitored, not administered, the chemotherapy and were not involved in the 4-day overdose.

Although the administrative proceedings for the 18 Dana-Farber nurses has finally concluded, civil litigation could follow. Chapter 3 focuses on civil litigation, in an attempt to assist nurses like those 18 nurses practicing at the Dana-Farber Cancer Institute and others in being more informed about the process.

End Notes

1. National Council of State Boards of Nursing, Inc (NCSBN). 1994. *Model Nursing Practice Act.* Chicago: National Council of State Boards of Nursing; pp. 5–6.
2. Ibid.
3. American Nurses Association (ANA). 1996. *Model Practice Act.* Washington, D.C.: American Nurses Association; p. 13.
4. NCSBN 1994, p. 2.
5. NCSBN 1994, p. 3.
6. ANA, p. 20.
7. NCSBN 1994, pp. 3–4.
8. NCSBN 1994, p. 9.
9. NCSBN 1994, p. 10.
10. ANA, p. 22.
11. Colorado Board of Nursing. 1995. *Colorado Nurse Practice Act.* pp. 4–5.
12. NCSBN 1994, pp. 12–15.
13. ANA, pp. 21, 22.
14. 454 So. 2d 1041 (Al. 1984).

15. No. 1-97-4560 (Ill. App. Ct. June 17, 1999).
16. ANA, p. 28.
17. NCSBN 1994, pp. 22, 23.
18. 244 N.W. 2d 683 (Ne. 1976).
19. ANA, p. 36.
20. ANA, p. 36.
21. NCSBN 1994, pp. 27–28.
22. ANA, p. 31.
23. ANA, p. 31.
24. 505 A. 2d 357 (Pa. 1986).
25. Oklahoma Board of Nursing. 1998. *Oklahoma Bard of Nursing Practice Act and Rules and Regulations.* pp. 38–40.
26. NCSBN 1994, pp. 29–32.
27. 403 S.E. 2d 582 (N.C. 1991).
28. NCSBN 1994, p. 33.
29. Willmann, J. 1998. *Annotated Guide to the Texas Nursing Practice Act*, 3rd ed. Austin, TX: Texas Nurses Association; pp. 13–16.
30. Willmann, p. 18.
31. Willmann, p. 24.
32. Willmann, p. 24.
33. Willmann, p. 25.
34. Available from URL: http://www.ncsbn.org/files/publications/positions/cdntoc.asp.
35. Ibid.
36. Ibid, p. 6.
37. 757 P. 2d 1167 (Co. 1988).
38. 457 So. 2d 931 (Ms. 1984).
39. ANA, p. 28.
40. ANA, p. 37.
41. 436 A. 2d 369 (D.C. 1981).
42. Oklahoma Board of Nursing, p. 38.
43. 593 P.2d 712 (Id. 1979).
44. 954 P. 2d 979 (Wy 1998).
45. NCSBN. 1998. *Mutual Recognition Talking Points & Speech Text.* Chicago: National Council of State Boards of Nursing; p. 7.
46. HCFA, proposed regulations, Vol 63, No. 119.
47. Chaffee, M. 1999. A telehealth odyssey. *AJN* 99(7): 27.
48, Milholland, D.K. 1997. Telehelath: A tool for nursing practice. *Nursing Trends & Issues* 2(4).
49. Available from URL: http://www.hpts.org/hpts97issueb....f28908525671a006b2179?OpenDocument
50. Gobis, L. 1996. Telenursing: Nursing by telephone across state lines. *Journal of Nursing Law* 3(3): 14.

51. Simpson, R. 1994. Ensuring patient data, privacy, confidentiality and security. *Nursing Management* 25(7): 18–20.

52. 5 U.S.C. §522a (1994).

53. Bibas, S.A. 1994. A contractual approach to data privacy. *Harvard Journal of Law and Public Policy* 17: 595.

54. O.C.G.A. 16-9-93.

55. Schmitt, B. 1999. Suit alleges university tapped into nurse's medical records. *Fulton County Daily Report* October 26; available from URL: http://www.lawnewsnetwork.com.

56. NCSBN. 1984. *Continued competence.* National Council Position Paper. Chicago: National Council of State Boards of Nursing.

57. Available from URL: http://www/ncsbn.org/files/publications/annualreports/ar1996/devcomp.asp.

58. Available from URL: http://www/ncsbn.org/files/publications/positions/cont1.asp, p 2 of 3.

59. deVries, C. 1999. Continued competence: Assuring quality health care. *AJN* 99(10): 61.

60. Moffett, S., Ferguson, A. 1998. Creating a professional profile. A Celebration of Nursing Practice in Oklahoma. 19(2).

61. Taskforce on Health Care Workforce Regulation. 1998. *Strengthening Consumer Protection: Priorities for Health Care Workforce Regulation.* Pew Health Professions Commission; p. iii.

The Nurse as a Civil Litigation Defendant 3

Introduction

With patients, nurses are expected to use reasonable care and skill reflective of the standard of care. Failure to adhere to those standards can lead to litigation, and to a determination that the nurse was negligent or committed malpractice in the delivery of patient care services.

Historically, nurses have rarely been named as defendants when civil lawsuits were filed. The nurses' employer, usually an acute care facility, was the named defendant. However, that trend is changing. Nurses are increasingly being named as defendants in lawsuits alleging that the nurse did or failed to do something that harmed the patient–plaintiff. Additionally, employers have begun to sue nurses in an attempt to recover damages awarded in negligence and malpractice causes of action.

In the *Journal of Nursing Law*, Mable H. Smith-Pittman, a nurse and attorney, studied nurses' involvement in the litigation process between 1990 and 1997, and found that nurses practicing in specific specialty units were more likely to be involved in civil litigation than were nurses practicing in other settings.[1] According to Smith-Pittman, nurses practicing in obstetrics and gynecology (ob/gyn) settings were more likely than nurses working in other specialty units to be involved in civil litigation. Next, nurses practicing in ob/gyn settings, nurses practicing in emergency rooms, the operating room, mental health units, postoperative settings, nursing homes, critical care units, pediatric, and medical-surgical units were more likely to be sued than nurses practicing in other specialty settings. Although the incidence was not as high, nurses practicing in newborn nurseries, recovery rooms, home health, preoperative, corrections, personnel agencies, occupational health settings, and hospices were also involved in civil litigation.[2]

Because nurses are involved in the litigation process, and because nurses are increasingly being named as defendants in lawsuits that allege failure to act as reasonably prudent health care professionals, it is important for nurses to understand the theories or causes of action that may be used to hold them legally responsible for the wrong that allegedly occurred. It is also critical for nurses to know what courts are holding them responsible for, and what can be expected during the litigation process. First, causes of action will be outlined. Next, doctrines and terms used in the civil litigation process will be identified. Finally, the civil litigation process will be discussed.

Causes of Action

Cause of action is defined as the fact or facts that give a person the right to seek judicial relief.[3] In patient care situations, the occurrence of a particular set of facts may give rise to a cause of action based on a specific legal theory. For nurses, the legal theories upon which most civil cases against them are based are negligence, negligence per se, malpractice, wrongful birth, wrongful death, defamation, assault and battery, loss of consortium, intentional infliction of emotional distress, and intentional indifference.

Negligence

Negligence is failing to act as an ordinarily prudent person under similar circumstances. For a negligence-based cause of action to exist, plaintiffs must prove that the four elements of negligence were present: duty, breach, causation, and damages. For a negligence cause of action to proceed against a nurse, there must have been a duty or obligation on the part of the nurse to conform to some standard that was breached. The breach, in turn, must have caused some damage or injury. Although negligence can occur whether or not an individual is acting in a personal or professional capacity, nurses commit negligence when they act in a manner that deviates from the standard of care, and the deviation results in harm to patients for whom they care. When nurses act negligently in their professional capacity, they are said to have committed malpractice. Malpractice will be discussed in more detail later in this chapter.

Duty

For a nurse–defendant to be found negligent, the patient–plaintiff must prove that the nurse breached some duty owed to the patient. Nurses assume a duty to provide care for patients that is consistent with the standard of care when a nurse–patient relationship is established. Providing care that is consistent with the standard of care encompasses a nurses' duty to protect patients from foreseeable injuries.[4] *Lunsford v. Board of Nurse Examiners*[5] exemplifies the way that courts deal with the duty nurses have to patients.

In *Lunsford*, a registered nurse was working in the emergency room at Willacy County Hospital in Raymondville, Texas, when Donald Wayne Floyd entered the emergency room complaining of chest pain and pressure, and pain and pressure radiating down his left arm. Francis Farrell, Floyd's traveling companion attempted to have Floyd examined by a physician and was told that he needed to initially be seen by a nurse. The physician was sitting at the emergency room nurse's station. When nurse Lunsford approached the nurse's station, the physician instructed the nurse to transfer Floyd to a neighboring hospital in Harlingen, Texas, 24 miles away because the emergency room's cardiac care equipment was already in use.

After interviewing Floyd, nurse Lunsford suspected cardiac involvement, but instructed Farrell to drive Floyd 24 miles to the neighboring hospital. Prior to sending them on their way, Lunsford allegedly suggested that Farrell drive with the car's emergency flashers on, and that she speed to get there. Lunsford also reportedly asked Farrell if she knew cardiopulmonary resuscitation (CPR) and indicated that Farrell might need to perform CPR prior to their arrival at the Harlingen hospital.

Approximately 5 miles from the Harlingen hospital, Floyd died. A complaint was subsequently filed with the Texas Board of Nurse Examiners. After a hearing on the matter, the Board of Nurse Examiners suspended Lunsford's license for 1 year. Lunsford appealed the board's decision. The case was eventually heard by an appellate court that determined that a nurse in Lunsford's position has a duty to evaluate the status of a sick person seeking his or her professional care. The court also determined that nurses like Lunsford have a duty to implement the care needed to stabilize a patient's condition, and to prevent complications. Lunsford, according to the court, breached her duty to Floyd when she failed to assess his condition, inform the physician of Floyd's life-and-death condition, and take appropriate action to stabilize his condition and prevent his death.

Lunsford is significant because it recognizes that a nurse–patient relationship exists and stems from the State of Texas issuing her license to practice nursing. In addition, the court pointed out that Lunsford's duty to Floyd could not be relieved by any hospital policy or physician order.

In addition to *Lunsford,* cases from a number of other states recognize the nurse–patient relationship as a separate and distinct relationship,[6] and as a prerequisite for determining whether or not a nurse owes the patient a duty to provide care in accordance with the requisite standard of care. If a nurse shows that he or she was not assigned to that particular patient on the date that the negligence allegedly occurred, or working the day or time the negligence allegedly occurred, no duty will be imposed on the nurse. Because no duty will be imposed on the nurse, negligence allegations will fail.[7]

Porter v. Lima Memorial Hospital[8] demonstrates how courts handle this. In *Porter,* an emergency room nurse provided care to the infant daughter of Rachel Porter who was eventually discharged after being examined for injuries sustained when she was thrown to the floor of an automobile. After Liesel, the infant had been discharged, Rachel, her mother noticed that the baby was breathing irregularly. The nurse examined Liesel, and determined that no treatment was necessary. By the time that Rachel arrived home, she noticed that Liesel was much worse, and took her to another emergency room. At that emergency room, a spinal cord injury and paralysis were diagnosed. Rachel sued the hospital where Liesel was taken initially, alleging that the emergency room nurse failed to repeat the taking of Liesel's vital signs, inform the physician of the Liesel's vital signs and irregular breathing patterns, and immobilize Liesel to prevent the deterioration of a spinal cord injury, which was diagnosed at another hospital. The court determined that liability would not be imposed against the hospital, because the nurse's actions were reasonable. With regard to the failure to immobilize claim, the court declared that nurses have no duty to immobilize apart from a doctor's instruction to immobilize a patient. The physician paid $2.5 million to the family prior to trial.

Although courts have determined that nurses have a duty to act reasonably when caring for patients, courts have limited the breadth of duties imposed on nurses in a number of specific instances. Nurses have been absolved of duties to assist patients who have no history of impaired mobility, insist that physicians conduct physical examinations, and intervene when a physician exceeds the scope of consent. Five cases discussing each of these limitations on a nurse's duty are discussed below.

First, in *Kimball v. St. Paul Ins. Co.,*[9] a Louisiana court concluded that nurses do not have a duty to assist patients with walking or sitting where patients have no history of health problems that would impair mobility, do not ask for assistance, and do not appear visually incapacitated. The second case discussing the limitations of a nurse's duty is *Daniel v. St. Francis Cabrini Hospital of Alexandria.*[10] In this case, another Louisiana court determined that the nurse has a duty to assist patients where the patient's physical and mental incapacities require assistance. In light of these Louisiana cases, a nurse's duty to assist patients depends on the patient's physical and mental condition. It is therefore important for nurses to properly assess patients to determine whether or not they need assistance.

With regard to insisting that a physician take a specific course action, courts in Minnesota and Missouri have determined that nurses do not assume that duty. *Mercil v. Mathers* and *Downey v. Mitchell* are the third and fourth cases included here that discuss the limitations on a nurse's duty.

In *Mercil v. Mathers,*[11] a Minnesota court decided that a nurse did not have a duty to insist or order a physician to conduct a physical examination on a patient. In *Downey v. Mitchell*[12] a Missouri court concluded that an operating room nurse had no duty to intervene where a surgeon, performing surgery on a patient, exceeded the scope of consent given by the patient.

The fifth case involves the issue of informed consent. Informed consent cases have consistently held that it is the physician's responsibility to obtain consent to perform any procedure performed by the physician. Contemporary cases, like *Mathias v. St. Catherine's Hospital, Inc.,*[13] continue to conclude that informed consent is a physician's responsibility, rather than a duty imposed upon nurses. In spite of these cases, where a nurse intends to perform any invasive procedure, it is advisable for the nurse to obtain the informed consent of patients. Failure to obtain the informed consent of patients by nurses who perform invasive procedures could result in nurses being defendants in failure to obtain informed consent cases.

Although courts have been willing to construct parameters around a nurse's duty to his or her patient, when a patient establishes that a particular nurse took care of him or her when negligence allegedly occurred, the nurse will have assumed a duty to provide reasonable care for the patient. A nurses' failure to provide reasonable care subjects the nurse to liability for negligence where the patient–plaintiff proves that the failure caused the patient to sustain damage or an injury. *Vassey v. Burch*[14] exemplifies this principle.

In *Vassey,* an emergency room nurse was accused of failing to obtain treatment for a patient who was ultimately diagnosed with appendicitis. Evidence was presented suggesting that the nurse was ruling out other possible causes, and the court concluded that the patient presented insufficient evidence to support his claim that the nurse failed to exercise reasonable care. In reaching its' decision, the court noted that the nurse was under a duty to exercise reasonable care and diligence in the application of his or her knowledge and skill to the care of the patient, and use his or her best judgment in the treatment and care of patients. According to the court, when a nurse fails to exercise reasonable care and diligence, and harm comes to the patient for whom the nurse is caring, negligence occurs.[15] In *Vassey,* the court determined that although the nurse has a duty to exercise reasonable care, the patient failed to show that the nurses' ruling out other possible causes of the patients' abdominal pain was unreasonable, and not diligent or indicative of the nurse exercising less than her best judgment.

What constitutes reasonable care has been the focus of many cases filed against health care professionals and the settings in which they practice. For nurses, there seems to be an emerging trend: Where the nurse assesses, plans, implements, and evaluates the care given to a patient in accordance with the requisite standard of care, reasonable care will have been provided. Where, however, the nurse fails to address any single component of the nursing process, care provided to a patient will be deemed insufficient, unreasonable, and negligent.

A nurses' *assessment-related failures* include the failure to assess and analyze the level of care needed by the patient and failure to ascertain the patient's wishes with regard to self-determination. *Planning-related failures* include the failure of the nurse to identify an appropriate nursing diagnosis and plan of care. *Implementation failures* include the failure to communicate patient findings in a timely manner, failure to take appropriate action, failure to document assessment findings and patient response to interventions, and failure to preserve patient privacy. *Evaluation failures* include the failure to act as a patient advocate. Each of these four types of failures is described below.

Assessment Failures: Failure to Assess and Analyze the Level of Care Needed by the Patient. Nurses have a duty to assess and analyze the level of care needed by the patient. Where a nurse allegedly fails to fulfill this responsibility, liability for negligence may be threatened. Two cases illustrate this duty.

The first case is *Alvis v. Henderson.*[16] In *Alvis,* Briana L. Alvis was born November 15, 1993, and sustained severe kidney damage during the birth process. After Briana's birth, the family sued the hospital and attending physician alleging that negligence had been committed during the birth process, and that Briana's kidney damage was the result of the negligence of the physician and hospital. Specifically, the hospital was allegedly negligent in permitting the administration of oxytocin (Pitocin) and in failing to detect the fact that Briana, prior to her birth, was in a breech position. The attending physician, Dr. William P. Henderson was allegedly negligent because he ordered the administration of oxytocin, which resulted in the rupture the mother's bag of waters prematurely, failed to discover the baby was in a breech position, and then used excessive force at delivery. The Illinois jury listened to the evidence presented and awarded Briana more than $2.9 million in damages. The jury determined that the physician and hospital were responsible for Briana's damages. The physician was deemed 75% responsible for her damages, and the hospital was 25% responsible. Although the physician was found to be predominately liable for the injuries sustained in this case, the nurse failed to assess and analyze the level of care Briana needed, and the hospital was also found to be partially responsible for her injuries.

Bell v. Western Pennsylvania Hospital[17] is the second case that discusses a nurses responsibility to assess and analyze the level of care needed by a patient. In *Bell*, a man was admitted to the hospital after fracturing his left leg in a motorcycle accident. One day after admission, surgery was performed on the fractured leg, and after surgery, orders were written to have hourly neurovascular checks of the left leg. Because of circulatory concerns, another physician was consulted, and vascular exploration of the left leg was performed later that evening. The next day, the patients' leg became swollen, and a fasciotomy was ordered. Two days after the fasciotomy, an incisional infection developed, and the exposed muscle tissue became necrotic. Antibiotics were administered.

During the next week, the patient seemed stable; however, the bacterial infection remained, and hyperbaric oxygen chamber treatments were thought to be indicated. For the patient to receive the hyperbaric oxygen chamber treatments, he had to be transferred to another hospital. The patient was transferred, and the treatments provided, but the patients' left leg had to be amputated. The patient filed a malpractice cause of action, asserting that his clostridial infection was neither diagnosed, nor properly treated; the failure to debride his wound allowed the clostridial infection to spread; there had been a failure to monitor his open reduction surgery; there was a failure to monitor the condition of his leg, which contributed to the continuing necrosis of the leg tissues; and that the inaction on the part of the hospital and nursing staff increased his risk of exposure to a clostridial infection, which led to the amputation of his leg.

The case was tried and a verdict was returned in favor of the hospital and physicians. The patient and his parents asked that a new trial be granted or that judgment be entered for them in spite of the jury's verdict. The court decided to grant a new trial citing errors that were made with regard to one of the expert witnesses. This decision was appealed by the defendant hospital and physicians to the Superior Court of Pennsylvania, but that court affirmed the decision to grant the patient and his parents a new trial. Subsequent proceedings regarding this matter are unpublished.

To withstand negligence allegations, it is not only important for nurses to assess and analyze the level of care needed by patients, but for them to document their assessment findings, as well as all actions taken to properly care for patients. Failure to assess and analyze, or the failure to document that assessment and analysis has occurred and that proper action has been taken, exposes a nurse to substantial malpractice liability.

Assessment Failures: Failure to Ascertain a Patient's Wishes With Regard to Self-Determination.   Health care professionals, including nurses, have a legal and ethical obligation to act in accordance with a patient's wishes with regard to self-determination. *Self-determination* refers an individual's right to make their own end-of-life treatment decisions. These wishes are reflected in legal documents called *advance directives*. Advance directives include a living will, health care proxy, and durable power of attorney for health care. Appendix B provides an example of an advanced directive, issued according to Oklahoma law, that serves as a living will and identifies individuals to serve as health care proxies.

Failure to abide by these wishes violates the federal Patient Self-Determination Act,[18] state self-determination acts, and can lead to disciplinary action and to civil liability. *Anderson v. St. Francis-St. George Hospital*[19] demonstrates how self-determination issues were handled by one Ohio court.

In *Anderson*, Edward H. Winter was admitted to St. Francis–St. George Hospital because he was having chest pain and was fainting. After George E. Russo, Winter's treating physician, discussed treatment options with Winter, the physician entered a do not resuscitate order in Winter's chart. Three days later, Winter began having ventricular tachycardia. A nurse defibrillated Winter, and upon his regaining consciousness, he thanked the nurse for saving his life. When Russo was informed of Winter's condition he ordered that lidocaine be administered. Two hours later Winter experienced another ventricular tachycardia episode, but it resolved spontaneously.

The next day, Russo ordered the discontinuation of Winter's lidocaine and heart monitor. The day after that, Winter suffered a stroke which paralyzed his right side. Edward H. Winter was eventually discharged, but his right side paralysis persisted until his death almost 2 years following his admission to St. Francis–St. George Hospital.

Prior to his death, Winter sued the hospital alleging the hospital was negligent in failing to obey the do not resuscitate order that had been issued. The case was eventually heard by the Ohio Supreme Court where the justices concluded that the interference in a person's right to die constituted a breach of the health care professional's duty to honor a patient's wishes. In spite of that, the court ruled that Winter was not entitled to damages for the reasonably foreseeable damages associated with the unwanted resuscitation because he did not suffer any damage as a result of the defibrillation.

Planning Failures: Failure to Appropriately Diagnose.   A health care professional's ability to plan an effective course of treatment depends on making a proper diagnosis. Historically, failure to diagnose cases have been filed against physicians, not nurses. However, because nurses do use nursing diagnoses and advanced practice nurses diagnose patient conditions, nurses may find themselves the target of a failure to diagnose case, and need to be aware of the consequences of making an erroneous diagnosis. *Vidana v. Garfield Medical Center*[20] is a failure to properly diagnose case, and illustrates the life-altering effects that diagnostic decisions can have on patients and their families.

In *Vidana,* a physician was accused of failing to complete diagnostic tests on a woman who was a 30 weeks pregnant and was suffering from high blood pressure, uterine tenderness, abdominal pain, and vomiting. Instead of ordering diagnostic tests to determine the source of the woman's abdominal pain, the obstetrician performed a cesarean section. The patient alleged that performing the proper diagnostic tests would have prevented the premature cesarean section delivery of twins who have been diagnosed with moderate cerebral palsy and mild retardation. A California jury heard the evidence and rendered a $6.4 million verdict against the obstetrician, agreeing that the physician failed to properly diagnose the patient prior to performing the cesarean section.

Although *Vidana* involved a physician, the implications are significant for advanced practice nurses who diagnose patients. *Adams v. Krueger, et al*[21] and *Fein v. Permanente Medical Group*[22] demonstrate that advanced practice nurses can and will be held accountable for making accurate diagnoses. In both cases, nurse practitioners were liable for incorrectly diagnosing a patient's condition. In *Fein,* a nurse practitioner and a physician diagnosed Lawrence Fein's chest pain as muscular in nature, rather than cardiovascular. Fein continued to have chest pain and was seen by a third physician who thought his pain was muscular, but ordered an electrocardiogram (EKG). The EKG showed that Fein was having a myocardial infarction. Consequently, Fein was admitted to an in-patient cardiac care unit.

Fein later sued Permanente Medical Group alleging that he suffered compensable damages after two health care providers misdiagnosed his condition. The case was tried by a jury. The jury issued a verdict in favor of Fein and awarded him $1,287,733 in damages. That award was later reduced to $1,037,733 because of a statutory cap on noneconomic damages.

Implementation Failures: Failure to Timely Communicate Patient Findings. Nurses spend more time with patients than any other health care professional. As a result, nurses are in the best position to promptly detect changes in a patient's condition. Detection, however, is only the first step. Nurses are required to promptly communicate troublesome patient findings. Failure to properly communicate patient findings can be devastating for patients, and can be the reason that patients file malpractice causes of action.

Gold v. United Health Service Inc.[23] is a failure to timely communicate patient findings case, and makes evident the effects that these kinds of cases have on patients, and on juries. Cases from a number of other states also make this point.[24]

In *Gold*, Abraham Gold was born 10 weeks early at Charles S. Wilson Memorial Hospital in New York. Abraham is a spastic quadriplegic, and his parents alleged that his condition resulted from the negligence of the health care providers involved in his birth. The events that gave rise to the lawsuit, which was filed on Abraham's behalf, occurred approximately 1 hour before Abraham was born. Abraham's mother, approximately 30 weeks pregnant, had been admitted for observation because she was having visual disturbances and headaches. Because of her pregnancy and neurologic condition, Kathryn Gold was being treated by her obstetrician, Donald Werner, and Jeffrey Ribner, a neurologist. At approximately 10:55 PM, Kathryn, Abraham's mother, began having seizures. The nurse documented that grand mal seizures were occurring, but did not call the obstetrician or neurologist for 20 minutes. When she did call the neurologist, he testified that he ordered that phenytoin (Dilantin) be administered. Phenytoin was never administered by the nursing staff, because the nurse reportedly failed to inform the oncoming shift that the order had been given by Dr. Ribner, the neurologist.

Abraham was finally delivered via cesarean section, and was cared for in the neonatal intensive care unit. While a patient there, Abraham developed an *Escherichia coli* infection, which caused him to go into septic shock. The defendant hospital and physicians alleged that Abraham's condition was a complication of this event, rather than any event surrounding his birth.

The New York jury listened to the evidence presented by both sides and rendered a verdict in favor of Abraham for $103,127,355. In reaching their conclusion, the jury exonerated the physician defendants but held the hospital responsible for the negligence of the nurse.

Implementation Failures: Failure to Take Appropriate Action. Cases from across the country continue to affirm that it is the nurse's responsibility to take affirmative action when it is indicated. Cases from New Hampshire, Louisiana, New Jersey, Oregon, Nebraska, Colorado, and Michigan describe more definitively what constitutes failure to take appropriate action and communicate what happens when failure to take appropriate action is proven.

In a New Hampshire case, *Brookover v. Mary Hitchcock Memorial Hospital*,[25] Ronald Brookover had significant seizure activity that resulted in his need to undergo two surgical procedures called a corpus callostomy. The operations are undertaken with the goal of diminishing or eliminating seizure activity. Three days after the second surgery, Mr. Brookover got out of bed, fell, and broke his hip. The medical record indicated that Mr. Brookover was unrestrained, and that he used his call light to indicate that he needed assistance. Based on this evidence, the hospital was found liable for Mr. Bookover's injury. Liability was imposed here because the nursing staff failed to take appropriate action in providing assistance to Mr. Brookover.

Three decisions from Louisiana illustrate how courts in that state handle failure to take appropriate action cases. In 1995, a Louisiana court decided *Gordon v. Willis Knighton Medical Center*.[26] In *Gordon*, Elizabeth Gordon was a 76-year-old grandmother when she began manifesting the signs and symptoms of a myocardial infarction. She was taken to the emergency room by paramedics who placed supplemental oxygen on Ms. Gordon. When she arrived at the emergency room, the supplemental oxygen was discontinued. Ms. Gordon was left unattended and was not assessed in the emergency room for more than 1 hour. It was only when Ms. Gordon's son started screaming for help because his mother passed out that resuscitation efforts were extended to Ms. Gordon. Unfortunately, those efforts were unsuccessful and Ms. Gordon was pronounced dead. The jury awarded $385,000 in damages.

Two years after *Gordon, Pellerin v. Humedicenters, Inc.*[27] was decided in Louisiana. In *Pellerin,* a patient had been admitted to the hospital because of chest pain. While in the hospital, the patient noticed that she experienced pain at the site of the intramuscular injection, and that the site was irritated, painful, and eventually encompassed an area of approximately 10 inches in diameter. Subsequently, the patient was diagnosed with right cutaneous gluteal neuropathy. Gwen Tangney, RN, was the nurse caring for the patient when the injection was reportedly given; however, Gwen Tangney did not remember giving it. Her documentation, on the other hand, from the day in question showed that an injection was given. Missing from the nurses notes was the site of the injection, and a description of the injection given. This missing information made it possible to infer that the drug had been administered improperly, and the jury awarded Ms. Pellerin more than $90,000 in damages.

Four years after *Gordon* and 2 years after *Pellerin, Odom v. State Department of Health and Hospital*[28] was decided in Louisiana. In *Odom,* 14-year-old Joseph Paul Odom (JoJo) was a resident at the Pinecrest Developmental Center because he was profoundly mentally retarded and suffered from spastic quadraplegia, hydrocephaly, asthma, a convulsive disorder, respiratory distress, and obstructive apnea. His ability to breathe was dependent on a well-functioning tracheostomy tube. Orders were written to change the tracheostomy collar or tie once each day, to change the tracheostomy tube itself each Wednesday, and to keep a tracheostomy tube at the young man's bedside. In addition, an apnea monitor was ordered. The alarm was to be activated to notify the staff if his heart rate decreased to below 60 beats per minute or increased to above 120 beats per minute, and a vital signs log was to be kept. The apnea monitor reportedly went off frequently, and was viewed as an annoyance. Sometimes the alarm would be turned off. One evening, a licensed practical nurse (LPN) found that the tracheostomy tube had been dislodged. She called for help, started cardiopulmonary resuscitation, and removed the apnea monitor leads so that the alarm would sound, but the alarm did not sound. The young man was transferred to a nearby emergency room where he was pronounced dead. The boys parents sued alleging that the nursing staff committed malpractice when they turned off the apnea monitor alarm and when they failed to monitor their son as his condition warranted. A jury heard the case and rendered a verdict in favor of the boy's parents. The court found that the nursing staff failed to exercise their duty to provide this patient with the degree of skill ordinarily required by nursing professionals in the same or similar situation, and awarded JoJo's family $174,386.34 in damages.

In New Jersey, *Chin v. St. Barnabas Medical Center*[29] was heard by a jury, who awarded a patient's family $2 million in damages because of the failure of the health care providers to take appropriate action. In *Chin*, a patient sustained an air embolus during a hysteroscopy procedure and died. After the patient died, it was discovered that the hysteroscope was attached to gas, rather than fluid. The infusion of air into the woman's uterus resulted in the woman sustaining a fatal embolus. The jury also determined that the surgeon bore 20% of the liability, and one nurse and the hospital bore 25% and 35% of the liability, respectively.

In *Fieux v. Cardiovascular & Thoracic Clinic, et al,*[30] an Oregon case, a serrefine clamp slipped off of a vein and fell behind Maurice Fieux's heart during open heart surgery. The clamp slippage was not noticed by the surgical team. The surgical team consisted of three surgical nurses, and one surgeon, George R. Wilkinson, MD. Following the surgery, the patient's chest was closed and the patient was transported to the recovery room. The postoperative x-ray taken after the patient had been transported to the recovery room showed the clamp lodged behind the patient's heart. Another surgery was performed shortly thereafter, and the clamp was removed. The missing clamp was not detected by the surgical team because surgical instruments were not counted. The hospital had a policy requiring the counting of sponges and needles, but not surgical instruments. Initially, the trial court granted the defendant's request for a verdict in their favor because the patient–plaintiff did not present expert testimony to support his malpractice claim. However, on appeal, the trial court's decision was characterized as erroneous, and the trial court was directed to allow a jury to hear this matter. Subsequent proceedings in this matter are unpublished.

Miles v. Box Butte County[31] was heard in a Nebraska courtroom. There, a $1,589,280 verdict was rendered in favor of the deceased patient's family. In *Miles*, a pregnant woman, Barbara Miles, was admitted with a diagnoses of preeclampsia. She was cared for by Jane McConkey, a nurse who worked in the hospital obstetrical unit and emergency room. After Barbara's baby, Traig Williams Miles, was born retarded and with cerebral palsy, the parents sued alleging that Nurse McConkey failed to correctly interpret the fetal heart monitor tracings, failed to properly hydrate and oxygenate the laboring mom, failed to notify the attending physician when presented with a nonreassuring tracing, failed to place the monitor strips in front of the examining physician, and failed to remain in the labor room with Barbara Miles after nonreassuring tracings were detected.

The case was eventually heard by the Nebraska Supreme Court, which affirmed the decision and award of the district court. As a result, the $1.589 million verdict against Box Butte General County Hospital was upheld.

In *Garcia v. United States,*[32] Candido Garcia was admitted to a Veteran's Administration Medical Center in Colorado for the removal of a subdural hematoma. He was operated on, moved to recovery, then to a medical surgical unit. He began making snorting noises, and white bubbles began to form at his mouth. Candido's wife reported the occurrence to the nurse caring for him. The nurse, Margaret John, reportedly told the wife that the extent of her responsibility was to ensure that the surgically inserted drainage tubes were kept clear. Doctors from a neighboring hospital were called, but they were not informed of the emergency nature of the call. In all, the patient did not receive proper medical assistance for a period of about 45 to 50 minutes. Following medical intervention, which included a return trip to the operating room, it was determined that Mr. Garcia was quadriplegic. At trial, the hospital was found to be negligent and liable for the damages sustained Candido Garcia, and awarded more than $2.3 million in damages, interest, and the cost of litigation to Garcia and his wife. In reaching its decision, the court found that the nursing staff should have recognized the emergency nature of the situation and taken proper steps to notify the attending physician.

In Michigan, *Boretti v. Wiscomb*[33] is a failure to take appropriate action case that concerned nurses practicing in a corrections environment. A prisoner, David G. Boretti, filed suit against two nurses who reportedly failed to provide him with proper care and treatment. The two nurses, Beverly A. Wiscomb, RN, and Wanda M. Baldwin, RN, were allegedly negligent because they failed to change the dressing at the site of a gunshot wound, and failed to administer pain medication. According to Boretti, he did not receive proper care and treatment between December 30, 1987 and January 4, 1988. Reportedly, when Wiscomb and Baldwin made rounds, they refused to change Boretti's dressing, administer pain medication, or obtain a mattress upon which he could rest. Wanda M. Baldwin was eventually dismissed from the case, but Beverly A. Wiscomb was not. At the trial court level, the court determined that a jury trial was unnecessary, because the prisoner did not state a cause of action that needed to be presented to a jury. However, the court of appeals reversed the decision of the trial court and observed that Boretti was the recipient of deliberate indifference. As a result a jury trial was ordered.

Implementation Failures: Failure to Document Patient Findings and Patient Responses to Interventions. Not only are nurses required to take appropriate action, they are required to accurately document their findings, interventions, and their patients' response to those interventions. Failure to thoroughly and accurately document any aspect of care gives rise to negligence causes of actions. Cases from Oklahoma, North Carolina, Georgia, and Arizona demonstrate how courts and juries deal with a nurse's failure to properly document.

In *Scribner v. Hillcrest Medical Center,*[34] Ronda Scribner had undergone a hysterectomy at Hillcrest Medical Center in Oklahoma. She was placed in bed B in one of the hospital's semi-private rooms. The patient who had been in bed A of that room was moved to another room. Approximately 22 hours after Ronda's surgery, an orderly, at the direction of the nursing staff, appeared at her room saying that he needed to transport her to the ultrasound laboratory for diagnostic testing. Ronda reportedly protested about being moved, and questioned the orderly about the testing, but after the orderly persisted, she was moved from her bed to a wheelchair. When she was moved to the wheelchair, Ronda testified that she felt excruciating pain in her abdominal area and almost passed out. She was transported to the ultrasound laboratory anyway, where the technicians there began the procedure by instilling cold water through a catheter into Ronda's bladder. This, according to Ronda, caused cramping pain.

It was only after Ronda's continued expressions of concern about the procedure being performed on her that the ultrasound technicians discovered the mistake, discontinued the ultrasound, and returned Ronda to her room. In spite of their discovery, the ultrasound staff did not inform Ronda's nurse of the mistake. It was only after a confrontation with the patient's physician that the transportation of the patient to the ultrasound laboratory and subsequent incident was recorded in Ronda's medical records. Two days after the incident, Ronda was discharged, but had to be readmitted after she experienced wound dehiscence and a hernia, complications she claimed stemmed from the negligently performed ultrasound testing.

Subsequently, Ronda sued alleging that the hospital was negligent. The trial court determined that the hospital exhibited a reckless and wanton disregard for the rights of Ronda Scribner, and the jury returned a verdict in Ronda's favor in the amount of $100,000 for actual damages, and $10 million in punitive damages. The hospital appealed, and the Oklahoma Supreme Court affirmed the verdict rendered by the jury, but reduced the punitive award to $5 million, concluding that the original punitive award was excessive.

In North Carolina, *Haney v. Alexander*[35] dealt with a nurse's purported failure to take appropriate action, as well as the nurse's failure to properly document care given to a patient. Originally, the trial court dismissed the hospital from the case. The physician–defendants later settled with the family. The family appealed the trial court's decision to dismiss the hospital, and, citing the negligence of the nurse, the court of appeals agreed that the hospital should not have been dismissed, and determined that a jury trial should be commenced.

In this case, a nurse caring for a patient experiencing atrial fibrillation failed to take, record, and communicate all of a patient's vital signs, and failed to properly document the order and administer chlordiaxepoxide (Librium). Reportedly, chlordiaxepoxide had already been administered, but the on-call physician was allegedly told that chlordiaxepoxide had not been administered, so the physician ordered, again, that chlordiaxepoxide be given. The nurse gave the medication, and 45 minutes later, the patient was found dead.

In reversing the trial court's previous decision to dismiss the hospital, the court of appeals concluded that the nurse was negligent in several respects. Specifically, the court of appeals observed that the events leading to the double administration of chlordiaxepoxide could have prevented the patient from being able to communicate about his worsening condition, and could have prevented him from receiving life-saving medical assistance.

In Georgia in *Ahrens v. Katz*,[36] parents of an infant sued the infant's treating physician and hospital alleging that documentation were fraudulent. In an attempt to prove the claim of the parents, nurses' notes were used to show the inconsistencies between what the physician recorded and what the nurse recorded. The physician recorded that the infant was lethargic and in distress, whereas the nurse recorded that the boy was acting normally. In addition, the nurse documented that the child was receiving oral feedings, whereas the physician reported that a nasogastric tube was used to administer feedings. In addition, some of the physician's progress notes had been obliterated because of the use of white-out. The court, in dismissing the case filed by the parents, recognized that the physician's documentation was improper, but decided that the documentation-related failures were not fraudulent.

Kenyon v. Hammer[37] is a case decided by the Arizona Supreme Court. In *Kenyon,* a nurse charted that a pregnant patient, Sharon D. Kenyon, had Rh-positive blood when the patient actually had Rh-negative blood. Sharon D. Kenyon delivered an Rh-positive baby who was otherwise healthy. Because of the erroneous Rh-positive entry, $Rh_0(D)$ immune globulin (RhoGAM) was not administered following the delivery of this infant. Five years later, Sharon D. Kenyon delivered a stillborn infant because of the destruction of the baby's blood cells by Sharon's Rh antibodies.

Approximately 1 year after the stillborn delivery, Sharon and her husband filed a wrongful death cause of action against Raymond E. Hammer, the obstetrician who was providing obstetrical care for Sharon. Sharon and her husband alleged that the obstetrician was vicariously liable for the negligence of the nurse, because the nurse was an employee at the obstetrician's office. The Kenyon's case was dismissed by the trial court, which concluded that the statute of limitations had expired.

The Arizona Supreme Court heard the case and determined that the trial court should not have dismissed, and ordered that the matter be heard by a jury. In reaching that conclusion, the court noted that medical malpractice defendants like Hammer, via statute, had effectively abolished the opportunity for those with the most meritorious claims to pursue them. That, according to the Arizona Supreme Court, violated Kenyon's fundamental rights, which were protected by the Arizona constitution, and required that the supreme court declare the statute unconstitutional.

Implementation Failure: Failure to Preserve Patient Privacy.   Nurses have a duty to preserve patient privacy. State and federal statutes and case law affirm this duty. Failure to preserve a patient's privacy can result in liability, and can be damaging for patients. *Doe v. Ohio State University Hospital and Clinics*[38] explores the issue.

In *Doe,* a nurse taking care of an HIV+ patient wrote his HIV status down on a laboratory requisition slip in the "other test" section of the form. This was done so that laboratory personnel could be alerted to the patient's HIV status. The patient was to have a complete blood count and potassium level drawn prior to having a lithotripsy performed to remove kidney stones. The laboratory staff interpreted the notation made by the nurse as an instruction to perform an HIV screen, and not a message regarding the patient's HIV status. The patient found out that the HIV screen had been done, and was outraged that the HIV testing had been done without his consent. This facility had a policy prohibiting HIV testing without informed consent being obtained by the physician.

The case was ultimately dismissed, but serves as a reminder to guard the privacy of every patient. Nurses can ensure that the privacy of patients is protected by following privacy-related policies and procedures, and by refraining from having discussions about specific clients with anyone except other health care professionals involved in the care of the client. When discussing specific patients with other health care professionals, it is imperative that those discussions occur in nonpublic settings. Discussions about specific patients are never appropriate in public areas like elevators, cafeterias, gift shops, and parking lots.

Evaluation Failures: Failure to Act as a Patient Advocate. From admission to discharge, nurses have a duty to act as a patient advocate. This duty imposes upon nurses the responsibility to analyze and evaluate the care that is being given to patients for whom they care. *NKC Hospitals, Inc. v. Anthony*[39] is illustrative. In this case, Margaret Anthony was approximately 30 weeks pregnant, and experiencing nausea, vomiting, and abdominal pain when her husband took her to the Norton Hospital Emergency Room. She was then transferred to the obstetrical unit where she was evaluated by a nurse, Rebecca Moore. Moore called Anthony's obstetrician to advise her of the patient's condition. The physician, Elizabeth Hawkins, ordered that an IV be started, blood work and other lab tests be completed, and that medication to treat Anthony's nausea be administered.

About an hour and a half later, Hawkins was called again so that the laboratory result could be given. Hawkins was also advised that Anthony was in extreme pain. Hawkins, based on the information she received, concluded that Anthony had a urinary tract infection, prescribed antibiotics, and ordered that Anthony be discharged.

Approximately 15 minutes later, Nurse Moore called Hawkins a third time reporting that Ms. Anthony was in severe pain, and expressing concern about discharging Anthony. At this point, Mr. Anthony also talked with Hawkins about the pain his wife was experiencing. Hawkins ordered that morphine sulfate be administered, but left the discharge order intact.

Morphine sulfate was administered, and Anthony rested comfortably for about 3 hours. When Anthony awoke, she was in pain again, and in spite of her pain, she was discharged 1 hour later without being examined by a physician.

Nurse Moore continued to express concern about the pain that Anthony was experiencing, and reportedly suggested that a resident physician examine Anthony. She also advised her supervisor, Nurse Hale. However, in spite of the concerns expressed by Moore, Anthony was still discharged in pain, and without ever being examined by a physician.

Later that morning, Margaret Anthony was readmitted to the hospital. Two days later, she was transferred to the intensive care unit. One day after she was admitted to the intensive care unit, her baby was delivered by cesarean section. It was then that Ms. Anthony's perforated appendix was discovered. Three weeks later, still hospitalized, Margaret Anthony died from complications associated with the delayed diagnosis and treatment of her appendicitis.

Subsequently, Margaret's husband filed a civil lawsuit against the hospital and Hawkins. The case was tried in front of a jury. The jury returned a $2,265.923.70 verdict against Hawkins and Norton Hospital. Hawkins was deemed 65% responsible for the death of Margaret Anthony, while Norton Hospital was deemed 35% responsible. Anthony's claim against Hawkins was settled prior to trial, so judgment against the hospital was in the amount of $793,073.29, and was later reduced to $780,265.83. The hospital appealed, but the Kentucky Court of Appeals affirmed the judgment, concluding that the hospital's negligence was based on acts of omission, as well as the affirmative act of discharging her in pain. The omissions included the failure on the part of the health care providers to check the respiratory status of Ms. Anthony, as well as their failure to have Anthony examined by a physician.

For nurses, *NKC Hospitals, Inc* should serve as a reminder that courts will look at the affirmative steps nurses take, as well as the steps that were not taken to determine whether or not the nurse acted as patient advocate. *NKC Hospitals, Inc.* and other cases continue to hold that the duty nurses have to act as patient advocate is nondelegable.[40]

Breach

Breach is the failure to act consistently with applicable standards of care. For a nurse to be found negligent, the patient must establish that the nurse had a duty to provide care, and that the nurse failed to provide care consistent with those standards. Further, the nurse's failure, or breach, must have caused the damage(s) for which the patient seeks redress. Cases from Georgia, Idaho, Illinois, and Louisiana illustrate the courts' willingness to conclude that breach did not occur where the actions of nurses meet or exceed the standard of care.

In Georgia, in *Deese v. Carol City County Hospital,*[41] Magdalene Deese and her husband filed a negligence cause of action against Tanner Medical Center, and Elsie Addison, the nurse. Magdalene Deese alleged that Elsie Addison administered an injection to her in a manner that fell below the standard of care.

A jury heard the case and returned a verdict in favor of the hospital and nurse. Magdalene Deese appealed that decision to the Georgia Court of Appeals. That court affirmed the decision of the trial court, concluding that the nurse acted with a reasonable degree of care and skill ordinarily exercised by members of the nursing profession under similar conditions and circumstances.

In Idaho, in *Sparks v. St. Lukes Regional Medical Center,*[42] the family of Thomas Sparks sued St. Lukes Regional Medical Center and treating physicians alleging that their negligence resulted in Thomas Sparks sustaining brain damage after he was extubated and after he experienced cardiac arrest. The trial court granted St. Luke's motion to have judgment entered in its' favor, and Sparks appealed the matter to the Idaho Supreme Court.

The Idaho Supreme Court reviewed the evidence presented by both parties and concluded that the nurses met the requisite standard of care. Therefore, no breach occurred. In fact, the court pointed out that Thomas Sparks presented evidence, which recognized that the standard of care regarding the extubation and subsequent hospital care was met by St. Luke's personnel. As a result, the ruling of the trial court was affirmed.

In Illinois, two cases address the issue of breach. First, in *Northern Trust Co. v. Louis A. Weiss Memorial Hospital*,[43] an Appellate Court of Illinois concluded that two nurses complied with the standard of care in observing, documenting, and communicating a baby's deteriorating condition to physician. The baby's parents alleged that the nurses were negligent in the care they provided to their infant daughter, and that their negligence caused their daughter to sustain brain damage. The hospital, however, was deemed negligent in failing to provide a specially trained nurse to supervise the nursery. Accordingly, the hospital breached the standard of care, and was liable for negligence. As a result, the $1.5 million jury verdict rendered against the hospital was affirmed.

Eight years later, in *Chiricosta v. Winthrop-Breon, et al*,[44] another Illinois jury determined that two nurses met the standard of care when it came to the administration of meperidine (Demerol) to a laboring patient. In this case, the mother of a baby boy who developed cerebral palsy sued alleging that the meperidine administration caused the injury to Nicholas, the baby boy who was delivered approximately 30 minutes after the injection.

The case was heard by a jury and during jury deliberation one physician defendant and one physician group involved in the case settled with the plaintiffs for $1.6 million. The jury exonerated all of the other defendants. Plaintiffs appealed the decision of the trial court to the Appellate Court of Illinois where the jury's verdict was affirmed.

In Louisiana, in *McClain v. Glenwood Regional Medical Center*,[45] a court of appeals determined that a jury verdict in favor of the defendant hospital concluded that the nursing staff complied with the standard of care in assessing, charting, and informing the physician of the patient's development of blisters underneath a plaster of paris cast, which had been recently applied.

Nurse Practice Acts. Nurse Practice Acts (NPAs) provide statutory authority for the practice of nursing in any jurisdiction. See Chapter 2 for an in-depth discussion of NPAs. Nurses, as licensed and regulated health care professionals, are required to abide by the requirements of the applicable practice act. Failure to act consistently with NPA requirements exposes a nurse to civil liability in negligence or malpractice causes of action because the statutory standard was breached.

In NPAs, the range of activities in which a registered nurse may engage are referred to as a nurses' scope of practice. Typically, scope of practice activities for registered nurses include assessing the health status of individuals and groups; establishing a nursing diagnosis and goals to meet identified health care needs; creating and implementing a plan of care; prescribing and implementing interventions to operationalize the plan of care; delegating nursing interventions to qualified others as the practice act permits; providing for the maintenance of safe and effective nursing care rendered directly or indirectly and evaluating patient responses to interventions; teaching the theory and practice of nursing; and collaborating with other health care professionals in the delivery of health care services.[46]

Professional Practice Standards.   Actions that are consistent with professional practice standards will be evidence that the nurse did not breach his or her duty to patients. It is, therefore, important to know what professional practice standards say is expected of nurses practicing in specific practice settings. *Koeniguer v. Eckrich*[47] indicates that those standards will be used in cases involving nurses and alleged breaches in the standard of care.

In *Koeniguer,* Winnifred Scoblic was admitted to Dakota Midland Hospital for surgical correction of incontinence. Two days later, J.A. Eckrich performed the surgery. Postoperatively, Ms. Scoblic had a temperature which fluctuated. On the day of discharge, Ms. Scoblic's temperature was 100.2° F. In spite of her temperature, Ms. Scoblic was discharged. Sixteen days after her original surgery, Ms. Scoblic was readmitted because of a fever and severe abdominal pain. She was diagnosed as septic. Two days later, Ms. Scoblic was transferred to the University of Minnesota Hospital. She died from multiple organ failure several weeks later.

On behalf of Ms. Scoblic, her daughter Patricia Koeniger filed a malpractice cause of action contending that the care rendered to her mother deviated from the standard of care. An expert retained by Koeniger used the standards published by the American Nurses Association (ANA) and other general nursing treatises to conclude that the nursing staff failed to adhere to standards of care applicable to Ms. Scoblic as a postoperative urologic patient. At the trial court level, the case was dismissed, but was later heard and reversed by the South Dakota Supreme Court. A trial was ordered so that jurors could have an opportunity to determine whether or not the actions on the part of the defendants caused the wrongful death of Ms. Scoblic. Subsequent proceedings are unpublished.

Job Descriptions/Contracts.   Although standards of care are usually derived outside of any one specific institution, a nurse's job description and/or employment contract may contain provisions that require a nurse to act or refrain to act in a specific manner, and within a specific period of time. Failure to adhere to those provisions could give rise to negligence causes of action where the patient–plaintiff asserts that the nurse failed to act in accordance with his or her job description or employment contract. Accordingly, job descriptions and employment contracts need to be reflective of the standard of care, and expectations articulated in a reasonable manner.

Policies, Procedures, Protocols, and Pathways.   Nurses and other health care professionals are required to act in a manner that is consistent with organizational policies, procedures, protocols, and clinical pathways. Failure to act consistently with those organizational guidelines gives rise to a substantial amount of litigation. In *Parker v. Southwest Louisiana Hospital Association,*[48] the parents of Leigh Ann Parker sued Lake Charles Memorial Hospital alleging that the nursing staff was negligent in leaving the well-baby nursery unattended while babies were being delivered to their mothers, and that their daughter was inadequately monitored during one of those delivery periods. They also alleged that the hospital's observation policy requiring patients to be observed every 10 to 15 minutes was below the standard of care. The policy, according to the Parkers, allowed Leigh Ann to be unobserved for 6 to 8 minutes, and that that length of time was sufficient for Leigh Ann to sustain permanent brain damage.

A jury heard this case and determined that the hospital did not breach its duty to Leigh Ann and was not negligent. The case was appealed, and the court of appeals affirmed the decision reached by the jury. For the court of appeals, one of the key findings in this case was that both the Parkers and Lake Charles Memorial Hospital presented evidence that indicated that the hospital's policy of having nurses circulate throughout the nursery every 10 to 15 minutes was well within known and accepted standards of care.

Parker is not the only case in which courts have reviewed a health care organization's policy. Cases from a number of other states indicate that an organization's policies and procedures will be instrumental in having a nurses action or failure to act considered a breach of the applicable standard of care.[49]

Causation

In negligence causes of action, patient–plaintiffs must prove that a health care professional breached his or her duty to the patient, and that the breach caused the patient to sustain injuries or damages for which they seek payment. Causation, as an element of negligence, is a pivotal element for patient–plaintiffs and for health care organizations and health care professionals. If causation is not proven by plaintiffs, there can be no recovery.

It should be no surprise, then, that many professional negligence cases focus on causation. If plaintiffs prove that the health care organization or health care professional did or failed to do something that caused an injury, then they have met their burden of proof. If, on the other hand, plaintiffs fail to establish that some act or omission directly resulted in the injuries for which they are seeking compensation, or if health care organizations or health care professionals show that the complained of injury was the result of something other than an action or omission that fell below the standard of care, then recovery will be denied. *McMullen v. Ohio State University Hospitals*[50] dealt with the causation issue, and was ultimately decided by the Ohio Supreme Court.

In this case, a patient was intubated and placed on a ventilator. Three days after she was intubated, her oxygen saturation level suddenly dropped, as did her blood pressure, and she became cyanotic and dyspneic. The patient also developed a squeak, which the nurse thought was a cuff leak on the endotracheal tube. The nurse believed that the patient was dying, and made a "stat" page so that the physicians on call could be notified. Prior to the arrival of the physicians, the nurse removed the patient's endotracheal tube.

When the physicians arrived, they attempted to reintubate the patient. It took more than 20 minutes for their reintubation attempts to be successful. The patient never resumed consciousness, and died 7 days later.

The patient's estate brought a wrongful death cause of action against the Ohio State University Hospitals. The case went to trial where damages were awarded to the patient's estate. Ohio State University Hospital appealed the award to the Franklin County Court of Appeals. The court of appeals reversed the award to the patient's estate. The patient's estate then appealed the case to the Ohio Supreme Court. The Ohio Supreme Court, among other things, concluded that the actions of the nurse directly caused the ultimate harm sustained by the patient. Her act of removing the patient's endotracheal tube was negligent, setting into motion a chain of events that directly caused the patient to die. As a result, the decision of the Franklin County Court of Appeals was reversed.

Damages

Damages, in professional negligence matters, are the sums of money that may be awarded for injuries sustained because of the negligence of a health care provider. Damages are classified as nominal, compensatory, or punitive. *Nominal damages* are awarded where there is no actual monetary loss, but where there is wrongdoing that must be rectified. Nominal damages are awarded when one party is injured in principle.

Compensatory damages represent the actual loss suffered in the present, past, and future. Compensatory damages are categorized as either general or special damages. *General damages* are the harms that flow from the natural, usual, and necessary result of the wrongdoing. Awards for emotional injury, pain and suffering, and mental anguish are examples of general damages. *Special damages* are those harms that flow naturally but not inevitably from the wrongdoing.

Punitive damages, on the other hand, are awarded as punishment for outrageous, grossly negligent, malicious, fraudulent, or reckless or indifferent conduct. Unlike nominal and compensatory damages, punitive damages are awarded in an effort to deter future transgressions. Therefore, the extent of the injury suffered by the plaintiff–patient is not the standard of measure; rather, the standard is the financial condition of the defendant. For health care professionals, another distinguishing feature of punitive damages is that generally there is no malpractice coverage for this kind of damage award.

In professional negligence cases against health care providers, how frequently do juries render verdicts in favor of patient–plaintiffs and how substantial are the jury awards? Although only about 36% of all medical malpractice cases filed in 1998 resulted in jury verdicts in favor of patient–plaintiffs, jury awards are getting larger. Jury awards represent the amount of money the jury believes it takes to alleviate the damages suffered by the patient–plaintiff. In 1997, the median jury award in medical malpractice cases was $515,738. In 1998, the median jury award was up 46% to $755,530. Median jury awards were highest in childbirth cases, at $2 million. Median awards in medication administration and misdiagnosis cases were more than $600,000, and median jury awards were $400,000, $300,000, and $230,000 in non-surgical treatment cases, surgical matters, and health care professional–patient relationship cases, respectively.[51]

The number of nurses being named defendants in these cases is increasing. Some estimate that the number of nurses being named as individual defendants has increased 10% since 1995.[52]

Although many of the cases that have been used to describe the elements of negligence have resulted in jury verdicts in favor of patients, nurses are not always deemed negligent in cases filed against them. *Eversole v. Oklahoma Hospital Founders Association*[53] exemplifies this. In *Eversole,* a patient, Anthony C. Eversole, Jr., sued the Oklahoma Osteopathic Hospital and Valorie Susan Clark Parris after he fell while being assisted by Valorie Parris, a nurse. Parris was assisting Mr. Eversole to the restroom because of his postoperative condition, and because he received meperidine and acetaminophen (Tylenol) with codeine prior to getting out of bed. In spite of the assistance rendered by nurse Parris, Mr. Eversole fell. The fall led to a series of complications that resulted in Mr. Eversole's being hospitalized for more than 8 months.

After hearing the evidence presented in this case, a jury returned a verdict in favor of Mr. Eversole in the amount of $1.2 million. During jury deliberations, Parris was exonerated, and the hospital was deemed responsible for the damages sustained by Mr. Eversole. Although the jury gave no rationale for exonerating Parris, it is clear that she acted in accordance with the applicable standard of care, and that the jury verdict reflected that. The hospital appealed, and the case was reviewed by the Oklahoma Supreme Court. One of the issues discussed by the justices was the contention, made by the hospital, that it could not be liable without the nurse being negligent. The Oklahoma Supreme Court disagreed, concluding that Parris acted in accordance with her education, experience, and best judgment, but that the hospital was negligent in its staffing of the unit in which Anthony C. Eversole, Jr. was located. As a result, the verdict rendered by the jury was affirmed.

Negligence Per Se

Most courts have ruled that a statutory violation is negligence per se. Negligence per se allows patient–plaintiffs to conclusively establish a presumption that a health care professional was negligent. However, a minority of courts have decided the issue differently. Some courts have held that statutory violations give rise to a rebuttable presumption, and a few other courts have determined that statutory violations are not conclusive evidence of negligence. Regardless of the jurisdiction, however, statutory violations do assist patient–plaintiffs in proving that negligence occurred. This was the case in *Lama v. Borras.*[54] In this case, a patient acquired a postoperative infection and the nurse failed to recognize the associated signs and symptoms. The court concluded that the nurse was negligent, and that the doctrine of negligence per se applied because the nurse's failure was a violation of Puerto Rico Health Regulations.

Malpractice

Malpractice is professional misconduct, or the failure to meet the requisite standard of care. The alleged professional misconduct may be intentional or unintentional. Unlike negligence, malpractice requires that the alleged wrongdoer have special standing as a professional. Where an individual acts in a personal rather than professional capacity, that individual would be subject to a negligence cause of action, but not a malpractice cause of action.

In health care cases, the terms malpractice and negligence are used interchangeably, although there are courts that distinguish between the two causes of action. The malpractice–negligence distinction was addressed in *Candler General Hospital Inc. v. McNorrill.*[55] The court concluded that malpractice was merely a professional negligence act. According to the court, nurses, when acting in their professional capacity, are subject to malpractice causes of action when patients assert that the nurse failed to meet the requisite standard of care.

In *Gould v. NY City Health and Hospital,*[56] the court looked at the elements that must be proven in a malpractice case, and determined that there were three duties inherent in a malpractice cause of action: to possess requisite knowledge and skill possessed by an average member of the profession; to exercise reasonable and ordinary care in the application of professional knowledge and skill; and to use best judgment in the application of professional knowledge and skill. These duties are consistent with the duties nurses have in traditional negligence-based causes of action.

Griffin v. The Methodist Hospital[57] illustrates that most courts treat malpractice cases like negligence cases. The only difference is that malpractice cases involve individuals with some special standing. In *Griffin,* Sharon Ann Griffin and her husband Dennis Griffin filed a malpractice cause of action against The Methodist Hospital and Sharon's treating physicians. They allege that Sharon sustained damages because of the negligent treatment of her treating physicians and nursing staff while she was a patient at The Methodist Hospital. Specifically, Sharon alleges that her development of an Achilles tendon contraction or foot drop was the result of negligence. The Methodist Hospital contended that, in spite of Sharon's development of foot drop, its staff fully complied with applicable standards of care. As a result, the hospital asked that the judge render a judgment in its favor. The judge agreed, and dismissed the matter. Sharon and her husband appealed the case. After reviewing the case, the court of appeals determined that the case should not have been terminated, and ordered that the matter be slated for trial. Subsequent proceedings are unpublished.

Wrongful Birth

Wrongful birth claims are filed by parents who contend that they would have terminated their pregnancy had they known that their child was going to be born with severe birth defects. Typically, parents allege that the pregnancy would have been terminated had they been timely informed, through prenatal diagnostic tests, of the possibility of having a child with severe birth defects. Wrongful birth claims are distinguished from wrongful life and wrongful conception cases in that wrongful life cases are usually commenced by the child born with birth defects, rather than the child's parents. Wrongful birth claims, on the other hand, are designed to compensate parents, not the child. Alternatively, wrongful conception can be brought by a healthy child or that child's parents and usually allege the failure to perform a contraceptive procedure.

Smith v. Cote[58] and *Duplan v. Harper*[59] are illustrative of the way that courts handle wrongful birth claims. In *Smith*, Linda J. Smith, in her second trimester, underwent a rubella titre. Test results indicated that she had been exposed to rubella. Approximately 5 months later, Linda J. Smith gave birth to a full-term infant, Heather B. Smith. Heather was born with rubella syndrome, suffered from cataracts, multiple congenital heart defects, retardation, and significant hearing impairment. Heather was also legally blind. Approximately 4 years after Heather was born, Linda and Heather filed suit alleging that Linda should have been tested for the disease in a timely manner, and Linda should have been advised of the potential for delivering a baby with rubella-related birth defects.

The case was eventually heard by the New Hampshire Supreme Court. The justices affirmed that wrongful birth actions would be recognized in New Hampshire, and that damages could be recovered for extraordinary medical and educational costs associated with raising the impaired child, as well as extraordinary parental care and tangible losses attributable to the parents' emotional distress.

In *Duplan*, Roseann Duplan learned that she was pregnant after a pregnancy test was performed at the obstetrics and gynecology clinic at Tinker Air Force Base in Midwest City, Oklahoma. At that time, Roseann Duplan worked at a child care center. Because she worked at the child care center, Roseann Duplan knew that she was at an increased risk for contracting cytomegalovirus (CMV), a virus that is harmless for many people, but can cause serious birth defects if it is contracted during pregnancy. Consequently, she requested to be tested for CMV. She made multiple requests to have the test performed. When the test was finally performed, it indicated that Roseann had contracted a CMV infection in the first trimester of her pregnancy. A clinic nurse, Elizabeth Reed, reportedly informed Roseann that the CMV test was positive, and that the positive result meant that she was immune to CMV. Months later, Roseann delivered a severely mentally retarded baby boy.

Roseann's treating physician allegedly failed to discuss the CMV infection with her and did not follow the virus' impact on the unborn fetus. The nurse failed to give accurate information about the laboratory test. As a result, the Duplans filed a wrongful birth cause of action. The United States District Court found the treating physician and clinic nurse negligent and awarded the Duplans $3,056,100 in damages. The case was appealed to the United States Court of Appeals. After reviewing the matter, the Court of Appeals affirmed the damage award.

Wrongful Death

Wrongful death claims are filed by the survivors of patients who allege that the patient died because of the negligence of health care organizations and/or health care professionals. *Reynolds v. Swigert*[60] and *Manning v. Twin Falls Clinic & Hospital*[61] provide insight into how courts handle wrongful death causes of action.

In *Reynolds,* a child had been seen three times as an outpatient. In spite of these visits, the girl died from meningitis. Initially, the child's mother took her to an ambulatory care clinic because she was listless and had a fever. Three days later, the mother took her daughter to an emergency room. There, she was cared for by a nurse who wrote that the child had a fever, but failed to record any vital signs. The treating emergency room physician determined that the child had bronchopneumonia. He prescribed medications, and dismissed the child. The next day, the mother returned with the daughter to the emergency room, but was seen by a different physician. By that time, the girl was not eating, and her neck was stiff. This time, the physician determined that the girl was suffering from meningitis. She was admitted to the hospital, but died 4 days later.

After the child's death, the mother filed a malpractice and wrongful death cause of action against the first emergency room physician and the hospital. The mother contended that the physician was negligent in failing to make the proper diagnosis while the child's illness was treatable and in failing to perform an adequate physical examination. The mother also alleged that the emergency room nurse failed to perform an adequate physical examination. Specifically, it was alleged that the nurse failed to take the little girls' vital signs. Expert testimony was used to establish that it was the responsibility of the emergency room nurse to take vital signs without being ordered to do so. Subsequent proceedings are unpublished.

In *Manning,* the outcome was not as favorable for an LPN. The court determined that the nurse failed to exercise reasonable care, and was deemed negligent in the death of her patient, Daryl Manning, a 67-year-old man. In 1987, Mr. Manning was admitted to the hospital in the last stages of chronic obstructive pulmonary disease (COPD), hypoxemia, and increased carbon dioxide retention. Mr. Manning was on continuous supplemental oxygen via a nasal cannula, and had a do not resuscitate order in place. His condition steadily deteriorated, so Virginia L. Anderson, LPN, discontinued Mr. Manning's supplemental oxygen and began to transfer him to a private room. The family requested that oxygen be administered during the move, but the nurse declined to apply it citing the proximity between the patients' current location and the private room. After the bed had been moved approximately 15 feet, Mr. Manning stopped breathing. Resuscitation was attempted, but upon the arrival of the physician, who was aware of Mr. Manning's "no code" status, resuscitative measures were discontinued. The family sued the hospital and two nurses. One nurse, Donna Gay Austin, RN, was relieved of all liability, but the jury determined that Virginia L. Anderson, LPN, had been negligent in transferring the patient without using supplemental oxygen, and awarded the Manning family $184,800 in compensatory, emotional distress, and punitive damages.

Defamation

Defamation causes of action can be filed against health care professionals where individuals believe that something the health care professional has said or written injures the patient's reputation. Any communication may be considered defamatory if it compromises a person's decency, integrity, or reputation. If the defamatory communication is in writing, *libel* has been committed. If, on the other hand, the defamatory communication is verbal, *slander* has been committed.

To be successful, individuals alleging that they have been defamed must prove that the defamatory communication came from the defendant, and that the defamatory language pertained specifically to the plaintiff. In addition, the defamatory communication must have been published to a third person, and the plaintiff must have suffered damage to his or her reputation. Where defamation involves a public figure or a matter of public concern, the plaintiff must prove that the defamatory communication was false and was made with malice.

Meuser v. Rocky Mountain Hospital[62] involved two claims of defamation filed by a nurse against Rocky Mountain Hospital and the hospital administrator. In that case, Virginia T. Meuser alleged that the hospital administrator, Robert Pierce, defamed her in a letter that was published to other employees and in a statement to employees. In reviewing Meuser's defamation allegations, a Colorado Court of Appeals concluded that she failed to present clear and convincing evidence that the allegedly defamatory statements made by Pierce were false or that the defendant hospital or administrator entertained serious doubts about the truth of the statements. As a result, the trial court could not resolve Meuser's defamation claims.

Assault and Battery

Assault and battery are two separate torts (civil wrongs) that can be alleged by patient–plaintiffs. *Assault* is any intentional act that creates reasonable apprehension of immediate harmful or offensive contact with the plaintiff. With assault, no actual contact is necessary. *Battery,* on the other hand, is any intentional act that brings about actual harmful or offensive contact with the plaintiff. In health care cases, assault occurs where a patient fears harmful or offensive touching. Harmful or offensive touching occurs where the patient has not consented to it. Battery occurs where the health care professional actually touches the patient in an unauthorized manner. Sexual misconduct and removing the wrong limb and other body parts constitute battery behaviors. Assault may be alleged in these instances, if the patient is aware that he or she is going to be touched in a manner not authorized by informed consent.

Historically, assault and battery allegations have been treated differently than traditional negligence-based causes of actions. Because assault and battery are considered intentional acts, these offenses have not been routinely covered by professional liability insurers. However, two cases recently decided by the Alabama and South Dakota Supreme Courts have indicated that some assault and battery cases may be considered malpractice because of unauthorized touching of the patient.[63,64]

False Imprisonment

False imprisonment is an intentional act or omission on the part of an individual that confines or restrains another to a bounded area. Acts that result in restraint include applying physical barriers, physical force, threats of force, failure to release, and the invalid use of legal authority. A bounded area is any area in which freedom of movement is limited in all directions, with no reasonable means of escape known to the person being confined. It is irrelevant how short the period of confinement is, and the person being confined must either know of the confinement or be harmed by it.

In health care settings, false imprisonment claims arise when patients are held against their will and in the absence of a court order to hold them, physically or chemically restraining patients in violation with organizational policies and procedures. *Bigtown Nursing Home v. Newman*[65] is a case that was decided in 1970, but it provides a striking example of false imprisonment in a health care setting.

In *Bigtown Nursing Home*, Howard Terry Newman, a 67-year-old man, was admitted by his nephew with the promise that he would not be kept there against his will. After Mr. Newman attempted to leave the facility and was forcibly returned to it, he was placed on a unit with people who had been declared insane and who were substance abusers. He was locked and taped in a restraint chair, prevented from using the telephone for 51 days, denied his personal clothing, told he could not be released from that unit until he began to obey the rules, and detained for 51 days in spite of his repeated demands to be released.

After 51 days, Mr. Newman escaped, and filed this false imprisonment case. A jury heard his case and awarded him $25,000 in damages. The award was appealed because the nursing home thought it was excessive. The Court of Civil Appeals in Tenth District in Texas agreed, and ordered that the verdict be reduced to $13,000. Mr. Newman agreed with the ordered reduction and the appellate court issued an order that affirmed the decision of the trial court to hold the nursing home responsible for false imprisonment.

Loss of Consortium

In addition to alleging negligence or malpractice, plaintiffs may also allege the loss of consortium where their relationships with their spouses, children, or parents have suffered because of the negligence of the health care organization and/or health care professional. *Loss of consortium claims* are based on the deprivation of an individual's right to enjoy the cooperation, companionship, affection, love, and aid of others. Historically, loss of consortium claims were limited to the conjugal relationship between a husband and wife. Today, loss of consortium claims are not limited to husbands and wives because courts have recognized that all family members suffer when one member of the family is injured.

Emotional Distress

Like loss of consortium claims, emotional distress claims can be added as causes of action in cases alleging that malpractice or negligence has occurred. Emotional distress claims may be classified as either intentional or negligent. *Intentional emotional distress claims* assert that the defendant acted in a way that intentionally caused emotional distress. *Negligent emotional distress claims,* however, do not contemplate an intentional act on the part of the defendant(s).

Regardless of the classification, emotional distress claims are alleged when an act is considered to be outrageous. Outrageous acts are reckless, intolerable, and have a tendency to shock the conscience. Consequently, emotional distress claims are difficult for plaintiffs to prove.

Intentional Indifference

Intentional indifference claims typically allege that the health care provider not only failed to provide care consistent with the standard of care, but that the health care provider did not attempt to provide appropriate care. These claims are typically filed by inmates in correctional facilities. Such was the case in *Ferris v. County of Kennebec.*[66] In this case, an inmate alleged that a corrections nurse was intentionally indifferent when the inmate reported that she thought she was having a miscarriage. The corrections nurse failed to recognize the signs and symptoms of a miscarriage, and the nurse dismissed the concern concluding that the inmate was simply menstruating. However, the court determined that alleged intentional indifference occurred when the nurse failed to provide the inmate with sanitary napkins.

Doctrines and Terms

There are a number of doctrines and terms used in civil litigation. To have a broad understanding of the civil justice system, these doctrines and terms should be familiar to nurses. They include assumption of risk, loss of chance, the respectable minority exception, honest error in judgment, Good Samaritan Acts, clinical innovation, contributory and comparative negligence, and statute of limitations.

Assumption of Risk

Assumption of risk is a doctrine that can be used by defendant health care providers and organizations to prevent the plaintiff–patient from recovering for damages sustained because of the alleged wrongdoing of a health care provider or organization. According to this doctrine, a plaintiff may not recover for injuries received when the patient voluntarily exposes him- or herself to known risks.

It is a doctrine that must be pled and proven by defendants as an affirmative defense. For defendants to be successful with the application of this doctrine, they must show that the plaintiff had knowledge of the facts that constituted the dangerous condition, knew that the condition was dangerous, appreciated the nature and extent of the danger, and voluntarily exposed him- or herself to the danger anyway.

Loss of Chance

The *loss of chance doctrine* permits recovery in some cases where negligence on the part of the health care provider probably caused the death of a patient whose condition was already perilous. As the name implies, the loss of chance doctrine can be used to seek compensation for acts of negligence that substantially diminished an ailing individual's chance of survival. The essence of this doctrine is the loss of the prospect of survival. Typically, the issue in these cases is whether liability should be imposed in a situation where death was probable. In a majority of jurisdictions, where the patient has less than a 50% chance of survival, the loss of chance doctrine will not result in liability being imposed. However, a growing number of jurisdictions are permitting loss of chance recovery in cases where the chance of recovery is less than 50%.

The Respectable Minority Exception

The *respectable minority exception* is a defense that may be asserted by a defendant health care professional where the provider insists that a variation in diagnosis, treatment, or judgment does not compromise the standard of care. It recognizes that variation in clinical judgment exists. Essentially, as the name implies, where there are two schools of thought regarding any aspect of care or treatment, the health care professional who embarks on a course of treatment supported by respectable minority of the profession will not incur liability. In addition to being used to defend malpractice causes of action, the respectable minority exception can be used in licensure hearings held by regulatory agencies. Many jurisdictions either do not recognize this defense or impose restrictions on the use of the doctrine.

Honest Error in Judgment

The *honest error in judgment* doctrine is closely associated with the respectable minority exception. According this doctrine, a health care provider is provided some leeway in choosing between uncertain but accepted treatment alternatives. This doctrine is based on the principle that health care providers are not guarantors of good results, and should not be responsible for an honest error in judgment.

Good Samaritan Acts

In an attempt to encourage health care professionals to render emergency aid, almost every jurisdiction has adopted Good Samaritan legislation. *Good Samaritan Acts* protect health care professionals from civil liability when health care professionals render emergency aid as a volunteer. Although the statutes do not limit where emergency aid can be rendered, they usually exclude emergency services rendered in acute care organizations, as well as emergency services rendered by health care providers who already have a provider–patient relationship established. However, it is important to remember that health care providers must act reasonably under the circumstances.

Clinical Innovation

Clinical innovation leads to many advances in the health care industry. However, courts are reluctant protect health care providers who experiment on patients. They do, however, protect health care professionals where an act is considered innovative, but not experimental. Courts recognize that the clinical judgment of health care professionals depends on a number of variable factors, including, but not limited to, the uniqueness of each patient for whom they care.

Contributory and Comparative Negligence

Contributory and comparative negligence are two doctrines which are used to defend negligence causes of action. Traditionally, *contributory negligence* worked to bar plaintiff's recovery where he or she contributed to the injury and damages for which he or she seeks recovery. Application of the contributory negligence doctrine proved to be harsh, and led courts around the country to fashion doctrines to bar its application. One such doctrine was the last clear chance doctrine. Under the *last clear chance doctrine,* a plaintiff could recover despite his or her own contributory negligence where the defendant had the last clear chance to avoid the resultant harm.

Like the last clear chance doctrine, the doctrine of *comparative negligence* evolved because of the harsh results of the contributory negligence doctrine. According to the doctrine of comparative negligence, a contributorily negligent plaintiff may recover a percentage of damages awarded in negligence cases. Today, most jurisdictions apply the doctrine of comparative negligence rather than contributory negligence. Some jurisdictions allow a plaintiff to recover under the doctrine of comparative negligence no matter how great the plaintiff's negligence. In those jurisdictions, if the plaintiff recovers any money, that percent of plaintiff's negligence is simply deducted from the plaintiff's monetary award. In most jurisdictions, however, a negligent plaintiff may recover under the doctrine of comparative negligence if his or her negligence is no more or less than that of defendant. That means that in some jurisdictions, plaintiffs can recover only if plaintiff's negligence does not exceed 50%. In other jurisdictions, plaintiff's negligence must be less than that of defendant's negligence. As a result, in those jurisdictions, plaintiff's negligence cannot exceed 49%.

Two cases demonstrate how courts apply these doctrines, as well as the impact of the doctrines on the outcome of the cases. The first case is *Sandejar v. Alice Physicians and Surgeons Hospital.*[67] The case was decided by a Texas Court of Civil Appeals. The second case, *Skar v. City of Lincoln,*[68] was a case decided by the eighth circuit United States Court of Appeals.

In *Sandejar,* Jose Sandejar, Jr. was 20 years old when he was involved in a car accident. His car overturned twice, and he was ejected from it. Jose had been drinking and was driving at approximately 70 miles per hours when his car left the road. When the emergency response team arrived on the scene, Jose was not moving any part of his body with the exception of his head.

Jose was taken to an emergency room where he was examined by D.R. Halverson. Halverson admitted Jose to the hospital and ordered that Jose's bed be elevated 30 degrees, that he be aroused every 2 to 3 hours, and that he have bathroom privileges the following morning. Additionally, Halverson ordered that Jose be admitted under the care of his family physician J.C. Gonzales.

Jose had been admitted to Alice Physicians and Surgeons Hospital on a Saturday evening, and did not see a physician until the following Monday morning. During that time he was cared for staff nurses who observed Jose every 2 hours. One nurse testified that she was on duty on Sunday when she noticed that Jose was unable to move his lower extremities when he was told to do so. On Monday morning, after unsuccessful attempts to reach J.C. Gonzales, the nursing staff contacted D.R. Halverson, the emergency room physician who admitted Jose. The nurses reported that Jose was complaining of back pain and said that he had not seen a doctor since he was admitted. Halverson ordered that Jose be given a sedative, but did not come to Jose's room to assess him.

Later on Monday, when J.C. Gonzales was contacted, he indicated that he could not see Jose, but that he would be seen by another physician. That physician arrived and determined that Jose was suffering from flaccid paralysis from the waist down. Jose was then transferred to another hospital for spinal cord injury treatment.

Subsequently, Alice Physicians and Surgeons Hospital, Inc. and D.R. Halverson were named as defendants in a medical malpractice cause of action filed on behalf of Jose. The petition alleged that Jose sustained complete and total paralysis from his chest down because of the negligence of the hospital and emergency room physician. The defendants asserted that Jose's injuries were not the result of any negligence on their part; rather, they were sustained because Jose was contributorily negligent by overturning and wrecking his car.

The case was tried in front of a Texas jury who agreed that Jose's injuries were the result of his own contributory negligence, and not the negligence of either defendant. Accordingly, a verdict was rendered in favor of the defendants.

Jose appealed the matter to a Texas Court of Civil Appeals. After reviewing the issues raised by Jose, the Court of Civil Appeals determined that no reversible errors had been committed and affirmed the ruling of the trial court. In reaching that conclusion, however, the court noted that the issue of contributory negligence should not have been presented to the jury because there was no evidence that Jose was guilty of any negligence that occurred simultaneously with the alleged negligence of the defendants. In spite of this error, the court affirmed the decision of the trial court characterizing the error as immaterial.

In Nebraska, *Skar* was decided by the eighth circuit United States Court of Appeals. In that case a highway patrol trooper found William T. Skar sleeping and intoxicated in his car. The car was stopped on a highway in Lincoln, Nebraska. Skar was unable to provide the trooper with any definitive information about himself, and produced only an address, which indicated that Skar lived in Longmont, Colorado.

The trooper arrested Skar and took him to the county jail in Lincoln, Nebraska. While Skar was incarcerated there his behavior became increasingly troubling. He was seen banging his head on the cell wall, removing his clothing neatly laying them on the floor. He had bowel movements in a number of locations around his cell. Skar was permitted to make a telephone call, but he was unable to communicate. He simply mouthed words into the telephone receiver. Later in the day, he was seen staring into space, and occasionally mumbled incoherently.

A corrections nurse finally decided to contact a physician who prescribed medication that was to be given to Skar, and arranged his admittance to a psychiatric unit. He was assessed by Robert Osborne, his treating physician, but was unable to give accurate historical information. In light of the admitting physician's findings, Skar was given a diagnosis of paranoid schizophrenia, and admitted to the psychiatric unit located on the third floor.

During his stay, Skar was uncommunicative, but cooperative. Early one morning Skar got out of bed and went to the nurses' lounge. From the lounge, Skar was accompanied back to his room by nurse Lorraine Stoklasa. When Skar approached his room he began to run. When he reached his room, he continued to run until he attempted to jump out of the reinforced window. The window was closed, so after Skar hit it he fell to the floor suffering a disabling spinal cord injury.

William Skar, through his father, sued the City of Lincoln as the operator of the jail and hospital, the emergency room physicians' service which provided emergency room physician services to the hospital, and Robert Osborne, the psychiatrist who treated Skar at the psychiatric unit. At the trial court level, the judge dismissed Skar's negligence claims against the jail, hospital, and emergency physicians service, but required Skar's claim with regard to Robert Osborne be tried by the jury. The jury returned a verdict in favor of Robert Osborne, and Skar appealed these trial court actions the eighth circuit United States Court of Appeals.

The Court of Appeals reviewed the matter and affirmed the rulings of the trial court. In reaching this conclusion, the appellate court noted that the nurses at the jail and hospital were negligent in rendering Skar timely assistance, but that their negligence was not the cause of the injuries sustained by Skar. With regard to Robert Osborne, the Court of Appeals reviewed Skar's objection to Robert Osborne's assertion that Skar was contributorily negligent because Skar failed to give accurate information to his treating physician. It recognized that contributory negligence was a valid defense to medical malpractice claims in Nebraska, and determined that Robert Osborne could raise the defense because Skar's case depended heavily on the premise that accurate historical information was essential to providing proper psychiatric care.

Sandejar and *Skar* are indicative of how the doctrine of contributory negligence is applied in professional negligence cases. Cases from other jurisdictions also address contributory negligence.[69]

Statute of Limitations

The *statute of limitations* identifies the time period within which a lawsuit must be filed. In some cases, that period of time is measured from either the time the wrong occurred or the time that the wrong should have been discovered. For professional negligence causes of actions, jurisdictions vary, but many require that cases be filed within a 2-year period. The 2-year period can be measured from the time that the injury occurred, or from the time that the injury was discovered or should have been discovered. Where governmental entities are involved, the statute of limitations is typically shorter. In some states, a claim must be filed within 1 year. In other states, the time period may be longer. In all states, the statue of limitations for patients under the age of majority is extended.

With regard to the statute of limitations, jurisdictions vary. For any case filed, it is important to know what the statute of limitations is, and to file the case prior to its expiration. Failure to timely file any cause of action can prevent the plaintiff from pursuing his or her claim.

The Civil Litigation Process

Plaintiff Files Petition/Complaint

When a patient thinks that he or she has suffered from the allegedly negligent acts of a health care provider, that patient may file a lawsuit against the health care provider and/or health care facility within which the wrong occurred. Prior to filing a lawsuit, however, the plaintiff may have to complete a mandatory pre-suit claims evaluation process. When a lawsuit is ready to be filed at the trial court level, the document that is filed by the patient–plaintiff is called a *complaint* if the case is filed in a state court, or a *petition* if it is filed in a federal court.

In either case, the patient–plaintiff must outline the facts that give rise to the filed lawsuit. Usually, patient–plaintiffs will allege that the defendant committed one or more of the following: negligence, malpractice, wrongful birth, wrongful death, defamation, assault and battery, false imprisonment, loss of consortium, emotional distress, or intentional indifference. In managed care settings, breach of contract and breach of fiduciary duty may be part of the patients petition or complaint. (See pages 81–83 for a discussion of comparative and contributory negligence.)

Defendant Files Answer/Response

After the patient–plaintiff files the lawsuit-instigating petition or complaint, and after the paperwork has been received by the defendant, that defendant must file what is called an answer or response to the petition or complaint filed by plaintiff. Where the case has been filed in a state court, the responding document filed by the defendant is called an *answer.* If the case has been filed in a federal court, the responding document is called a *response.* In the document, the defendant responds specifically to each of the enumerated items included in the patient–plaintiff's complaint or petition. In addition, the defendant may allege that the statute of limitations has expired, that an unavoidable accident occurred, that the plaintiff was comparatively or contributorily negligent, or that the patient assumed the risk of the injury that he or she now complains of.

Discovery

Following the filing of defendant's response/answer, the period referred to as discovery commences. *Discovery* is that period of time within which the parties to a lawsuit may collect information from each other about the case. During discovery, several things occur. Written documents are traded, and witnesses are interviewed. Written documents that are exchanged between the parties include interrogatories, requests for production, and requests for admission. Witness interviews occur in settings called depositions.

Interrogatories

Interrogatories are written questions submitted by one party to another. Typically, the questions begin by asking general, biographical information, and end with very specific questions about the case at hand. Questions will likely be varied with some open-ended and some closed-ended questions. In an attempt to streamline the discovery process, many jurisdictions limit the number of interrogatories one party may forward.

Interrogatories request background information, seek to identify witnesses to be called at trial, and ask the other party to disclose relevant information about the case at issue. They must be answered under oath. In addition, parties have an affirmative obligation to supplement the answers given to interrogatories where additional information is uncovered after interrogatories have been answered.

Interrogatories

In professional negligence cases involving a registered nurse, that nurse will have to respond in writing to a series of questions asked by the patient–plaintiff. Questions posed by the patient–plaintiff may include

- State your full name, age, social security number, current residential address, the address of all places at which you have practiced nursing, and the unit/department in which you practiced, as well as the dates of employment at each of those places.
- State the nursing school you attended, its address, the date you graduated, the degree you obtained, and every state in which you have been licensed as a registered nurse.
- Have you ever been the subject of an investigation by any state board of nursing? If so, state each board of nursing, the facts surrounding each investigation, and the disposition of each investigation.
- Have you at any time been certified in any specialty? If so, state the specialty certification, the organization from which certification was obtained, as well as the dates of certification, and requirements for recertification.

- Have you every published, written, or contributed to a nursing book, paper, or article? If so, list the complete bibliographic information for each publication and contribution.
- Have you at any time obtained any information concerning the plaintiff's prior medical history or records? If so, from whom did you obtain that information?
- With regard to the care rendered plaintiff, did you make any written notes? If so, state where the notation was made and whether it has been produced for the plaintiff.
- State the name, address, title, and specialty of any expert or other witness who will be called to render any opinion evidence at trial.
- Do you have any records or notes concerning the plaintiff? If so, where are those records or notes? For each record or note, state its identity, the subject matter, who made the record or note, date of each record or note, whether each record or note has been produced for the plaintiff, and who now has control and custody of each record or note.
- Do you have or know of the existence of any report, correspondence, or other record relating to the treatment of plaintiff rendered at any time? If so, where are those records or notes? For each record or note state its identity, the subject matter, who made the record or note, date of each record or note, whether each record or note has been produced for the plaintiff, and who now has control and custody of each record or note.
- With regard to the nursing care you rendered to plaintiff, state how you believe you met the standard of care.
- Do you have any information that plaintiff's injuries are not as he claims? If so, list what information you have, and who has custody and control of that information.
- List all insurance policies and their limits of coverage that could be used to satisfy any judgment against you in this case.
- Have you ever been involved in any other civil or criminal lawsuit, other than this one? If so, state the case name for each case, as well as the case number, the role you played in each case, and the disposition of each case.

Requests for Production

Requests for production are written requests to turn over or produce documents and other tangible items needed to prove or defend the case being prepared for trial. Typically, requests for production apply to medical records, medical supplies, medical devices, bookkeeping records, photographs, x-rays, bylaws, organizational charts, personnel files, internal telephone directories, credentialing files, policies and procedures, index of training and educational programs, laboratory logs and equipment records as well as other tangible items.

Requests for Production

Plaintiffs alleging that they have been the recipient of malpractice will request that defendants produce the following documents and other items for their inspection:

- Copies of plaintiff's complete medical record and other records including, but not limited to, billing records, appointment records, telephone memoranda, office records, reports, logs, photographs, slides, correspondence, referrals and consultation documentation, as well as any other documentation that concerns plaintiff.
- All documents and correspondence from plaintiff to defendant.
- Copies of all insurance policies that insure defendant for professional negligence claims, as well as the liability limits for each policy.
- Copies of all lawsuits your hospital has been involved with that concern acts of negligence toward patients.
- Copies of all items and documents referred to in answering your interrogatories.

Requests for Admission

Requests for admission are written requests from one party to another to admit or deny certain facts. This document is used to help narrow the issues to be tried, and are usually written as closed-ended statements that require the person answering the question to do so affirmatively or negatively. Sometimes, requests for admissions may be submitted, along with interrogatories asking the other party to state the reasons, facts, and evidence upon which the other party relied in refusing to admit any specific request.

Depositions

Depositions are opportunities for the counsel for the parties in a lawsuit to interact with witnesses. Depositions usually occur as interviews, but can be done in writing. Whether the deposition is completed via interview or in writing, the person being interviewed or deposed needs to remember that depositions require the witness to be under oath; that is, the witness must swear to tell the truth. Failure to do so could result in the witness being subjected to perjury charges.

During depositions, it is important for the person being questioned to

- speak clearly;
- listen carefully to the question being asked;
- be completely honest;
- clarify any inaccurate or unclear responses;

Requests for Admission

Requests for admission are used to narrow the issues at trial. Nurses who are parties in a professional negligence case will be asked to admit or deny statements posed by the plaintiff. Here are examples of statements that nurses will likely be asked to admit or deny certain facts.

- That on April 22, 2001, from 3:00 PM until 11:00 PM, you provided nursing care services to plaintiff.
- That on April 22, 2001, from 3:00 PM until 11:00 PM, you provided nursing care services to plaintiff and to 10 other patients.
- That on April 22, 2001, from 3:00 PM until 11:00 PM, plaintiff needed nursing care services.
- That on April 22, 2001, from 3:00 PM until 11:00 PM, you were the only registered nurse providing nursing care services to plaintiff and to 10 other patients.
- That on April 22, 2001, from 3:00 PM until 11:00 PM, the patient's condition deteriorated.
- That as a registered nurse, it was your responsibility to assess the neurologic status of plaintiff while he was being cared for by you on April 22, 2001.
- That as a registered nurse, it was your responsibility to intervene as the neurologic condition of plaintiff changed.
- That as a registered nurse, it was your responsibility to act as plaintiff's advocate.
- That on April 22, 2001, the nurse's notes do not indicate the frequency with which you performed any neurologic assessment on plaintiff.
- That on April 22, 2001, plaintiff was admitted to your unit because he sustained a closed head injury.
- That on April 22, 2001, at 11:15 PM, the plaintiff was unresponsive in his bed.
- That on April 22, 2001, at 11:47 PM, the plaintiff was pronounced dead.

- refrain from guessing or approximating;
- stay calm; and
- be aware of nonverbal mannerisms or habits that might be distracting.

Pre-Trial Conference

During or at the conclusion of discovery, a pre-trial conference is usually scheduled. This conference occurs with the judge who will hear the case, as well as the attorneys for the patients to the lawsuit. Deadlines are established and a date for trial set. It is during this conference that a judge will encourage the parties to resolve the matter without taking it to trial, and plans for mediation or arbitration will be discussed. Many jurisdictions require a pre-trial attempt at settlement, so the parties need to be prepared to have their case heard in this alternative dispute resolution process prior to proceeding to trial.

Trial

Cases that are not settled or dismissed prior to trial are usually decided by a jury at trial. At *trial,* a jury will be selected, opening statements will be made by the attorneys for each party, and the plaintiff's case will be presented, followed by the presentation of defendant's case. Then, closing arguments will be made by the attorneys for the parties. The judge will then give the jury the instructions they are to follow. Once jury instructions are given, the jury is dismissed from the court room to commence their deliberations. Once the jury reaches a decision in the case, the judge and attorneys for the parties are informed, and a verdict is rendered. Following the rendering of the jury's verdict, the losing side will likely ask the judge to render a decision in their favor notwithstanding the decision of the jury, and will ask the judge to allow them to file an appeal. Each of these phases of a civil jury trial will be discussed in more detail.

Jury Selection

Jury selection is the phase of the litigation process where individual jurors are selected to decide a specific controversy. The process used to select a jury depends on the jurisdiction and the court. Sometimes judges question the jurors to determine which are best suited to hear the evidence that will be presented. However, most of the time, attorneys of the parties question jurors. Questioning jurors is called *voir dire.*

Jurors are questioned to identify those who are best suited to decide the case. The primary objective of jury selection is to select a jury that can be objective and fair to all parties. As advocates for their clients, plaintiff attorneys will be looking for jurors who appear to understand their client, and the situation the client finds him- or herself in; defense attorneys will be looking for jurors who are sympathetic to their client. Following voir dire, attorneys have an opportunity to eliminate jurors. Each side has an equal number of strikes. In addition, potential jurors can be eliminated by either side for bias or prejudice.

Opening Statements

After the jury is selected, attorneys for both parties make *opening statements.* The plaintiff's attorney presents his or her opening statement first, followed by the counsel for the defense. During opening statements, attorneys for both parties state what they believe the facts are, and unveil their theme for the case. In their opening statements, attorneys attempt to be clear, forceful, and positive about their case, but are required to refrain from being argumentative and stating their personal opinions.

Plaintiff's Case

Following the presentation of the parties' opening statements, the plaintiff presents his or her case. Here, witnesses are called to assist the plaintiff to prove his or her case against the defendant(s). Witnesses called by the plaintiff are questioned or directly examined by plaintiff's counsel. Sometimes, a witness called by the plaintiff will be considered *hostile,* and the plaintiff will be permitted to proceed as if the witness was called by the opposing party.

Through the witnesses called, the plaintiff attempts to present a clear, logically organized, scenic description of the events that gave rise to the case being tried. Weaknesses in the plaintiff's case are likely to be addressed, so that the jury can be prepared for what plaintiff's counsel anticipates that defense counsel will raise as reasons to disallow recovery.

Following the direct examination of each of plaintiff's witnesses, defense counsel has an opportunity to question or *cross examine* these witnesses. During cross examination, inconsistencies in the witnesses testimony are exposed, and the credibility of the witness is called into question.

Following the plaintiff's presentation of their case, counsel for the defendant typically asks that the judge issue a judgment in favor of the defendant because the plaintiff failed to prove his or her case. Although courts usually deny these motions, there are instances where the court will grant a defendant's motion to enter a judgment in favor of defendant.

Defendant's Case

After the plaintiff completes the questioning of witnesses called to assist in proving the case on behalf of the plaintiff, plaintiff's counsel will announce that the "plaintiff rests." At this point, the defendant has the opportunity to present his or her case to the jury. Witnesses called by the defense are directly examined by the defense counsel, and cross examined by the plaintiff's counsel. After all of the defense witnesses have been directly examined and cross examined, defense counsel will announce that the "defense rests."

Closing Arguments

After the parties conclude the questioning of witnesses, both parties are provided an opportunity to present their closing arguments to the jury. Unlike opening statements, closing arguments are argumentative. Attorneys are permitted to argue their theory of the case. They argue that the facts require the jury to return a verdict in their favor, and are likely to remind the jury of their theme; they articulate how the witnesses provided evidence that supports their theme, and thus the conclusion that a jury verdict be in their favor.

Jury Instructions

After the attorneys for both parties complete their closing arguments, the judge will review the jury instructions with the jury. *Jury instructions* are a list of laws to be followed in a particular case and are used to help the jury make a decision in the case.

Jury Deliberation

After the trial court judge reviews the jury instructions with the jurors, the jury begins its *deliberation.* During this discussion and decision-making time, the jury is secluded in a jury room and given the time they need to reach a decision in the case. A jury foreperson is selected, and the jurors begin reviewing the evidence and the jury instructions to decide whether or not the plaintiff is entitled to recovery.

Verdict

After a jury reaches a decision in a professional negligence matter, they return to the courtroom to announce their verdict. Once a verdict is rendered, the members of the jury are thanked for their service, and dismissed. Typically, the party that the jury renders a verdict against will ask the judge to enter a verdict for that party in spite of the decision of the jury. Courts will usually deny such motions.

Appeal

Parties losing any pre-trial motions may seek review by the appellate courts. In addition, after the jury enters a verdict in a civil matter, the losing party has the right to appeal the case to the applicable court of appeals. Courts of appeals will either affirm or reverse the decisions made by the trial court. The party losing at the court of appeals may request to appeal the matter to the state supreme court. State supreme courts generally have discretion as to whether to accept or reject the review of a civil case. Courts deciding to review the issues that have been properly reserved for them either affirm, reverse, or modify the decisions of the preceding courts. Where state supreme courts accept the review of a civil matter and reverse a decision of a lower court, the court will remand the matter to the trial court for entry of the reversal decision in the record, trial, or re-trial on the issues outlined by the state supreme court. Unless the issues in a civil matter involve constitutional matters, the decision of the state supreme court is final and not appealable. When the case involves constitutional issues, it can be appealed to the U.S. Supreme Court. The U.S. Supreme Court, however, has complete discretion to determine whether or not it will hear those cases.

Summary

With increasing frequency, nurses are being named as defendants in professional negligence causes of action. As a result, it is important for nurses to know what actions and omissions give rise to nursing-focused litigation, and to understand the doctrines and terms that are likely to be used. Should a nurse find him- or herself involved in any civil lawsuit, familiarity with the civil litigation process will also be needed. Nurses need to seriously consider purchasing malpractice insurance in the event that they find themselves a named defendant in a professional negligence cause of action.

This chapter outlines the common causes of action that nurses face in civil litigation. By far, negligence is the most common cause of action leveled against nurses and/ or the organizations at which they practice; therefore, a significant portion of this chapter was devoted to discussions of negligence. The nursing acts and omissions commonly pointed to as evidence that a nurse breached his or her duty to a patient were organized using the nursing process. This was done in an attempt to underscore the importance of practicing in a way that reflects that the nurse is attentive and acting in accordance with the standards of care when assessing, planning, implementing, and evaluating care given to patients. Assessment failures include a nurse's failure to assess and analyze the level of care needed by the patient and failure to ascertain the patient's wishes with regard to self-determination. Planning failures included the failure to diagnose appropriately. Implementation failures included the failure to timely communicate patient findings, failure to take appropriate action, failure to document assessment findings and patient responses to interventions, and failure to preserve patient privacy. Evaluation failures include the failure to act as a patient advocate.

Failing to act as a patient advocate can not only lead to civil litigation and to disciplinary action, it can also lead to criminal action where the nurse's actions violate criminal laws. Chapter 4 focuses on the criminal litigation process and the nurse as a criminal defendant.

Endnotes

1. Smith-Pittman, M.H. 1998. Nurses and litigation. *Journal of Nursing Law* 5(2): 7–19.
2. Ibid, p. 12.
3. *Black's Law Dictionary*, 5th ed. 1979. St. Paul, MN: West Publishing Co; p. 201.
4. *Simmons v. U.S.*, 841 F.Supp. 748 (W.D. La. 1993).
5. 648 S.W. 391 (Tx. App. 1983).
6. For example, *Ybarra v. Spangard*, 154 P.2d 687 (Cal. 1944); *Woods v. Rowland*, 592 P.2d 1332 (Co. 1978); *Larrimore v. Homeopathic Hospital Association*, 176 A.2d 362 (De. 1962); *Daniel v. St. Francis Cabrini Hospital of Alexandria*, 415 So. 2d 586 (La. 1982); *Plutshack v. University of Minnesota Hospital*, 316 N.W. 2d 1 (Mn. 1982); *Hunsaker v. Bozeman Deaconess Foundation*, 588 P.2d 493 (Mt. 1978); *Vassey v. Burch*, 262 S.E. 2d 865 (N.C. 1980); *Baur v. Mesta Machine Co.*, 176 A.2d 684 (Pa. 1962); *Childs v. Greenville Hospital Authority*, 479 S.W. 2d 399 (Tx. 1972).; and *Stone v. Sisters of Charity of the House of Providence*, 469 P.2d 229 (Wash. 1970).
7. *Clough v. Lively*, 387 S.E. 2d 573 (Ga. 1989).
8. 995 F.2d 629 (6th Cir. 1993).
9. 421 So. 2d 309 (La. 1982).
10. 415 So. 2d 586 (La. 1982).
11. 517 N.W. 2d 328 (Mn. 1994).

12. 835 S.W. 2d 554 (Mo. 1992).

13. 569 N.W. 2d 330 (Wi. 1997).

14. 262 S.E. 2d 865 (N.C. 1980).

15. Ibid.

16. 592 N.E. 2d 678 (Il. 1992).

17. 437 A. 2d 978 (Pa. 1982).

18. 42 U.S.C. Section 1394 CC(a)(1)(1990).

19. 671 N.E. 2d 225 (Oh. 1996).

20. Los Angeles County Super. Ct. No. GC 011 608, August 16, 1995.

21. 856 P. 2d 864 (Id. 1993).

22. 695 P. 2d 674 (Ca. 1985).

23. 98 LWUSA 51 (January 11, 1999).

24. *Lambert v. Sisters of Mercy Health Corporation,* 369 N.W. 2d 417 (Ia, 1985); *Brannan v. Lankenau Hospital,* 417 A.2d 196 (Pa.1980); *Agustin v. Beth Israel Hospital,* 586 N.Y.S. 2d 252 (N.Y. 1992); *Washington v. NY City Health Hospital Corporation,* No. 8606/89 (N.Y., Bronx County Sup. Ct. October 21, 1995); *Karney v. Arnott-Ogden Memorial Hospital,* 674 N.Y.S. 2d 449 (N.Y. 1998); *Morse v. Flint River Community Hospital,* 480 S.E. 253 (Ga. 1994); *Sullivan v. Sumrall by Ritchy,* 618 So.2d 1274 (Ms. 1993); *Berdyk v. Shinde,* 613 N.E. 2d 1014 (Oh. 1993); *Ramsey v. Physicians Memorial Hospital,* 373 A.2d 196 (Md. 1977); *Karrigan v. Nazareth Convent and Academy, Inc.,* 510 P.2d 190 (Kan.1973); *Flores v. Cyborski,* 629 N.E. 2d 74 (Il. 1993).

25. 893 F.2d 411 (1st Cir. 1990).

26. 661 So. 2d 991 (La. 1995).

27. 696 So. 2d 590 (La. 1997).

28. 733 So. 2d 91 (La .1999).

29. 734 A. 2d 778 (N.J. 1999).

30. 978 P. 2d 429 (Or. 1999).

31. 489 N.W. 2d 829 (Ne. 1992).

32. 697 F. Supp. 1570 (Co. 1988).

33. 930 F. 2d 1150 (6th Cir.1991).

34. 866 P.2d 437 (Ok. 1992).

35. 323 S.E. 2d 430 (N.C. 1977).

36. 575 F. Supp. 1108 (Ga. 1979).

37. 688 P.2d 961 (Az. 1979).

38. 663 N.E. 2d 1369 (Oh. 1995).

39. 849 S.W. 2d 564 (Ky. 1993).

40. *Sultan v. Kings Highway Hospital,* 562 N.Y.S. 2d 204 (N.Y. 1990); *U.S. v. Vamos,* 797 F.2d 1146 (N.Y. 1986); *Poluski v. Richardson Transportation,* 877 S.W. 2d 709 (Mo. 1994); *Wingo v. Rockford Memorial Hospital,* No. 922 345 (Il.Winnebago County Cir. Ct. July 3, 1996); *Jack v. State,* 671 So. 2d 26 (La. 1996); *Utter v. United Hospital Center,* 236 S.E.2d 213 (Va. 1977); *Justin v. Santa Monica Hospital Medical Center,* SC019-167, Ca.; *Ortega v. Public Health Trust of Dade County,* No. 91-04089 (Fl. Dade County Cir. Ct. June 5, 1995); *Wall v. Fairview Hospital,* 584 N.W. 2d 395 (Mn. 1998); *Wendland v. Sparks,* 574 N.W. 2d 327 (Ia. 1998).

41. 416 S.E. 2d 127 (Ga. 1992).

42. 768 P. 2d 768 (Id. 1989).

43. 493 N.E. 2d 6 (Il. 1986).

44. 635 N.E. 2d 1019 (Il. 1994).

45. 602 So. 2d 240 (La. 1992).

46. National Council of State Boards of Nursing, Inc (NCSBN). 1994. *Model Nursing Practice Act.* Chicago: National Council of State Boards of Nursing; pp. 3, 4.

47. 422 N.W. 2d 600 (S.D. 1988).

48. 540 So. 2d 1270 (La. 1989).

49. *Harris County Hospital District v. Estrada,* 872 S.W. 2d 759 (Tx. 1993); *Elizabeth Hospital v. Graham,* 883 S.W. 2d 433 (Tx. 1994); *Hurlock v. Park Lane Medical Center, Inc.,* 709 S.W. 2d 872 (Mo. 1985); *Battles v. Aderhold,* 430 So. 2d 307 (La. 1983); *Alvis v. Henderson,* 592 N.E. 2d 678 (Il.1992); *HCA Health Service v. National Bank,*745 S.W. 2d 120 (Ar. 1988).; *Goldsby v. Evangelical Deaconess Hospital,*74-004-754 (N.M. 1978).

50. 725 N.E. 2d 1117 (Oh. 2000).

51. Jury Verdict Research Report, April 12, 2000.

52. Stein, T. 2000. On the defensive. *NurseWeek/HealthWeek.* Available at URL: http://www.nurseweek.com/features/00-05/malpract.html

53. 818 P.2d 456, 461 (Ok. 1991).

54. 16 F.3d 473 (1st. Cir. 1994).

55. 354 S.E. 2d 872 (Ga. 1987).

56. 490 N.Y.S. 2d 87 (N.Y. 1985).

57. 948 S.W. 2d 72 (Tx. 1997).

58. 513 A. 2d 341 (N.H. 1986).

59. 188 F.3d 1195 (Ok. 1999).

60. 697 P. 2d 504 (N.M. 1979).

61. 830 P. 2d 1185 (Id. 1992).

62. 685 P. 2d 776 (Co. 1984).

63. *Mock v. Allen, Alabama,* No. 1980985. June 30, 2000.

64. *Martinmaas v. Engelmann,* South Dakota, No. 2000. June 28, 2000.

65. 461 S.W. 2d 195 (Tx. Civ. App. 1970).

66. 44 F. Supp. 2d 62 (Me. 1998).

67. 55 S.W. 2d 879 (Tx. 1977).

68. 599 F.2d 253 (8th Cir. 1979).

69. *Martineau v. Nelson,* N.W. 2d 409 (Mn. 1976); *Kaspar v. Schack,* 237 N.W. 2d 414 (Ne. 1976); *Mecham v. McLeay,* 227 N.W. 2d 829 (Ne. 1975); *Grippe v. Momtazee,* 705 S.W. 2d. 551 (Mo. 1986); *Faile v. Bycura,* 374 S.E. 2d 687 (S.C. 1988); *Welker v. Scripps,* 16 Cal. Rptr. 538 (1961); *Wisker v. Hart,* 766 P.2d 168 (Ks 1988); *Hunter v. U.S.,* 236 F. Supp. 411 (Tn. 1964); *Matthews v. Williford,* 318 So. 2d 480 (Fl. 1975); *Whitehead v. Linkows,* 404 So. 2d 377 (Fl. 1981); *Cowan v. Doerning,* 522 A.2d 444 (N.J. 1987); *Lamoree v. Binghamton General Hospital,* 329 N.Y.S. 2d 85 (N.Y. 1972); *Los Alamos Medical Center v. Coe,* 275 P.2d 175 (N.M. 1954); *Owens v. Stokoe,* 485 N.E. 2d 537 (Il. 1985).

The Nurse as the Accused in Criminal Litigation

4

Introduction

Nurse Convicted of Killing 6 Patients[1] . . . this and headlines from many community newspapers serve as reminders that nurses can be accused of committing crimes. When a crime is committed, the person who is said to have committed the crime is called the *defendant,* and the party pursuing the matter is either the state or federal government, or both. Typically, at the state level, the district attorney files criminal charges when state crimes are committed, and federal prosecutors from the Department of Justice file criminal charges on behalf of the federal government. In criminal proceedings, district attorneys represent the state, and federal prosecutors represent the United States. This chapter will outline doctrines associated with criminal litigation, as well as the criminal litigation process, and crimes that have been committed by nurses.

Doctrines and Terms

Because nurses commit crimes, sometimes knowingly and other times unknowingly, it is important to be familiar with doctrines and terms that are used. Below are key doctrines and terms used in the criminal justice system.

Bail

Bail is a mechanism used by judges and magistrates to guarantee an accused person's attendance at a criminal proceeding and continuing presence in the jurisdiction. Typically, money is paid by the defendant to a court or other authorized public officer to ensure that the criminal defendant will attend all criminal proceedings. Where the defendant fails to abide by the directives of the court, the money paid to secure his or her release from jail will be forfeited.

Sometimes, no money is required for a criminal defendant to be released from jail prior to trial. Where a judge or magistrate is satisfied that the defendant will appear voluntarily, the defendant may be released on his or her own recognizance.

In some cases, bail is denied, and the arrested individual is required to remain incarcerated. This occurs when the crime is particularly heinous, and when the person may attempt to flee the jurisdiction.

Double Jeopardy

Double jeopardy is the doctrine that prohibits anyone from being prosecuted more than once for the same offense. The doctrine of double jeopardy arises out of the fifth amendment to the U.S. Constitution.

Due Process

Due process is a guarantee of the fifth and fourteenth amendments to the U.S. Constitution, and promises that individuals will be provided a meaningful opportunity to be meaningfully heard in a meaningful manner. In criminal cases, due process requires that the state prove guilt beyond a reasonable doubt.

Fifth amendment due process rights limit the actions that can be taken by the federal government; fourteenth amendment due process rights protect people from unreasonable state actions. Due process is considered either procedural or substantive due process. *Procedural due process* requires that the judicial process be fair; *substantive due process* protects a person's property from unfair government interference.

In the criminal procedure context, due process requires that self-incriminating statements be voluntary and not the result of compulsion, duress, or force. Due process also requires that trials be conducted in a manner that is unbiased. Because of this, due process is denied if the criminal defendant is compelled to stand trial in prison clothing and if it is unlikely that the jury gives reasonable consideration to all of the evidence presented.

Exclusionary Rule

The *exclusionary rule* commands that evidence be excluded at trial where the evidence is obtained in violation of the U.S. Constitution. This rule works to keep the jury from hearing about any evidence gathered in the midst of an unreasonable search and seizure, or in violation of any of the accused's other Constitutional rights.

Exculpatory Evidence

Exculpatory evidence entitles the accused person to present evidence that tends to indicate that the accused individual is innocent or mitigate the seriousness of the crime. Failure to provide criminal defendants with evidence that indicates that he or she may be innocent violates the defendant's due process rights and may be grounds for reversing a decision to convict someone for a crime, if there is a reasonable probability that the nondisclosed evidence would have affected the outcome of the trial.

Expectation of Privacy

An individual has a legitimate and reasonable *expectation of privacy* in the place searched where the individual owns or has a right to possess it. In addition, an individual has a reasonable expectation of privacy in his or her home, whether or not the individual owns it. Finally, an individual has an expectation of privacy in the place where he or she was an overnight guest of the owner of the place searched.

Alternatively, there is no reasonable expectation of privacy in the sound of an individual's own voice or handwriting, or in the paint on the outside of the individual's vehicle. Also, there is no expectation of privacy in bank account records, the location of one's vehicle on public roads or its arrival at a private residence, as well as areas outside the individual's home and associated buildings. Finally, there is no legitimate expectation of privacy in garbage left for collection, land visible from a public place including an airplane or helicopter, the smell of one's luggage, and the thermographic patterns emitted from a house.

Extradition

Extradition occurs when one jurisdiction surrenders an individual to another jurisdiction because that individual is accused or convicted of committing a crime outside the surrendering jurisdiction. In most cases, the surrendering jurisdiction issues an order signed by the governor of that state to transport the accused to another jurisdiction.

Grand Jury

In federal criminal cases, the fifth amendment to the U.S. Constitution permits indictment by grand jury. A *grand jury* is a body of citizens summoned to determine whether probable cause exists that a crime was committed and whether an indictment should be issued against a particular individual for committing the crime. Grand jury proceedings are conducted in secret, and witnesses subpoenaed to testify before a grand jury do not have the right to receive Miranda warnings or to have an attorney present. In addition, grand juries may base their decision to indict someone on evidence that would be inadmissible at trial. This body of citizens is called a grand jury because the number of people who comprise this body is greater than the number of jurors in a civil or criminal trial. In addition to the federal government's use of the grand jury, most states east of the Mississippi River use grand juries in the criminal charging process. However, states in the western part of the United States typically charge an individual with a crime by having the prosecutor file an *information*, a written accusation that the charged individual committed the crime that is recorded in the information.

Indictment

An *indictment* is a written accusation, by a prosecutor or grand jury, that a crime has been committed, and that the crime was committed by a specific person. It is the document that is used to assert that a specific individual committed a specific crime. It is used to require that a specific individual be tried for committing a specific crime.

Insanity

Insanity may be asserted as a defense to crime that is alleged to have been committed. The term is synonymous with having a mental illness, which negates the individual's ability to be held legally responsible or accountable for the crime allegedly committed.

There are four tests that are used by the courts to determine whether a defendant was insane when the crime was committed. (1) Under the *M'Naghten Rule,* the defendant will be acquitted if he or she had a mental illness or defect that caused the defendant to not know right from wrong when the crime was committed. (2) Under the *Irresistible Impulse Test,* a defendant will be acquitted only if, because of a mental illness, he or she was unable to control his or her actions or to conform his or her conduct to the law. (3) Using the *Durham Test,* a defendant will be acquitted if the crime was the product of his or her mental illness. (4) According to the *Model Penal Code Test,* a person is not responsible for the criminal conduct he or she is allegedly accused of if, at the time, because of mental disease or defect, the accused individual lacks substantial capacity either to appreciate the criminality or wrongfulness of the conduct or to conform his conduct to the requirements of law.[2]

Intent

Crimes almost always require some bad act occur, and that the individual actor possess a certain mental state or *intention* to act badly in violation of criminal statutes. The required level of intent varies with the crime which is alleged to have been committed. There are four levels of intent: malice, general, specific, and strict liability. *Malice* crimes are those in which the wrongdoer did something intentionally, willfully, and wrongfully. Malice crimes include murder and arson. *General intent* crimes require the wrongdoer to act in a manner that is knowingly prohibited. General intent crimes include battery, rape, kidnapping, and false imprisonment. *Specific intent* crimes require the wrongdoer to intentionally commit the crime alleged. Specific intent crimes include solicitation, attempts to commit crimes, conspiracy, first degree premeditated murder, assault, larceny, robbery, burglary, forgery, false pretenses, and embezzlement. Finally, *strict liability* crimes are those that only require that the wrongdoer do the criminal act. No intent is required. Strict liability offenses include selling liquor to minors and statutory rape.

Mistake of Fact

Mistake of fact is one of the defenses that can be used to excuse the actions of the criminal defendant where it shows that the criminal defendant did not have the state of mind necessary to commit the crime. For instance, where a crime requires specific intent, if the defendant did not have that specific intent in mind when the crime was committed, the defendant cannot be guilty of that specific intent crime.

Plea Bargaining

Plea bargaining is used to expedite the resolution of criminal matters. It may occur at any stage during the criminal litigation process. Typically, the accused individual agrees to plead guilty to a more minor offense than the original charge, or to only certain offenses when multiple charges have been filed. Judges may or may not accept a plea bargaining agreement reached between the prosecutor and defendant.

Probable Cause

Probable cause is the standard of proof that must be met for searches and seizures in any criminal matter. Governmental seizure of any person, including making an arrest, is a seizure within the scope of the fourth amendment and must be reasonable. A seizure occurs when a reasonable person believes that he or she is not free to leave or discontinue an encounter with a government official. Although a seizure may not constitute an arrest, an arrest is a seizure of the person and must be based on probable cause. That is, there must be trustworthy facts or knowledge sufficient for a reasonable person to believe that a suspect has committed or is committing a crime.

Reasonable Doubt

In all criminal matters, the government must establish guilt by presenting that a criminal defendant committed a crime beyond a reasonable doubt. Proving that someone has committed a crime requires that prosecutors meet the highest of evidentiary standards. In civil cases, the standard of proof is less rigorous; the plaintiff or party suing must show that he or she was damaged, using a preponderance of the evidence standard. The preponderance of evidence standard requires that plaintiff's introduce evidence that slightly tips the scales in their favor.

Right to Counsel

Once criminal charges have been filed, the sixth amendment to the U.S. Constitution guarantees the right to have the assistance of counsel in all criminal proceedings. The fifth amendment extends the right to counsel to the time that the accused person is in custody and prior to interrogation. A person is considered to be in custody when his or her freedom is restricted in any way. As a result, a person who has been arrested is considered to be in custody.

Self-Incrimination

The fifth amendment to the U.S. Constitution protects criminal defendants from making statements that would amount to a confession or admission of guilt. Because of this fifth amendment guarantee, any person in custody must be informed, prior to being interrogated, that individual has the following rights, known as the Miranda rights: the individual has the right to remain silent; anything said can be used against him or her; he or she has the right to the presence of an attorney; and if an attorney cannot be afforded, one will be appointed. These rights stem from *Miranda v.*

Arizona,[3] a case that was decided by the U.S. Supreme Court in 1966. In *Miranda,* Ernesto Miranda was arrested at his home and taken to a Phoenix police station where he was identified as the individual who had kidnapped and raped the victim. Miranda was subsequently taken into an interrogation room where he was questioned by two officers for 2 hours. During the interrogation, Miranda signed a confession statement. At the top of the statement was a paragraph stating that Miranda's confession was voluntary, without duress or the promise of immunity, and made with the full knowledge of his legal rights, understanding that the statements he made could be used against him.

The case was eventually tried in an Arizona state court, and the signed confession statement was admitted as evidence in the trial. Miranda was convicted of kidnapping and rape, and that conviction was eventually appealed and affirmed by the Arizona Supreme Court.

It was then consolidated with three other cases and heard by the U.S. Supreme Court. The issue that the Supreme Court dealt with was whether or not the confession made by Miranda, while he was interrogated in police custody, should have been admitted as evidence at his trial. The allegation was that the written confession was self-incriminating, in violation of Miranda's fifth amendment constitutional rights

The U.S. Supreme Court agreed with Miranda. Chief Justice Warren, writing for the majority, concluded that the failure on the part of law enforcement officials to warn Miranda that he had the right to remain silent and to have an attorney present during the custodial interrogation violated his fifth amendment right to be free from compelled self-incrimination.

Criminal Litigation Process

The litigation process for criminal defendants is different from the litigation process used in civil litigation. Accordingly, a brief overview of the litigation process in the criminal justice system is provided.

Investigation

Typically, law enforcement authorities commence a criminal investigation once they become aware that a crime may have been committed. Law enforcement officers commence investigations by analyzing the facts surrounding the crime and by talking to those who may have information about the crime. When talking to those who may have information about a crime, law enforcement officers may detain that person or persons if the officer has a reasonable suspicion that the person or persons being detained were involved in the commission of the crime being investigated. However, reasonable suspicion must be accompanied with facts articulated by the officer. Where a person has been detained, the detention can be no longer than necessary to conduct a limited investigation.

If a nurse becomes the focus of any criminal or quasi-criminal investigation, it is imperative that steps be taken to preserve his or her constitutional rights. First, and foremost, nurses should not speak with any investigators without seeking advice from an attorney. Second, no statements should be given to law enforcement officials without an attorney being present. When a nurse is detained because there is reasonable suspicion that he or she was involved in a crime, the nurse should not resist the detention but should clearly indicate to the detaining officers that no statements will be made until after the advice of an attorney is given and until an attorney is present.

Search and Seizure of Evidence

During the criminal investigation, law enforcement officers may collect evidence. However, search and seizure activities must be reasonable to ensure that they comply with the fourth amendment to the U.S. Constitution. A search complies with the fourth amendment if it was conducted after a proper search warrant had been properly executed or if the search was within one of the warrantless search exceptions. A search warrant is proper if it was based on probable cause, was precise with regard to the place to be searched and items to be seized, and was issued by a neutral and detached magistrate. A warrant is properly executed if it was obtained without unreasonable delay, after law enforcement officers knock and announce the purpose of their being on the premises, and the person or place searched and evidence seized is within the scope of the warrant.

Although a search warrant is usually needed for law enforcement officers to search any place or thing in which an alleged wrongdoer has an expectation of privacy and seize evidence, there are times when warrants are unnecessary. Warrantless searches are permitted where the alleged wrongdoer has no expectation of privacy, the search is incident to a lawful arrest, and where there is probable cause to believe that a vehicle contains evidence of a crime. In addition, warrantless searches are permitted where law enforcement officers, lawfully on the premises, discover evidence that is in plain view and gives them probable cause to believe that it is evidence of the commission of a crime. Warrantless searches are also permitted when a law enforcement officer stops someone he or she thinks is armed and dangerous. In this case, the law enforcement officer is permitted to conduct a protective frisk of the stopped individual. Finally, law enforcement officers may make a warrantless search and seizure when the officer is in hot pursuit of a fleeing felon, when evidence is likely to disappear before a warrant can be obtained, in instances where evidence consists of contaminated food or drugs, when children are in trouble, and when fires are burning.

If a nurse is asked to allow a law enforcement officer to search his or her belongings, body, or residence, the nurse should ask to see the search warrant permitting the requested search. If no search warrant is presented, the nurse may decline the officer's request to search. The officers may search anyway, citing one of the warrantless search exceptions, or they may leave, and return later with a search warrant. If the nurse grants a request to search the nurse's belongings, body, or residence, any evidence gathered will be considered valid and used against the nurse.

Arrest

To *arrest* someone is to deprive that individual of his or her liberty. Accordingly, to be arrested, there must be probable cause to believe that the individual committed a crime. Probable cause can be determined a number of ways. First, a police officer, or other officer of the law, can arrest someone without an arrest warrant when the officer believes that there is probable cause. Second, a district attorney may, if statutorily authorized, request that an arrest warrant be issued. Third, a grand jury may be assembled to determine if there is probable cause to issue an arrest warrant.

Using the arrest warrant, law enforcement officers arrest and book the person or persons charged with committing the criminal offense. *Booking* is the procedure that is used to register the individual in the police records. It is during this procedure that the person arrested is fingerprinted and photographed. Immediately after law enforcement officers arrest someone, *Miranda* warnings must be given.

Preliminary Hearing

Where an arrest is based on probable cause (either by a warrant or indictment issued by a grand jury), a preliminary hearing to determine probable cause is unnecessary. However, where probable cause has not been determined and where the accused individual is in jail or out on bail, a preliminary hearing will be scheduled to determine if there is probable cause that the accused individual committed the crime. Preliminary hearings are usually scheduled within 48 hours and are informal.

Arraignment

Arraignment is the procedure used to determine whether the arrested person is going to plead guilty or not guilty to the crimes being charged. Should the arrested person plead guilty to the crimes charged, a sentence is determined, and incarceration for the term of the sentence commences. Pleading guilty at this stage of the process results in the arrested person's waiving of his or her constitutional rights. That being the case, the judge should make sure that the arrested person understands the consequence of pleading guilty and seeks to ensure that the arrested person is entering the guilty plea voluntarily and knowingly. If, on the other hand, the arrested individual pleads not guilty to the crimes charged, bail may be set, along with a trial date.

Trial

The sixth amendment to the U.S. Constitution guarantees criminal defendants the right to a speedy, public trial by jury once he or she is arrested or charged with a crime. The right to a public trial, however, depends on the proceeding, and not solely on the wishes of the criminal defendant. The defendant also has the right to confront witnesses.

The criminal defendant is promised a trial by jury where conviction for criminal offenses results in imprisonment for more than 6 months. Jurors must represent a cross-section of the community, and must be unbiased.

The criminal defendant has a constitutionally based right to counsel. A criminal defendant's right to counsel may be exercised at custodial police interrogations, postindictment interrogations, preliminary hearings, the arraignment, post-charge line-up, when rendering a guilty plea, at sentencing, at felony trials, at misdemeanor trials when imprisonment is imposed, overnight recesses during trial, and on appeal from conviction for the criminal offense. Violating a criminal defendant's right to counsel at trial requires that a criminal conviction be reversed on appeal.

In a criminal trial, a jury is selected or empaneled, and the prosecutor and defense attorney make opening statements. First, the prosecutor lays out the facts and law that tend to prove beyond a reasonable doubt that the criminal defendant committed the crime with which he or she has been charged. Then, the defense attorney presents the facts and law he or she thinks exonerates the defendant or that suggest that the beyond reasonable doubt standard has not been met.

After the opening statements have been made, the prosecutor puts on the witnesses he or she thinks help to prove their case. The defense attorney has an opportunity to question or cross examine the prosecutions' witnesses to point out the weakness and missing links in the testimony given. Allowing the criminal defendant an opportunity to cross examine witnesses that are testifying against him or her ensures that the criminal defendant is exercising his or her sixth amendment right to confront witnesses.

After the prosecution calls all of its witnesses, the defense attorney will usually ask the judge to dismiss the charges filed against the criminal defendant because the prosecution failed to meet its burden of proof. The judge will either grant or deny the defense attorneys' request. If the request is granted, the trial is concluded, and the criminal defendant is freed. If the judge denies the defense attorneys' motion, the defense will have the opportunity to call witnesses who suggest that the defendant did not commit the crime or that the prosecution did not meet its burden of proof. The prosecution has the opportunity to cross examine or question witnesses called by the defense so that weakness in the testimony are exposed. In most criminal cases, the prosecution does not have an opportunity to cross examine the criminal defendant because the U.S. Constitution permits criminal defendants the option to not testify at trial. This constitutionally protected right is not intended to be an indicator of a criminal defendant's guilt or innocence, and jurors are cautioned not to misinterpret a criminal defendant's decision to not testify.

After the prosecutor and defense have an opportunity to present all of their witnesses, the prosecutor and defense attorney make closing arguments. It is here that the case is summarized and that the prosecutor asks that the jury convict the defendant of the alleged crime or crimes. The defense attorney will ask jurors to acquit the defendant because the prosecution did not prove beyond a reasonable doubt that the defendant committed the alleged crime or crimes because the criminal defendant did not, in fact, commit the crime or crimes he or she has been charged with committing.

Conviction and Sentencing

After both sides make their closing arguments, the judge give the jury instructions, and the jury begins to deliberate the guilt or innocence of the defendant. Once the jury decides whether a defendant is guilty or innocent, they return to the court room, where their decision is read. If they decide that the criminal defendant is not guilty, the trial is over, and the criminal defendant is free to leave. If the jurors convict the defendant of the alleged crime or crimes, sentencing is imposed. In some cases, sentencing occurs concurrently with the rendering of a guilty jury verdict. In other cases, the sentencing phase of a criminal trial occurs later in a separate proceeding.

Incarceration

After the conviction and sentencing phases are complete, the side that loses will consider appealing the decision to convict or not convict the defendant, or decisions made by the judge during the course of the trial. If a criminal defendant is convicted of a criminal offense or of committing multiple criminal offenses, the incarcerated defendant may elect to appeal the conviction. However, there is no Constitutional right to counsel during an appeal unless the defendant is indigent. If the criminal defendant is indigent, he or she must be provided the assistance of counsel, at state expense, during the first appeal.

Release

Once a criminal defendant is found not guilty, and after a criminal defendant serves the duration of the prison sentence imposed on the defendant, the criminal defendant is released from custody. If the defendant is released because of a not guilty verdict, the defendant can never be tried again for the same offense. If the defendant is released after serving a prison sentence of longer than 1 year, he or she will remain a convicted felon, and be required to live with the associated limitations and restrictions, including the inability to vote or be issued certain vocational licenses.

Crimes

Crimes are defined as any act or failure to act that violates those duties an individual owes to the community and for the breach of which the law provides that the offender shall make satisfaction with the public.[4] Crimes may be punishable by death or imprisonment; torts (civil wrongs) are not.

Crimes are commonly categorized as felonies or misdemeanors. *Felonies* are more serious crimes and are generally punishable by death or imprisonment for more than 1 year; all other crimes are classified as misdemeanors. *Misdemeanors* are considered less serious offenses and are usually punishable by a fine or confinement in jail for a period of less than 1 year. To be convicted of a crime, the defendant must have acted or failed to act consistently with a legal duty to act or refrain from acting in a specific manner. Further, the criminal defendant must have acted or failed to act in accordance or in concert with the requisite mental state. Finally, the state and federal government must show that the defendant's action or failure to act caused the harmful, unlawful, criminal result.

Murder

Murder is the unlawful killing of another human being with malice aforethought. *Malice afterthought* is the act of deliberation or planning to inflict serious bodily harm, regardless of the length of time spent deliberating or planning. *Premeditation,* the act of deliberating or planning, is the hallmark of the crime of murder. Malice aforethought connotes purposeful, intentional behavior. Felony murder is the crime that is committed when someone dies during the commission of, or in an attempt to commit, a felony. For example, felony murder occurs when, in the midst of a robbery, the person being robbed dies.

Murder can be classified as either first or second degree. Murder in the first degree is associated with malice aforethought or premeditation. On the other hand, if a killing is classified as murder in the second degree, it is because the purpose to kill was formed instantaneously, rather than in a premeditated manner.

Orville Lynn Majors was a nurse who was convicted of committing murder. Majors used to be a licensed practical nurse, but his license to practice was revoked in 1995 by the Indiana State Board of Nursing. More than 4 years and 7 months later, Majors was convicted for killing six critically ill patients in his care. The judge was so outraged that someone killed those who were sick and defenseless that he imposed a stiff sentence: 360 years in prison.[5] The result is that Majors will spend the rest of his life in prison, unless his convictions are overturned on appeal.

The investigation began in 1994 when the Indiana State Police were informed of a quadrupling of deaths in the rural Indiana hospital in which Majors worked. More than 165 hospital deaths were investigated, and prosecutors filed criminal charges in cases that offered the best chance of conviction. In all, Majors was working when 121 of the 165 deaths occurred, and 16 patient bodies were exhumed to determine whether they had been poisoned with potassium chloride, epinephrine, or another toxin.[6]

Manslaughter

Like murder, *manslaughter* is the unlawful killing of another human being. Unlike murder, however, manslaughter occurs when someone is killed without malice aforethought or premeditation. Manslaughter is usually classified as either voluntary or involuntary. *Voluntary manslaughter* is charged when a killing would be murder except for the fact that the killer was provoked. *Involuntary manslaughter,* on the other hand, is the killing of another human being committed with criminal negligence or during the commission of another unlawful act. *State of New Jersey v. Laura Winter*[7] and the *Somera* case, discussed in the fifth edition of Helen Creighton's book, *Law Every Nurse Should Know,*[8] illustrate how nurses can be convicted of manslaughter.

Laura Winter, a registered nurse, was indicted for aggravated manslaughter. The charge stemmed from the death of a patient for whom she was caring at Beth Israel Hospital in Newark, New Jersey. Winter allegedly transfused Anna Mudryj, a patient, with incompatible blood. Mudryj developed a transfusion reaction and died. Reportedly, Winter attempted to conceal the mistake by failing to inform the physician of the mistake, disposing of the incompatible blood, changing Mudryj's medical record information, and denying that she gave the transfusion. After a lengthy trial, a jury found Laura Winter guilty of manslaughter. She was fined and sentenced to 5 years in prison.

In *Somera,* a patient had a seizure and died after a nurse administered an injection of 10% cocaine solution and epinephrine. Prior to administering the medication, the nurse repeated the order to the surgeon. The injection was given and minutes later the patient, who had been scheduled to have a tonsillectomy, was dead. In retrospect, the surgeon meant to order procaine rather than cocaine. The nurse, because she administered the fatal injection, was convicted of manslaughter. She did not intend to kill the patient, but her acts were considered reckless and wanton, and were the direct cause of the death of the patient.

To avoid a *Somera* situation, nurses need to question, clarify, and possibly even refuse to give medication if necessary. Prescribed drugs that are unclear, incomplete, or in any way deviate from the standard of care should not be administered. Reviewing the rights of medication administration before administering any medication is a good place to start. Giving the right dose of the right drug, to the right patient, at the right time, using the right route will go a long way to ensuring that patients do not sustain life-threatening and life-ending medication administration injuries, and that nurses will not be convicted for manslaughter or other medication administration-related criminal offenses.

Assault and Battery

Criminal assault and battery usually occur together, but one is not required for the other to have been committed. *Assault* in the criminal context is either an attempt to harmfully or offensively touch another or the intentional creation of a reasonable apprehension, in the mind of the victim, of imminent bodily harm. *Battery* is the unlawful application of force to the person of another resulting in bodily injury or an offensive touching. Simple battery is usually considered a misdemeanor; however, aggravated battery is considered a felony.

Moore v. State[9] illustrates the courts' longstanding willingness to hold nurses responsible for assault and battery. In this case, a nurse was caring for a child in the child's home. Moore, the nurse, reportedly removed the child from the home and later returned to the home with the child, whereupon it was noted that Moore may have severely whipped the child.

Whereas *Moore* alleged that the nurse was the person who committed assault and battery, *Records v. Aetna*[10] concerned a nurse who believed she was the victim of assault. Nurse Koch, believing that she had been assaulted by Records, a doctor, filed a civil cause of action against Records. At the time of writing, the resolution of this matter had not been published.

Larceny and Robbery

Larceny is the taking and carrying away of the tangible personal property of another by trespass with the intent to permanently deprive that person of his or her interest in the property. Larceny requires that the person doing the taking be illegally in the place of the taking. This is the crime that is committed when residences are broken into when no one is home, or when automobiles are broken into and driven away. Larceny can also occur in the health care profession when a health care provider illegally deprives an entity such as a third-party payor of money that is due them. In *People of the State of New York v. Chaitin*,[11] a physician practicing in New York was found guilty of 28 counts of grand larceny when he submitted invoices seeking reimbursement from Medicaid for services not rendered by him. Nurses billing Medicaid and Medicare need to be aware of the potential consequences of seeking reimbursement when services are not rendered. Grand larceny is a felony and can result in the nurse spending time in prison, losing his or her license to practice nursing, and having to repay the money wrongly received.

Robbery is distinguished from larceny in that robbery involves the taking of tangible personal property of another from the other's person or presence, by force or threats of immediate death or physical injury with the intent to permanently deprive the other person of the property. Pick pocketing is a frequently cited example of larceny, but where the victim resists the attempt to pickpocket, the taking is considered a robbery. Health care providers commit robbery when they forcibly take the personal property of another person.

False Imprisonment

False imprisonment is the unlawful confinement of a person without valid consent. False imprisonment is closely related but distinguished from kidnapping because kidnapping requires that the person be moved from one place to another.

For nurses, false imprisonment can occur where isolation and restraints are used as interventions. It is imperative that isolation and restraint procedures be explicitly followed and that those policies abide by current regulatory requirements. In addition, the patient's medical record should clearly indicate that the nurse has complied with restraint policy and procedures. Where documentation fails to reflect the requisite standards delineated by state, federal, and private regulatory agencies, the facility and health care providers may be liable for falsely imprisoning the isolated or restrained patient.

Forgery

Forgery consists of making or altering any writing with apparent legal significance so that it is false. With forgery, there is an intent to defraud or deceive. According to a published report in *Modern Healthcare,* a nurse in California reportedly tried to kill, by overdosing, a patient who had been diagnosed with AIDS. She did this after she withdrew money from the patient's checking account. She was convicted of two crimes: attempted murder and forgery.[12] Forgery is also committed when individuals not authorized to do so write prescriptions for themselves or others by prescribing and dispensing medication and signing an authorized prescriber's name to the prescription form.

Fraud

Fraud is the intentional perversion of the truth for the purpose of inducing another to rely on the fraudulent representation, so that the individual who has been induced parts with some valuable thing belonging to that individual. According to the Health Care Financing Administration (HCFA), fraud is the intentional deception or misrepresentation that an individual knows to be false or does not believe to be true, knowing that deception could result in some unauthorized benefit to himself or herself or some other person.[13] *Health care fraud* is a specific type of fraud and is defined as knowingly and willfully executing, or attempting to execute, a scheme or artifice to defraud any health care benefit program or to obtain, by means of false pretenses, representations, or promises, any of the money owned by, or under the custody or control of, any health care benefit program.[14] Typically, this kind of fraud occurs when a false statement or misrepresentation is made that is material to entitlement or payment under the Medicare or Medicaid programs. In a fee-for-service environment, economic incentives exist for providers to commit fraud by billing for services not rendered, billing for more expensive services than were actually provided, and providing medically unnecessary treatment. In a managed care environment, economic incentives exist for providers to submit false cost data, to not provide necessary medical services, to enroll fictitious patients in a plan, place patients in a Diagnosis Related Group (DRG) category that is too high, to bill separately for services that should be billed together, to waive coinsurance and deductibles, to enter into incentive agreements that reward the health care provider for limiting or denying care, and to enter into agreements that make payments for the referral of patients. HCFA considers all of these actions to be fraudulent.

Stamping out fraud has been the goal of the federal government's investigation of health care providers who improperly bill federal health care programs. Investigations have been effective; the federal government collected more than $1 billion in health care fraud fines and settlements from individuals and organizations that improperly billed the federal government. In addition, in 1997, the Department of Justice initiated 243 civil health care fraud cases against individuals and entities accused of committing health care fraud. In 1996, the Department of Justice initiated half as many health care fraud cases.[15]

Fraud investigations continue to sweep through the health care industry. Investigations have been launched against individual providers, acute care organizations, laboratory companies, medical device manufacturers, Medicare carriers, management companies, schools of medicine, home health companies, and medical equipment suppliers, among others. Nurses, although not currently the targets of fraud and abuse investigations, are potential targets, so great care needs to be taken to ensure that accurate information is submitted for reimbursement. Some settlements reached during fraud and abuse investigations have been staggering, in terms of dollars that are being paid back to the government (see sidebar, next page).

The settlements and judgments reached in favor of the government suggest that fraud and abuse investigations will continue. The cost of stamping out health care fraud and abuse has been significantly less than the income realized from fines, penalties, and settlements. It is estimated that the federal government receives approximately $22 in fines, penalties, and settlements for every $1 enforcement dollar it spends.[16]

So far, fraud and abuse investigations have focused on physicians, health care organizations, home health agencies, and medical device companies. Nurses can avoid being the target of investigations by becoming more informed about health care fraud and abuse. In addition, where health care fraud and abuse is suspected to be occurring, nurses should report it. To report fraud and abuse, contact the Office of Inspector General Hotline at the Department of Health and Human Services at P.O. Box 17303, Baltimore, Maryland, 21203. The toll-free, nationwide hotline telephone number is (800) 368-5779. Also, where nurses are involved directly or indirectly in claims processing, nurses should ensure that claims are processed accurately and in accordance with the directives issued by federal and state enforcement agencies.

According to HCFA, the most common forms of fraud include

▌ billing for services not furnished.
▌ misrepresenting the diagnosis to justify payment.
▌ soliciting, offering, or receiving any payment to a person or entity that is intended to induce or influence the future purchases of the person paid. These payments are referred to as kickbacks.
▌ billing for separate parts of a single procedure to obtain a higher payment (unbundling).
▌ falsifying certificates of medical necessity, plans of treatment, and medical records to justify payment.
▌ billing for services not furnished as billed (upcoding).[17]

In *Nursing Economic$*, Mary Chaffee identified the following as additional forms of fraud:

▌ providing services more often than indicated (overutilization);
▌ billing for unnecessary services;
▌ making a single visit while billing for multiple visits;
▌ exhausting insurance benefits for one family member, then billing another (looping);
▌ falsifying the identity or credentials of an unlicensed or noncovered provider so that services are billed at a higher rate (phantom billing); and

Fraud and Abuse Settlements

Amount	Case
$700,000.00	Peter Embriano, MD—an ophthalmologist who was accused of falsely billing Medicare for performing laser surgery when there was no equipment to perform the procedure and for not performing billed tests.
$1 million	OrthoLogic Corporation—a medical device manufacturer for billing Medicare, TRICARE, and Medicaid for non-FDA approved devices.
$1.5 million	David Yedidson, MD—a physician who billed Medicare for home visits for patients who were deceased or in nursing homes.
$1.75 million	U.S. HomeCare Corporation—a home care firm that agreed to settle fraud allegations after fraud charges were brought by the attorney general's office in New York.
$2.6 million	Invacare Corporation—an Elyria, Ohio, medical equipment supplier that agreed to settle an allegation that it failed to pass on government discounts to commercial customers.
$3.1 million	Emergency Physicians Billing Service—two subsidiaries of this emergency room management company agreed to this settlement, the third for this company, which allegedly billed Medicare, Medicaid, TRICARE, and the Federal Employees Health Benefits Service for more expensive services than were actually provided.
$4.3 million	Grady Memorial Hospital—an Atlanta, Georgia, hospital agreed to settle an allegation that it submitted false prescription claims to Medicaid.
$4.75 million	Charter Behavioral Health—an acute inpatient psychiatric hospital elected to settle allegations that it fraudulently admitted and extended the stay of hundreds of Medicare beneficiaries.
$5.6 million	Yale University School of Medicine—agreed to this settlement package after it was accused of improperly handling patients' credit balances.
$7.3 million	Paracelsus Healthcare Corporation—Orange County Community Hospital and Bellwood General Hospital were suspected of paying kickbacks to physicians and improperly billing Medicare for psychiatric services.

$9.4 million	Twenty-five hospitals in Ohio elected to settle claims that they overbilled Medicare and Medicaid for outpatient laboratory testing.
$15 million	Quest Diagnostics, Inc.—a laboratory testing company agreed to settle after it was accused of fraudulently billing for unnecessary laboratory tests.
$17.5 million	Baptist Medical Center—this Kansas City, Missouri, health care facility was accused of receiving $59.8 million in Medicare reimbursements for treating patients referred by two osteopaths in a kickbacks-for-referrals agreement.
$38.5 million	Highmark, Inc.—the corporate successor to Pennsylvania Blue Shield agreed to settle claims that Pennsylvania Blue Shield submitted false claims under its Medicare carrier contract.
$61 million	Olsten Corporation—a subsidiary of Kimberly Home HealthCare was accused of violating federal anti-kickback laws and committing conspiracy and mail fraud in connection with deals it made with Columbia.
$144 million	Blue Cross and Blue Shield of Illinois—the organization was accused of shredding 10,000 railroad workers claims, deleting 1 million documents in the computer system, misleading government evaluators, doctoring documents, and submitting false reports on telephone efficiency.
$325 million	SmithKline Beecham Clinical Laboratories—this clinical laboratory agreed to settle claims that it overbilled Medicare and other insurers by adding unneeded tests to bills, inventing diagnoses, and charging for work it did not do.

■ billing Medicare and a private insurer for the same treatment or procedure (double billing).[18]

Nurse–attorneys have identified the following actions as violations of fraud and abuse statutes:

■ deliberately billing twice for the same service;
■ billing multiple funding sources for the same service;
■ billing for supplies or services never provided;
■ billing for a higher level of care than actually provided;
■ hiring too many executive staff members;
■ paying excessive salaries to administrators;

- providing lucrative employee expense accounts;
- leasing or buying luxury automobiles to make home visits;
- soliciting, offering, or receiving a kickback, bribe, or rebate;
- charging excessively for products or services; and
- making claims for products or services not medically necessary.[19]

In addition to the actions identified above, HCFA has delineated 33 ways in which it can impose monetary penalties and render an offender excluded for program non-compliance. The 33 items delineated by HCFA can be categorized as those that apply as follows: general, nonassignment, durable medical equipment suppliers, non-participating physicians, physicians, insurers, and employers. They are listed in Appendix C.

False Pretenses

False pretenses requires the misrepresentation of a material fact that causes the victim to voluntarily pass title to his property to the wrongdoer. False pretenses requires the wrongdoer to know the representation to be false and intend to defraud the victim. A nurse commits the crime of false pretenses when or she causes a patient or a patient's family member to pass the title to any of the patient's personal property to the nurse asserting that the title must be transferred before care can be rendered.

Embezzlement

Embezzlement occurs when an individual who has lawful possession of another's property takes for their own use the other's money or property. With embezzlement, there is an intent to defraud another. In a nursing context, embezzlement occurs when nurses take medications or other property owned by patients or health care facilities with the intent of using the property themselves.

Rape

Rape is nonconsensual intercourse. *State v. Lora*[20] defines rape as the act of sexual intercourse between a man and a woman, not his wife, without her consent, committed when the woman's resistance is overcome by force or fear, or under other prohibitive conditions. Although *Lora* suggests that rape cannot occur between husbands and wives, that trend is changing. In most jurisdictions, if intercourse is not consensual, the crime of rape may have been committed.

Unfortunately, nurses have been accused of committing the crime of rape. The November 11, 1999, edition of *The San Francisco Chronicle* reported that Jeffrey Leodones, a licensed vocational nurse, was accused of raping a disabled patient at a San Mateo County mental health facility. Leodones is innocent until proven guilty; however, the story illustrates the fact that nurses can and do find themselves accused of crimes like rape.

Rape, although a crime, may also result in civil liability for a health care organization. *Samuels v. Southern Baptist Hospital, et al*[21] is demonstrative. In *Samuels*, a

16-year-old female patient was admitted to the Baptist Hospital psychiatric unit after she attempted suicide. While she was hospitalized, she reported that she was raped by Raymond Steward, a nursing assistant. The nursing assistant was subsequently terminated, and entered a guilty plea to the crime of rape approximately 5 months later. About 10 months after Steward pled guilty to rape, a civil trial concerning the matter commenced. The 16-year-old and her parents sued the hospital, the hospital's insurance company, and Steward. After listening to the evidence, the jury returned a $450,000 verdict in favor of the patient who had been raped. The hospital appealed, contending that it could not be held responsible for the actions of Steward and that the jury award was excessive. The Louisiana Court of Appeals disagreed with the hospital and affirmed the verdict.

Statutory Rape

Statutory rape is defined as having sexual intercourse with a female under the age of consent. Reasonable mistakes as to age and consent are irrelevant and ineffective as defenses. It is a strict liability offense, which means that all the wrongdoer has to do is commit the act. The age of consent varies from state to state, but is typically either 18 or 21. Health care professionals caring for patients who have not yet reached the age of consent commit statutory rape when they have sexual intercourse with a patient under the age of consent, whether or not the patient verbally consented.

Mayhem

Mayhem has been abolished in most jurisdictions. Historically, it was considered a felony and was the offense used when dismemberment or disablement of a body part occurred. Today, dismemberment and disablement of body parts usually lead to aggravated battery charges being filed.

Aggravated battery is considered a felony in most jurisdictions. It is the crime that is committed when battery with a deadly weapon resulting in serious bodily harm occurs and when battery of a child, woman, or police officer occurs. A nurse may be accused of committing aggravated battery when he or she uses instrument to unlawfully touch a patient. The instrument may be as small as a hypodermic needle or as large as a piece of machinery.

Narcotics Violations

Narcotics violations occur when state and/or federal narcotics or controlled substances statutes are violated. At the federal level, the Comprehensive Drug Abuse Prevention and Control Act of 1970 (The Controlled Substances Act) classifies drugs into five schedules.

> ∎ *Schedule I drugs* have no accepted medical use, are to be used for research purposes only, and have high abuse potential. Administration of Schedule I drugs requires clearance from the Food and Drug Administration. Schedule I drugs include heroin, marijuana, LSD, peyote, mescaline, tetrahydrocannabinols,

ketobemidone, levomoramide, racemoramide, benzylmorphine, dihydro-morphine, nicocodeine, and nicomorphine.

- Schedule *II drugs* are those with high abuse potential, but acceptable therapeutic use. Schedule II drugs require a written prescription; no telephone renewals are allowed, except in emergency situations. Opium, morphine, codeine, hydro-morphone, methadone, pantopen, meperidine, cocaine, oxycodone, and oxy-morphone are examples of Schedule II narcotics. Schedule II also includes amphetamines, methamphetamines, phenmetrazine, methylphenidate, amo-barbital, pentobarbitol, secobarbital, methaqualone, elorphine, hyrochloride, dipehnoxylate, and phencyclidine.

- *Schedule III drugs* are those with a lower abuse potential than those listed in Schedules I and II, and which have current acceptable therapeutic use in the United States. Schedule III prescriptions must be rewritten after 6 months or after five refills. Unlike Schedule II drugs, Schedule III drugs may be prescribed over the telephone and include glutethimide, methyprylon, chlorhexadol, benzphetamine, butabarbital, sulfondiethylmethane, sulfomethane, and talbutal.

- *Schedule IV drugs* have a low abuse potential when compared to drugs listed in Schedules I through III, and have an acceptable therapeutic use in the United States. Schedule IV drugs include longer acting barbiturates, tranquilizers, and some depressant drugs. Among the drugs included in Schedule IV are barbital, phenobarbital, methylphenobarbital, chloral hydrate, ethinamate, meprobimate, paraldehyde, methohexital, fenfluraine, diethyloproplon, phentermine, chlordiazepoxide, diazepam, flurazepam, clonazepam, prazeam, lorazepam, mebutamate, and dextropropoxyphene.

- *Schedule V drugs* are those drugs which have the least abuse potential than drugs listed in Schedules I through IV. Schedule V drugs may contain limited amounts of certain narcotic drugs generally for antitussive and antidiarrheal purposes.

- *Schedule VI drugs* are those that are listed in an approved formulary.

For nurses, it is important to know whether authorization exists to prescribe medications. Prescribing any medication without authorization to do so may result in regulatory, civil, and criminal penalties. Unfortunately, state statutes regarding prescriptive authority vary significantly and must be reviewed to determine whether prescriptive authority is authorized. In spite of the lack of uniformity, trends were detected by analyzing a "1999 Prescriptive Authority Chart" prepared by Winifred Carson, Nurse Practice Counsel at the American Nurses Association.[22] For instance, all jurisdictions that extend prescriptive authority to nurses do so to at least one category of advanced practice nurse. In 11 jurisdictions (Arizona, California, Georgia, Maryland, Mississippi, New Hampshire, North Carolina, Oregon, South Dakota, Washington, and Guam), prescriptive authority is limited to nurse practitioners only. Georgia and Guam do not authorize any nurse to have prescriptive authority. Collaborative agreements, protocols, or consultation plans addressing prescriptive authority issues are not required in Iowa, Montana, New Hampshire, New Mexico, Oregon, or Washington, and advanced practice nurses in 29 jurisdictions may apply for their own Drug Enforcement Agency (DEA) number. Jurisdictions permitting nurses to apply for and use a DEA number are Alaska, Arizona, Colorado, Connecticut, Delaware, District of Columbia, Iowa, Maine, Maryland, Massachusetts, Minnesota, Montana, Nevada, New Hampshire, New Jersey, New Mexico, New York, North Carolina, North Dakota, Ohio, Oregon, Pennsylvania, Rhode Island, South Carolina, Tennessee, Vermont, Washington, West Virginia, and Wisconsin.

Where any advanced practice nurse is granted prescriptive authority, the drugs that may be prescribed are limited. According to a review of the "Prescriptive Authority Chart" prepared by Winifred Carson, prescriptive authority limitations fall into one of four categories: noncontrolled drugs, Schedule II–V drugs, Schedule III–V drugs, and other. Prescriptive authority is limited to noncontrolled drugs in 13 jurisdictions. Those jurisdictions are Alabama, California, Florida, Hawaii, Kansas, Kentucky, Mississippi, Missouri, Nevada, Ohio, Rhode Island, Texas, and the Virgin Islands.

Schedule II through V drugs may be administered by nurses who meet the prescriptive authority criteria in 22 jurisdictions. These jurisdictions are Alaska, Arkansas, Colorado, Connecticut, District of Columbia, Idaho, Indiana, Iowa, Maryland, Michigan, Minnesota, Montana, New Hampshire, New Mexico, New York, North Carolina, North Dakota, Oregon, Pennsylvania, Tennessee, Vermont, and Wisconsin. Six jurisdictions permit statutorily authorized nurses to prescribe Schedule III through V drugs. Those jurisdictions are Maine, Nebraska, Oklahoma, Utah, West Virginia, and Wyoming.

Eight jurisdiction have other prescriptive authority limitations. South Dakota permits Schedule III and V drugs to be prescribed by nurse practitioners. South Dakota also permits nurse practitioners to apply for their own DEA numbers; however, nurse practitioners are prohibited from using them. In Virginia, nurse practitioners and clinical nurse specialists (licensed as advanced practice nurses) may prescribe Schedule VI drugs. In Delaware, nurses classified as advanced practice nurses, clinical nurse specialists, and nurse practitioners may prescribe all drugs, including controlled Schedule II through IV drugs. In Illinois, nurse practitioners, clinical nurse specialists, and certified nurse midwives are authorized to prescribe noncontrolled drugs, and Schedule III through V drugs so long as the prescription is within the nurse's practice specialty. In Louisiana, nurse practitioners, clinical nurse specialists, and certified nurse midwives are limited to prescribing only the noncontrolled drugs that are authorized by the joint board of nursing and board of medical examiners committee appointed to determine which drugs may be prescribed.

Although every effort has been made to ensure that the foregoing information is current, it is important to note that legislative activity continues to occur in this area. Nurses seeking prescriptive privileges need to contact their state board of nursing to receive definitive information.

Conspiracy

A *conspiracy* is an agreement between two or more parties to commit a crime. To be found guilty of conspiracy, there must be an agreement between two or more persons, an intent to enter into the agreement, and an intent by at least two persons to achieve the objective of the agreement. A nurse could be found guilty of conspiracy if he or she participated in a plan to defraud a federal program like Medicare.

Solicitation

Solicitation is inciting, counseling, advising, urging, or commanding another to commit a crime, with the intent that the person solicited commit the crime. Not only could a nurse be found guilty of conspiracy where he or she participated in a plan to defraud Medicare, but that same nurse could be found guilty of solicitation if he or she asked or advised someone else to commit health care fraud.

Bribery

Bribery is the corrupt payment or receipt of anything of value for official action. Nurses in decision-making positions could be found guilty of bribery if they offer someone money or anything of value for doing something fraudulent.

Compounding a Crime

Compounding a crime consists of agreeing, for valuable consideration, not to prosecute another for a felony or to conceal the commission of a felony or the whereabouts of a felon. If a nurse knows that a felony has been committed and conceals it, that nurse may be found guilty of compounding a crime.

Perjury

Perjury is intentionally making material false statements under oath. The material component of this requirement is one that might affect the outcome of a judicial proceeding. Nurses may find themselves testifying in front of state boards of nursing and in court rooms. It is important to understand that in those settings, and in other settings in which the nurse swears to tell the truth, that failing to tell the truth could result in perjury charges being filed against the nurse.

Subornation of Perjury

Subornation of perjury is committed when someone induces or procures another person to commit perjury. In other words, asking someone to testify in a way that is not truthful could result in that person being found guilty of the crime of perjury, and the person who asked that the false testimony be given could be found guilty of subornation of perjury. As a result, nurses should refrain from asking anyone to testify falsely in any judicial proceeding.

Summary

Nurses have been convicted of crimes, and if fraud and abuse investigations continue at the pace that has been unfolding over the past few years, nurses will likely find themselves the primary target in some of those investigations. To avoid the imposition of sanctions that accompany judicial findings that fraud and abuse or other offenses have been committed, it is imperative that nurses understand the law and commit themselves to practicing nursing in accordance with those laws.

Professionals in the health care industry are not only having to pay substantial fines for alleged Medicare fraud, but some are facing incarceration. Robert Whiteside, the former Columbia/HCA Healthcare Corporation director of Columbia's single markets division was sentenced to 2 years in prison and was ordered to pay a $7,500 fine and $645,000 in restitution after he was convicted of Medicare fraud.[23]

Two months after the conviction of Whiteside was reported, *Modern Healthcare* disclosed that Jay Jarrell, a second former Columbia/HCA Healthcare Corporation executive, had been ordered to report to a federal prison in North Carolina because of alleged Medicare fraud. Jarrell is a former chief executive officer of Columbia's southwest Florida division, and was ordered to pay almost $1.7 million in restitution and a $10,000 fine.[24]

Approximately 6 months following the reported convictions of Whiteside and Jarrell, *Modern Healthcare* published another article that discussed the alleged commission of Medicare fraud by Dennis McClatchey, a former chief operating officer at Baptist Medical Center in Kansas City, Missouri. McClatchey was convicted of participating in a conspiracy to pay and accept bribes for Medicare referrals, but was later acquitted by the U.S. District Court judge. That decision, however, was subsequently overturned by a federal appellate panel. The judge who acquitted McClatchey affirmed the convictions of Dan Anderson and Ronald and Robert LaHue. Anderson was a former chief executive officer at Baptist Medical Center, and Ronald and Robert LaHue were osteopathic physicians who referred their nursing home patients to Baptist Medical Center, as well as other area hospitals. All four men were reportedly involved in the referral agreement. All four defendants have filed appeals, and face paying monetary fines and serving time in prison if their convictions are upheld.[25]

These criminal convictions, and other more classic criminal offenses committed by nurses, make it imperative that nurses understand what actions may give rise to criminal prosecution. Familiarity with doctrines and terms used in criminal litigation, the criminal justice system, and criminal offenses is a good initial step to avoid committing crimes. The next and most important step, however, is for nurses to practice in accordance with all applicable state and federal statutes, regulations, and case law.

End Notes

1. Associated Press. 1999. *Washington Post.* October 18; p. A4.
2. Model Penal Code, Section 4.01.
3. 384 U.S. 436 (1966), *rehearing denied*, 385 U.S. 890 (1966).
4. *Black's Law Dictionary*, 5th ed. 1979. St. Paul, MN: West Publishing Co.; p. 334.
5. Kelly, J. November 16, 1999. Available from URL: http://web.lexis-nexis.com/ln.universe/search. Associated Press.
6. Harris, C. November 13, 1999. Available from URL: http://web.lexis-nexis.com/ln.universe/search. Louisville, KY: The Courier-Journal.
7. 477 A.2d 323 (N.J. 1984).
8. Creighton, H. 1986. *Law Every Nurse Should Know*, 5th ed. Philadelphia: W.B. Saunders; pp. 231–232.
9. 64 Ga. 449 (1879).
10. 294 N.J. Super. 463 (App. Div. 1996).
11. 462 N.Y.S. 2d 61 (N.Y.S. Ct. App. Div., 1983).
12. Anonymous. Nurse sentenced to nine years for murder attempt, forgery. *Modern Healthcare* 1988. August 12: 67.
13. Available from URL: http://www.hcfa.gov/medicare/fraud/DEFINI2.HTML.
14. Pub. L. No. 104-191.
15. http://www.modernhealthcare.com:80/current/topten10.html.
16. Michael, J., Summers, C. 1998. What should nurses know about fraud and abuse? *Journal of Nursing Law* 5(2): 41.
17. Available from URL: http://www.hcfa.gov/medicare/fraud/DEFINI2.HTML.
18. Chaffee, M. 1998. Health care fraud: Hemorrhage from the health care system. NURSING ECONOMIC$ 16(3): 140–143.
19. Michael and Summers, pp. 44, 45.
20. 515 P.2d 1086 (Ks. 1973).
21. 594 So. 2d 571 (La. 1992).
22. Carson, W. 1999. *1999 Prescriptive Authority Chart.* Washington, D.C.: American Nurses Association.
23. Taylor, M. 1999. Convicted Columbia exec gets two years. *Modern Healthcare* December 6: 4.
24. Taylor, M. 2000. Second Columbia exec going to prison. *Modern Healthcare* January 3: 12.
25. Moore Jr., D.J. 2000. Court restores guilty verdict. *Modern Healthcare* June 19: 2–3.

The Nurse Practicing as Employee 5

Introduction

An *employee* is a person who is in the service of an employer where that employer has the right to direct and control the employee in the material details of how the work is performed. This is distinguished from an *independent contractor*, who contracts to perform a specific service or to complete a specific project. With an independent contractor, the focus is on the outcome or final product, not the intervening process. The distinction is important, because many liability determinations depend on the alleged wrongdoer being considered an employee, and not an independent contractor. When a health care professional is considered an independent contractor and not an employee, liability for alleged wrong doing on the part of the organization at which the health care professional is practicing may be reduced or eliminated. In addition to employment-status issues faced by nurse-employees, contemporary clinical issues and a number of federal and state laws that protect employees will be discussed in this chapter.

Contemporary Clinical Issues Faced by Nurse-Employees

Abandonment

Because of inadequate staffing and mandatory overtime policies that are in place, nurses have been faced with either working longer than they were scheduled to work, facing prolonged exposure to work hazards, fatigue and stress, or risking disciplinary action being taken by their employers and state boards of nursing. *Husher v. Commissioner of Education of the State of New York*[1] and *Hainer v. American Medical International, et al*[2] are illustrative.

In *Husher*, Darlene Husher was charged with professional misconduct because she abandoned her employment at St. Joseph's Hospital in Queens County. She reportedly walked off her assigned nursing unit after working 8 hours from 7:00 AM until 3:00 PM. Evidence introduced suggested that Darlene knew that there was a staffing shortage, and that one nurse was going to have to stay and work the evening shift from 3:00 PM until 11:00 PM. The hospital had a mandatory overtime policy that required the least senior nurse to stay. Husher reportedly told her supervisor that she would stay until she was relieved. However, after 3:00 PM she left the hospital without informing the staff on the unit. She left the 29-patient unit staffed with only one nurses aide, orderlies, and one respiratory therapist.

After listening to the evidence in this case, Darlene Husher's license was suspended for 1 year. Husher appealed that decision and a New York court affirmed the disciplinary decision concluding that Darlene's failure to give reasonable notice of her leaving, in spite the fact that she previously agreed to stay was sufficient to show that she abandoned her professional employment.

In *Hainer*, Anne T. Hainer was a registered nurse who practiced at East Cooper Community Hospital until she resigned. Approximately 8 months after she left the hospital, the hospital filed a complaint with the board of nursing contending that Hainer resigned without notice and that in so doing she committed patient abandonment. Hainer contended that the hospital filed the complaint in bad faith and with malice because Hainer was planning to testify on behalf of another nurse who had been terminated for patient abandonment. The case was tried, and a jury returned a verdict in favor of Hainer, agreeing that the hospital inflicted intentional emotional distress and abused the legal process. They entered a verdict in the amount of $75,000 for compensatory damages and $225,000 in punitive damages. The hospital appealed the decision of the jury, and the case was eventually decided by the South Carolina Supreme Court. The South Carolina Supreme Court affirmed the court of appeals decision to reverse the jury verdict, saying that Hainer did not meet her burden of proof with regard to the causes of action she filed against the hospital. In spite of this decision, one South Carolina Supreme Court Justice wrote a strongly worded dissenting opinion asserting that Hainer met her burden of proof, and that there was ample evidence to indicate that the hospital embarked on a course of action that was motivated by retaliation. The judge pointed out that it was not until after the hospital discovered that Hainer was going to testify in another nurse's case against the hospital that the hospital filed the complaint with the board of nursing.

Although the verdicts against the nurses in *Husher* and *Hainer* were adverse, nurses have been exonerated where they have left the care of patients because they were fearful of their physical safety. Such was the case in *Bosch v. Perry*.[3]

In *Bosch*, Sandra Perry, a licensed practical nurse (LPN), was working in the emergency room at Parkway Regional Hospital when a physician brought a patient in to suture the patient's chin laceration. During the procedure, the patient raised up suddenly striking Sandra Perry, throwing her against the wall. Sandra was in the treatment room alone with the physician and patient because another nurse had already left the room to call their supervisor because the two nurses were concerned that both the physician and the patient were intoxicated, and that the physician did not appear capable of suturing the laceration. After Perry was struck, she left the treatment area, and she and the other nurse refused to return to the treatment area. Their refusal was supported by their superiors, who advised the nurses to do nothing to aggravate the situation.

Whereas *Husher, Hainer,* and *Bosch* demonstrate how the issue of abandonment is handled in U.S. Courts, no case better underscores the impact that abandonment has on patients than *Czubinsky v. Doctor's Hospital.*[4] In *Czubinsky,* a patient sustained a catastrophic brain injury because she was abandoned by the circulating nurse and operating room technician during the most critical postoperative period. The circulating nurse left the patient's side in violation of the hospital's policy that directed that the circulating nurse remain with the patient at all times while the patient was in the operating room. In addition, the operating room technician was at the instrument table, rather than observing the patient. As a result, the anesthesiologist was left alone to attempt to resuscitate the patient. The case was tried, and a jury returned a verdict against the hospital because of the abandonment of the circulating nurse and operating room technician. Because the patient was abandoned, the jury determined that the hospital was required to pay $982,000 in damages.

Employment Status

Nurses need to be clear about whether they are practicing as employees at will or as independent contractors. The distinction has significant implications for the nurse and for setting in which the nurse is practicing. So that the differences are better understood the following two sections discuss what it means to be an at-will employee and independent contractor.

Employee At Will

Employees who work without a contract guaranteeing a specific position, for a definite period of time, and at a designated pay rate are referred to as *employees at will.* Until the late 1970s, this kind of employment arrangement allowed employers to terminate any at-will employee for any reason or for no reason. Now, employers do not enjoy that kind of unbridled latitude. Although the absence of job security continues to be an issue for at-will employees, many state legislatures and Congress have enacted laws to ensure that employers treat employees fairly, regardless of the employee's status as a contract or at-will employee. One of the key limitations on an employers' ability to terminate an at-will employee is called the *public policy* exception. This exception permits a terminated at-will employee to pursue a wrongful termination claim against the employer where the employee has been terminated in violation of a clear mandate of public policy. Such was the case in *Kirk v. Mercy Hospital Tri-County.*[5]

Pauline Kirk worked as a registered nurse at Mercy Hospital Tri-County until she was terminated. She was an at-will employee who reportedly told a family member of one of the patients for whom she cared and died that the physician hastened the death of the woman and offered to obtain a copy of the patient's medical record for the family. When hospital officials were informed about this, they terminated Kirk.

Kirk filed a wrongful termination cause of action and the trial court dismissed her case against the hospital. The case was appealed to a Missouri Court of Appeals where the case was sent back to district court for trial. In recognizing Kirk's right to pursue her wrongful termination lawsuit, the appellate court determined that Kirk simply attempted to report serious misconduct that could constitute a violation of the law, and that kind of activity was what the public policy exception was designed to protect. The outcome of this trial is unknown; subsequent proceedings are unpublished.

Independent Contractor

An *independent contractor* is a person who contracts with another to do something, but is not controlled by the other. Nurses have traditionally worked as employees, but more and more nurses are working as independent contractors. This is especially true of advanced practice nurses who are obtaining admitting privileges at health care facilities, and who are working as practitioners in private practice or as partners in a group practice. In addition, nurses working through temporary or staffing agencies are generally considered independent contractors. Independent contractor issues are addressed in more detail in Chapter 6, but independent contractor status is introduced here so that the nurse-employee has a better understanding of the impact of being considered an independent contractor and not an employee.

Although *Hansen v. Caring Professionals, Inc.*[6] does not involve an advanced practice nurse, it examines whether a nurse retained by a temporary staffing agency is an employee or independent contractor of that agency. The distinction was fundamental in determining whether or not the agency was going to be held liable for the allegedly negligent acts of the nurse. In *Hansen,* Mr. Hansen alleged that malpractice occurred when a central venous catheter that was inserted into his wife's jugular vein became dislodged, air entered the intravenous line, and an air embolus caused her to sustain severe brain damage and total disability

Eileen Fajardo-Furlin, RN, was named as a defendant in the case, because she cared for Mrs. Hansen while she was in the hospital. Nurse Furlin was working at the hospital on temporary assignment through Caring Professionals, Inc., another defendant. The patients' husband sought to hold Caring Professionals, Inc. responsible for the alleged negligence of Nurse Furlin. Caring Professionals sought to be removed from the case, asserting that there was no employee–employer relationship, but rather a liability-absolving independent contractor relationship between them and Nurse Furlin. The trial court agreed, as did the appellate court. In fact, the appellate went on to say that it was only the hospital that had the responsibility to supervise Nurse Furlin, implying that the hospital might be liable for negligent supervision of this independent contractor should the nurse be found negligent. The court pointed out that it was the hospital, not Caring Professionals, Inc., that decided which unit and patients Nurse Furlin would be assigned to. In addition, it was the hospital's protocols and procedures under which the nurse was working, and it was the hospital's equipment that was being used in the provision of patient care services. As a result, the dismissal of Caring Professionals, Inc. was affirmed.

This wall of insulation for temporary staffing agencies exists even when the nurse–independent contractor is driving to and from a patient care assignment. *Rhoney v. Fele*[7] is characteristic of how courts handle this issue. In *Rhoney*, Tony Fele, a registered nurse, was on his way to a temporary assignment when he attempted to drive into a gasoline station to call the hospital to which he had been assigned. He was involved in a motor vehicle accident that killed Vincent Rhoney. The family of Vincent Rhoney sued Tony Fele, as well as Nursefinders, the staffing agency through which Tony was providing temporary staffing services when the fatal accident occurred. The family alleged that Nursefinders should be a co-defendant because Mr. Fele and Nursefinders were in a joint venture, that an employee–employer relationship existed, and that Nursefinders was negligent in supervising Tony. They pointed out that Mr. Fele was not paid a lump sum for a particular assignment, nor was he able to freely select the assistants with whom he worked, or choose his own work hours. The family also contended that Nursefinders, not Fele, received payment for services rendered, and that state and federal income taxes were deducted from Fele's paycheck.

Nursefinders claimed that they should be excluded from the case because Tony Fele was an independent contractor, and not an employee. The North Carolina trial court and the court of appeals agreed. The court of appeals concluded that Nursefinders exercised no control over the nursing care delivered by Mr. Fele, and could not compel him to take any particular assignment. Nursefinders' role was considered to be like that of a broker or middleman. Moreover, the joint venture claim failed because Fele did not have an equal, legal right to control Nursefinders' conduct.

Mandatory Overtime

Mandatory overtime is the unilateral mandate by a supervisor that an employee work overtime. Increasingly, nurses are reporting a dramatic increase in the use of mandatory overtime in an effort to solve staffing problems.[8] Failure to work mandatory overtime has multiple implications: an employer does not have the staff needed to provide safe patient care and a nurse is subject to the health and safety issues associated with mandatory overtime (prolonged exposure to hazards, stress, and fatigue). Nurses can also be recipients of disciplinary action, including termination by employers, and sanctions by state boards of nursing for unprofessional conduct and/or patient abandonment. As a result, state boards of nursing have begun to identify what constitutes patient abandonment. Advisory opinions to clarify the issue have been issued in Alabama, California, Ohio, and Oregon.

Currently, there is an absence of state and federal laws that limit the amount of overtime worked by health care professionals. The same is not true to the aviation and transportation industries. As a result, state and federal initiatives are underway to codify overtime limitations for nurses and other health care workers. In 2001, legislation prohibiting mandatory overtime was introduced in California, Connecticut, Hawaii, Illinois, Maine, Maryland, Minnesota, New Jersey, New York, Ohio, Rhode Island, Washington, and West Virginia.

Needlestick and Sharps Injuries

Between 600,000 and 1 million preventable needlestick injuries are sustained from conventional needles and sharps every year and at least 1000 health care workers contract serious infections—hepatitis B, hepatitis C, and HIV—annually from needlestick and sharps injuries.[9] Nurses, as a health care professional group, sustain the overwhelming majority of these injuries. Denise Cardo, a physician and Chief of the HIV Infections Branch of the Hospital Infections Program at the Centers for Disease Control and Prevention (CDC) in Atlanta, Georgia, reported that, through 1999, nurses have sustained 23 of a total of 56 of the occupationally acquired AIDS/HIV infection; clinical laboratory technicians and physicians have sustained 16 and 6 of those injuries, respectively.[10] Patient rooms, operating rooms, emergency rooms, and intensive care units seem to be the places in which the injuries occur.[11] In spite of these alarming numbers, less than 15% of all U.S. hospitals use safer needle devices and systems. Reportedly, safe needle devices cost only about $0.28 more than conventional systems. Proponents of these systems argue that the marginal cost difference is well worth it when this cost is compared to the $3000 per needlestick injury follow-up cost.

Lawsuits filed by health care workers alleging that their needlestick and sharps injuries were sustained by the negligence or wrongdoing of others began to be decided in courts around the country in the 1990s. Courts, in cases decided between 1990 and 1996, have been reluctant to allow health care workers to pursue their cases outside of the worker's compensation systems. The cases below indicate the hesitancy with which courts deal with needlestick and sharps injuries sustained by health care professionals.

In 1990, *Burk v. Sage Products Inc.*[12] was decided by the U.S. District Court for the Eastern District of Pennsylvania. In *Burk,* a paramedic was stuck by a needle protruding through a sharps container. He sued the manufacturer of the sharps container contending that the needles should not have been protruding from the container. Even though the paramedic tested negative five times for HIV, he developed a fear of contracting AIDS because several AIDS patients had been seen on the floor on which he was stuck. However, the paramedic could not prove that the needle that stuck him was from an AIDS patient. In light of those facts, the court expressed a reluctance to allow someone to recover for the fear of contracting a disease after it became apparent that he was not substantially likely to develop the illness.

In 1993, four additional cases were decided and subsequently published. In California, *Willits v. Superior Court of Santa Clara County and Health Dimensions, Inc.*[13] involved Kathryn Willits, a critical care nurse at San Jose Medical Center who became HIV positive after she stuck herself while attempting to inject blood from a syringe into a blood collection tube. The case went to the sixth appellate district court of appeals in an attempt to resolve a dispute over what information Kathryn Willits had a right to obtain from San Jose Medical Center. The court noted that quality of care records and proceedings were generally immune from discovery, and said that the precise nature of the documents requested needed to be ascertained by the trial court judge so that medical staff candor was protected, and the nurse was given the information needed to pursue her case against the facility.

In Montana, the Montana Supreme Court decided *Blythe v. Radiometer America, Inc, Community Medical Center, and Michael Biggins.*[14] In this case, Michael Blythe was a respiratory therapist employed by the Community Medical Center when he was stuck by an arterial blood gas (ABG) needle that had been used to collect a sample from a patient with AIDS. ABG kits at the facility were known to be defective, but were the only ABG kits available for use in the respiratory care unit. After sustaining the injury, Michael became psychotic and eventually became disabled and unable to work. He filed a negligence and breach of employment contract against his employer and immediate supervisor.

Michael Blyth's case was eventually heard by the Montana Supreme Court where the court concluded that worker's compensation was Michael's exclusive remedy. In reaching that conclusion, the justices feared that allowing Michael's claim to proceed would undermine the state's worker's compensation system.

In Louisiana, *Vallery v. Southern Baptist Hospital*[15] concerned a security guard called to subdue a patient. During the event, the patient's IV became dislodged, and the patient bled on the security guard's hand. The patient had AIDS, but the security guard did not know that until the day after the incident. He and his wife were subsequently enrolled in an HIV testing program, and both were negative for 2 years. The security guard and his wife filed suit against Southern Baptist Hospital. They allege emotional distress associated with the year they waited to confirm that they were HIV negative. They also sued alleging loss of consortium stemming from having to have protected sex for a year.

The case was heard by a Louisiana Court of Appeals, which determined that the security guard's case had been properly dismissed because worker's compensation was his exclusive remedy. Mrs. Vallery's emotional claim, however, was allowed to proceed, and the court of appeals directed that the matter be tried.

In Ohio, Gina Seimon was a registered nurse and Assistant Director of Nursing for Education at Richmond Heights General Hospital when she was stuck during a patient's demonstration of insulin self-injection. Gina filed a products liability cause of action against Becton Dickinson and Company. The case[16] was heard by the court of appeals for the eighth appellate district, which observed that Gina was required to show that Becton Dickinson and Company breached its duty to provide needle caps that would protect Gina from injury, and that Becton Dickinson and Company's breach caused her to sustain the injury for which she sought compensation. After reviewing the evidence presented, in light of Gina's evidentiary responsibility, the court determined that Gina presented no evidence that she was exposed to HIV or that the defective cap was the proximate cause of her emotional distress. Therefore, her case was dismissed.

In 1994, two cases filed by health care workers were decided and published: *Doe v. Aliquippa Hospital Association*[17] and *Doe v. Yale.*[18] Health care workers in both cases elected to pursue their cases anonymously. In the case against Aliquippa Hospital

Association, an operating room technician was stuck by a needle while working in the operating room. She was tested and was told she was HIV positive. She was put on a leave of absence until the HIV positive results were determined to be falsely positive. Later, she was stuck again.

She resigned and sued the hospital, alleging that federal law had been violated and that her confidentiality rights had been breached when it was disclosed that the technician had been put on a leave of absence because she tested HIV positive. She also alleged that she suffered emotional distress.

The case was dismissed by the United States District Court for the Western District of Pennsylvania. The court concluded that the operating room technician failed to establish that she was an individual with disability protected by the Rehabilitation Action, and she failed to show that her right to confidentiality had been violated. In addition, the court noted that Pennsylvania courts had been reluctant to declare the hospital's conduct as outrageous, and determined that the conduct complained about by the technician did not amount to anything that could be considered outrageous or atrocious. As a result, the emotional distress claim, along with the technician's other claims, were dismissed.

In *Doe v. Yale,* a physician who was infected with the AIDS virus during her internship at Yale-New Haven Hospital saw six jurors award her more than $15 million. The award was reduced by approximately $3 million because the physician was partially responsible for the needlestick injury.[19]

In 1995, two additional needlestick and sharps injury cases were decided. In Tennessee, *Stout v. Johnston City Medical Center Hospital*[20] concerned a nurse, Marcia Stout, who had been exposed to HIV, hepatitis A, hepatitis B, and hepatitis C when she stuck herself with a needle that had been used on a patient who died from AIDS. She pursued the matter as a worker's compensation case, and was awarded benefits based on a 62.5% permanent, partial disability determination. A component of Marcia Stout's claim involved a mental illness she developed following the exposure. The Special Worker's Compensation Appeals Panel of the Tennessee Supreme Court affirmed the award, concluding that mental illnesses were compensable under Tennessee's worker's compensation.

In Pennsylvania, *Riley v. Becton Dickinson Vascular Access, Inc.*[21] was decided by the U.S. District Court for the Eastern District of Pennsylvania. In that case, a 23-year-old nurse contracted HIV after she was stuck by a needle that had been contaminated with HIV. The nurse had been attempting to start an IV. She sued the manufacturer, contending that the company should be responsible for the injury she sustained. The court, however, disagreed with her, and granted the company's motion for summary judgment. The angiocath involved was deemed dangerous, but not unreasonably so, and the court determined that the costs of these kinds of injuries should be borne by employers, via worker's compensation, not manufacturers.

In 1996, two cases were decided and published by courts involving health care workers and their injuries sustained because of needlestick and sharps punctures. In

Brown v. New York City Health and Hospitals,[22] the Second Department Supreme Court heard a case involving a nurse, Lillian Brown, who was the Head Nurse on a Pediatric Unit at Queens General Hospital when she stuck herself with a needle. She was caring for nine infants, including one baby with hepatitis C and HIV. She stuck herself with a needle that had been left in the crib of the baby with hepatitis C and HIV. She was treated for her exposures, was prescribed AZT, and told to assume she was HIV positive. In that regard, she was told to use condoms and avoid kissing as well as the sharing of utensils. Two years after her exposure, Lillian Brown continued to be HIV negative.

After her exposure, she developed a fear of contracting AIDS, and sued the hospital for the negligent infliction of emotional distress. At the trial court level, the hospital was awarded a summary judgment. The New York Supreme Court, however, concluded that Lillian Brown could recover for her fear of contracting AIDS for 6 months following her exposure. The court observed that Lillian Brown had actually been exposed to HIV and that a jury may consider her fear of contracting AIDS reasonable.

In *Murphy v. Abbott Laboratories,*[23] Mary Murphy was a nurse at a hospital in Philadelphia when she was stuck using a needleless system manufactured by Abbott Laboratories. She stuck herself while she was caring for a patient who had hepatitis B and was HIV positive. She sued the manufacturer, seeking to recover damages she sustained when she injured herself. Surprisingly, the U.S. District Court for the Eastern District of Pennsylvania permitted Mary Murphy to pursue her claim against the manufacturer, in spite of previous ruling that limited employees like Mary Murphy to recovery under the state's worker's compensation system.

Although most courts have affirmed that on-the-job accidents, including needlestick and sharps injuries, can only be redressed in that state's worker's compensation system, at least one state supreme court has recognized that a health care organization's negligent treatment following a compensable injury can be pursued outside of worker's compensation. The case was *Dyke v. Saint Francis Hospital, Inc.,*[24] and it was decided by the Oklahoma Supreme Court.

In *Dyke,* Judy Dyke was a nurse working at Saint Francis Hospital in Tulsa, Oklahoma. While at work, she was exposed to hepatitis and was directed to the Employee Health Department for treatment. Her treatment included the administration of a series of Heptavax-B injections. After she had received five injections, she became seriously ill with Guillain-Barré syndrome. Subsequently, Jane and her husband, Dave, brought a malpractice cause of action against the hospital and her treating physicians. Her case was dismissed at the trial court level, but was reversed on appeal. The court of appeals agreed that Jane's case should not have been dismissed because the *dual persona doctrine* could provide Dyke with a tort remedy.

According to the court, the dual persona doctrine applied when an employer like Saint Francis stepped into a role other than that of employer. The Oklahoma Supreme Court agreed with the court of appeals, noting that employers like Saint Francis could not shield themselves from liability asserting the exclusivity of the worker's compensation system when that employer assumes a second persona. Here, the second persona of Saint Francis was that of health care provider. Because Saint Francis assumed a second persona, it could be held responsible for the injuries sustained by Dyke that were severable from her worker's compensation claim.

Staffing

Although staffing issues continue to be contentious and frustrating for nurses, hospital administrators, and patients, courts have consistently held that hospitals are responsible for staffing their institutions consistent with the needs of the patient. Two cases, one from New York, and the other from Arkansas demonstrate how courts address these issues.

In *Horton v. Niagra Falls Memorial Medical Center,*[25] an appellate court in New York upheld a verdict rendered in favor of a patient, Willard B. Horton, and his family after he fell while hospitalized at the Niagra Falls Memorial Medical Center. Mr. Horton was initially admitted to the facility because of a fever of unknown origin, lack of coordination, and blurred vision. Later, he was given a medical diagnosis of pneumonitis. During his hospital stay, Mr. Horton was noted to be confused, and at one point he was found outside his second story room asking construction workers on the first floor to hand him a ladder. Mr. Horton was escorted back to his room where soft wrist restraints and a posey belt were applied. Following this incident, the charge nurse reported the incident to Mr. Horton's attending physician who ordered that the staff keep an eye on Mr. Horton, keep him restrained, and, if necessary, transfer him to a secure room. Following that conversation, the charge nurse called Mrs. Horton to ask that she come to sit with Mr. Horton because the nursing staff was unable to provide that kind of supervision. Mrs. Horton told the charge nurse that she would call another family member who could be at the hospital within approximately 5 minutes. Prior to the conclusion of the conversation between Mrs. Horton and the charge nurse, Mrs. Horton asked that someone remain with her husband until someone arrived. The charge nurse reportedly indicated that the hospital was understaffed and that there was no one available to do that.

When the family member arrived in Mr. Horton's room, she noticed that a group of construction workers on the first floor were standing around someone lying on the ground. She quickly realized that it was Mr. Horton, and that he had fallen from the second floor window in his room.

Subsequently, the Hortons filed a civil lawsuit against the hospital alleging that the hospital was negligent in the care it provided Mr. Horton. After listening to the evidence, a jury rendered a verdict in favor of Mr. Horton and his family. The hospital appealed this decision, arguing that it acted reasonably under the circumstances.

The appellate court noted that although the hospital followed the physician's order with regard to the use of restraints and had no obligation to provide 24-hour supervision, that the hospital did have an independent duty to supervise patients to ensure that they do not injure themselves. Accordingly, the appellate court concluded that the hospital's failure to provide Mr. Horton with the level of supervision he needed until family members arrived was negligent and that the hospital was responsible for the injuries sustained by Mr. Horton and his family.

In 1988, the Arkansas Supreme Court heard *HCA Health Services of Midwest, Inc. v. National Bank of Commerce.*[26] In this case, the parents of James Talley alleged that Doctors Hospital in Little Rock, Arkansas, and three newborn nursery nurses, Elaine Firestone, Frances Tully, and Brenda Swayze, committed medical malpractice after James was born and was a patient in the newborn nursery. The Talley family specifically alleged that the nursery was inadequately staffed and that the nurses failed to adequately monitor James' condition.

The events that gave rise to this lawsuit were as follows: after 11:00 PM on September 7, 1982, nurses Elaine Firestone, Frances Tully, and Brenda Swayze were working in the newborn nursery, where 18 newborn infants were located. One patient was located in the admissions room, and the other 17 newborn infants were located in one of three nursery rooms. The rooms were connected to each other, and were separated by glass walls from the ceiling to the middle of each wall. After report and assignments were made, Frances Tully began caring for the newborn infant in the admissions room, while Elaine Firestone and Brenda Swayze proceeded to the second room where 11 babies were located. After Frances Tully finished her work with the baby in the admissions room, she proceeded to the third room where 6 babies were located. Upon her arrival in that room, Tully immediately noted that James was not breathing and rushed him to the intensive care unit. Although James was successfully resuscitated, he sustained permanent brain damage.

The family sued the hospital and the three nurses, and the case was eventually tried by an Arkansas jury. During the course of the trial, it was disclosed that the hospital had a policy in place that prohibited newborn infants from being left alone in the newborn nursery. It was also disclosed that hospital administrators had been told of a continuing need for nurses in the newborn nursery, and that the number of staff on duty the night James arrested was below the hospital's stated standards. Consequently, the jury rendered a verdict in favor of the Talley family. The jury exonerated Elaine Firestone, and the trial court judge issued directed verdicts in favor of Frances Tully and Brenda Swayze. However, the hospital was deemed negligent and ordered to pay $2.62 million in compensatory damages and $2 million in punitive damages.

The hospital appealed alleging that nine reversible errors had been committed. After considering the alleged reversible errors, the Arkansas Supreme Court ordered that the case be re-tried because of prejudicial remarks made by the attorney representing the family. In reaching this decision, the Arkansas Supreme Court concluded that the evidence clearly supported the jury's finding that the hospital's negligence caused the injury to James, as well as the resultant compensatory damage award. The Arkansas Supreme Court also determined that punitive damages could be awarded

According to the Principles for Nurse Staffing, *Staffing Systems Need to Reflect the Following:*

▮ an analysis of individual and aggregate patient needs, as well as the needs of the nursing staff;

▮ use of a unit of measure that accurately calculates the intensity of nursing care needed by patients;

▮ integration of support services needed to deliver quality patient care services;

▮ that the specific needs of patient populations and the competencies needed by nurses providing care to that patient population are incorporated;

▮ that registered nurses have the support of nursing administration at the operational and executive levels;

▮ that there is readily available clinical support for less proficient nurses from more experienced registered nurses;

▮ the operationalization of policies and practices that indicate that the health care organization values registered nurses and other employees as valuable assets;

▮ the implementation of the competencies of the nursing staff, including temporary, agency, supplemental or traveling staff.

American Nurses Association (ANA). 2000. *Principles for Nurse Staffing.* Available from URL: http://www.nursingworld.org/readroom/stffprnc.htm.

in this matter and that Frances Tully and Brenda Swayze should not have been dismissed by the trial court judge.

These and other cases indicate that courts are treating staffing seriously, and are holding nurses as well as health care organizations accountable for staffing in a way that is consistent with the standard of care. Now that principles for nurse staffing have been articulated by the American Nurses Association (ANA; see sidebar), courts will likely look to see if those standards, as well as institutional standards have been adhered to.

Whistleblower Protection

Whistleblower protection shields employees from retaliation for reporting unsafe conditions within their workplaces. Although whistleblower protection is addressed more extensively in Chapter 8, it is introduced here so that nurse-employees can better understand the protection afforded by the passage of whistleblower legislation.

Whistleblower protection conceptually protects employees from retaliation when they report unsafe conditions to appropriate agencies. The scope of this protection was recently tested in Texas. In that state, three registered nurses were demoted after they insisted that a licensed vocational nurse at their agency be reported to the Board of Vocational Nurse Examiners (BVNE) because of a medication error that resulted in the death of one patient. When the three registered nurses insisted that the matter be reported to the BVNE, they were immediately removed from the agency's Peer Review Committee and relieved of their administrative responsibilities.[27] The three registered nurses resigned and filed a civil lawsuit against the agency alleging that it had wrongfully retaliated against them in violation of the whistleblower protection provision contained in the Texas Nurse Practice Act. The case was eventually decided by the Texas Supreme Court, which determined that the conduct of the employer in this case was the kind of behavior the whistleblower protection legislation was designed to prohibit, and that the employer's adverse action with regard to those nurses was retaliatory. In reaching this conclusion, the justice observed that whistleblower protection would be significantly diminished if employers were permitted to retaliate against employees simply because the employer actually filed a complaint before employees do. The employer had argued that whistleblower protection did not extend to the three registered nurses in this case because they had not filed their report with the proper agency. In addition, the justices commented that employees should be encouraged to inform their employers that another employee poses a potential threat to patients, and that this informing activity furthers the legislative intent of whistleblower protection.

Although U.S. courts are beginning to hear and decide whistleblower cases, many states do not yet have legislation in place that prohibits employer retaliation in instances where an employee reports unsafe conditions within the workplace. In an attempt to extend whistleblower protection to employees in healthcare institutions, six states are contemplating the passage of whistleblower protection: Hawaii, Illinois, New York, Oregon, Rhode Island, and West Virginia.

Federal Laws Protecting Employees

Age Discrimination in Employment Act

As the name implies, the Age Discrimination in Employment Act (ADEA)[28] protects individuals from being discriminated against because of their age. The ADEA protects individuals who are over the age of 40, and who work for employers with at least 20 employees. It applies to hiring, termination, lay-off, promotion, demotion, pay, insurance benefits, and pension accrual decisions, as well as other terms and conditions of employment.

The ADEA was amended by the Older Workers' Benefit Protection Act (OWBPA). The OWBPA requires that any waiver of rights be made knowingly and voluntarily. Waiver of rights issues arise when employees are asked to sign agreements to forego their right to pursue their case in court.

The ADEA is enforced through the Equal Employment Opportunity Commission (EEOC). The EEOC is the federal agency charged with investigating discrimination (age, race, sex, ethnic, religious, or disability) claims filed against employers with 15 or more employees. The EEOC has the power to investigate employer records, examine witnesses, and bring legal action against the employer. If the EEOC elects not pursue the case, a right to sue later can be issued, so that a private attorney can litigate the matter.

Americans with Disabilities Act

The Americans with Disabilities Act (ADA)[29] was passed in 1990, while President George H. Bush was in office. When it was passed, it offered individuals with disabilities more protection than had previously been extended. The ADA is a federal anti-discrimination law designed to remove barriers that prevent qualified individuals with disabilities from enjoying the same employment opportunities available to persons without disabilities. The ADA applies to all aspects of employment, including recruitment, hiring, termination, pay, promotion, training, layoffs, leave, and benefits, as well as to government services, and public accommodations. The ADA applies to all employers with 15 or more employees.

In a nutshell, the ADA protects people who are (1) qualified and (2) disabled. A person is qualified under the ADA if he or she satisfies the job requirements and can perform the essential job tasks/functions. A person has a disability under the ADA if he or she has a present physical or mental impairment that substantially limits a major life activity, has a record of substantially limiting physical or mental impairment, or is regarded as having a substantially limiting impairment. Examples of people qualified for ADA protection include individuals who use assistive devices for hearing, seeing, communicating, and transportation, and people with handicaps or chronic and acute diseases. In addition, the ADA provides protection to people who are mentally ill and to those with temporary impairment. The ADA also protects those who assist disabled individuals.

Although the ADA extends employment protection to a large group of individuals, it does not cover everyone. The following groups are excluded from ADA protection: chemically dependent people who are not in recovery, people who have psychoactive substance-induced organic and mental disorders, and people with one of the following conditions: transvestism, pedophilia, transexualism, exhibitionism, voyeurism, compulsive gambling, kleptomania, pyromania, and gender identity disorders.

The disabled individual who is protected under the ADA is deemed "qualified" if that person satisfies the job requirements, and can perform essential job tasks/functions. The question then becomes, what are essential job tasks/functions? Answers to three questions are used to determine whether a particular task/function is essential. First, is this task the reason this position exists? If the answer is "yes," then that particular task/function is essential. Second, are there other employees available to perform the task/function? If the answer is "yes," then it might not be essential that this individual be able to perform the task/function. Third, what is the degree of expertise or skill required to perform the task/function? If there are no other employees available to perform the task/function and the task/function is of a highly technical nature, then it would be essential for this person to be able to perform it.

Information used to determine whether a task/function is essential comes from a variety of sources. Employer judgment is given a great amount of weight, as are written job descriptions, work experience of present and past employees, time spent performing the task/function, as well as the consequences for not requiring an employee to perform the task/function.

The issue of essential job functions was the focus of *Deane v. Pocono Medical Center.*[30] Here, a nurse claimed that her employer regarded her as disabled because she could no longer lift patients, and terminated her because she could no longer perform all of the functions of her job. The third circuit judge declared that the nurse did not have to perform all of the functions, simply the essential functions. In reaching this decision, the court implied that lifting patients may not be an essential job function. However, because the facility regarded the nurse as disabled, it was obligated to reasonably alter the work environment.

If an individual is disabled and qualified for protection under the ADA, the employer may need to make some sort of revision to the work environment so that the individual can successfully perform in it. According to the ADA, when an employer alters the work environment so a disabled, qualified person can successfully perform in it, that employer is making an accommodation. Employers are not required to make an accommodation unless it is reasonable. A *reasonable accommodation* is any change or adjustment to a job or work environment that permits a qualified applicant or employee with a disability to participate in the application process, perform essential job tasks/functions, or enjoy the benefits and privileges of employment equal to those enjoyed by employees without disabilities. Reasonable accommodations include things like the employer making the workplace accessible, acquiring or modifying equipment or devices, job restructuring, modifying work schedules, reassigning the affected individual, adjusting or modifying examinations, policies, and other information so that they can be given to the disabled applicant or employee, and providing readers and interpreters.

Depending on the financial and human resources available to employers, what may be a reasonable accommodation for one employer may not be reasonable for another employer. Should an employer characterize a requested accommodation as unreasonable, the employer must show that the requested accommodation would be too costly, extensive, substantial, disruptive, or fundamentally alter the nature or operation of the business. In short, the employer must make reasonable accommodations for qualified, disabled applicants and employees unless the accommodation would cause the employer undue hardship. The factors that are used to determine whether an accommodation is an undue hardship include the cost of the accommodation, the employer's size, financial resources available to the employer, as well as the nature and structure of the accommodation.

Although the burden on employers seems great, 93% of the ADA discrimination cases heard by trial courts were decided in favor of employers.[31] In addition, the U.S. Supreme Court has recently decided three cases that significantly restrict the reach of the ADA. Following these decisions, a person does not have a disability (with ADA protection) if that individual has a medical condition that is corrected, for example, with glasses, hearing aids, or medication. The rationale was that these kinds of corrected conditions do not limit major life activities.

Nevertheless, substantial awards have been returned for individuals who have been adversely affected by ADA violations. For example, a jury returned a $7.1 million verdict in favor of a Coca-Cola executive employee who was terminated while he was in outpatient treatment for alcoholism.[32] The award included $109,000 for back pay, $700,000 for front pay, $300,000 for mental anguish, and $6 million in punitive damages.

Unfortunately health care facilities, health plans, and health care professionals have had to pay significant penalties for ADA violations. An Ohio hospital violated the ADA when an emergency room physician refused to treat a patient with AIDS.[33] In that case, the judge upheld a verdict against the hospital in the amount of $512,000 and ordered that the hospital post a sign in the emergency room pledging that treatment would not be denied because of an AIDS diagnosis.

In *Henderson v. Bodine Aluminum, Inc.,*[34] the eighth circuit court of appeals ordered a health plan and insurance provider to cover costs associated with the administration of high-dose chemotherapy treatment (HDCT) for insureds with a breast cancer diagnosis. It was proven that HDCT is an accepted form of breast cancer treatment, and that it was covered for other forms of cancer. Not covering the cost of HDCT in breast cancer patients was discriminatory, based on disability type, and violated the ADA.

ADA violations have not been limited to health care facilities, and health care plans. Health care providers have been cited for violating the ADA. One case, *Bragdon v. Abbott,*[35] went to the U.S. Supreme Court. In this case, a dentist, Randon Bragdon, refused to treat a patient in his office because the patient was HIV positive. Bragdon reportedly had a policy of not treating people with infectious diseases in his office because he contracted dysentery from a patient, and had to quit treating patients for 3 weeks. The U.S. Supreme Court determined that Ms. Abbott was protected by the ADA, and that Bragdon's refusal to treat her in his office violated the act.

Although the cases discussed here were decided in favor of the individual alleging that they had been discriminated against because of their disability, many cases are decided in favor of the employer or entity alleged to have violated the ADA. For instance, in *Mauro v. Borgess Medical Center,*[36] the court determined that the termination of an HIV-positive surgical assistant did not violate the ADA because this employee was not qualified for ADA protection. He was disabled, but he was not qualified because he posed a direct threat to others, which could not be eliminated by a reasonable accommodation. The surgical assistant attempted to show that the primary focus of his job was handing instruments to a surgeon, but other evidence showed that he was occasionally required to manually retract tissue around incisions while a surgeon was operating. This activity was deemed to be invasive and exposure prone.

Civil Rights Act

The Civil Rights Acts and its amendments are perhaps the most significant pieces of legislation to ever be enacted. The Civil Rights Act of 1870, The Civil Rights Act of 1964, and the Civil Rights Act of 1991 will be discussed.

Passed following the Civil War, the Civil Rights Act of 1870 has one section in it that will be discussed here: Section 1981. Section 1981, for the first time in U.S. history, afforded African-Americans equal benefit of the law. Following the passage of this law, the U.S. Supreme Court narrowed the application of this provision to discrimination in hiring. However, amendments to the Civil Rights Act have extended discrimination protection to all aspects of employment.

In 1964, additional civil rights protections were added. Title VII of the Civil Rights Act of 1964 prohibits discrimination or termination based on race, sex, religion, handicap, age, marital status, color, ancestry, or national origin. Employers with at least 15 employees are subject to Title VII.

In 1991, the Civil Rights Act was amended once again. This time, the amendments primarily affected Title VII. Title VII protection was extended to all aspects of employment, including hiring, firing, discipline, promotion, demotion, compensation, and benefit accrual, as well as other terms and conditions of employment. In addition, women, people with disabilities, and members of religious minorities were afforded the opportunity to sue for damages with intentional discrimination, and to request a trial by jury.

Although amendments to the Civil Rights Act have broadened individual protection from discrimination, Title VII does not apply where there is a bona fide occupational qualification (BFOQ). A BFOQ is narrowly construed and applies in only a few circumstances. For instance, a BFOQ exception applies where a male actor is sought to play a male role.

Title VII is enforced by the EEOC. Complaints must be filed within 180 days of alleged violation. Private lawsuits may be pursued within 90 days after receiving a right to sue letter from the EEOC.

Sexual harassment is a Title VII violation. It is considered a form of sex discrimination. The EEOC defines *sexual harassment* as unwelcome sexual advances, requests for sexual favors, and other verbal or physical conduct of a sexual nature that is made an explicit or implicit term or condition of employment, is used as a basis for making employment decisions, or unreasonably interferes with an individual's work performance, creating an intimidating, hostile, or offensive working environment.[37] Sexual harassment is classified as either quid pro quo or hostile work environment. *Quid pro quo sexual harassment* is the explicit exchange of a tangible job benefit for sexual favors. On the other hand, *hostile work environment sexual harassment* occurs when sexual behavior becomes so pervasive that the work environment negates an employee's ability to do his or her job.

The automotive industry has been hit hard with sexual harassment claims; three of the largest sexual harassment verdicts have been against automakers. Sexual harassment cost Mitsubishi $34 million; Chrysler and Ford have had to pay $21 million and $7 million, respectively, for sexual harassment incidents.

Although automakers have been hit hard with sexual harassment claims, the health care industry has its share of sexual harassment incidents. *Farpella-Crosby v. Horizon Health Care*[38] and *Helmuth v. Alaska Psychiatric Institute*[39] are examples. In *Farpella-Crosby,* a female treatment nurse was subjected to sexually harassing comments by her male director of nursing. Apparently, the director made inappropriate sexual comments, asked the treatment nurse about her sexual habits, and continued making these kinds of comments in spite of the treatment nurses' requests that he stop. The male director also insisted that the female nurse perform tasks not related to her job description. The treatment nurse reported the situation to the human resources director, who made no effort to investigate the matter. The U.S. Circuit Court of Appeals for the Fifth Circuit upheld the nurse's sexual harassment claim, saying that there was substantial evidence that her employer, the nursing home, failed to take prompt remedial action once the nurse made a good faith sexual harassment complaint.

In *Helmuth,* a nurse was awarded $463,000 in damages, $79,400 in interest, and $56,500 in attorney fees after she was laid off for reporting that she was sexually harassed. Nurse Helmuth's male supervisor reportedly subjected Helmuth and other female employees to vulgar sexual harassment and discrimination. Helmuth reported her supervisor, and he was suspended for 2 weeks. After that, the supervisor was promoted to hospital administrator. The state then began investigating Helmuth and the other women who had been interviewed prior to the supervisor's suspension. Helmuth and another nurse took the matter to a local television station, and approximately 1 month later, Helmuth was laid off. Reportedly, the lay off was for reorganization purposes. The court determined that Helmuth had been sexually harassed, and that she had been retaliated against for filing the sexual harassment complaint.

Employees who think they have been subjected to sexual harassment should carefully follow the procedural steps outlined in the employer's sexual harassment policy and procedure. Once a complaint is filed in accordance with the employer's policy and procedure, an investigation should commence. During the investigation, facts will be gathered and witnesses interviewed. Following the investigation, disciplinary action decisions will be made. Should an employee think that his or her sexual harassment complaint is being ignored, minimized, and not taken seriously by the employer, the employee may file the complaint with the EEOC. Sexual harassment complaints must be filed with the EEOC within 180 days of the incident, and private lawsuits cannot proceed until the EEOC issues a right to sue letter.

Consolidated Omnibus Budget Reconciliation Act

The Consolidated Omnibus Budget Reconciliation Act (COBRA)[40] requires employers with 20 or more employees to offer terminated employees continued health insurance benefits for at least 18 months. The law requires that employers notify employees of COBRA coverage when they are hired and when they are terminated from employment. Employers are not required to pay COBRA premiums. In addition, COBRA benefits expire when premiums are not paid or when the terminated employee becomes eligible for coverage in another health insurance plan. COBRA is enforced by the Internal Revenue Service (IRS), and where COBRA violations are found, the employer becomes liable for medical expenses incurred because of the violation.

Equal Pay Act

The Equal Pay Act[41] applies to employers with two or more employees and mandates equal pay for equal work. However, the Equal Pay Act does not extend to gender-neutral merit or seniority systems that are based on quality or quantity of production. The Equal Pay Act is enforced by the EEOC. Unlike other discrimination charges, individuals who allege that the Equal Pay Act has been violated are not required to register their complaint with the EEOC; a private lawsuit may be filed without going to the EEOC. However, once an Equal Pay Act violation has been reported to the EEOC, a private lawsuit cannot be filed unless the EEOC issues the complaining individual a right to sue letter.

Fair Labor Standards Act

Theoretically, the Fair Labor Standards Act (FLSA)[42] applies to every employer. It requires that minimum wages be paid, establishes rules for payment of overtime, and designates limits on hours worked for some populations. Many states have laws that designate higher minimum wages and stricter controls on hours worked for certain groups of employees. In those cases, the state law applies.

Not every employee is afforded FLSA protection. Professional, executive, and administrative employees who are typically paid salaries are exempt from the FLSA. In addition, labor commissioners can authorize employers to pay certain learners, apprentices, and trainees less than minimum wage.

The FLSA is enforced by the U.S. Department of Labor. FLSA violations must be filed with the U.S. Department of Labor within 2 years of the alleged violation. The time period is extended 1 year for willful violations of the FLSA. Private lawsuits may be filed for FLSA violations without filing a complaint with the U.S. Department of Labor. However, if an FLSA violation is reported to the U.S. Department of Labor, a private lawsuit cannot proceed unless the U.S. Department of Labor elects not to pursue the matter on the employee's behalf.

Employees who do have FLSA protection are entitled to sanctions for violations of the Act. However, remedies available under the FLSA continue to be a matter of great dispute.

Family and Medical Leave Act

The Family and Medical Leave Act (FMLA)[43] applies to employers with 50 or more employees within a 75 mile radius. It allows employees who have worked for an employer for at least 1 year to take up to 12 weeks of unpaid leave in any 12-month period for the birth or adoption of a child, or the serious illness of the employee or the employee's spouse, child, parent, or other dependent. When an employee requests to use FMLA leave, an employer may request that an employee provide documentation from the health care provider. If the employer has reason to doubt the validity of the documentation, a second opinion may be requested, but must be paid for by the employer. Employees must provide this requested documentation to employers that have requested it. Leave may be taken for 12 weeks in a row, or intermittently. Upon the employee's return to work, the employer is obligated to assign the employee to the same or equivalent job with equivalent pay and benefits. The FMLA is enforced by the U.S. Department of Labor, and alleged infractions must be reported within 2 years of the violation.

Recently, the first FMLA and gender discrimination case reached trial. In that case, a Maryland paramedic, Kevin Knussman, won a $375,000 verdict because the state of Maryland denied his request for parental leave for the birth of his first child. Knussman was reportedly told that the leave he requested for the birth of his first daughter was available only to women.[44]

National Labor Relations Act

Enacted in 1935, the National Labor Relations Act (NLRA)[45] governs the relationship between employers and unions. The NLRA created the National Labor Relations Board (NLRB), but did not extend coverage to voluntary, nonprofit hospitals until 1974. In 1974, a number of amendments were made to the NLRA to prevent potentially disruptive effects of unionization in health care environments.

The NLRB is an independent federal agency, composed of five members who are appointed by the U.S. President to 5-year terms. The agency is charged to administer and enforce the NLRA, and does so by overseeing the more than 35,000 charges that are filed each year. Recently, the reach of the NLRB was extended to workers in settings where collective bargaining agreements are absent. The case was *Epilepsy Foundation of Northwest Ohio*.[46] The NLRB determined that employees not practicing in a collective bargaining environment have the right have a co-worker present during investigatory interviews the employee reasonably believes could result in disciplinary action. In 1975, under *NLRB v. J Weingarten*,[47] the U.S. Supreme Court extended unionized workers this same privilege.

According to the NLRA, employers may not interfere with or restrain employees who exercise their rights to organize or bargain collectively. Neither are employers permitted to interfere in the formation of any labor organization. Moreover, employers may not discharge or discriminate against employees who file charges or testify in accordance with provisions of the NLRA, nor are employers permitted to refuse to bargain with the majority representative of the group chosen by employees.

For nurses in some parts of the United States, the option to unionize is being considered with growing frequency. Staffing inadequacy, mandatory overtime, dissatisfaction with the work environment, and a marginalized role in patient care decision making have been identified as occurrences that have led to nurses to consider using a collective bargaining agreement. Proponents believe that this mechanism works to more effectively address the concerns of nurses; collective bargaining opponents claim that the voice of nurses is simply channeled through an expensive third party. Regardless of the method used, it is imperative that nurses be considered a vital and integral part of the health care team, that they are permitted to practice in accordance within the full scope of practice, and that health and safety issues be addressed so that the workplace is safe and healthy for patients and employees. The excellence-focused Magnet Nursing Services Recognition Program discussed in Chapter 11 offers a framework that can be beneficial for patients, employees, and employers whether or not the employment setting is a collective bargaining environment.

The Needlestick Safety and Prevention Act

The Needlestick Safety and Prevention Act was introduced in the U.S. House of Representatives by Representatives Cass Ballenger from North Carolina and Major Owens from New York, and in the U.S. Senate by Senators James Jeffords from Vermont, Michael Enzi from Wyoming, Edward Kennedy from Massachusetts, and Harry Reid from Nevada. The bill sought to amend the Occupational Safety and Health Administration's Bloodborne Pathogen Standard to require employers to use safer devices in an effort to protect employees from needlestick and sharps injuries. The bill also sought to require employers to keep a sharps injury log, and to involve non-managerial direct care staff in the identification, selection, and evaluation of safety-engineered sharps and needleless systems designed to reduce the risk of sharps and needlestick injuries.

The bill was unanimously approved by the U.S. House of Representatives on October 4, 2000. The U.S. Senate then approved the bill on October 24, 2000. President Clinton signed the Needlestick Safety and Prevention Act on November 6, 2000.

Although the Needlestick Safety and Prevention Act represents a significant step forward in the elimination of preventable sharps and needlestick injuries sustained by health care workers, device manufacturers, and the hospital industry are concerned about being able to comply with the legislated mandates. Ed Lovern wrote an article published in *Modern Healthcare* discussing some of the concerns.[48] According to Lovern, manufacturers like Becton Dickinson are concerned about their ability to produce enough safe devices to meet the demand for syringes, although blood collection devices and intravenous catheters were expected to be produced in adequate quantities. Becton Dickinson, however, anticipated that the demand for syringes could be met, so long as hospitals did not convert to safer syringes at the same time.[49]

Because of the anticipated shortage of syringes some hospitals expressed concern about their being able to comply with the legislation. Should the shortage of devices actually occur, a spokeswoman from the Occupational Safety and Health Administration said that inspectors would take shortage into consideration so long as employers have acted in good faith with the implementation of the mandates of the Needlestick Safety and Prevention Act.[50]

To ensure that legislative mandates are complied with, employers need to have a process in place to begin using safer devices, including blood-drawing devices with shielded, retracting, or self-blunted needles, and IV catheters. Policies also need to be implemented that prohibit recapping and removal of needles from blood drawing devices; use of a needle to withdraw blood from a peripheral IV, arterial, or central line; and changing of needles when obtaining blood for blood cultures. Policies also need to be in effect that require blood to be collected directly in vacuum and other laboratory tubes, identifies the procedures to be followed when disposing of sharps, and outlines the postexposure process that is to be followed.

At the state level, state nurses associations have been tireless proponents of legislation introduced in state legislatures to prevent needlestick injuries. In 2000, needlestick legislation was introduced in Alabama, the District of Columbia, Florida, Illinois, Michigan, Missouri, Nebraska, New York, Pennsylvania, Rhode Island, Utah, Washington, and Wisconsin. By mid-2000, Needlestick legislation was enacted in 11 states, including Alaska, Connecticut, Georgia, Iowa, Maine, Massachusetts, Minnesota, New Hampshire, New York, Ohio, Oklahoma, and West Virginia. Six states had legislation which was passed in previous years, including California, Hawaii, Maryland, New Jersey, Tennessee, and Texas.[51]

If an employer needs to establish a postexposure plan or wishes to evaluate a plan that is currently in place, the Exposure Prevention Information Network (EPINet) at the University of Virginia has a checklist for establishing or evaluating post-exposure plans (available at http://www.med.virginia.edu/epinet). In addition, the American Nurses Association has posted a needlestick prevention program at http://www.needlestick.org.

Occupational Safety and Health Act

The Occupational and Safety Health Act (OSHA)[52] requires employers to comply with safety and health standards promulgated by the Occupational Safety and Health Administration. Because of OSHA, employers have to ensure that the workplace is free from ordinary hazards. Ordinary hazards are those things that are likely to cause serious injury or death. In health care settings, ordinary hazards include latex allergies, polluted air, needlestick and sharps injuries, back injuries, and ergonomic issues. Failure to rid the workplace of these hazards can result in the imposition of fines as much as $1,000 a day.

State Laws Protecting Employees

Immunity

Historically, governments and charitable organizations enjoyed immunity from liability for torts committed by these entities. Federal and state governments, cities, and towns were immune from tort liability because of the doctrine of sovereign immunity. The charitable immunity doctrine extended immunity from tort liability to charitable organizations. Today, both of those doctrines have been abolished or greatly restricted. Instead, immunity is extended through torts claim legislation codified at the federal and state levels. Immunity extended through these statutes is referred to as *governmental immunity*. Governmental immunity is addressed below; sovereign and charitable immunity are addressed in Chapter 8.

The Federal Torts Claims Act of 1945,[53] with the exception of specifically listed exclusions, confers general immunity from liability associated with alleged acts of negligence committed by federal government employees. All states have enacted some type of government immunity legislation for state government workers. For nurses working in government facilities, immunity from liability for alleged acts of negligence is a benefit not enjoyed by nurses working in the private sector. The effect of this benefit is significant. When a nurse employed at a government facility is named as an individual co-defendant in a negligence case against a government hospital, the nurse will be dismissed from the lawsuit because he or she is a government employee and is immune from personal liability.

However, *Bivens v. State of Oklahoma*[54] provides an example of what can happen if an activity is considered outside the scope of employment. In *Bivens,* Rosemary Williams died after suffering complications from a bone marrow transplant. The procedure was performed at a hospital owned by the state. During the procedure, the Hickman catheter that was being inserted pierced Ms. Williams' superior vena cava and she bled to death. Representatives of Ms. Williams' estate filed suit against the state, the hospital, five residents, and four attending physicians. The five residents and four attending physicians were dismissed as co-defendants by the trial judge. Ms. Williams' representatives appealed this decision to the Oklahoma Supreme Court. The Oklahoma Supreme Court determined that the trial court committed an error when the residents and attending physicians were dismissed from the case. In reaching its decision, the Oklahoma Supreme Court asserted that immunity from liability did not extend to the residents and attending physicians because they were practicing medicine. They drew a distinction between practicing medicine and teaching and administrative responsibilities. In their view, the teaching and administrative responsibilities of the attending physician were covered by the Governmental Torts Claim Act, but providing medical or surgical services to patients was within the scope of their employment as faculty members at this state-sponsored health care facility.

Because of the *Bivens* decision, it is crucial for employees of governmental entities to have the provision of patient care activities included in employment contracts and job descriptions. Inclusion of patient care activities in these two documents will help to show that providing patient care services is within the scope of employment and protected under applicable governmental torts claim acts.

Employment Security

Each state, along with the federal government, has statutes in place to provide short-term financial assistance to individuals who find themselves unemployed and eligible for the benefits. In most states, individuals eligible for benefits include those who: have worked for at least 3 months during the past year, meet the minimum earnings requirement, are physically and mentally capable of working, are available to work, and make reasonable efforts to get a job. Those who are ineligible to receive this short-term financial assistance include those who are fired for just cause, repeated willful misconduct, or committing a felony in the course of employment. Other grounds for ineligibility include quitting a job without sufficient work-related cause, taking part in an illegal strike, serving a prison sentence of longer than 30 days, and voluntarily retiring.

Employers may or may not contest an individual's application to receive these benefits. If an employer believes that an employee should be ineligible for benefits, the employer may be more likely to contest the application. Employers win some of the cases that are contested, but the system is remedial, and the presumption is that an individual is eligible for short-term unemployment benefits. In some states, more than 90% of all individuals who apply for these unemployment benefits are awarded benefits at their initial hearing.[55]

The remedial nature of the system can be seen in the case of *Warren v. Caro Community Hospital*.[56] In *Warren*, Cindy Warren worked as a nurse's aide at Caro Community Hospital. Ms. Warren worked full-time until she became pregnant and her physician recommended that she discontinue working. She then requested a leave of absence. Caro Community Hospital denied her leave of absence request citing a provision in a collective bargaining agreement that did not permit employees employed less than 1 year to take a leave of absence.

After Warren delivered, her doctor released her to return to work. Ms. Warren notified the hospital. However, the hospital did not respond to the notification tendered by Ms. Warren, and did not offer to allow her to work in any capacity.

Ms. Warren filed a claim for unemployment benefits, which was contested by Caro Community Hospital. The hospital contended that Ms. Warren was ineligible for benefits because she voluntarily left the employment of Caro Community Hospital. The case was eventually heard by the Michigan Supreme Court. The state court justices said that where an employee, like Ms. Warren, is willing to continue working but is advised to cease working by a doctor because of a temporary or short-term, self-limited medical condition, and that employee is not allowed to return to work as soon as medically possible, that the employee has not voluntarily quit, and is eligible for unemployment benefits.

Nondiscrimination Statutes

Title VII of the Civil Rights Act of 1964,[57] as well as state-based nondiscrimination statutes, prohibit employers from discriminating against applicants and employees because of the applicant's or employee's race, color, religion, sex, or national origin. The federal statutory scheme has been enacted in various forms, and to various degrees in each state, and the District of Columbia. Generally, state-based nondiscrimination statutes extend federally articulated prohibitions to small, private employers that might not have to comply with federal nondiscrimination laws.

Although every state has passed nondiscrimination legislation, the extent to which these laws apply to small employers varies. In Alabama, Georgia, Mississippi, and Virginia, no minimum number of employees was delineated. The implication is that virtually every employer in those states is obligated to abide by the state nondiscrimination statutes. Virginia has done something no other state has done, and that is to say that where an employee has a claim for discriminatory termination, the employer can be sued in state court if the employer has more than 5, but less than 15 employees.

Thirteen states and the District of Columbia exempt from their nondiscrimination statutes only those businesses with no employees. In addition to the District of Columbia, the 13 states are Alaska, Colorado, Hawaii, Iowa, Maine, Michigan, Minnesota, Montana, New Jersey, Oregon, South Dakota, Vermont, and Wisconsin. Wisconsin and Connecticut require all private employers with at least two and three employees, respectively, to comply with their nondiscrimination laws.

Private employers with four or more employees must abide by the nondiscrimination statutes in Delaware, Kansas, New Mexico, New York, Ohio, Pennsylvania, and Rhode Island. California and Idaho nondiscrimination statutes apply to employers with five or more employees. However, the California law says that where mental disability is concerned, private employers with at least 15 employees have to comply with the state nondiscrimination statutes.

Nondiscrimination statutes in Indiana, Missouri, and New Hampshire exempt private employers with five or less employees, whereas Kentucky, Tennessee, and Washington exempt private employers with seven or less employees. In Arkansas, North Dakota, and West Virginia, state nondiscrimination laws apply to employers with at least 9, 10, and 12 employees respectively.

Although most states have nondiscrimination statutes that reach small employers who are not required to comply with federal nondiscrimination statutes, there are 12 states that do not significantly extend the reach of federal antidiscrimination laws. Federal laws prohibiting discrimination apply only to private employers with 15 or more employees. This is the minimum employee requirement articulated in Title VII of the Civil Rights Act. States in this group include Arizona, Florida, Illinois, Louisiana, Maryland, Nebraska, Nevada, North Carolina, Oklahoma, South Carolina, Texas, and Utah.

Discrimination complaints are investigated by the EEOC. Complaints must be in writing, detailed, signed, and notarized. Complaints must be filed within 180 days of the act(s) that is the subject of the complaint. Once the complaint is filed, the EEOC has 10 days to notify the employer that a complaint has been filed. With regard to investigation, the EEOC usually defers the investigation of the complaint to the local agency designated to investigate such claims. This may be either a local division of the EEOC or a state's Human Rights Commission.

Pay and Hours Worked

Federal laws governing pay and hours worked are the FLSA,[58] and the Equal Pay Act.[59] In addition to the federal laws, each state has passed legislation that identifies the minimum wage that must be paid to employees. In most states, there are some workers who do not have to be paid the minimum wage. These exemptions include volunteers in charitable or nonprofit institutions, cleaning people in private homes, agricultural workers, people who work on commission, babysitters, newspaper delivery people, and members of the employer's immediate family.

Nurses do not generally have to worry about receiving minimum wage for the jobs they have, but they do need to be sure that overtime is paid appropriately. Nurses who are salaried are exempt from wage and hour laws. Generally, this encompasses administrative or executive level professionals. Nurses, paid on an hourly basis are more likely to be considered non-exempt, and employers must comply with wage and hour laws. Non-exempt employees must be paid overtime. Usually, the overtime rate is no less than one and one-half times the employee's regular pay. Thirty-two states use 40 hours per week as the standard against which overtime is paid. Fifteen states (Delaware, Georgia, Indiana, Iowa, Louisiana, Mississippi, Nebraska, Oklahoma, South Carolina, Tennessee, Texas, Utah, Virginia, and Wyoming) have no overtime statute. Accordingly, employers subject to the Fair Labor Standards Act must pay overtime for employees who work more than 40 hours in a week.

When it comes to "taking call," some nurses receive on-call pay and others do not. Generally, if calls are so numerous that on-call time cannot be used effectively, overtime pay should be received.

Pay and issues related to hours worked are enforced by the United States and each state's Department of Labor. There is a 2-year time period within which claims for pay can be filed. The time starts to run from the time you knew or should have known that the violation occurred. If back pay is awarded, it is limited to 2 years worth of unpaid or underpaid time. Where there has been a willful violation of the law, the employer may have to pay back pay for 3 years' worth of unpaid or underpaid time. In addition to back pay, damages, attorney fees, and costs are also available. Damages are limited to an amount equal to the unpaid or underpaid time, and attorney fees can be awarded, so long as the fees are reasonable.

Workplace Violence Prevention Statutes

The Workplace Violence Prevention Act[60] was passed in California to deal with the rising incidence of workplace violence. Between 1992 and 1996, more than 2 million people each year were victims of workplace violence. Assault was the most common form of workplace violence. There were 396,000 aggravated assaults, 84,000 robberies, and 1000 homicides each year. Approximately 60% of the violent acts were committed by strangers. Nine out of 10 victims were white, and 70% of all victims were between 25 and 49 years of age. In addition, more than half of all victims of workplace violence were employed by private companies. Mental health professionals had the sixth riskiest job. The top five riskiest jobs were held by police officers, private security guards, taxi cab drivers, prison guards, and bartenders.[61] Abdool Azeez was one of those mental health professionals. He was a registered nurse practicing as a psychiatric mental health nurse when he died after trying to pull a patient off of another employee. The patient shoved Azeez against a wall. The experienced psychiatric nurse suffered massive head injuries and died 2 days later.[62]

Although mental health professionals are at risk for workplace violence, that risk extends to health care workers in a variety of practice settings. Nurses working in emergency rooms and primary care settings are also threatened by workplace violence. Unfortunately, the risk does not stop there. Nursing administrators are also victims. The children of Sherry Crandell know the personal pain of workplace violence. Their mother, the nursing administrator at Prince George's Hospital Center in Cheverly, Maryland, was working late in her office one evening when she was brutally raped and strangled. She was murdered January 13, 1998, but her murderer has not been arrested.

Unfortunately, workplace violence affects a significant number of nurses. The Colorado Nurses Association became so concerned about workplace violence that a task force was convened to study the issue. Survey results were analyzed and more than 30% of the nurse respondents reported that they were victims of workplace violence in the previous year.[63]

Preventing workplace violence should be a priority at every health care organization. The first step toward having a safe workplace is to assess the workplace so that potential security problems can be identified and corrected. Next, employers need to create, distribute, and follow written aggressive policies addressing workplace violence issues. Third, employees need to be educated so that the proper procedural steps can be taken in a potentially violent situation. Fourth, employers need to staff properly so that there is follow up on reported incidents, and work as a team.

Cases around the country illustrate the court's willingness to support termination decisions when an action on the part of an employee threatens the safety of the workplace. In Florida, an employer's decision to terminate an employee was upheld after that employee brought a loaded gun to work.[64] In Massachusetts, a court determined that an employer properly terminated an employee who shouted obscenities, cleared another employee's desk of everything that was on it, threw office equipment and furniture, and knocked down several office partitions. The judge declared that a fundamental requirement of any job was that an employee must not be violent or destructive.[65]

Summary

Nurses continue to work as employees in a growing number of practice settings. As a result, nurses need to understand federal and state laws that have been created to protect nurse-employees. At the same time, more nurses are working as independent contractors. It is important that nurses and health care organizations understand and relate to each other in a way that respects those differences, and that is consistent with the actual employment status of the nurse. Confusion about a nurse's employment status can have devastating effects for the nurse and organization.

Whether practicing as an employee or independent contractor, there are contemporary clinical issues that face nurses, including being subject to abandonment allegations, working mandatory overtime, needlestick and sharps injuries, inadequate staffing, and retaliation for reporting unsafe conditions. It is only through the collective effort of nurses in every state that these issues are going to be resolved. State and federal legislative initiatives are underway, but nurses need to be sure that their perspectives and experiences are shared with policymakers so that proposed legislation becomes part of the statutory landscape that protects nurses.

End Notes

1. 591 N.Y.S. 2d 99 (N.Y. 1992).
2. 492 S.E. 2d 103 (S.C. 1997).
3. 311 S.E. 2d 481 (Ga. 1983).
4. 139 Cal.App. 3d 361 (Ca. 1983).
5. 851 S.W.2d 617 (Mo. 1993).
6. No. 1-95-2346 (Appeal from the Circuit Court of Cook County, February 20, 1997).
7. No. COA98-1299 (N.C. Ct. App. Aug. 17, 1999).
8. American Nurses Association (ANA). 2000 *Opposing the use of mandatory overtime as a staffing solution.* Washington, D.C.: ANA House of Delegates Action Report, CNPE-2, American Nurses Association.
9. American Nurses Association. 1999. *Nursing Facts: Needlestick Injury.* Available from URL: http://www.nursingworld.org/readroom/fsneedle.
10. Cardo, D.M.. November 3, 2000. *Needlestick injuries and bloodborne infection.* A presentation at the annual meeting of the Intravenous Nurses Society. Kissimmee, FL: Needlestick Safety Issues in Infusion Therapy.
11. The Exposure Prevention Information Network (EPINet) at the University of Virginia, Charlottesville, Virginia. Available from URL: http://www.med.virginia.edu/epinet.
12. 747 F. Supp. 285 (Pa. 1990).
13. 24 Cal. Rptr. 2d 348 (1993).
14. 866 P.2d 218 (Mt. 1993).
15. 630 So. 2d 861 (La. 1993).
16. 632 N.E. 2d 603 (Oh. 1993).
17. 1994 U.S. District Court, LEXIS 21284.
18. 1994 Connecticut Superior Court, LEXIS 2621.

19. 1997, LWUSA, "Connecticut: Yale Med Student Who Got HIV Wins $12.2 million."

20. 1995 Tennessee, LEXIS 601.

21. 913 F. Supp. 879 (Pa. 1995).

22. 648 N.Y.S. 2d 880 (N.Y. 1996).

23. 930 F. Supp. 1083 (Pa. 1996).

24. 861 P.2d 295 (Ok. 1993).

25. 380 N.Y.S.2d 116 (N.Y. 1976).

26. 745 S.W.2d 120 (Ar. 1988).

27. Willmann, J. 1998. Texas Supreme Court upholds "whistle blower" protections. *Texas Nursing.* Available from URL: http://texasnurses.org/service...ications/tn_mag/jun98-whistle.html.

28. 29 U.S.C. Section 621.

29. 42 U.S.C. Section 1201 et seq.

30. No. 96-7174. (United States Court of Appeals, 3rd circuit, April 15, 1998).

31. Colker, R. 1999. The Americans with Disabilities Act: A windfall for defendants. *Harvard Law Review* 34: 99.

32. *Burch v. Coca-Cola Co.,* June 30, 1995, U.S. District Court for the Northern District of Texas.

33. *Howe v. Hull,* 3:92CV7658 November 21, 1994, U.S. District Court for the Northern District of Ohio.

34. No. 95-2469, 1995 WL 566954 (8th Circuit, September 27, 1995).

35. No. 97-156, June 25, 1998.

36. 137 F.3d 398 (6th Cir. 1998).

37. EEOC Guidelines on Discrimination Based on Sex, Section 1604.11.

38. 97 F.3d 803 (5th Cir., 1996).

39. No. 3AN-93-10461 Civil (Third Judicial District Superior Court of Alaska, June 28, 1995).

40. 29 U.S.C. Section 1162.

41. 29 U.S.C. Section 206(d).

42. 29 U.S.C. Section 201 et seq.

43. P.L. 103-3.

44. Conklin, R. 1999. Father denied parental leave; Wins $350,000. *LawyersWeekly USA* March 22: B10 (99LWUSA 282).

45. 29 U.S.C. 151 et seq.

46. 331 NLRB 92 (2000).

47. 420 U.S. 251 (1975).

48. Lovern, E. 2000. New sharps law may stick some providers. *Modern Healthcare* November 13: 6.

49. Ibid.

50. Ibid.

51. American Nurses Association. 2000. Available from URL: http://www.nursingworld.org/gova/state/2000/needllg.

52. 29 U.S.C. Section 651 et seq.

53. 28 U.S.C.A. Section 1346 et seq.

54. 67 Oklahoma Bar Journal 206 (January 20, 1996).

55. Joel III, L.G. 1996. *Every employee's guide to the law.* New York: Pantheon Books; 279.

56. 579 N.W.2d 343 (Mi. 1998).

57. 42 U.S.C Section 2000e.

58. 29 U.S.C. Section 201 et seq.

59. 29 U.S.C. Section 206(d).

60. California Code of Civil Procedure Section 527.8, January 1, 1995.

61. Lardner, G. 1998. Violence at work is largely unreported. *The Washington Post* July 27: A2.

62. American Nurses Association. 1998. Nurse killed in Florida. *The American Nurse* November/December: 8.

63. Carroll, V., Morin, K. 1998. Workplace violence affects one-third of nurses: Survey of nurses in seven SNAs reveal staff nurses most at risk. *The American Nurse* September/October: 15.

64. *Hindman v. GTE Data Services, Inc.,* 11th Cir, No. 93-1046-CIV-T-17C.

65. *Mazzarella v. U.S. Postal Service,* 849 F. Supp. 89 (Ma. 1994).

The Nurse as an Independent Contractor 6

Introduction

Although nurses have traditionally worked as employees in acute care settings, expanded practice opportunities in less traditional settings have seen many nurses move from employee to independent contractor status. For many, working as an independent contractor is preferable to working as an employee. As an independent contractor, an individual enjoys a level of autonomy that is uncharacteristic of employee status, determining the manner and means by which the services being rendered are performed. For organizations, independent contractors are also appealing. Additional expert human resources can be added on a short-term, project-by-project basis, payroll taxes do not have to be withheld, no health or retirement benefits have to be paid, and there is no obligation to pay unemployment taxes. In addition, the number of individuals working on behalf of an organization can vary depending on the needs of the organization.

However, problems result when individuals categorized as independent contractors are actually treated like employees. Microsoft recently dealt with this issue. At Microsoft, a number of individuals signed independent contractor agreements, agreeing to work on specific projects. When the Internal Revenue Service (IRS) audited Microsoft's payroll records, however, it concluded that the independent contractors should have been classified as employees, and required Microsoft to pay back taxes and overtime associated with the misclassification. The IRS reclassified the individuals as employees because the independent contractors were integrated with the Microsoft workforce at large, worked the same core hours and as team members with other Microsoft employees, reported to the same supervisors as did permanent Microsoft employees, and used office equipment, space, and supplies provided by Microsoft. Microsoft reclassified the individuals and paid the required taxes and overtime. Then, eight of the individuals who had previously been considered independent contractors asked that they be given employee benefits that should have accrued while they were considered independent contractors.

The matter was eventually heard by the Ninth Circuit Court of Appeals, where the court determined that the previously classified independent contractors could not be excluded from the employment benefits afforded to permanent Microsoft employees.[1] As a result, these previously reclassified individual were allowed to participate in Microsoft's generous and lucrative 401(k) and stock option programs.

As practice options are explored by nurses, it is important to clearly establish whether nurses are going to be considered independent contractors or employees. Following that determination, the details associated with the working relationship can be addressed. This is especially true for advanced practice nurses. Now that nurse practitioners and clinical nurse practitioners can be directly reimbursed by Medicare regardless of the geographic setting in which they practice, these advanced practice nurses will have an opportunity to forge independent contractor agreements with health care organizations, health plans, and practice groups. To protect their interests, it will be important for advanced practice nurses to have a better understanding of the contractual issues that surround independent contractor agreements.

In an effort to provide nurses with a basic understanding of contracts and to outline some of the key terms in independent contractor agreements, this chapter provides background information about contracts, identifies key contractual terms that are likely to be addressed in independent contractor agreements, and outlines some of the legal issues courts are addressing when it comes to independent contractor agreements. First, different types of contracts will be discussed. Then, some of the contractual terms that should be included in independent contractor agreements will be addressed. Finally, a number of the legal issues that arise for independent contractors will be explored.

Contract Types

Contracts are promises or sets of promises that outline the rights and responsibilities of the parties to it. Where one or more party fails to perform in accordance with their articulated rights and responsibilities, that failure is termed a *breach*. When a breach occurs, remedies outlined in the agreement are available to the nonbreaching party. In addition, courts will award remedies to nonbreaching parties.

Contracts are usually categorized by the way in which they are formed as either express, implied, or quasi. *Express contracts* are promises or sets of promises that are agreed to verbally or in writing. *Implied contracts* are promises or sets of promises that are formed by the conduct of the parties to the contract. *Quasi-contracts* are really not considered contracts, but are used by courts to allow one or more parties to the quasi-contract to avoid unjust enrichment at the expense of the other party or parties.

Some contracts, whether express or implied, are considered invalid and are not enforced by courts. Unenforceable contracts are categorized as void, voidable, or unenforceable. A *void contract* is one that, when created, was without any legal force or effect. For example, a contract to commit a crime is void and unenforceable. A *voidable contract* is a contract that one or more parties may elect to void. This is the kind of contract that is created when minors or the mentally ill are parties. *Unenforceable contracts* are those that may be valid but not enforced because of the defenses that may be asserted by one or more party to the contract. This kind of contract exists when one party argues that the contract was entered into by mistake.

For any contract to be enforced, the parties must have reached a meeting of the minds about the terms of the contract. This process is called mutual assent. *Mutual assent* is achieved when one party makes an offer, and the other party unequivocally accepts the offer.

An offer that makes acceptance possible only by performing a specific act results in the formation of a *unilateral contract*. On the other hand, if there is an exchange of promises between the contracting parties, a *bilateral contract* is formed. The distinction is important because offerors are generally thought to be in an advantageous position with unilateral contracts. Courts recognize this and will generally consider a contract to be unilateral where the terms of the contract clearly indicate that a unilateral contract is being executed.

In addition to offer and acceptance, contracts will be enforced only if consideration is given. Consideration is bargained for exchange. In a bilateral contract, the parties exchange promises, whereas in a unilateral contract, the parties exchange a promise for an act.

With independent contractor agreements, mutual assent will be achieved when the parties to the agreement sign it. That contract will usually be considered a bilateral contract—one in which both parties agree to exchange promises. For nurses, they will agree to provide a specific set of services in exchange for payment for the delivery of those services. Because of the agreement to exchange promises, the agreement will be considered enforceable because it is supported by consideration.

Contractual Terms Included in Independent Contractor Agreements

Independent contractor agreements can be struck with a handshake or with the stroke of a pen. Agreements struck with a handshake, although honorable, may prove to be frustrating, unworkable, and largely unenforceable because many of the issues addressed in written agreements are absent. To avoid the distractions that arise with implied or verbal contracts, it is advisable to execute express contracts in writing.

Written agreements can be brief, confined to a few pages, or they can be lengthy, detailed documents. The length and terms of the contract depend on the specific agreement being negotiated, as well as the needs of the parties. Regardless of the length of an independent contractor agreement, there are terms that are typically included. Among the usual provisions are the following: Scope; Effective Date; Relationship and Responsibilities of the Parties; Confidentiality; Conflict of Interest; Compensation; Indemnification and Subrogation; Dispute Resolution; Term, Renewal and Termination; Remedies for Breach; Notices; Modifying and Assigning the Agreement; Severability; Conflict of Laws; Legal Authority; Force Majeure; Covenant Not to Compete; and Signatures.

Scope

This section of an independent contractor agreement introduces activities governed by the agreement. For a nurse who is seeking to become an independent contractor, it is in this section that the services he or she will provide are identified. The services may be stated very broadly, or they may be listed individually. A broadly written scope statement for an advanced practice nurse might state that an independent contractor agrees to provide services as an advanced practice nurse that are consistent with the scope of practice in place in that jurisdiction, and consistent with national practice standards such as the ANA *Scope and Standards of Advanced Practice Registered Nursing*.[2] Another approach, though, is to specifically list the individual services that will be incorporated into the agreement. Either approach can be effective, depending on the circumstances within which the agreement is executed.

Effective Date

It is in this section, the date on which the agreement commences is identified. It is also the date against which timeframes identified in the agreement may be measured. Dates identified in this and other sections of an independent contractor agreement should be clearly written, with numbers and other symbols used sparingly to avoid confusion.

Relationship of the Parties

It is the in *Relationship of the Parties* section that the working relationship of the parties is identified. It is here that the nurse will be identified as either an independent contractor or employee. If the nurse is going to be considered an independent contractor, it is important to keep that status in mind as other contractual provisions are written. Classifying an individual as an independent contractor but prescribing when, where, and how the service will be performed subjects an organization or other entity to having that independent contractor reclassified as an employee and having to pay back taxes, accrual of employment benefits, and penalties.

When a nurse is going to function in an independent contractor role, that nurse will not be eligible for the accrual of sick leave, annual leave, health insurance, and other benefits extended to the organization's employees, unless those issues are addressed in the independent contractor agreement. As a result, it is likely that a statement articulating the list of benefits not extended to the independent contractor as well as those benefits that will be extended will be included in the agreement.

Responsibilities of the Parties

Once the relationship of the parties has been established, the responsibilities of each party can be more easily identified. Like other provisions, this section may be brief, or quite lengthy, comprehensively listing the expectations of each party. Where a nurse is going to work as an independent contractor, it is imperative that the nurse maintain the decision-making ability with regard to the manner and means by which services will be provided. Should a nurse be identified as an independent contractor and then be required to operate in a manner proscribed by the other party, it is likely that the nurse will be considered an employee, and not an independent contractor. If, on the other hand, the agreement being executed is for a nurse who will be considered an employee, it may be reasonable to identify when, where, and how the nurse is to function.

Typically, nurse–independent contractors will have a responsibility to ensure that they are and remain properly credentialed, that they have adequate liability insurance, and that they perform contractual services in a manner that complies with professional practice and ethical standards, as well as applicable local, state, and federal regulations, statutes, and case law. In addition, independent contractors may be asked to promptly disclose any disciplinary action taken against them.

Usually, the organization will ask that the nurse assist with the collection of data that affirms that the nurse is competent. Data will likely be requested regarding a nurse's educational preparation, acquisition of specialty certifications, prior employment, history with requesting practice privileges, liability, criminal and licensure history, membership in professional associations, and issuance and action taken against his or her Drug Enforcement Agency (DEA) number. In addition, nurse–independent contractors may be asked to provide information regarding the nurses' population of clients previously served, charge per encounter, visits per hour, visit frequency, incidence of diagnostic procedure use, admission and readmission rates, complication and mortality rates, outcomes, accessibility and availability history, appointment waiting times, and after hours coverage history. Credentialing aspects of the nurse's practice are dealt with in more detail in Chapter 11.

Although nurses will have their responsibilities delineated in independent contractor agreement, organizations with whom they contract should also have their responsibilities delineated. In that regard, it is the organization's responsibility to execute contracts that are consistent with the organization's bylaws. It is also the organization's responsibility to have sound corporate compliance programs in place, and to provide the independent contractor with the information he or she needs to provide the agreed to services. These and other organizational responsibilities can be stated broadly, or can be delineated specifically and in detail.

Confidentiality

The confidentiality section of independent contractor agreements deals with information and documents that are considered confidential. The responsibilities of the parties with regard to this information and these documents will also be outlined. Some confidentiality provisions simply state that confidential, proprietary, and trade secret information shall not be disclosed to third parties. Although this approach is concise, the question then becomes what specific information is confidential, or proprietary, and what documents contain trade secrets. If there are questions about what specific information is protected, it is prudent to have the issue clarified so that potential breaches of confidentiality are minimized.

Conflict of Interest

Conflict of interest provisions are added to independent contractor agreements in an effort to ensure that both parties are acting in the best interest of the party. Potentially conflicting loyalties can be problematic, and should be avoided. Typically, conflict of interest provisions require the party who becomes aware of a potential conflict to promptly disclose it to the other party. Where these provisions are included in a nurses' independent contractor agreement, it is important for nurses to consider ensuring that the conflict of interest clause does not affect clients or business relationships. For instance, a nurse's prescribing habits ought to reflect what medication is most effective for the patient, not an interest or investment the nurse has in a specific drug or drug company.

Compensation

Compensation provisions in independent contractor agreements delineate the payment that will be rendered once agreed to services are provided. The sum may be listed as a total amount of money that will be paid over the course of the contract, or it may be listed as an incremental amount, paid according to established benchmarks. Typically, caps will be identified that limit the total amount of money that will be paid over the course of the agreement, as well as any bonus payments. In addition, health care organizations, plans, and practice groups will likely include a statement conveying that it is the responsibility of the independent contractor to pay all taxes associated with contracted services being provided.

Nurses executing independent contractor agreements need to consider adding specific dates upon which payments will be made to them. When those payments are not forthcoming, a late fee can be imposed so long as it is included in the agreement.

Indemnification and Subrogation

Indemnification and subrogation issues are typically addressed in independent contractor agreements. *Indemnification* is a promise extended from one party to another to hold each other harmless for the wrongdoing of the other party. Typically, contracts extended to nurses contain an indemnification provision. It is important, however, to ensure that the provision is reciprocal, and that both parties are extended the same level of protection.

Subrogation, on the other hand, permits the substitution of one party for another. In health care matters, the doctrine of subrogation has been used by health care facilities to recover monetary losses from nurses sustained after finding the health care organization liable for the negligence or malpractice of the nurse or other employee. Like indemnification, a subrogation provision will likely be included in contracts offered to nurses. Unlike indemnification, subrogation works to impose potential liability on the independent contractor. That being the case, it is important to ensure that the provision, if included at all, is reciprocal, with both parties having a right to subrogation.

Dispute Resolution

Dispute resolution provisions describe the process to be used when the parties disagree about any aspect of the independent contractor agreement. Usually, this provision states that both parties will make their best efforts to promptly resolve all disagreements. Where the resolution of a disagreement proves to be elusive, independent contractor agreements may identify mediation or arbitration as alternative dispute resolution mechanisms. Resolutions identified through one of these mechanisms may or may not be binding on the parties, and may have to be accessed prior to filing a cause of action in court.

Term, Renewal, and Termination

Term, renewal, and termination provisions in independent contractor agreements specify the length of the contract, usually in months or years, as well as the process to be used to renew and terminate the agreement. Renewal clauses typically require one or both parties to notify the other party within a certain period of time of their intention to renew the contract. Some independent contractor agreements approach the issue differently by providing for the automatic renewal of agreements for a specific period of time if one party does not notify the other of its intent to not renew the agreement.

With regard to the termination of agreements, independent contractor agreements commonly require the terminating party to notify the other party within a specific period of time, usually 60 or 90 days, of that party's intent to terminate the agreement. Agreements may be terminated without or with cause. Termination without cause provisions permit the independent contractor to be terminated for any reason or no reason. If it is reciprocal, the independent contractor may terminate the agreement for any reason or no reason. Alternatively, agreements terminated with cause usually result in the immediate termination of the independent contractor agreement. Terminations for cause are typically limited to instances where the independent contractor commits a crime, breaches his or her fiduciary duty to the organization, or acts in a manner that potentially compromises the standing of the organization in the community. Like termination without cause provisions, termination with cause may be exercised by an independent contractor, so long as an identifiable "for cause" event has occurred and the provision permits termination. It is, therefore, important to ensure that termination clauses are reciprocal. For cause events can be any prohibited occurrence, for instance, conviction for any felony, any restriction placed on one's license, or conduct that poorly reflects on the organization.

Remedies for Breach

Independent contractor agreements will likely identify the remedy or consequence of breaching or failing to perform the services as indicated in the agreement. In an attempt to limit the circumstances that can give rise to a breach, and to minimize the amount of money to be paid because of a breach, one party may attempt to limit the definition of breach to one specific provision in the agreement. Where a limited definition of breach is acceptable to the independent contractor, it is important to ensure that the limited definition is reciprocal.

Notices

The notices clause in independent contractor agreements identifies the individuals who are to receive notice from the other party, and contains contact information for each of the individuals listed. The provision also outlines the process to be used when notifying the other party of any occurrence requiring notification. It is important that the notification information be current so that the proper individuals are apprised of any communication between the parties to the agreement.

Modifying the Agreement

Modification provisions in independent contractor agreements permit the parties to modify the terms of the agreement without having to execute a new contract. For multi-year contracts, modification clauses are important because they permit an independent contractor to renegotiate the compensation package, or any other aspect of the agreement on an annual or other agreed to basis. Any specific term of the contract may be modified, so long as the modification provision states that the contract may be modified at any time, so long as both parties agree to the modification. Sometimes, however, modifications will limit the terms that can be modified during the course of the contract. Typically, modifications that do occur throughout the contract term accompany the agreement in the form of an addendum.

Assigning the Agreement

Assignment provisions in independent contractor agreements either permit or prohibit the assignment of the contract from one of the parties to another individual or entity. Where assignment is permitted, one party may pass a contract on to a third party. That third party would then assume the responsibility for performing in accordance with the terms of the contract. Where, on the other hand, assignment is prohibited, the agreement cannot be sold or transferred to another party.

Severability

Severability clauses help to keep noncontested and enforceable provisions of the independent contractor agreement in effect. Sometimes, one specific provision of an agreement will be disputed, and deemed unenforceable, and severability clauses permit that to occur without affecting the remainder of the contract.

Conflict of Laws

The conflict of laws clause in an independent contractor agreement usually identifies the jurisdiction within which the agreement was executed, as well as the jurisdiction that will govern any contractual disputes that may arise. It is important for nurses to know what jurisdictions are listed because that is the jurisdiction that the nurse is consenting to be subject to, and is the place wherein contract-based disputes will be heard.

Legal Authority

The legal authority section of an independent contractor agreement states that the parties to the contract have the authority to enter into the agreement. This provision ensures that only the individuals with the authority to bind the parties are participating in the negotiation and execution of the independent contractor agreement.

Force Majeure

The force majeure clause of an independent contractor agreement ensures that the contract will not be considered to be breached where an act of God prohibits one party from performing in accordance with the terms of the contract. Acts of God include natural disasters like floods, earthquakes, tornados, hurricanes, wars, and riots, and have the effect of putting the performance requirements on hold until performance can be reasonably completed.

Covenant Not to Compete

Covenants not to compete limit an independent contractor's ability to enter into any ventures that would compete with the interests of the organization, plan, or practice group with whom they are contracting. Typically, covenants not to compete are time limited. That is, an independent contractor will be prohibited from entering into any ventures that directly or indirectly compete with the other party for a period of 2 years.

When a covenant not to compete is included in an independent contractor agreement, it is important for the independent contractor to know what organizations or entities the other party considers to be within the scope of the covenant not to compete. It is also important to clarify what the other party means by the use of the term *interests*, and to limit the applicable period to as narrow a time as possible.

In exchange for retaining this covenant in an agreement, an independent contractor should give serious consideration to requiring the other party to execute an exclusive agreement. The independent contractor might also ask for the right of first refusal on all projects for which the independent contractor is qualified.

Signatures

The signatures section of an independent contractor agreement is the place where the parties sign and date the document. After the parties sign the agreement, it is considered to be executed. An agreement that is executed signifies that the parties have reached a meeting of the minds and that both parties intend to interact with each other in accordance with the terms of the contract.

Although most independent contractor agreements contain some combination of provisions identified, there are contemporary issues that need to be addressed by nurses who wish to work as an independent contractor. Those issues include the proprietary rights of the parties and incentives.

Proprietary Rights and Incentives

Proprietary rights of the parties should be discussed by the parties considering entering into a contractual relationship. Who owns what tangible and intangible property is important to clarify at the beginning of contractual relationship so that royalty arrangements can be explored, and restrictions on use, if any, can be articulated. Tangible personal property might include equipment, supplies, or furnishings. Intangible property includes things like intellectual property and good will. Where these issues have been addressed during the contract negotiation period, when the contract expires or is terminated, the parties are clear about what property they each own.

With regard to incentives, it is important for nurses to avoid agreeing to participate in any incentive arrangement that is based on the denial or rationing of care or schemes to acquire new patients. Incentive arrangements that fit into this category include any limitations on the numbers of diagnostic tests that can be performed, admissions ordered, patients seen in clinic settings, or drugs prescribed within any specific period of time. Engaging in these kinds of activities subjects health care professionals to fraud and abuse allegations and to breach of fiduciary duty causes of action. However, incentives can be based on the achievement of quality outcomes, and can be beneficial for nurses, the organizations for whom they are working, and for the patients for whom they are caring. These quality-based incentives can stimulate an improved quality of care.

Legal Issues Associated with Independent Contractor Agreements

Independent contractor agreements are executed in an effort to establish the ground rules the parties agree to follow. However, these agreements are the subject of some litigation. To date, independent contractor litigation in health care has focused almost exclusively on physicians. This trend is expected to change as more nurses begin to function as independent contractors.

Usually, in independent contractor litigation, one party alleges that the other has breached the contract. In other instances, agreements may be deemed illegal. In still other cases, these agreements are the focus in litigation that seeks to hold health care organizations liable for negligent acts committed by independent contractors. Organizations typically argue that they should not be liable for the negligence of independent contractors. Courts, however, have determined that there are circumstances that warrant the imposition of liability against health care organizations. The cases that follow involve physicians, but have been included as instructive examples of how courts resolve legal issues concerning independent contractor health care professionals. Nurses can expect that, as independent contractors, they will be treated similarly.

In 1999, juries in two Florida case awarded health care professionals a total of $24.8 million for breach of contract cases filed against the health care organizations with which the health care professionals had been working. In the first case, a jury awarded $22.8 million to two oncologists, Jerome J. Spunberg and Bruce W. Phillips, who had their practice agreements terminated by Columbia/JFK Medical Center in Atlantis, Florida.[3] The second case was decided in Dade County, Florida. In that case, a jury awarded Ho Chung Tu, a neonatologist, $2 million in damages after it determined that Mt. Sinai Medical Center of Greater Miami breached his contract by directing patients to other physicians.[4]

The agreements at issue in *Spunberg* and *Tu* were not only enforceable, but damages were awarded to the health care professionals because the agreements were breached. However, not all breach of contract cases are resolved in favor of the health care provider.

In *Zipper v. Health Midwest*,[5] a physician had his clinical privileges terminated and sued alleging that in so doing the hospital breached its contract arguing that hospital bylaws were not followed. The case was heard by the Missouri Court of Appeals, which ruled that Health Midwest was not liable for breach of contract. In reaching that conclusion, the court noted that Health Midwest had a preexisting duty to adopt bylaws. That duty, according to the court, was independent of Health Midwest's relationship with the physician. As such, there was no valid consideration. Consequently, Midwest Health was permitted to terminate the physician's privileges.

Although some agreements entered into by health care professionals are not only unenforceable, some are considered illegal. When that occurs, health care professionals are subject to civil and criminal sanctions. Jeremy N. Miller makes that point in an article published in the June 28, 1999, edition of *American Medical News*.[6] In the article, Miller talked about the importance of health care professionals ensuring that their agreements adhere to the Medicare-Medicaid anti-kickback law.[7] Robert LaHue and Ronald LaHue, brothers and osteopathic physicians, were convicted because an agreement they entered into violated the Medicare-Medicaid anti-kickback law. According to the agreement entered into by the LaHues and a hospital, the osteopaths received an annual fee for referring nursing home patients to the hospital at which they were administrators. Receiving money or other remuneration in return for referring Medicare or Medicaid patients is prohibited. If their convictions are affirmed, the osteopathic physicians face spending 35 years in prison and paying sizable monetary fines.

Liability imposed on the LaHues is indicative of the willingness of courts to hold independent contractors responsible for their actions. Typically, independent contractor agreements impose liability on individual health care providers rather than on the health care organization in which independent contractors practice. There are exceptions. *Jackson v. Power*[8] illustrates this principle.

In *Jackson,* 16-year-old Brett Jackson was seriously injured when he fell from a cliff. He was airlifted to the emergency room at Fairbanks Memorial Hospital (FMH). Brett was examined by John Power, MD. Dr. Power's examination revealed multiple lacerations and abrasions of Brett's face and scalp, multiple contusions and lacerations of the lumbar area, several broken vertebrae, and gastric distention suggesting possible internal injuries. Dr. Power ordered several tests, but failed to order certain procedures that could have been used to ascertain whether there had been damage to Brett's kidneys. This damage was undetected for approximately 9 to 10 hours after Brett's arrival at FMH, and ultimately caused Brett to lose both of his kidneys.

Brett Jackson and his mother, Linda Estrada, filed suit. In their complaint they alleged negligence in the diagnosis, care, and treatment Jackson received at FMH. Brett sought to hold FMH vicariously liable as a matter of law for the medical care rendered by Power. Dr. Power was not a Fairbanks Memorial Hospital employee, but an independent contractor employed by Emergency Room, Inc. Brett Jackson asserted that the even though Dr. Power was not an employee at FMH, the doctrine of apparent or ostensible authority should be used to imposed liability on the hospital for Dr. Power's failure to provide proper care and treatment.

In considering the issue, the court looked at cases decided in other jurisdictions. They found a strong trend toward imposing liability against hospitals that permitted or encouraged patients to believe that independent contractor–physicians were, in fact, authorized agents of hospitals. The court observed that other courts consistently held hospitals vicariously liable under a doctrine called ostensible or apparent agency.

The court pointed out that two factors were relevant to a finding of ostensible agency: (1) whether the patient looked to the institution, rather than the individual physician for care; and (2) whether the hospital held out the physician as its employee. Using these factors, the court determined that ostensible agency applied in Brett's case, and that FMH had a nondelegable duty to provide non-negligent physician care in its emergency room and, therefore, may be liable, in spite of the fact that Dr. Power was not an employee. The Alaska Supreme Court asserted that a jury could have concluded that FMH held itself out as providing emergency care services to the public, and Jackson reasonably believed that Dr. Power was employed by the hospital to deliver emergency room service.

Although *Jackson* focused on the care delivered by an independent contractor physician, nurses can expect that courts will use a similar decision-making process to determine whether or not to hold a health care organization responsible for the alleged acts of negligence of the independent contractor nurse. Where a patient receives care at health care organizations, because of the service the organization offers, and where that care is delivered by an independent contractor nurse, the organization, like FMH, may be responsible for acts of negligence committed by the independent contractor nurse.

The justices, in determining that Brett could pursue his negligence claim against FMH because of the alleged negligence of Dr. Powers, noted that neither Brett nor his mother chose FMH as their preferred place of treatment. They noted that a jury might conclude that FMH held itself out as a hospital that provided emergency care to the public, and that Brett reasonably believed that Dr. Powers was employed by FMH, and given the authority to render emergency care at the hospital. As a result, a jury should be able to hear the evidence presented by both parties and make their decision accordingly.

This emergency room exception was recently considered by the South Carolina Supreme Court. The case was *Simmons v. Tuomey Regional Medical Center*[9] and was filed after a man died because of an alleged failure to properly treat the man's head wound. In that case, the court followed *Jackson* and cases out of Florida and New York, concluding that hospitals have a nondelegable duty to provide non-negligent care in their emergency departments. This duty is likely to extend to anyone providing care, including independent contractor nurses.

Summary

Traditionally, nurses have practiced as employees and not independent contractors. However, this trend is changing as more and more nurses embark on private practice careers and develop entrepreneurial opportunities. Because independent contractor is a relatively new concept, it is important to understand the basic, foundational issues that need to be addressed in independent contractor agreements. This chapter has identified a number of those issues. There may be other issues that are addressed in independent contractor agreements. This is especially true where one party has unique needs or requests. The challenge for both parties is to create a comprehensive agreement in a way that meets the needs of both parties.

Although independent contractor agreements can provide nurses with great flexibility and autonomy, they can also result in the nurse–independent contractor, rather than the employer, being held liable for alleged acts of negligence. In addition, independent contractor agreements may be the focus of litigation themselves. Cases discussed in this chapter demonstrate how courts resolve cases involving independent contractors. It is, therefore, important to have the agreements memorialized in writing, reviewed for compliance with federal and state laws and regulations, and to have the agreements clearly articulate the agreement reached by the parties.

End Notes

1. *Vizcaino v. Microsoft*, 97 F.3d 1187 (9th Cir. 1996).
2. American Nurses Association (ANA). 1997. *Scope and Standards of Advanced Practice Registered Nursing*. Washington, D.C.: American Nurses Publishing.

3. *Spunberg v. Columbia/JFK Medical Center Inc.*, No. CL-97-008937 (Fl. 1999).
4. *Tu v. Mt. Sinai Medical Center of Greater Miami, Inc.*, No. 93-03552 (Fl. 1999).
5. No. 51357. August 4, 1998.
6. Miller, J.N. 1999. Is your medical director agreement illegal? *American Medical News.* June 28: 24–25.
7. 42 U.S.C. 1320 a-7b.
8. 743 P.2d 1376 (Ak. 1987).
9. No. 25143. June 5, 2000.

The Nurse Practicing as Educator 7

Introduction

Courts around the country extend a significant amount of discretion to schools when it comes to evaluating the academic performance of students. However, courts insist that schools, whether public or private, have reasonable, nondiscriminatory, non-arbitrary admissions and academic standards in place, and that those standards be followed. Where admissions and academic standards are not in place, are not followed, or are deemed unreasonable, discriminatory, or arbitrary, liability may be imposed, dismissal decisions reversed, or both. Issues that give rise to significant amount of litigation include catalogs, students with disabilities, dismissing students from an academic program, the responsibility of the school to provide students with a safe environment, warning third parties, and clinical experiences. These areas will be discussed in more detail in this chapter. In addition, intellectual property and the privacy of academic records as emerging issues in academia will be discussed.

Catalogs

Generally, catalogs will be viewed as a contract between an educational institution and student. *Lidecker v. Kendall College*[1] and *The University of Texas Health Science Center at Houston, School of Nursing, et al v. Joy Ann Babb*[2] illustrate this point. In *Lidecker*, Kendall College promised that graduates from the school of nursing would be ". . . prepared to take an examination for licensure and would be prepared for nursing practice."[3] The catalog also indicated that the school of nursing was empowered by relevant agencies to offer the nursing program, but made no reference to its' status as an accredited institution.

The National League for Nursing, a private accrediting body, denied accreditation status to Kendall College. The nursing students were informed of the denial by the National League for Nursing, and of the College's intent to appeal. The matter was appealed, but like the initial accreditation decision, the appeal was denied.

Subsequently, a lawsuit was filed alleging that fraud had been committed by Kendall College. The trial court decided the matter in favor of the College, and the students appealed. The appellate court affirmed the decision of the trial court when it determined that the students failed to prove that the college or its officials committed fraud. The court noted that the college did not breach any promise it made in the course catalog, but observed that colleges will generally be held accountable to present a program to its students in accordance with the descriptions and representations set forth in the catalog.

In *University Health Science Center at Houston,* Joy Ann Babb asked that a temporary injunction be issued against The University of Texas Health Science Center at Houston so that she could complete her course of study in accordance with the 1978–1979 catalog. The injunction was granted, and the Health Science Center appealed the decision. The court of appeals heard the matter and affirmed the trial court's decision to issue an injunction. In making its' decision, the court of appeals observed that schools have the right to change their catalogs. In this case, however, The University of Texas Health Science Center allowed students who began studying under the 1978–1979 catalog description to continue through the program under that same catalog, so long as the student completed the degree requirements within a 6-year period.

Lidecker and *Babb* underscore the importance of catalogs to accurately reflect what it is that students can expect from an educational institution, as well as the court's propensity to hold both parties to the terms of the document. *Lidecker* and *Babb* also serve as reminders to refrain from making guarantees about academic progression or graduation, and to reserve the right to require a student to withdraw from the school for any reason it deems sufficient. Behaviors such as academic failure, failure to meet specific course requirements, failure to meet the specific conditions of probation, moral delinquency, and gross misconduct are viewed as typical grounds for required withdrawal.

Students with Disabilities

Schools of nursing must provide qualified students with disabilities that substantially limits a major life activity with reasonable accommodations. This obligation stems primarily from the passage of the Americans with Disabilities Act (ADA) discussed in Chapter 5.

Students with disabilities who qualify for ADA protection must be given the opportunity to succeed in educational environments. However, educational institutions are not required to fundamentally alter the nature of the program, lower their academic standards, or substantially alter their academic requirements. When a qualified student with a disability requests an accommodation, the reasonableness of the request must be considered, as well as whether or not the request adversely effects one of the essential elements of the program. Where the request is reasonable and does not adversely effect one of the essential elements of the program, the accommodation must be granted. Failure to grant a request for reasonable accommodation can subject the educational institution to an investigation and sanctions by the Civil Rights Division, Disability Rights Section of the U.S. Department of Justice.

Darian v. University of Massachusetts[4] explores the application of the ADA in educational settings, and in the context of the facts presented, identified what constituted a reasonable accommodation extended by the University. In *Darian,* a pregnant nursing student in the last semester of the nursing program at the University of Massachusetts, began experiencing significant complications associated with her pregnancy, including severe pelvic bone pain, uterine irritation, contractions, and pain, as well as back pain. The U.S. District Court for the District of Massachusetts determined that these conditions qualified Darian for ADA protection.

After finding that Darian was a qualified student with a disability, the court contemplated whether or not the accommodations proffered by the university were reasonable. In outlining its rationale, the court reviewed the series of events that transpired between the time that Darian requested that she not be required to see patients in the clinical portion of the community health course in which she was enrolled and Darian's filing of this lawsuit.

In concluding that the university extended Darian a reasonable accommodation, the court found that the university made arrangements for Darian to

▌ make up missed clinical time;
▌ not have patient assignments in three clinical experiences;
▌ see one patient per clinical day, in accordance with the order of her physician;
▌ take an incomplete in the clinical portion of the course and completing it the following semester, while completing the classroom portion of the course in the current semester; and
▌ retake the course, so that she could complete the requirements for a nursing degree.

These steps, according to the court, suggested that the university made a diligent assessment of the options available and offered accommodations that were considered reasonable. As a result, Darian was prohibited from pursuing her ADA claim against the university.

To protect educational institutions from ADA violations, schools of nursing should process requested accommodations with the diligence of the University of Massachusetts in the *Darian* case. Schools that exercise that level of diligence substantially increase the likelihood of being exonerated like the University of Massachusetts.

Dismissing Students

Dismissing students is unpleasant, and often contentious for students and faculty members. As a result, a significant amount of litigation occurs following the dismissal decision. It is, therefore, imperative that clear, reasonable, nondiscriminatory policies and procedures govern the disciplinary, grievance and dismissal processes. *Morin v. Cleveland Metropolitan General Hospital School of Nursing*[5] illustrates the willingness of courts to uphold dismissal decisions where those decisions are made conscientiously, with clear deliberation, and based on an evaluation of a students' entire academic career.[6]

In *Morin,* Victoria Morin was expecting to graduate from the 3-year nursing program in which she was enrolled. Approximately 2 months before graduation, on April 2, Morin began the clinical component of a Medical/Surgical III course. Her clinical instructor was Mary Pannitto, RN. Over the course of the next 2 days, instructor Pannitto observed six separate instances of Morin practicing unsafely. As each instance was observed, Pannitto provided Morin with instruction and evaluation. On April 4, Pannitto informed Morin that the matter would be brought to the attention the Admissions and Standards Committee. On April 5, Pannitto provided Morin with written notification of her failure to meet seven course objectives, of Pannitto's intent to take the matter to the Admissions and Standards Committee, and of Morin's right to make a 15-minute presentation to the Admissions and Standards Committee. On April 6, after hearing the presentations from Pannitto and Morin, the Admissions and Standards Committee recommended that Morin be dismissed from the nursing program. Three days later, on April 9, the recommendation of the Admissions and Standards Committee was reviewed by the entire nursing faculty. In addition, the faculty reviewed Morin's entire record as a student. Thereafter, the nursing faculty voted unanimously to dismiss Morin based on her unsafe nursing practice, and poor pattern of performance.[7]

Following the vote of the faculty, Morin filed a lawsuit against the Cleveland Metropolitan General Hospital School of Nursing asserting that her dismissal from the nursing program was arbitrary and capricious, constituting a due process violation.[8] Morin thought that her dismissal was arbitrary and capricious because it occurred in the final course of her senior year after only three clinical experiences. The trial court disagreed with Morin, and granted the School of Nursing's request to dismiss the case. Morin appealed, but the court of appeals affirmed the decision of the trial court. In affirming the trial court's decision to dismiss this matter, the court of appeals noted that judicial intervention occurs in academic decision-making cases only where the dismissal is clearly shown to be arbitrary and capricious. In this case, the court of appeals determined that dismissal decision did not meet the arbitrary and capricious standard. The School of Nursing

▌ clearly advised the student of the requirements for completing the nursing program and the consequences for failing to comply with those requirements;

- advised the student of her deficiencies and gave her an opportunity to respond;
- referred the matter to the Admissions and Standards Committee, and then was considered by the entire nursing faculty;
- dismissed the student based upon her failure to meet curriculum guidelines and her poor pattern of performance as a whole; and
- permitted the student the opportunity to reapply for admission.[9]

Prudent academic environments have dismissal policies and procedures in place that are consistent with the principles delineated in *Morin*. Schools that do not yet have such policies and procedures in place should give serious consideration to creating and beginning to follow *Morin*-like processes when dismissing students.

Providing Students a Safe Environment

Although schools are not insurers of a students' complete safety, they do have an obligation to exercise reasonable care in the protection of students. Where reasonable care is not taken, schools may find themselves negligent in providing a safe educational environment. *District of Columbia v. Jane Doe, et al*[10] illustrates this point. In this case, a 10-year-old student was taken at knife point from the school premises by an unknown intruder to a wooded section of a nearby park and raped. After she was raped, she ran back to the school where she reported the incident. The student was taken to a hospital where she was examined and received psychiatric treatment. Subsequently, the student's mother sued on behalf of the student alleging that the school failed to provide her daughter a safe environment. The jury found the school negligent and awarded the student more than $250,000 in damages.

Although the *District of Columbia* case involved a minor and a grade school, the safety principles delineated in the case should be incorporated in schools across the educational continuum. A security expert who testified on behalf of the student that a school's normal security procedures should include

- locking entrances (including gates and doors) that are not used to enter and exit the school when school is in session;
- maintaining and using properly functioning locking mechanisms on doors;
- visually monitoring and screening all visitors;
- issuing passes to visitors; and
- maintaining properly functioning communication systems.[11]

To ensure that school premises are safe, educational institutions should have a regular procedure in place to inspect and maintain the building and grounds. Doors, windows, and gates need to be properly functioning, as do alarm and communication systems. In addition, individuals on the school property should be readily identifiable.

Warning Third Parties

In any number of classes, students will have opportunities to disclose personal matters. *Brooks v. Logan*[12] suggests that there are times when such disclosures should be reported to third parties. Disclosures that need to be reported to third parties include those indicating that the student may injure himself or another person. In *Brooks*, a high school student committed suicide and his parents sued the student's teacher and the school district alleging that they failed to warn the student's parents and take appropriate action with regard to this student's suicidal tendencies. The Idaho Supreme Court determined that the student's parents could pursue this case against the school district and teacher because there was a statutory duty to exercise reasonable care in supervising students. The Idaho Supreme Court specifically determined that the school district was not immune to liability under the state torts claims act, and that the duty to warn the student's parents or seek appropriate assistance was an operational responsibility for which the school district could not escape liability.

Clinical Experiences

Clinical experiences are unique to schools preparing students for a career in health care. They provide an opportunity for students to apply principles and perform skills taught in the classroom. It is in the clinical experience that some students experience difficulty. When that occurs, it is important for schools to clearly articulate what the consequences are for unacceptable clinical performance. *Gasper v. Bruton*[13] is the landmark case in this area. In *Gasper*, a licensed practical nurse (LPN) student was dismissed from a practical nursing program for poor clinical performance. The student's academic performance in the classroom was acceptable; however, she had been counseled on numerous occasions for, among other things, the inability to organize and complete assignments, and the unsafe handling of a newborn. Prior to her dismissal, Gasper was placed on probation, and was told that if her performance did not improve, that she would be dismissed from the program. Two months later, Gasper was dismissed. After unsuccessfully attempting to have the dismissal reversed with the school, Gasper sued, asserting due process violations. The case was heard in a 10th circuit court and the court determined that Gasper's due process rights had been protected, because she was advised of the consequences of continuing to perform below acceptable standards in the clinical environment.

Because the clinical experience is potentially problematic for students, schools, and patients, most schools of nursing require students to have professional liability insurance. The actions of students may result in a negligence cause of action being filed against the student, schools of nursing, and the clinical setting. *Carter v. Anderson Memorial Hospital*[14] involves such a situation.

In *Carter*, Thomas Carter was recovering from serious abdominal surgery in which approximately 15% of his stomach was removed when two nursing students brought a portable x-ray machine into his room so that an abdominal x-ray could be taken. The machine cord became entangled with the machine wheels, and the machine fell on the patient's abdomen. The 24-square-inch machine head landed on Mr. Carter's surgically repaired abdomen, which contained large metal surgical sutures. After the incident, Mr. Carter had to undergo a second surgery because he began hemorrhaging and vomiting blood.[15] Mr. Carter contended that the second operation was needed because of the incident, but hospital representatives asserted that the second operation was needed because Mr. Carter developed an ileus. The jury agreed with Mr. Carter and awarded him $17,500 in actual damages.

It is unclear why Mr. Carter chose to sue only the hospital. He could have sued the hospital, as well as the school of nursing the nursing students were attending, the nursing students themselves, and the clinical faculty member. That being the case, it is important for students to be knowledgeable about every aspect of a patient's treatment, and that students know how to operate any machine or device that is indicated for a particular patient. If a student does not know how to operate a particular machine or device, the student should refrain from attempting to use it for the first time on any patient. When a student has not performed a particular skill or procedure previously, that skill should be supervised when performing it for the first time. Knowledgeable faculty members should closely supervise students in the clinical setting, and ensure that students are prepared to provide competent care to the patients to whom they are assigned. Students who do not come to clinical experiences prepared or knowledgeable about the patient(s) they are to provide care for should not be permitted to provide patient care services. Allowing unprepared students to provide patient care services is dangerous, and can be disastrous for patients, students, the faculty member, the clinical setting, and the school of nursing.

Intellectual Property Issues

Intellectual property is used to refer to the law as it relates to patents, trademarks, and copyrights. *Intellectual property* is any product of the human intellect that is embodied in the goods and services a company offers and by which the company is known. It is a right to exclude others from acting in a certain way toward objects that others may own. Its major forms are patents, copyrights, and trademarks. Patents, trademarks, and copyrights comprise intellectual property, and are distinctive intellectual property rights.

Governed by the Patent Act of 1994,[16] a *patent* is an exclusive right given to an inventor by the U.S. Patent and Trademark Office to make, use, or sell an invention for approximately 17 years throughout the United States. The U.S. Patent and Trademark Office is a division of the U.S. Department of Commerce. A patent is an entitlement to make and market the invention, as well as to exclude others from doing so. Any new and useful process, machine, manufacture, or composition of matter or any new and useful improvement to a current process, machine, or manufacture may be patented. Patent protection can extend abroad if conduct abroad actively induces or contributes to infringement occurring with in the U.S. territory.[17] Many higher education institutions have research departments dedicated to inventing new machines, medicines, and other processes that can improve the quality of life. In these settings, it is important to know whether it is the researcher or the school that will hold the patent on the invention. Not doing so can result in protracted litigation, and can cause the testing and use of the patented item to be delayed for years.

A *trademark,* on the other hand, is the right to prevent others from using a company's product name, slogan, or identifying design. It is any work, name, symbol, or device adopted and used by a company to identify goods and distinguish those goods from those sold by others. Not every word, shape, or symbol receives trademark protection. However, words, shapes, or symbols used in combination and with the purpose of identifying and distinguishing a product may qualify for trademark protection. Trademarks used by service organizations like educational institutions are called service marks. A *service mark* is a trademark used in the sale or advertising of services to identify the services of one person or organization and distinguish them from the services of another person or organization. Failure to obtain trademark or service mark protection permits others to use the name, slogan, or identifying design.

While patents and trademarks are two important intellectual property categories, copyrights are receiving a significant amount of attention in academic settings. Attention to copyright has occurred because of the development of distance education. Generally, a *copyright* is the right to exclude others from using or marketing forms of expression. It is also legal protection given to authors for their original writings (see sidebar).

According to the 1976 Copyright Act, a copyright in any work created after January 1, 1978, begins when the work is fixed in tangible form—when a book is written down or a picture is painted—and lasts for the life of the author plus 50 years after

---

Rights of Copyright Owners

Copyright owners have the right to

- reproduce or make copies of the work;
- prepare adaptations of the work;
- distribute copies of the work to the public;
- perform the work in public; and
- display the work to the public.

The Stevens Institute of Technology Policy

Faculty members:

- are paid to develop online courses;
- own the material in the courses they develop;
- control how the material can be used; and
- receive one-third of the revenue from the purchased use of the course.

The school:

- retains the copyright to the course;
- markets the course;
- receives two-thirds of the revenue from the purchased use of the course.

Anonymous. 2000. The chronicle of higher education. *Online* December 8: A35.

his or her death. Specifically, the Copyright Act of 1976 protects books, newspapers, magazines, music, drama, choreography, films, art, sculpture, computer software, and sound recordings. Each copy of the work to be copyrighted must contain a copyright notice, the date of first publication, and the name of the copyright owner, an application and two copies of the work must be filed with the Copyright Office in Washington, D.C. The two copies that are filed with the Copyright Office are added to the holdings of the Library of Congress.

In educational and other settings, copyright ownership has been the subject of discussion and debate. Some institutions have policies in place requiring that the institution retain the copyright to courses taught, whereas others have policies allowing faculty members to hold the copyright to the course being taught, and still others have shared copyright agreements.

The focus on copyright protection signifies that faculty members and educational institutions both have an interest in holding the copyright on courses developed and taught whether courses are taught in traditional or electronic formats. The challenge, then, is to create a policy that is beneficial to faculty members and to the school. One such policy has been proposed by the Stevens Institute of Technology (see sidebar). Whatever the arrangement, it is important for copyright issues to be addressed early in the faculty member–institution relationship. Failure to clarify these issues can lead to protracted litigation, and can compromise the faculty member–institution relationship in a way that compromises the relationship that faculty members and institutions have with students.

Privacy of Academic Records

The Family Educational Rights and Privacy Act[18] (FERPA) ensures that current and former students have access to their educational records; protects those records from disclosure without the student's voluntary, written consent; and provides parents access to their children's educational records. Educational records include any information, record, file, or document that directly relates to a specific student and is maintained by the institution or an individual acting on behalf of the institution.[19] When disclosing student-specific information, consent of the student is not required when

- disclosures are made internally to school officials or employees who have a legitimate educational interest in inspecting the records;
- records are sent to officials at other schools in which the student intends to enroll; or
- parents request educational records and the student is a claimed dependent for income tax purposes.

FERPA is enforced by the Secretary of Education, and institutions violating FERPA can lose federal funding. FERPA violations have been found to exist when students are asked to grade another student's work. *Falvo v. Owasso Independent School District, No. I-011, et al*[20] is illustrative.

In *Falvo*, several teachers in the Owasso school district in Oklahoma had their students grade another student's assignment or test. The assignment or test would be handed back to the student whose name was on the assignment or test, and each student would call out their own grade to teachers. The mother of three sibling-students filed a class action lawsuit against the school district, the superintendent, assistant superintendent, and principal alleging the practice of having students grade assignments or tests of other students violated the U.S. Constitution and FERPA. The practice of having other students grade papers was the focus of the alleged constitutional and FERPA violations, because the plaintiff-mother said that the process of having children call out grades really did not matter.[21] The mother contended that the initial disclosure to the grading student resulted in constitutional and FERPA violations.

The school district asserted that the grading practice did not violate either the U.S. Constitution or FERPA. The U.S. Court of Appeal agreed with the school district, concluding that the practice did not constitute a constitutional violation. However, the U.S. Court of Appeals disagreed with the school district with regard to FERPA. In concluding that the grading practice violated FERPA, the Court of Appeals observed that the grades students place on each other's assignments or tests are educational records subject to the requirements of FERPA, and disclosure in the manner described by Falvo constituted a FERPA violation.

In light of *Falvo*, what can educators do to continue to involve students in the teaching–learning process, and avoid a FERPA violation? Two alternatives are to obtain parental consent where students are minors, or ask students to not put their names on their assignments or tests that are to be graded by another student.

Summary

Educators value academic freedom, and the U.S. judicial system affords educational institutions significant discretion so long as admissions and academic standards are reasonable, nondiscriminatory, and nonarbitrary. Courts readily enforce the terms contained in catalogs, so great care needs to be taken in drafting the document, and in carrying out promises made in it. In addition, grievance, disciplinary action, and dismissal policies and procedures need to be closely followed. Where those policies and procedures are followed by the institution and not invalidated by a reviewing court because of constitutional or public policy concerns, dismissal decisions will be upheld, even if those decisions are made in the final weeks of a student's academic experience.

Not only do educational institutions need to ensure that the learning environment is reasonable, nondiscriminatory, and reflective of making reasonable accommodations when requested by students with disabilities, they need to ensure that the physical environment safe. Failure to provide a safe environment can yield disastrous results for the school and students. In addition, attention needs to be made to warning third parties when a student's communication with an educator warrants it. Clinical experiences for students need to be closely supervised and regularly evaluated if dismissal decisions are based on clinical performance.

With regard to emerging academic issues, having a clear intellectual property policy and a commitment to protecting academic records are of paramount importance. Distance education has afforded educational institutions new opportunities to meet the educational needs of students around the world. To make the most of these opportunities, clear copyright policies need to be in place and student privacy should be protected.

End Notes

1. 550 N.E. 2d 1121 (Il. 1990).
2. 646 S.W. 2d 502 (Tx. 1982).
3. Ibid, p. 502.
4. 980 F. Supp. 77 (Ma. 1997).
5. 516 N.E. 2d 1257 (Oh. 1986).
6. Ibid, p. 1262.
7. Ibid, p. 1258.

8. Ibid, p. 1259.

9. Ibid, p. 1257.

10. 524 A.2d 30 (D.C. 1987).

11. Ibid, p. 31.

12. 903 P.2d 73 (Id. 1995).

13. 513 F.2d 843 (10th Cir. 1975).

14. 325 S.E. 2d 78 (S.C. 1985).

15. Ibid.

16. 35 U.S.C. §§ 1-376.

17. 35 U.S.C. § 271(b)(c).

18. 20 U.S.C. § 1232.

19. 21. 20 U.S.C. §1232g(a)(4)(A).

20. 229 F.3d 956 (10th Cir. 2000).

21. Ibid, p. 957.

The Nurse Practicing as Administrator   8

Introduction

Nurses practicing in administrative roles are faced with balancing the coordination of patient care services with the consequences that may result when something goes wrong. Inevitably, things go wrong. Sometimes decisions are made without having time to thoroughly identify all of the possible ramifications of pursuing one course of action rather than another. Accordingly, it is important for nurses practicing in administrative positions to be aware, prior to decision-making time, of legal doctrines, causes of action, and steps that can be taken to avoid making decisions that may jeopardize the nurse, patient, employee, and facility. In this chapter, legal doctrines encountered by nurse-administrators and causes of action filed by nurses because of the alleged wrongdoing of nurse-administrators and other executive level decision makers are discussed so that nurse-administrators are better informed about the legal implications of the decisions they make.

Doctrines

Captain of the Ship Doctrine

This doctrine worked to impose liability on surgeons while in the operating room. It was applied when any of the surgeons' assistants, including nurses, acted in an allegedly negligent manner. The *captain of the ship doctrine* concluded that operating room assistants were under the surgeon's control, and that the surgeon should bear the responsibility of that negligence whether or not that assistant was a hospital employee. *Ravi v. Williams*[1] applies the doctrine. In *Ravi,* Elly Williams went to a clinic complaining of back and pelvic pain, as well as vaginal bleeding. Dr. P.B. Ravi performed a hysterectomy on Ms. Williams 2 days later. Nine days after the surgery, Ms. Williams began experiencing severe abdominal pain and emergency surgery was performed. During the surgery, a surgical sponge was removed from Ms. Williams' abdomen. Ms. Williams sued Dr. Ravi, the hospital, and another physician alleging that negligence occurred when the surgical sponge was left inside her abdomen. Dr. Ravi claimed that he was not negligent because he relied on the sponge count being correct, and that he did not close the Ms. Williams' abdomen until he was told that the sponge count was correct. Applying the captain of the ship doctrine, the court determined that it was the physician who bore the responsibility for removing sponges from the patient's body and that responsibility was not one that could be delegated, in spite of the fact that the task of counting was done by a scrub and circulating nurse.

However, in *Franklin v. Gupta,*[2] the captain of the ship doctrine was rejected. The court determined that the doctrine would not be applied because surgeons do not always have the authority to control all operating room personnel. Instead, the court declared that each defendant—the surgeon, anesthesiologist, certified registered nurse anesthetist (CRNA), and hospital—would be required to show that they acted as reasonable practitioners in this circumstance. The effect of this ruling was to hold the hospital, anesthesiologist, and CRNA accountable for their actions. Historically, surgeons bore the burden of paying for the wrongs that occurred in the operating room. That is no longer the case. *Franklin* and other cases serve as a stark reminder that the captain of the ship can no longer be used to excuse acts of alleged negligence in the operating room. As a result, nurse-administrators need to take aggressive steps need to ensure that all operating room personnel are practicing in accordance with the prevailing standard of care.

Immunity

Immunity was introduced in Chapter 5, and it is included here to ensure that nurse-administrators are aware of the protection from liability nurses have when working as an employee at a governmental entity. For nurses who are employees at governmental entities, they are shielded from liability because of a doctrine called *governmental immunity,* which evolved out of the historical applications of doctrines that are no longer used or that have been significantly restricted: the charitable and sovereign immunity doctrines.

Until the 1940s, courts in many U.S. jurisdictions used the doctrine of charitable immunity to relieve charitable organizations of liability when negligence occurred. In 1946, a Maryland court, in *President and Directors of Georgetown College v. Hughes*[3] explored the charitable immunity doctrine and rejected its application, contending that charitable organizations need to respond as other corporations do for the wrongs inflicted by persons acting on the corporation's behalf about corporate business, and within the course of their employment. In reaching its decision, the court observed that the doctrine of charitable immunity was not needed in contemporary society because modern charity was "big business" and had the capacity to absorb losses.[4] In making that decision, the court looked at how the doctrine of charitable immunity had been applied in other jurisdictions, and determined that the doctrine had been eroding, and was no longer needed.

In spite of the demise of charitable immunity, governmental immunity continues to be asserted in cases brought against governmental entities. Governmental immunity, like charitable immunity, works to shield government employees as well as governmental entities from liability in some negligence causes of action. In *Hyde v. University of Michigan Board of Regents*,[5] the Michigan Supreme Court decided that to the extent that the diagnosis, treatment, and care of patients at a public general hospital or medical facility were activities expressly or impliedly mandated or authorized by the Michigan constitution, statutes, or case law, the hospital or facility was entitled to immunity from tort liability. Immunity from tort liability was not extended to activities conducted primarily for profit. Even though a public hospital had excess revenue, the court determined that it did not operate its hospitals primarily to produce a profit. The history of the hospital revealed that it was established to provide hospital and medical care to the communities surrounding the hospital.

Immunity can be an important defense for nurses, and nurse-administrators practicing in government-affiliated institutions should not underestimate the importance of this doctrine when delineating the benefits of working at a government health care organization. Immunity is what caused one trial court to dismiss nurse-defendants in a case where the nurse-defendants were accused of failing to assess, evaluate, and advise other health care professionals of the status of the patient. In that case, the trial court judge noted that the nurses were dismissed because a statute shielded them from liability. They were shielded because their alleged acts of negligence were committed within the scope of their employment as employees at a government-affiliated health care organization. Although the court pointed to a sovereign immunity act as statutory support for dismissing the nurses, the status of the hospital as a governmental entity is what shielded these nurses from personal liability. The case was *Jones v. Baptist Memorial Hospital-Golden*,[6] and was eventually heard by the Mississippi Supreme Court. The Mississippi Supreme Court Justices affirmed the trial court judge's dismissal, concluding that the nurses were immune from liability.

Corporate Negligence

This doctrine imposes liability on a corporation because of the acts of individuals working on behalf of the corporation. For health care organizations, corporate negligence imposes liability on the organization for acts of negligence committed by those practicing at the organization. Corporate negligence is imputed against health care organizations because they have a duty that cannot be delegated to ensure that the safety and well-being of patients are protected. The landmark case on corporate negligence is *Darling v. Charleston Community Memorial Hospital*.[7] In *Darling*, Dorrence Kenneth Darling II was admitted to the emergency room at Charleston Community Memorial Hospital, in Charleston, Illinois, after sustaining an injury to his right leg in a college football game. X-rays revealed that Dorrence sustained a comminuted fracture of his right tibia and fibula. Dorrence was taken to the operating room so that the fractures could be reduced. Dr. Alexander, the physician treating Dorrence, then applied a full-length leg cast. X-rays were taken again, and good bone alignment was seen. Dorrence was then taken to a hospital room where his casted leg was elevated on pillows, and a heat cradle was used to help dry the cast. The heat cradle was removed, as ordered, approximately 24 hours after it had been placed over the cast.

Right away, the nurses' notes contain entries that refer to the pain Dorrence was in, as well as the swollen nature of his toes. In fact, 6 hours after surgery the nurses' notes characterize the toes of Dorrence to be very edematous. Nineteen hours later, the nurses' notes record that Dr. Alexander notched the cast and elevated Dorrence's foot on more pillows. Fifteen hours after Dr. Alexander notched the cast, the nurses' notes show that there was a large blister on Dorrence's right foot. Four hours after that, Dorrence's toes were said to be cyanotic and cold to touch. Five hours later, Dr. Alexander cut the cast again. This time, the cast was cut approximately 3 inches up the foot. The next day, Dr. Alexander split the cast on both sides, and opened some of the blisters on Dorrence's right foot.

The nursing staff made regular references to the pain that Dorrence was in, as well as to attempts made to relieve Dorrence of this pain. However, the pain persisted. Then, approximately 10 days after surgery, one nurse recorded the presence of a foul odor coming from the fractured leg. Four days later, Dorrence was transferred to another hospital. Ultimately, his leg had to be amputated.

Dorrence filed suit, alleging, among other things that the hospital failed to conform to the standards customarily required by accredited hospitals. Allegedly, the hospital failed to provide

1. a licensed, graduate professional nursing service available to Dorrence at all times.
2. qualified personnel adequate to supervise and conduct the supervision of medical patients.
3. adequate hematology and serology examinations.
4. modern and adequate medical library relating to modern orthopedic methods and casting techniques.
5. adequate supervision of the medical treatment rendered to Dorrence.
6. sufficient numbers of licensed, graduate, professional nurses for the bedside care of all patients at all times, and thus failed to have such nurses available for bedside care of Dorrence at all times capable of recognizing the progressive gangrenous condition of Dorrence's right leg, and of bringing the same to the attention of the hospital administration and to the medical staff so that adequate consultation could have been secured and rectified.

The jury agreed with Dorrence and rendered a verdict in his favor. The doctrine of corporate negligence was used to hold the hospital responsible for the acts of the nursing staff and others acting on behalf of the hospital.

The doctrine of corporate negligence is still used today to hold health care facilities responsible for the negligent acts of its employees. Because of that, health care facilities have a economic interest in ensuring that an adequate professional nursing staff is used to provide bedside care. They also have an interest in knowing that the nursing staff is proactive when it comes to detecting, and treating complications, like the postoperative infection. In the *Darling* case, this highly treatable complication, combined with the passiveness of the nursing staff, cost Dorrence his right leg.

Although *Darling* represents the hallmark case in which the corporate negligence is applied, health care organizations need to be aware that current clinical issues could lead to health care organizations defending more corporate negligence cases. Nurse-administrators can minimize the health care organization's risk of being liable under the doctrine of corporate negligence by having staffing systems that respect the rights of staff members and meet the physical and emotional needs of patients. For instance, staffing systems that disregard the religious beliefs of employees could subject the organization to a corporate negligence cause of action. In addition, where a nurse's negligence can be attributed to inadequate or inappropriate staffing, the health care organization could ultimately be found responsible under the theory of corporate negligence.

Res Ipsa Loquitur

Res ipsa loquitur literally means "the thing speaks for itself." It is a doctrine invoked by patients that requires that the defendant show that negligence did not occur, rather than requiring that patients show that negligence did occur. For res ipsa loquitur to apply, the patient must show that he or she was injured, the injury was directly caused by a device or procedure that was solely in the control of the defendant, and the injury was one that did not ordinarily occur in the absence of negligence. If the court determines that the doctrine applies, it presumes negligence on the part of the defendant health care provider and/or facility. It then is up to the defendant to prove that negligence did not occur. That is what happened when the doctrine of res ipsa loquitur was applied in *St. John's Hospital and School of Nursing, Inc. v. Ben D. Chapman.*[8] Here, the Oklahoma Supreme Court applied the doctrine of res ipsa loquitur for the first time in a medical malpractice case.

In *Chapman*, Ben D. Chapman was the guardian for Rose Belle Stand, and he alleged that Rose's right femur was broken when she was improperly turned by the nursing staff at St. John's Hospital. The case went to trial and the jury returned a verdict in favor of Mr. Chapman. The hospital appealed, and the case was heard by the Oklahoma Supreme Court. In deciding to apply the doctrine of res ipsa loquitur, the Court asserted that it was extremely hard to think of a situation any more appropriate for the application of the doctrine than the situation presented in this case. Ms. Stand suffered a stroke, and was unconscious when her leg was broken while being turned in bed by a nurse's aide. The court observed that Ms. Stand could not have done anything to contribute to the breaking of her leg. The entire situation, even Ms. Stand, was under the control of the hospital. As a result, justice demanded application of the res ipsa doctrine in this case

Res ipsa loquitur was also the subject of case recently heard by the Mississippi Supreme Court. In *Coleman v. Rice*,[9] a doctor left a sponge in a patient's body during surgery. The patient asserted that the doctrine of res ipsa loquitur applied, but the trial court disagreed. The Mississippi Supreme Court disagreed with the trial court judge, and concluded that a layperson could understand that the leaving of an object inside a patient during surgery is negligence. As a result, the patient could assert the burden-shifting doctrine of res ipsa loquitur.

The doctrine of res ipsa loquitur continues to be used in cases filed against health care facilities and health care professionals. Nursing administrators should be aware that the doctrine could be asserted by any patient whose level of consciousness is compromised. Historically, the majority of cases invoking the doctrine of res ipsa loquitur involved care delivered in operating rooms. Today, the doctrine can be invoked in cases that do not involve operating rooms. Ambulatory care settings are just as susceptible to res ipsa litigation, especially where conscious sedation and other consciousness-altering medication is administered. As a result, it is imperative that health care organizations permit their health care providers to practice consistent with the standard of care.

Vicarious Liability

Vicarious liability allows liability to be imposed against health care facilities indirectly. Because of the vicarious liability, a health care employer can be held responsible for a negligent act of an employee, and the health care organization can be liable as a principal for the acts of an agent. It is the theory under which the doctrine of respondeat superior arises. *Respondeat superior* literally mean "let the master answer." It is used to impose liability on the master when wrongful acts are committed by the master's servant(s).

Beeck v Tucson General Hospital[10] is a case in which the doctrine of vicarious liability is applied, and the facility held responsible for the actions of a health care provider. In *Beeck*, Carolyn Beeck got pneumonia after a needle was inserted into her spine during a lumbar myelogram while she was a patient at Tucson General Hospital (TGH). An x-ray machine collided with the procedure needle. Beeck brought a malpractice suit against TGH and the radiologists who administered the myelogram.

Dr. Rente and his colleagues were the only authorized radiologists at TGH. Ms. Beeck did not have a choice of radiologists; TGH chose for her. TGH furnished the radiology equipment, and the radiologists paid no rent. Working hours, vacation time, billing, and employment of technicians were all controlled by TGH. It was also TGH that had the right to control the standards of performance for Dr. Rente. Radiology services were an inherent function of the hospital. All facilities, instrumentalities, and administrative services were provided by the hospital. Because of these things, the court determined that an employee–employer relationship existed between Dr. Rente and TGH, and that TGH could be vicariously liable, based on the respondeat superior doctrine, in spite of the fact that TGH claimed that Dr. Rente was an independent contractor.

Causes of Action

Failure to Protect the Patient

For nursing administrators, causes of action can come from a variety of sources, including patients and employees. When a case is filed by a patient, at least one issue will revolve around the alleged failure of the health care facility to protect the patient. *Washington v. Washington Hospital Center*[11] provides an example of how courts deal with patient protection issues.

On November 7, 1987, LaVerne Alice Thompson, a healthy 36-year-old woman underwent elective surgery a the Washington Hospital Center (WHC) for an abortion and tubal ligation. At about 10:45 AM, nurse anesthetist Elizabeth Adland, under the supervision of Dr. Sheryl Walker, the physician anesthesiologist, inserted an endotracheal tube into Ms. Thompson's throat so that oxygen could be delivered and carbon dioxide removed from her lungs. Plaintiffs allege that Nurse Adland inserted the tube into Thompson's esophagus instead of the trachea. After inserting the tube, Nurse Adland ventilated the patient while Dr. Walker observed the rise and fall of Ms. Thompson's chest and listened to breath sounds. Dr. Walker found that breath sounds were equal at the left and right lung fields. Carbon dioxide monitoring was not part of the anesthesiology protocol at WHC. However, Dr. Dermot A. Murray, WHC's Chairman of the Anesthesiology Department testified that he requested carbon dioxide monitors in December, 1986 or January, 1987. In the requisition Dr. Murray submitted, he stated that the end tidal carbon dioxide units were necessary to monitor the administration of anesthesia in each of the hospital's operating rooms, stating that if the monitors were not provided, the hospital would fail to meet the national standard of care. According to the requisition, the monitors were to be fully operational in July, 1987. To bolster his request for monitors, Dr. Murray attached a copy of an August, 1986 article from the *Journal of American Medical Association* entitled "Standards for Patient Monitoring During Anesthesia at Harvard Medical School."

At about 10:50 AM, while the surgery was underway, Dr. Nathan Bobrow, the surgeon noticed that Thompson's blood was abnormally dark, and reported the condition to Nurse Adland, who checked Thompson's vital signs and found them to be stable. As Dr. Bobrow began the tubal ligation part of the operation, Thompson's heart rate dropped. She suffered a cardiac arrest and was resuscitated, but the lack of oxygen caused catastrophic brain injuries. At the time of trial, Ms. Thompson was reported to be in a persistent vegetative state and was totally incapacitated. Her legal guardian brought suit against WHC. The court determined that the reasonable standard of care required WHC to supply monitors as of November, 1987, so that surgical patients, like Ms. Thompson, could be cared for safely.

Whereas *Washington* illustrates the kind of case that is typically filed by patients, there are cases that are filed by employees or previous employees that may prove to be equally troubling for nursing administrators and the facilities in which nurse-administrators work. Hiring, supervision, and termination decisions give rise to many lawsuits. It is imperative that nursing administrators know what to do to avoid being negligent in making hiring, supervisory and termination decisions. Negligent hiring, supervision, and termination are explored below.

Negligent Hiring

Negligent hiring occurs when hiring decisions are based on race, color, religion, age, sex, national origin, or physical or mental handicap. It also occurs when an inappropriate person is hired or when credentialing processes are either inadequate or not followed. In addition, some states have passed more extensive laws prohibiting discrimination based on marital status and sexual preference. In those states, hiring decisions that are based on marital status or sexual preference are considered unlawful and subject employers to litigation.

Because of the legal issues faced by employers, it is important for great care to be taken during the interview process. Employers should consider reviewing appropriate, lawful interview questions that can be asked, as well as those that should not be asked. Permissible interview questions include those that elicit the following information about an interviewee:

- if they have worked using another name;
- their current address;
- if they are the minimum age required to perform the job;
- if they have the license required to work in the position that requires a license;
- to demonstrate or describe how they would perform job-related functions;
- if they are a citizen of the United States, or authorized to work in the United States; and
- if membership is held in professional, trade, or other job-related organizations.

Although the foregoing list identifies permissible interview questions, there are a number of prohibited interview topics. Prohibited interview questions include asking the interviewee about their:

- marital status;
- living arrangements;
- plans regarding having children;
- health status;
- disability rating;
- prescription drugs currently being taken;
- consumption of alcohol;
- treatment for mental health or substance abuse problems;
- use of sick leave in previous positions;
- religious affiliation;

- elderly parents; and
- dangerous hobbies.

After the interview process is completed, and the final candidate selected. Employers need be aware that there are post-interview issues that need to be addressed. One of the important issues is the post-offer physical examination.

Employers may make an employment offer contingent on the results of a physical examination so long as all employees in the same job category are subjected to the examination and the information obtained in the examination is kept in a separate, secured file and considered confidential. After making an offer of employment, questions about sick leave usage, illnesses, as well as general physical and mental health may be asked. However, it is crucial to stay away from these and other prohibited subjects during the interview process.

Prohibited interview questions are also prohibited when checking an applicant's references. Prior to checking references, it is wise to ask the applicant to sign a statement authorizing the prospective employer to contact previous employers and academic institutions, and allowing previous employers and academic institutions to release information about the applicant.

When it comes to obtaining and receiving references, it is wise to have a written policy on the issue. It should specify the information to be obtained and received. The policy should require that requests for references be in writing and authorized by the person whose reference information is being sought. The policy should also identify the individuals authorized to respond to reference requests.

When obtaining references on a prospective employee, it is vital that the confidentiality of personnel files and medical records be protected. In addition, it is important to obtain and record only factual, job-related information so that defamation and civil rights laws are not violated. If reference information is being given to an individual or organization that has been authorized by a present or former employee, it is important to be factual, and release only job-related information. In most instances, it is best to give only the dates of employment, and indicate whether the previous employee is eligible for rehire.

Historically, it has not been customary for employers to conduct criminal checks on all health facility personnel; however, that is changing. Many states have begun passing legislation that requires that criminal checks be done on certain classes of workers—for example, criminal background checks may be required for those working with vulnerable populations.

Negligent hiring allegations can arise when an employee does something criminal to a patient or other employee, after having done it previously. For instance, the health care facility that hires a nurse who commits a sexual offense with a patient or other employee may be liable for negligent hiring practices, if it is shown that the nurse who committed the offense was previously convicted of a sexual offense, and the employer failed to inquire about or discover it. Accordingly, health care facilities need to seriously consider performing criminal background checks on all employees. Failing to detect a previous conviction could be ruinous for the institution.

Negligent Supervision

Negligent supervision issues occur when adequate supervisory safeguards are not in place. For instance, a staff nurse who fails to turn a patient as ordered can be deemed negligent should the patient develop decubitus ulcers. In addition, an administrative nurse may be negligent in supervising the care this staff nurse was supposed to provide. Steps need to be taken to show that nurses have the skill, knowledge, and ability to care for the patient population to which they are assigned.

Although *Valentin v. La Societe Francaise De Bienfaaisance Mutuelle De Los Angeles*[12] was decided in 1946, it provides a classic example of negligent supervision. Here, August Valentin, an otherwise healthy 20-year-old was admitted to the hospital to surgically repair a hernia. The first 8 days following the surgery, August's recovery was uneventful. For 3 days thereafter he was febrile, flushed in appearance, and dyspneic. He complained of soreness in his chest and of his inability to chew. Eventually, a resident examined August and found that he had tightness in his throat and pain in his jaws when he attempted to open his mouth. On the third day, a physician determined that August had tetanus and ordered that he be transferred to another facility. August died approximately 8 hours later.

The nurse's notes clearly showed that August was progressively deteriorating. In addition, the notes indicated that the head nurse and night supervisor were aware of the situation. About 12 hours before his death, the resident physician who examined August informed the nursing supervisor that he thought August might have tetanus, and instructed her to call an attending physician. More than 9 hours elapsed before an attending physician examined August, confirmed the tetanus diagnosis, and arranged for his transfer to another hospital.

The court discussed the nursing staff's actions, and determined that the supervisory nurse was negligent in failing to adequately supervise the care given to August. The court asserted that the supervisory nurse was negligent because she permitted August, a postoperative patient, to display the symptoms he had for 3 days, without seeing that proper medical care was administered.

Wrongful Termination

In most cases, wrongful termination claims arise when an employer terminates an employee in violation of federal or state law. For instance, Title VII of the Civil Rights Act of 1964 prohibits discrimination or termination based on race, sex, religion, handicap, age, marital status, color, ancestry, and national origin. The Family and Medical Leave Act (FMLA) allows qualified workers to take unpaid leave for family or medical emergencies without risking job loss. The National Labor Relations Act (NLRA) ensures a worker's right to unionize and protects workers from arbitrary discipline and dismissal should organization be sought. The Fair Labor Standards Act (FLSA) not only guarantees the right to certain wage and hour considerations, but also the right to assert them without fear of retaliation in the form of disciplinary action or discharge. The Occupational Safety and Health Act (OSHA) outlines the requirements for a safe workplace. Termination decisions involving violations of these and other laws are unlawful, retaliatory, and subjects employers who are required to adhere to these laws to significant wrongful termination liability. *Stelkoff v. St. John's Mercy Health Systems*[13] is illustrative.

In *Stelkoff,* Debbie Stelkoff practiced as a psychiatric nurse at St. John's Mercy Health Systems until she was terminated for what St. John's Mercy Health Systems called "job abandonment." After Stelkoff had gotten into an argument with her supervisor, she told supervisor that she was too upset to continue working and that she was going to have to leave. She received a doctor's note saying that she should not return to work for 2 weeks. She placed the note in her supervisor's mailbox, and left the unit. Eight days later, she was terminated.

In the lawsuit Stelkoff filed against St. John's Mercy Health System, she alleged that her termination was wrongful because it violated the FMLA. The trial court judge initially issued judgment in favor of the hospital. Debbie Stelkoff appealed that decision and the U.S. Court of Appeals for the Eighth Circuit determined that Stelkoff's leave was protected by the FMLA. This was in spite of the fact that Stelkoff was able to work as a psychiatric nurse for another employer. The Court of Appeals determined that Stelkoff did not have to show that she was unable to perform the essential job functions of her other job. Her claim was against St. John's Mercy Health Systems, and the appellate court justices determined that the inquiry in these kinds of cases should focus on the employee's ability to perform the essential job functions of her work environment at St. John's Mercy Health Systems, and not any other employer.

Like Debbie Stelkfoff, Barry Adams, was involved in wrongful termination litigation. Barry Adams, RN, was terminated in 1996 from a hospital in Cambridge, Massachusetts after he and two other nurses documented several incidents of patient neglect and substandard care. Inadequate staffing was the alleged cause of the neglect and substandard care. Following his documenting these incidents, Mr. Adams was terminated. His employer based the termination on insubordination. However, in November, 1997, an administrative law judge found no evidence to support the employer's charge, and concluded that the termination was motivated by the employer's desire to silence and retaliate against him.[14]

Barry Adams received whistleblower protection because he was part of a group that sought to modify working conditions, according to the NLRA. Other sources of federal protection include the federal Whistleblower Protection Act and the False Claims Act. At the state level, some laws have been passed to safeguard employees who report illegal, unethical or unjust activities from retaliation. Arkansas, California, Colorado, Connecticut, Florida, Illinois, Kentucky, Minnesota, New Jersey, North Dakota, Ohio, Rhode Island, Texas, Utah, and Washington have passed whistleblower protection legislation extending protection from retaliation to healthcare workers who report quality of care and patient safety concerns.

In Texas, whistleblower protection is part of Texas Nurse Practice Act. According to the Texas law, any person subject to the provisions of the Texas Nurse Practice Act who receives disciplinary action, is discriminated against, suspended, or terminated because they made a good faith report about unlawful activity may recover actual damages, as well as damages for mental anguish whether or not other damages exist, exemplary damages, court costs, and reasonable attorney's fees. Where an employee has been suspended or terminated in violation of the whistleblower section of the Texas Nurse Practice Act, that employee is entitled to reinstatement in the previous position or 3 months salary as severance pay, lost wages. The Texas Nurse Practice Act goes even further by saying that where an employee is suspended, or terminated within 60 days after making the report, it is presumed that the suspension or termination was due to the report the employee made.[15]

Unfortunately, the Texas whistleblower law represents the exception, rather than the general rule, when it comes to state law. Most states do not have whistleblower protection for health care workers. The absence of this legislation can be significant for nurses who report incidents. For instance, Cathleen Kyle, a nurse who practiced at Massachusetts General Hospital for 10 years was allegedly terminated because she filed unsafe staffing incident reports. The hospital disagreed that Ms. Kyle was terminated for that reason, contending she was not terminated by Massachusetts General Hospital. However, *The Boston Globe* reported that 3 months before Ms. Kyle's involuntary separation from the hospital, she received an outstanding performance review, which complimented her clinical decision making and excellence in nursing science.[16]

What are the costs associated with whistleblowing? The jury in *Page v. Goodman-Wade Enterprises, Inc.*[17] awarded Ms. Page $695,000 including $75,000 in punitive damages against each defendant. Interest and attorneys fees were added, and the total judgment in the case was approximately $1.16 million. In *Page,* Ms. Page was an administrator of a chain of residential psychiatric mental health treatment facilities owned by defendant Goodman and his two companies. Ms. Page informed Mr. Goodman that she believed that there were a number of things occurring within the residential treatment facilities that were not in compliance with state law and regulations. Two weeks later, based on information the state received from Ms. Page about Goodman and his companies, the state banned him and his companies from operating mental health care facilities in the state for a period of 10 years. That same day, Goodman terminated Ms. Page.

Ms. Page sued Goodman and his two companies. She alleged that she had been terminated in violation of a Texas health and safety code that prohibited terminating a person for reporting resident abuse or neglect at health care facilities to supervisors or enforcement agencies. The jury agreed, and Ms. Page received a judgment in her favor in the amount of $1.16 million.

Page symbolizes the seriousness with which courts treat whislteblowing and retaliation. The U.S. Supreme Court has even expanded the grounds on which whistleblowing cases can be brought. The case was *Haddle v. Garrison*.[18] The Supreme Court Justices determined that where an employee is deterred from testifying in a federal investigation by two or more supervisors acting together, the deterred employee can sue the employer for damages and attorney fees under 42 U.S.C §1985(2). In *Haddle,* Michael Haddle was a manager of a private health care organization. In 1994, the government began investigating the health care organization. Eventually, the president and other top-level officials were indicted for Medicare fraud. The company then filed for bankruptcy, and fired Mr. Haddle claiming their need to cut costs. Mr. Haddle believed that he was terminated because he cooperated with the government investigation. He sued the company under 42 U.S.C §1985(2) because the statute created a cause of action where two or more persons conspire to deter any party or witness from attending any court in the United States or from testifying to any matter pending in any U.S. court. The statute also creates a cause of action where the party or witness is injured in his person or property because of his or her attendance or testimony.

Page and *Haddle* represent what happens when an employee whistleblows, and an employer retaliates. To minimize the chances that a retaliation claim will succeed, it is important to take immediate action when an employee is performing in less than a satisfactory manner. Where an employee complains about something that violates a regulation, case law, or legislation, reiterate to the employee's supervisor the organization's "no retaliation" policy. When terminating an employee, or when denying a promotion, bonus, or salary increase, be sure the written record indicates that this action is fair and consistent with action taken with other employees.

Although retaliation against whistleblowers can be devastating, so can wrongful termination claims for other reasons. For instance, wrongful termination claims can arise when an employer fails to follow the guidelines delineated in an employee handbook. Southwestern Vermont Medical Center, in *Trombley v. Southwestern Vermont Medical Center*[19] heard a jury order the health care facility to pay a nurse, Judy Trombley, $125,000 because she was wrongfully terminated. The problem in *Trombley* was that there were two versions of the employee handbook being referred to. Judy Trombley relied on a previous version of the employee handbook that delineated disciplinary action procedures. The employer, on the other hand, referenced a version of the handbook that had been in use only 4 months at the time of Judy Trombley's discharge. The court found that the employer used the handbook in effect at the time of Trombley's discharge, but that the counseling report that recommended Ms. Trombley's termination contained the exact language used in the disciplinary action procedures outlined in the version of the handbook relied upon by Ms. Trombley. Accordingly, the jury verdict in favor of Ms. Trombley was affirmed.

Wrongful terminations claims are probably the most frequently type of case filed against nurse-administrators. Knowing and understanding the federal and state laws that extend various protections to employees helps to avoid wrongfully terminating an employee. In addition, terminations occurring as the final component of progressive discipline, based solely on performance and an employee's continued failure to adhere to institutional standards affords nurse-administrators the best protection from wrongful termination liability.

Right to Privacy Violations

The right to privacy extends to every American. It was one of the rights promised in the U.S. Constitution. The U.S. Supreme Court first heard a right to privacy case when *Union Pacific Railway v. Botsford*[20] was argued. It was not until *Whalen v. Roe*[21] that the U.S. Supreme Court suggested that the right to privacy extended to patient records. In *Whalen,* a New York statute required physicians to identify patients to whom they prescribed Schedule II controlled drugs. The patient name and address, as well as the prescription drug, were to be recorded in a centralized database maintained by the New York Department of Health. Patients regularly receiving Schedule II drugs and doctors who prescribed the drugs filed suit, alleging that the statute was unconstitutional because it violated the patient's right to privacy. When the case came to the U.S. Supreme Court, the justices unanimously determined that the statute was constitutional, and favored disclosure of the information, rather than nondisclosure. Their reasoning was that the state had a sufficient interest in collecting this information, and that the threat of identification was remote enough that the right to privacy was not violated. As a result, prescriptive patterns continue to be monitored in New York. Other states collect comparable data. Now that advanced practice nurses have prescriptive privileges, their prescriptive practices will also be monitored, so nurse-administrators need to be prepared to facilitate the dissemination of that information to the required reporting agencies.

Not only do patients have a constitutional right to privacy, a new federal law recently enacted strengthens the privacy protections patients have in their medical record information. Signed by President Clinton, the law is known as the Health Insurance Portability and Accountability Act (HIPAA). HIPAA requires that patient information be secured, and that procedural and technological safeguards be in place to maximize patient privacy and prevent the unauthorized disclosure of any information that could identify the patient. HIPAA is a comprehensive piece of legislation prohibiting discrimination against employees and their dependents because of their health status. HIPAA also requires insurers to cover employees who change jobs if their last employer provided insurance coverage, and limits the length of time insurers may refuse to cover preexisting conditions.

Although the aforementioned implications of HIPAA are significant, for nurse-administrators, the most important aspect of HIPAA is the privacy protection afforded patients with regard to the use and disclosure of the information contained in their medical record. Medical information with HIPAA privacy protection includes any oral or recorded information that is created or received by health care providers, health plans, public health authorities, employers, life insurers, schools or universities, or health care clearinghouses that relates to any past, present, or future physical or mental health condition of an individual.

To secure medical record information, HIPAA requires that significant technology-based, procedural, and physical protections be in place at every health care organization to ensure that patient-identifiable health information is secure and free from disclosure to any third party without the patient's consent. HIPAA applies to every health care organization, regardless of the size or location of the organization. Health care organizations subject to the mandates of HIPAA include private practice offices, employers, rehabilitation and assisted living centers, nursing homes and other long-term care settings, public health authorities, billing agencies, some service organizations, and universities. HIPAA also applies to most health care providers, insurance companies, and health data clearinghouses. Entities subject to HIPAA must be in compliance by February 28, 2003.

To be in compliance, security, privacy, and electronic transaction standards need to be in place. Security measures must include comprehensive administrative procedures, physical safeguards, and technical security mechanisms designed to guard data integrity, confidentiality, and availability. Privacy standards must address a patient's right to informed consent prior to the release of information, to access his or her health information, to correct information that is incorrect, and to an accounting for all disclosures. Electronic transaction standards require that individuals and entities subject to the provisions of HIPAA have policies, procedures, and technologies in place that are compliant with HIPAA and that reflect standardized codes recognized by HIPAA. Direct care providers must also obtain the patient's consent before using or disclosing patient-identifiable health information, and patients must receive written patients' rights information from the health care provider. In addition, administrative policies need to be implemented that safeguards patient-identifiable information, including the delineation of a complaint process. A privacy officer also needs to be identified, and employees educated about privacy policy and procedures. Failure to comply could result in the imposition of a $25,000 fine for multiple violations within the same calendar year. Knowing misuse of patient-identifiable health information can result in a $250,000 fine and imprisonment for up to 10 years. To avoid these sanctions, nurse-administrators should work to see that HIPAA compliance is achieved on or before February 28, 2003.

As a result, health care professionals, health plans, public health authorities, employers, life insurers, schools or universities, and health care clearinghouses should establish compliance programs and begin crafting policies and procedures to ensure adherence with HIPAA mandates. Failure to comply could result in the payment of significant fines and incarceration.

False Claims Act Violations

The False Claims Act[22] has been used to prosecute health care fraud in the United States. Health care professionals are going to prison and paying millions of dollars in fines because of False Claims Act violations. Although nurses have not yet been targets of investigation, it is anticipated that more nurses will become targets. Advanced practice nurses who receive direct reimbursement for Medicare and

Medicaid, as well as nurse-administrators who oversee billing practices are at greatest risk.

Although fraud was discussed in Chapter 4, nurse-administrators need to be aware of the growing number of qui tam claims alleging fraud that are being filed under the False Claims Act. In health care settings qui tam claims are those False Claims Act cases in which someone with nonpublic first-hand information files suit against a health care organization alleging that the organization committed fraud against the federal government. The individual filing the suit is referred to as the relator, and that individual files the suit on his or her behalf, and on behalf of the United States.

Qui tam claims are filed under seal at the applicable federal district court so the defendant health care organization does not know that a claim has been filed against them. At the same time that the case is filed at the district court, the complaint and the evidence that the relator has that serves as evidence that fraud has been committed must be delivered to the Attorney General of the United States and the U.S. Attorney for the district in which the action is filed. The complaint and evidence possessed by the relator stays under seal for at least 60 days so that the government can investigate the claim. Once the government completes their investigation, the government decides whether it will pursue the matter. Where the government elects to pursue the case, the relator will receive 15 to 20% of the recovery obtained by the government. Where, on the other hand, the government elects to not pursue the matter, the relator will receive 25 to 30% of any recovery. Recovery in these kinds of cases can be substantial. Recently, a qui tam case filed in Philadelphia, Pennsylvania, alleging health care fraud yielded the government $325 million.[23] In addition, the average recovery in qui tam cases has been $7.2 million.[24]

Because more than $100 billion is lost annually to health care fraud, the government's quest to eliminate fraud will likely continue. To avoid being the subject of fraud and abuse investigations, it is important for nurse-administrators to oversee the systems used in an organization, and that safeguards be in place to ensure that the False Claims Act is not violated. It is also important to know that relators in qui tam actions and others assisting with the investigation should not be retaliated against. Retaliation claims could result in job reinstatement, and a damage award that is twice the amount of the employee's lost back pay.

Summary

Nurse-administrators, like the nurses they supervise, face federal and state litigation when the plaintiff believes they have been wronged and damaged because of negligence. Unlike nurses providing direct patient care, nurse-administrators are also subject to litigation filed by subordinate staff members. So that nurse-administrators better understand the kinds of cases that may be filed against them, frequently used doctrines and causes of action have been outlined. Doctrines discussed included the captain of the ship doctrine, immunity, corporate negligence, res ipsa loquitur, and vicarious liability. Causes of action delineated included the failure to protect the patient, negligent hiring, negligent supervision, wrongful termination, right to privacy violations, and False Claims Act violations.

Nurse-administrators not only have to understand the wide range of causes of action that might be filed against them, they also face scrutiny by state boards of nursing. State boards of nursing are beginning to discipline nurse-administrators for making administrative decisions that compromise patient care. *Tryon v. Colorado State Board of Nursing*[25] illustrates this point.

In *Tryon*, Ellen Tryon was a registered nurse who served as the vice president of patient care services at Littleton Hospital in Colorado. She and two nurses involved in the care of two patients were sanctioned by the Colorado State Board of Nursing. These sanctions were imposed following an investigation by the Colorado Department of Public Health and the Colorado Board of Nursing. Tryon was issued a letter of admonition. She appealed the disciplinary action to an administrative law judge. The administrative law judge affirmed the decision of the Colorado Board of Nursing. Ellen Tryon then appealed to a Colorado Court of Appeals. The court of appeals vacated the decision made by the administrative law judge, and concluded that Ellen Tryon's administrative responsibilities did not constitute the practice of nursing as it was defined in the Colorado Nurse Practice Act.

Although Ellen Tryon was ultimately exonerated, disciplinary action taken by the Colorado Board of Nursing could have been affirmed had the Nurse Practice Act included broader supervision language. The implication is significant. Nurse-administrators need to clarify whether or not their administrative decisions subject them to disciplinary action by boards of nursing. In addition, proposed changes to nurse practice acts need to be closely monitored so that the impact of the proposed changes in definitions and other substantive provisions can be analyzed. Once the impact of proposed changes is ascertained, strategies can be implemented to support or oppose the proposed changes.

End Notes

1. 536 So.2d 1374.
2. 567 A.2d 524.
3. 3. 130 F.2d 810.
4. Ibid, p. 820.
5. 393 N.W.2d 847.
6. 735 So. 2d 1099 (Ms. 1999).
7. 211 N.E. 2d 614 (Il. 1974).
8. 434 P.2d 160.
9. No. 94-CT-00807-SCT
10. 500 P.2d 1153.

11. 579 A.2d 177.

12. 172 P.2d 359.

13. 218 F. 3d 858 (8th Cir. 2000).

14. Available from URL: http://www.ana.org/pressrel/1998/whist.html.

15. Willmann, J. 1998. *Annotated guide to the Texas Nurse Practice Act,* 3rd ed. Austin, TX: Texas Nurses Association; pp. 16–17.

16. Kong, D. 1999. Ex-nurse: MGH firing was payback. *The Boston Globe* January 21: A18.

17. Tarrant County 153rd Judicial District Court, No. 352-150345-93, August 23, 1996, reported in 39 *Law Reporter*, December 1996, p. 396.

18. No. 97-1472. December 14, 1998.

19. No. 97-320, July 16, 1999.

20. 141 U.S. 250 (1891).

21. 429 U.S. 589 (1977).

22. 31 U.S.C. 3729 et seq.

23. Lovitky, J. 1999. Qui tam litigation: A practical primer. *Trial* January: 68.

24. Ibid.

25. 989 P.2d 216 (Co. 1999).

The Nurse as Counselor 9

Introduction

Counseling, according to the American Nurses Association's (ANA) *Scope and Standards of Psychiatric-Mental Health Nursing Practice* is:

> a specific, time-limited interaction of a nurse with a patient, family, or group experiencing immediate or ongoing difficulties related to their health or well-being. The difficulty is investigated using a problem-solving approach for the purpose of understanding the experience and integrating it with other life experiences.[1]

This definition contemplates counseling occurring in a variety of settings and specialties, and suggests that counseling is an important part of every nurse's practice, whether or not a nurse considers him- or herself to be a psychiatric-mental health nurse.

Although counseling occurs in a number of settings and is an important intervention for nurses regardless of specialty practice, the focus of this chapter will be on the legal issues faced by nurses practicing in psychiatric-mental health settings. In psychiatric-mental health settings some of the most frequently litigated legal issues include breach of confidentiality, failure to warn third parties, sexual misconduct, improper hospitalization, failure to protect suicidal patients, failure to properly administer medication, negligent patient supervision, and negligent discharge/release of patients. So that psychiatric-mental health nurses are aware of the legal issues faced in their practice settings, these issues, as well as the emerging issue of third-party suits, are discussed in greater detail.

Breach of Confidentiality

Nurses have an ethical and legal obligation to keep patient information confidential. Failure to honor the confidential nature of patient information can result in a nurse being liable for harm that is caused by the unauthorized and illegal release of confidential patient information.

Berger v. Sonneland[2] illustrates that courts are serious about a health care professional's obligation to keep certain patient information confidential. In *Berger*, a physician disclosed a patient's use of narcotic pain medications to the patient's ex-husband without her consent. The ex-husband then filed a request to modify the couple's child custody agreement based on the information obtained from the physician. The patient sued her physician alleging that she had been wronged by the unauthorized release of confidential patient information. The trial court determined that the physician could not be sued for the disclosure, but the court of appeals disagreed, concluding that the physician disclosed confidential information that was obtained within the context of the physician–patient relationship. As a result, the physician could be sued and held liable for damages arising out of the wrongful release of confidential patient information.

Although nurses are obliged to keep patient information confidential, there are exceptions to that requirement. These exceptions consistently reflect an interest in public safety that outweighs an individual's right to privacy. Although the issue will be discussed in more detail later in this chapter, one exception is the duty to warn when a patient threatens to harm another. In addition to this exception, there are others. They include consent of disclosure by patients, as well as laws requiring the mandatory reporting of violence inflicted gun and knife wounds, child abuse, elder abuse, and occurrences of sexually transmitted and contagious diseases.

On the other side of the confidentiality spectrum is a patchwork of state laws that protect mental health- and substance abuse-related information, as well as genetic testing results, HIV status, and adverse underwriting decisions by insurers. These and other state laws, combined with the Health Insurance Portability and Accountability Act (HIPAA) make it imperative for nurses to know when to disclose and when to not disclose patient information. See Chapter 8 for a more detailed discussion regarding HIPAA.

Failure to Warn Third Parties

In 1976, the landmark case of *Tarasoff v. The Regents of the University of California*[3] dramatically affected the health care professional's responsibility to keep patient information confidential. In *Tarasoff*, the California Supreme Court determined that mental health care professionals have a duty to warn third parties that their client has threatened to harm them. In that case, Prosenjit Poddar was a student enrolled at the University of California at Berkley. He became interested in another student, Tatiana Tarasoff. Tatiana told Prosenjit that she was not interested in him, and he subsequently began counseling at the school's counseling center in an effort to deal with Tatiana's rejection.

After a number of sessions, the counseling psychologist determined that Prosenjit might harm Tatiana, and consulted two other psychologists who told the psychologist that Prosenjit Poddar needed to be admitted to an inpatient psychiatric unit. The psychologist asked campus police officers to detain Poddar so that his eligibility for civil commitment could be ascertained. The campus police officers interviewed Poddar, determined that he was rational, and released him after he promised to stay away from Tatiana. One of the consulting psychologists then ordered that no action be taken with regard to Prosenjit Poddar's emergency ordered detention.

Subsequently, Poddar terminated treatment with the university counselor. Two months later, after Tatiana returned from her summer break, Prosenjit Poddar went to Tatiana's home, shot, and repeatedly stabbed her. Tatiana's wounds were fatal. After she died, Tatiana's parents sued the university, the psychologist, the consulting psychologist, and the campus police alleging that their actions resulted in Tatiana's wrongful death. Tatiana's parents asserted further that the defendants had a duty to warn Tatiana that Prosenjit Poddar threatened to harm her. The California Supreme Court agreed with the parents, concluding that therapists have a duty to warn identifiable third parties their clients threaten to harm, even if that disclosure is made in an otherwise confidential therapist–patient relationship.

Following the California Supreme Court's *Tarasoff* ruling, *McIntosh v. Milano*[4] was decided in New Jersey. In *McIntosh*, a 17-year-old patient revealed to his therapist that he had feelings of inadequacy and that he fantasized about using a knife to become a hero or important villain. The patient brought a knife to show the therapist what he was talking about, and also revealed that he had fired a BB gun at a car in which a neighborhood girl was riding with her boyfriend. The 17-year-old subsequently shot and killed the neighborhood girl who was previously riding in the car at which the BB gun was fired. The girl's family sued the therapist alleging that the therapist knew that the 17-year-old was dangerous and owed a duty to protect their daughter. The therapist contended that the 17-year-old never threatened to harm the victim and asked that the judge enter judgment in the psychiatrist's favor. The judge denied the request of the therapist and asserted that *Tarasoff* applied, and that therapists not only owed a duty to identifiable third parties, but that the therapist owed a more general duty to protect society.

One year after *McIntosh, Lipari v. Sears, Roebuck and Co.*[5] was decided by a Nebraska court, and the reach of *Tarasoff* and *McIntosh* was expanded even further. In *Lipari,* a patient who had been in and out of day treatment at a Veteran's Administration hospital purchased a gun, walked into a crowded nightclub, and fired the gun. Ms. Lipari and her husband were at the nightclub when the gun was fired. Ms. Lipari was injured by the gunshots, and her husband was killed. Ms. Lipari sued Sears, Roebuck and Company because that is where the gun was purchased. The court, after listening to the arguments of both parties, determined that there was a duty to protect society and that foreseeable violence was not limited to an identified, specific victim. As a result, the duty to warn was extended to society at large, rather than limited to a specific, identifiable victim.

Three years after *Lipari*, and 7 years after *Tarasoff*, a California court heard another "duty to warn" case, *Hedlund v. Orange County*.[6] In *Hedlund*, during the course of couple's therapy, a man disclosed to the therapist his intent to harm his girlfriend. The disclosure was made when the girlfriend was not present. Subsequently, the man shot the woman while she was in a car with her young son. The woman survived and sued, seeking damages for herself and her son. The California court determined that not only was there a duty to warn third parties whom a client threatened to harm, but that there was a duty to warn foreseeable persons in close relationship to the person threatened to be harmed. Accordingly, Ms. Hedlund was allowed to pursue emotional distress damages on behalf of her son who witnessed the shooting.

Although cases from *Tarasoff* to *Hedlund* result in therapists being held responsible for the wrongful death of individuals killed after their clients disclosed that they intended to harm the eventual victims, *Emerich, et al v. Philadelphia Center for Human Development, et al*[7] illustrates that therapists are not always found liable when a client kills someone. In *Emerich*, Teresa Hausler was murdered by her former live-in boyfriend, Gad Joseph. When Gad committed the murder, he was being seen at the Philadelphia Center for Human Development. The morning that Gad killed Teresa, he called Anthony Scuderi, his counselor, and said that he was going to kill Teresa. Scuderi immediately scheduled and held a therapy session with Gad. Scuderi suggested that Gad voluntarily commit himself to a psychiatric hospital. Gad declined, saying that he was in control of his emotions and that he would not harm Teresa. With that pledge, Gad was allowed to leave the center. About 15 minutes later, Teresa called Scuderi. She asked the counselor where Gad was and said that she was on her way back to the apartment she previously shared with Gad to get her clothes. Scuderi advised Teresa not to go to the apartment and instructed her to return to her new residence in a neighboring city. Teresa went to the apartment anyway. At the apartment, Gad shot and killed Teresa. Approximately 5 minutes after the shooting, Gad called Scuderi, who called the police.

Teresa's family sued the counseling center, the counselor, and other individuals and entities associated with the center alleging that Teresa's death was wrongful. The case made its way to the Pennsylvania Supreme Court, where the justices decided that Pennsylvania would follow *Tarasoff* because the state had an interest in protecting its citizens. In spite of that holding, the Pennsylvania Supreme Court observed that Scuderi was not liable because sufficient warnings had been given.

Although *Tarasoff* represents the majority view when it comes to the duty to warn, not all jurisdictions follow the landmark case. Jurisdictions like Colorado, Florida, Georgia, Maryland, and Texas have elected to take different approaches.

In Colorado, *Brady et al v. Hopper*[8] involved the attempted assassination of President Reagan. After the plaintiffs were shot by John Hinckley, they contended that Hinckley's therapist should have known that he was dangerous and that they were in a class of reasonably foreseeable victims. The court disagreed, concluding that therapists do not owe a duty to the world at large. Rather, the court limited a therapist's duty to warn to those that involve specific threats to specific individuals.

In Florida, *Boynton v. Burglass*[9] was decided by the court of appeals. In this case, Lawrence Blaylock shot and killed Wayne Boynton, Jr. Lawrence had been seeing psychiatrist Milton Burglass on an outpatient basis, and after the shooting, Wayne's parents sued Burglass alleging, among other things, that Burglass failed to execute his duty to warn Wayne. The court of appeals disagreed with Wayne's parents, calling the duty to warn third persons like Wayne unreasonable, unworkable, and potentially fatal to an effective patient–therapist relationship.

In Georgia, *Ermutlu v. McCorkle et al*[10] was a duty to warn case decided by the court of appeals. In *Ermutlu*, Ilhan Ermutlu was a psychiatrist who was employed by the North DeKalb Mental Health Center. In the course of his employment, he saw Camille Watkins. Camille suffered from a long-term psychiatric-mental condition that required ongoing treatment. Two days after a manic episode, Camille was driving when she hit a car being driven by Lisa McCorkle. Camille and Lisa were both killed in the collision.

A negligence cause of action was subsequently filed by Lisa's family against Camille's psychiatrist. Among the allegations, was assertion that Ilhan Ermutlu failed to execute his duty to warn. The court disagreed, concluding that Ilhan Ermutlu had no control over Camille, and had no reason to know that Camille was likely to harm herself or others. Therefore, Ilhan Ermutlu could not be liable for the death of Lisa McCorkle.

In Maryland, the court in *Shaw v. Glickman*[11] declined to adopt or reject *Tarasoff.* In this case, Daniel Shaw was a dentist who married Mary Ann Billian. Mary Ann Billian had previously been married to Leonard Billian. Prior to the Billian divorce, Mary Ann and Leonard were in marital counseling. During the course of marriage therapy, Mary Ann Billian disclosed that she was seeing Daniel Shaw. All three were participants in group therapy. The day after the last group therapy session that Daniel Shaw and Mary Ann Billian attended, Leonard Billian broke into the home of Daniel Shaw. At the time that Leonard Billian broke into the home, Mary Ann and Daniel were nude and asleep in the same bed. After seeing this, Leonard Billian shot Daniel five times. None of the wounds proved to be fatal.

Subsequently, Leonard Billian was convicted of assault, the Billians were divorced, and Danial Shaw sued Leonard Billian to recover damages sustained in the shooting. Daniel Shaw also sued the estate of the then deceased psychiatrist, Leonard J. Gallant, a psychiatric nurse, Patricia Hencke, and Joseph Napora, a psychologist, for the injuries he sustained at the hands of Leonard Billian. Daniel Shaw claimed that the psychiatric team failed to warn him of Leonard's unstable and violent condition. Daniel also asserted that Leonard's violent act was foreseeable and that resulted in Daniel being in immediate danger. The trial court dismissed Daniel's case against the psychiatric team because the court determined that Daniel assumed the risk of being injured by voluntarily placing himself in a situation in which the danger was obvious and apparent. Daniel then appealed the trial court's decision to the Maryland Court of Special Appeals. In reviewing the matter, the court discussed *Tarasoff* and decided that it was not applicable to the case at hand. The court observed that

Leonard Billian revealed no threats to the psychiatric team, nor were there any conversations between any member of the psychiatric team and Leonard in which Leonard disclosed any ill will or animosity toward Daniel Shaw. As a result, the Daniel Shaw matter was considered to be strikingly different than *Tarasoff*. In addition, the court ruled that it would have been a violation of Maryland confidentiality statutes for any member of the psychiatric team to disclose to Daniel Shaw any propensity Leonard Billian had to inflict harm on Daniel. Accordingly, the trial judge's decision to dismiss the matter was affirmed.

In Texas, *Thaper v. Zezulka*[12] was decided in 1999. In that case, Freddy Ray Lilly shot and killed Henry Zezulka approximately 1 month after being hospitalized for in-patient psychiatric treatment. Freddy Ray Lilly was a long-term patient of psychiatrist Renu K. Thaper, and during the course of treatment, Freddy disclosed that he felt like killing his stepfather Henry Zezulka. Following the disclosure, Renu K. Thaper noted that Freddy would not kill Henry Zezulka, in spite of his desire to do otherwise. Thaper, following Freddy's disclosure, never warned anyone about Freddy's threats to harm Henry.

Following the shooting, Lyndall Zezulka, Henry's wife, sued Thaper for the wrongful death of her husband. Among other things, Lyndall Zezulka contended that Thaper failed to properly exercise his duty to warn. The case was eventually reviewed by the Texas Supreme Court where the justices expressly declined to follow *Tarasoff*. Instead, the court looked at the state confidentiality statute governing communications between therapists and patients. The statute classified therapist–patient communications as confidential and prohibited third-party disclosure, except in limited circumstances, and none of the exceptions permitted therapist disclosure of communications to third parties whom the client threatened to harm. The Court observed that if it created case law requiring disclosure, a "catch 22" would exist resulting in therapists being liable whether or not the disclosure was made. As a result, the Texas Supreme Court declined to impose a *Tarasoff* duty to warn. As a result Lyndall Zezulka was unable to impose liability on Renu K. Thaper for the death of her husband.

In spite of decisions like *Thaper*, *Tarasoff* represents the standard of care for mental health professionals. It is important to know, however, what the specific rule of law is in any given jurisdiction. Also, the duty to warn may not extend to nurses and other health care professionals if *Charleston v. Larson*[13] is deemed the standard of care.

Charleston v. Larson is an Illinois Court of Appeals case involving a failure on the part of a patient's admitting physician, John Larson, to disclose the dangerousness of a patient to Vita Charleston, a nurse. The patient, Andrew Thain, had been voluntarily admitted to an in-patient psychiatric unit for alcohol, drug, and sexual abuse and for a history of self-mutilation. A month after Thain had been admitted, he threatened to break Vita Charleston's neck. Later that same day, Thain attacked and beat Vita Charleston.

Vita Charleston sued John Larson asserting that Larson should have known that Thain posed a danger to staff and that a duty to warn was indicated. Larson argued that he owned no special duty to Charleston. The trial court agreed with Larson and dismissed the case against him. On appeal, the court observed that Larson's duty to warn extended only to patients. The court agreed that there was no special duty owed to Charleston. Even if there had been a special duty Larson owed Charleston, the court determined that the attack did not seem to be reasonably foreseeable.

Nurses who counsel patients, whether or not they are practicing as psychiatric-mental health professionals, need to know what the duty to warn standard is in the jurisdiction in which they practice. Where the nurse has a duty to warn and fails to do so, that nurse will have breached his or her duty to the third party. Breaching that duty could lead to liability for negligence.

Sexual Misconduct

Courts have consistently held that therapists who engage in sexual activity with their clients will be held responsible for that conduct. Civil, criminal, and administrative sanctions may be imposed, and can result in the therapist serving time in prison, revocation of the therapist's license to practice, as well as the payment of monetary fines, judgments, and court costs.

Zipkin v. Freeman[14] exemplifies the courts' longstanding disapproval of sexual activity between therapists and their patients. In *Zipkin*, Ada Margaret Zipkin sued Robert F. Freeman, a psychiatrist after she alleged that Freeman mishandled the transference phenomenon and aroused her emotions to the point that she began to love him, moved in with him, left her husband, made investments controlled by Freemen, and became his mistress and travel companion. Ada Margaret Zipkin asserted that Freeman's behavior amounted to negligence and caused her to suffer remorse, humiliation, mental anguish, loss of respect of friends and family, to develop insomnia, to suffer headaches, and to compromise her financial condition. The case was presented to a jury who agreed that Robert F. Freeman was negligent and liable for the damages suffered by Ada Margaret Zipkin.

Whereas *Zipkin* provides historical perspective, *Roy v. Hartogs*[15] is the landmark case in this area. In *Roy*, Julie Roy alleged that the Renatus Hartogs engaged in unlawful sexual activity with her for about 13 months. Julie contended that Renatus Hartogs committed malpractice and that he assaulted her. Because of the emotional distress associated with this experience, Julie Roy had to be hospitalized twice.

The case was prepared for a jury trial, but following opening statements, Hartogs moved to dismiss the case because the allegations were barred by state statutes. The trial judge denied Hartogs' motion to dismiss, and issued an opinion that permitted Julie Roy to pursue her case. The judge concluded that patients like Julie Roy can pursue civil remedies against therapists like Renatus Hartogs so that the wrongs perpetrated against them can be vindicated and so that public interest is protected from malicious and deliberate abuse of power and breach of trust by therapists.

Like *Hartogs, Palazzolo v. Ruggiano*[16] focused on the alleged sexual misconduct of psychiatrist John R. Ruggiano. Unlike the plaintiff in *Hartogs,* Donna M. Palazzolo sued John R. Ruggiano alleging that federal law had been violated. According to Palazzolo, Ruggiano repeatedly initiated sexual, physical contact with her. Palazzolo alleged that the sexual touching violated the Violence Against Women Act.[17] Because this federal law was implicated, the case was filed in federal, rather than state, court. The federal court determined that although the conduct complained of was unwelcome, it was not a crime of violence within the meaning of the Violence Against Women Act. The Violence Against Women Act, according to the judge, required physical force or coercion. Physical force or coercion was determined to be absent in the Palazzolo matter, and the case was dismissed.

Sexual misconduct is never appropriate. Nurses who engage in this kind of activity subject themselves to liability for violating civil and criminal state and federal laws. Nurses convicted of sexual misconduct are considered sex offenders and are required to comply with the reporting obligations and restrictions associated with that status.

Improper Hospitalization

Mentally ill patients are admitted to psychiatric-mental health settings either voluntarily or involuntarily. Voluntary admissions are usually uneventful and do not give rise to a significant amount of litigation. On the other hand, involuntary admissions are often contentious and can be traumatic for patients and staff. Involuntary admissions are permitted because of a state's responsibility to protect individuals who are unable to care for themselves, as well as the state's duty to protect its citizens from individuals who are thought to be dangerous. Every state permits involuntary psychiatric admissions so long as the patient's constitutional right to due process is protected. The U.S. Supreme Court had an opportunity to confirm this principle in *Youngberg v. Romeo.* In that case, the Supreme Court Justices determined that involuntarily committed patients enjoy constitutionally protected interests in having reasonable and safe care.[18] Typically, these constitutional rights are protected in part by requiring states to hold a due process hearing prior to rendering treatment to a patient who has been admitted involuntarily. Where procedural safeguards are ignored and where competent patients are not released when they express a desire to leave the in-patient setting, improper hospitalization allegations may arise. *Felton v. Coyle*[19] is an example.

In *Felton,* Ernest Felton, Sr., a patient hospitalized at South Chicago Community Hospital, sued John Coyle, his treating physician, alleging assault and false imprisonment. The situation arose after Felton kicked a nurse's aide. The aide then threw tea on Felton. In response, Felton then threw soup at the aide. John Coyle was called and was asked to come to the hospital because Felton was out of control. Upon Coyle's arrival to Felton's room, Felton was standing in the doorway partially dressed, saying that he wanted to leave the hospital. The physician said that he simply led Felton from the doorway to the bed. Not surprisingly, Felton's recollection about the altercation with the nurse's aide and Coyle was different. The jury heard the evidence presented by Felton and Coyle, and determined that, in spite of the fact that Coyle took Felton by the left arm and led him back to bed, the action of the doctor was justifiable. In light of that, the jury rendered a decision in Coyle's favor. Felton appealed to an Illinois Appeals Court, but that court affirmed the jury's verdict.

Nurses caring for competent patients who originally subjected themselves to treatment voluntarily, but who do not wish to remain hospitalized, must refrain from keeping the patient against their will. Most health care organizations have policies and procedures that indicate how to proceed when this occurs. It is important for nurses to know what their organization's policy is, and that the nurse follow that policy. If an organization does not have a policy, it is prudent to create one and follow it. Failing to follow the policy, or denying a voluntarily admitted, competent patient's request to leave a facility may subject the nurse and facility to liability for false imprisonment, as well as for other causes of action.

Nurses caring for incompetent patients or for patients who have been admitted involuntarily need to be sure that they know what state laws govern the admission of that patient. A nurse's failure to follow governing state laws can also subject the nurse and facility to liability.

Failure to Protect Suicidal Patients

The American Psychiatric Association estimates that almost one-third of all claims filed by those seeking damages from mental health professionals are those concerning a patient committing suicide.[20] Cases from Missouri, Louisiana, Texas, Washington, and Illinois illustrate the ways in which courts deal with cases brought because a patient committed suicide.

In *Honey v. Barnes Hospital, et al*,[21] a Missouri jury found Barnes Hospital liable for the wrongful death of a suicidal young man who jumped from a the 10th-floor window of a psychiatric intensive care unit. The young man's parents were awarded $350,000 in damages because the jury determined that the young man's death was wrongful. The court held that the hospital failed to provide adequate supervision of the patient and failed to safeguard the 10th-floor window, given that hospital staff knew of the patient's suicidal condition.

Palermo v. NME Hospital, Inc.[22] offered an opportunity for the Louisiana courts to address the "failure to protect a suicidal patient" issue. In *Palermo*, Lucille Palermo jumped from a 4th-floor window the morning she was to be discharged. She had been admitted to Jo Ellen Smith Medical Center for treatment for Parkinson's Disease and Depression. In the 6-week period prior to her admission to the hospital, Lucille twice attempted to commit suicide. She was initially admitted to the psychiatric unit but was transferred to a medical/surgical unit after her attending physician determined that she exhibited no suicidal symptoms and after ensuring that Lucille's family supported the transfer. While Lucille was on the medical/surgical unit, a family member stayed with her. At night, a family member slept in her hospital bed while the patient slept in a day bed in the room.

On the night before Lucille was to be released from the hospital, she told a nurse, Julie Gravois, that she felt wonderful and was happy about being discharged the next day. When Lucille was checked throughout the night, she was sleeping on the day bed in her room until 4:50 in the morning. At that time, it was discovered that she was no longer sleeping on the day bed. However, her family member remained asleep in the patient's hospital bed.

The window in Lucille Palermo's 4th floor room was completely open, and Lucille was found dead on the concrete below. Lucille Palermo's family sued the hospital alleging that the hospital was responsible for the patient's wrongful death. The Louisiana court dismissed this case in favor of the hospital, but noted that hospitals have a duty to exercise the requisite amount of care that a specific patient's condition requires. The court also concluded that it is the hospital's duty to protect patients from dangers that may result from their physical and mental infirmities and from the external circumstances within the hospital's control.

Texas addressed the failure to protect suicidal patient issue in *Hatley v. Kassen.*[23] In this case, Pennie Johnson was chronically mentally ill, had been admitted to long-term psychiatric facility, but was changed to outpatient status after the treatment team decided that long-term in-patient treatment was not having beneficial effects on her. After she had been discharged from the in-patient setting, a difficult patient file was developed, recommending that Pennie Johnson be discharged whenever she presented herself for in-patient treatment unless she displayed significantly different symptoms than those she had displayed in the past.

One evening, a highway patrol officer found Pennie walking along the Dallas North Tollway. The trooper questioned Pennie, and she indicated that she intended to harm herself. The officer took Pennie to Parkland Hospital where she was voluntarily admitted. After she had been admitted, the staff noted that Pennie reported a heightened sense of depression and had been taking her prescription medication improperly, more than she had previously been prescribed. The medication was taken from Pennie, and when she was discharged, the medication was not returned to her in spite of Pennie's request to have the medicine returned to her. The refusal to have her medication returned to her resulted in Pennie's becoming verbally abusive and threatening to throw herself in front of a truck. Lisa Kassen, a charge nurse in Parkland's psychiatric emergency room, was asked to determine whether or not it was appropriate to return the medication to Pennie. Lisa Kassen, another nurse, Robert L. Knowles, and Gurjeet S. Kalra, a third year resident decided not to return the medication to Pennie. Gurjeet S. Kalra then discharged Pennie in accordance with the difficult patient file. Thirty minutes later, Pennie Johnson did what she said she would do. She stepped into traffic on Interstate 35, was hit, and died at the scene.

Following her death, Pennie's parents sued the resident, charge nurse, and hospital. Initially, the district court granted summary judgment in favor of the resident and hospital and directed a verdict in favor of the nurse. The parents appealed, and the court of appeals determined that a jury trial should occur and that Lisa Kassen and Gurjeet S. Kalra should not be granted governmental immunity. Subsequent opinions in this case have not yet been published.

In Washington, *Lewis v. Long View School District No. 122*[24] dealt with the duty to warn a student's parents of the student's threat to commit suicide. In *Lewis,* a psychologist for the school district became aware that a student threatened to commit suicide. In response to that information Batzle, the psychologist, did nothing. That afternoon, the 15-year-old high school shot and killed himself in his bedroom. The student's family sued the school district for the wrongful death of the student. The school district contended that the psychologist met the standard of care and claimed that the student's stepfather was at fault because he kept a loaded gun in the house. In spite of the defenses asserted by the school district, the school district elected to settle the case before it was tried by a jury.

In Illinois, *Martino v. Illinois Masonic Medical Center*[25] was heard by a jury. In *Martino,* a patient committed suicide after she was denied admission to a psychiatric unit. Her brothers sued the medical center alleging that the admission was denied because the woman did not have insurance and that admission denial led to their sister's suicide. A jury agreed with the brothers and rendered a verdict in their favor.

Courts hold health care organizations and health care professionals responsible for protecting patients. When it comes to suicidal patients, courts continue to readily hold organizations and individuals involved in the death of suicidal patients liable. To avoid liability, great care should be taken to protect vulnerable populations, including those patients who are suicidal.

Improper Medication Administration

In 1977, the U.S. Supreme Court decided *Ingram v. Wright.*[26] In *Ingram,* the Supreme Court Justices determined that compulsory medication administration was deemed to be intrusive upon a person's liberty interest. As such, it violated an individual's 14th Amendment constitutional rights. *Ingram v. Wright* remains intact and continues to represent the standard of care when it comes to compulsory medication administration.

Three years after *Ingram, Davis v. Hubbard*[27] was addressed by an Ohio court. In *Davis,* a number of patients at Lima State Hospital filed a lawsuit challenging, among other things, Lima State Hospital's excessive and forced use of psychotropic drugs. The patients claimed that they had a constitutional right to treatment in a humane and therapeutic environment and that Lima State Hospital was infringing on those rights. The Ohio Federal District Court agreed with the patients and determined that mentally ill patients who have not been declared a danger to themselves or others had a due process right to refuse medications. In fact, the court concluded that there was no legitimate reason to administer psychotropic drugs without informed consent of competent patients unless the patient was a danger to him- or herself or others. However, the court recognized that a patient's right to refuse medication was not absolute. Medication, according to the court, could be administered involuntarily after the patient was afforded a due process hearing. To preserve the patients' constitutional right to due process, the Ohio Federal District Court ordered Lima State Hospital to follow a due process procedure including holding a hearing before it can involuntarily treat a patient.

Sixteen years after *Davis,* and 19 years after *Ingram, Bushey v. Derboven*[28] was heard in Maine. In *Bushey,* Beatrice Dobson had been admitted 17 times to Bangor Mental Health Institute between 1957 and 1993. During her last admission, Beatrice Dobson was given medications intended for another patient. When a nurse discovered this, the on-call physician, Paul Derboven, was immediately notified. Paul Derboven ordered that all medications be held until the next morning.

During the night, Beatrice began experiencing cardiac and respiratory distress. The nurse noted these occurrences and properly documented four sets of vital signs throughout the night. However, the on-call physician was not called.

At 3:00 in the morning, approximately 90 minutes after the onset of these cardiac and respiratory distress symptoms, Beatrice was found not breathing. She was transferred to Eastern Maine Medical Center but was pronounced dead within the hour. Following her death, the on-call physician, nursing staff, and the Bangor Mental Health Institute were sued by the family who alleged that Beatrice's constitutional due process right to receive adequate medical care had been violated. The U.S. District Court for the District of Maine heard the matter. The district court judge dismissed the case against Bangor Mental Health Institute because the Institute was a state agency and not subject to liability for the alleged federal civil rights violation. However, the judge declined to dismiss the on-call physician. As a result, Paul Derboven was still subject to liability in the death of Beatrice Dobson. Subsequent proceedings in this case have not yet been published.

Nurses, regardless of their practice setting, must ensure that the right patient gets the right medication at the right dose using the right route at the right time. Failure to administer medication without adhering to these five rights can be devastating for patients and nurses. However, compulsory medication is unconstitutional. Therefore, it is important for nurses to refrain from administering medication to patients who do not consent to the administration of the medication.

Negligent Patient Supervision

Courts around the country require that patients be adequately supervised. Failure to properly supervise patients can have serious implications. Cases from Florida,

Georgia, New Jersey, and New York enforce the duty of health care facilities and the staff at these facilities to adequately supervise patients entrusted to their care.

Kirkland v. State Department of Health[29] is a Florida case that involves a patient injuring herself while she was walking around the grounds at Northeast Florida State Hospital. While on the pass, Brenda Kirkland threw herself in front of a truck and suffered multiple serious injuries.

Subsequently, Brenda Kirkland sued the state of Florida and Northeast Florida State Hospital alleging, among other things, that Northeast Florida State Hospital had been negligent in supervising her. The court of appeals determined that Northeast Florida State Hospital was immune from the malpractice claim brought by Brenda Kirkland but was required to defend the negligent supervision claim. Subsequent proceedings were unpublished.

Although hospitals have a responsibility to appropriately supervise patients, *Brooks v. Coliseum Park Hospital, Inc.*[30] makes it clear that health care facilities are not obligated to furnish any patient a constant attendant and that an injury to a patient does not necessarily constitute negligence. In *Brooks,* Lucille M. Sterling was a 69-year-old Alzheimer's patient in the special care unit at Coliseum Park Hospital because she was having delusions, hallucinations, severe mood swings, and was refusing to take her medication. One evening Lucille was given flurazepam (Dalmane) to help her sleep. During the night Lucille was found out of bed. One time when she was out of bed, Lucille ran into a door frame and fell to the floor. X-rays were taken and revealed that Ms. Sterling had fractured her hip.

Her family sued on Lucille's behalf alleging that Coliseum Park Hospital failed to provide her adequate protection. Lucille's case was built around the idea that the side rails of her bed should have been up so that she could not have easily gotten out of bed and that she was not provided adequate supervision by the staff. Coliseum Park Hospital argued that the use of side rails would have increased the risk of injury to Lucille and would have resulted in her falling further to the floor should she climb over them. The case was tried and a Georgia jury returned a verdict in favor of the hospital. Upon affirming the jury verdict, the court of appeals concluded that it was not the law of Georgia that one patient was entitled to a constant attendant at all times, even if the patient was semi-conscious or under the influence of medications.

Approximately 7 years after *Brooks* was decided, *Ahn v. Kim*[31] was decided by a New Jersey court. In *Ahn,* Ho Ahn's wife, Kejoo Ahn, filed suit against the psychiatric hospital, doctors, nurses, and others she thought responsible for the wrongful death of her husband. With regard to the nursing staff, Kejoo Ahn asserted that there was inadequate supervision.

While at the psychiatrist's office, Ho Ahn tried to hang himself. Following the attempted suicide, he was hospitalized. He was assigned a room between noon and 1:00 PM. In spite of the fact that Ho Ahn was admitted because of suicide ideation, his belt was not removed, nor was he placed on suicide precautions. Mary Manuella, RN, the charge nurse on the unit saw Ho Ahn at 3:00 PM and Ho Ahn's roommate saw him at 5:00 PM. No one saw Ho Ahn after 5:00 PM. Ho Ahn disappeared from the unit and was never found. He was later declared dead.

The case was tried by a jury, which found that Mary Manuella, RN, the nursing staff at the Carrier Clinic, and the security staff were negligent. However, the jury determined that Keejoo Ahn failed to prove causation and wrongful death. Judgment, therefore, was entered in favor of the defendants. The matter was appealed to the Appellate Division of the Superior Court of New Jersey where the judgment of the jury was reversed and a new trial ordered because the jury was charged to presume that Ho Ahn did not commit suicide. In addition, the judge should have permitted Keejoo Ahn to add Carolyn Barter, RN, as a defendant because she was the charge nurse of the unit when Ho Ahn was admitted and should not have dismissed Irvin Kelly, the Director of Security. Subsequent proceedings in this case have not yet been published.

Three years after *Ahn,* a New York Court heard *Genao v. State.*[32] In that case, Jacqueline Genao was a 20-year-old patient at South Beach Psychiatric Center. She had ongoing psychiatric problems that required multiple hospitalizations. During one stay at South Beach Psychiatric center, Jacqueline was raped by another patient. Evidence was presented suggesting that the whereabouts of Jacqueline were unknown for approximately 3 hours. According to the center's observation policy, Jacqueline was supposed to be observed every 30 minutes. Center employees attempted to use the patient accountability record (PAR) to show that Jacqueline had been observed in accordance with South Beach's 30-minute observation rule. For approximately 2 1/2 hours, there were six "U" entries indicating that Jacqueline was on the unit. However, neither the therapy aide nor the nurse on staff could identify the whereabouts of Jacqueline for a 3-hour period.

The staff did come to the assistance of Jacqueline after the rape, after they heard her crying. Following the incident Jacqueline sued the State of New York asserting that South Beach Psychiatric Center had been negligent in providing her a safe environment. She was awarded $250,000 in damages. The award was later reduced to pay for uncompensated care provided to Jacqueline.

Nurses and health care organizations have an affirmative responsibility to adequately supervise patients. Failure to appropriately supervise patients subjects the nurse and facility to liability. Nurses and health care organizations are required to act reasonably in the supervision of patients, and are not generally required to provide patients with a constant attendant or with care until they are cured. In addition, where a nurse-defendant can show that his or her inability to adequately supervise a patient stemmed from inadequate staffing, or from other corporate acts, the facility and not the nurse can be found liable.

Negligent Discharge and Release

Negligent discharge and release cases are heard regularly by courts around the country. When it comes to the negligent discharge of patients, courts have held that hospitals may not keep a competent patient against his or her will and cannot confine institutionalized patients to in-patient settings when less restrictive settings are available and more appropriate. Two U.S. Supreme Court cases and cases from Oklahoma and Kansas indicate that a patient's constitutional rights must be protected. Failure to protect these rights can be costly, as demonstrated in *O'Connor v. Donaldson*.[33]

In *O'Connor*, Kenneth Donaldson was civilly committed to Florida State Hospital in 1957 after being diagnosed with paranoid schizophrenia. He was also declared incompetent. Kenneth remained a Florida State Hospital patient for almost 15 years. Throughout his confinement, Kenneth demanded his release from the facility. He eventually filed a class action lawsuit on behalf of himself and fellow patients alleging that this confinement against his will violated his constitutionally protected liberty interests. The case was tried in front of a jury, who returned a verdict in favor of Kenneth Donaldson. They also awarded compensatory and punitive damages.

The case made its way to the U.S. Supreme Court. The Justices agreed to hear the case and concluded that a person may not be involuntarily confined if he or she is not a danger to anyone and can live safely in freedom. They asserted that a mental illness diagnosis alone could not justify a state's confinement of a person against his will and do so indefinitely. In response to this decision, state legislatures created statutes identifying criteria to be used to treat a person involuntarily.

Twenty-five years after *O'Connor*, *Wofford v. Mental Health Services, Inc. d/b/a Parkside Hospital*[34] was heard by an Oklahoma Court. In *Wofford*, Dawn Wofford was detained for more than 3 days after she requested in writing to be released from Parkside Hospital. She was originally admitted because she was suicidal and in need of immediate treatment. Later the same day she was admitted, Dawn requested in writing that she be discharged. Four days later, on November 2, 1990, Parkside filed an order seeking to detain Dawn Wofford. Dawn obtained a writ of habeas corpus and was released at mid-day, November 2, 1990.

After her release, Dawn Wofford's mother filed suit against Parkside Hospital contending that she had been falsely imprisoned. The trial judge agreed with Wofford that Dawn had been unlawfully restrained. It was unclear whether the order entered by the trial judge meant that she had been unlawfully restrained past the 3-day statutory time period or whether she had been unlawfully restrained and falsely imprisoned consistent with case law on the matter. The reviewing judge determined that the matter of false imprisonment had not been decided and slated the matter for a jury trial. At trial, the jury returned a verdict for the hospital, because they concluded that the hospital acted reasonably.

Two years after *Wofford*, *Hesler v. Osawatomie*[35] was decided by the Kansas Supreme Court. In *Hesler*, Ronald Hesler was given a weekend pass so that he could spend time with his parents. He had previously handled a 4-hour pass without difficulty, was observed to be responsible and interactive, and did not seem to be overly anxious about going home with his parents. While on the weekend pass, Ronald Hesler and his parents were in their car when Ronald suddenly and unexpectedly grabbed the steering wheel and forced the car into a head-on collision with another car. One person in the other car was killed, and several others were injured.

Individuals in the other car sued Ronald's physician, Robert Hwang, as well as three nurses involved in his care, and Ossawatomie State Hospital, the facility at which Ronald was hospitalized for treatment for paranoid schizophrenia. He had committed no crimes, and no violent behavior was exhibited. However, Ronald was considered to be impulsive. During his course of treatment at Ossawatomie, Ronald's behavior was notably improved after his medication had been changed from haloperidol (Haldol) to risperidone (Risperdal). Following that change, Ronald was compliant with his treatment, interacted with others, and demonstrated no impulsive behaviors. Approximately 11 days later a 4-hour pass was given to Ron so that he could have lunch with his parents. The outing went well and was uneventful. Five days later, Ron was given another pass. This time he was allowed to spend the weekend with his parents. It was during this pass that Ronald grabbed the steering wheel.

Plaintiffs alleged that Ronald had been negligently released. The trial court dismissed the case, and it was appealed to the Kansas Supreme Court. The Kansas Supreme Court affirmed the decision of the trial court concluding that although health care professionals have a responsibility to keep patients in custody so long as they pose a danger to others and must warn persons in harm's way when a dangerous patient has left custody, no one on the treatment team had any reason to anticipate that this patient would commit a violent and self-destructive act.

In the same year that *Hesler* was decided, the U.S. Supreme Court heard *Olmstead v. L.C.*[36] In that case, the U.S. Supreme Court determined that states are required to provide community-based treatment for mentally disabled individuals when such placement is appropriate and can be reasonably accommodated. In *Olmstead*, two mentally retarded women continued to be institutionalized in spite of the fact that their needs could be met in a community-based treatment program. The women sued state officials saying that their civil rights had been violated as well as the Americans with Disabilities Act (ADA). The matter was argued in front of the Justices, and an opinion was issued later. The opinion issued by the U.S. Supreme Court concluded that the isolation of disabled people like the plaintiffs was unjustified and discriminatory.

Nurses have a responsibility to be patient advocates and in that role, need to ensure that patients are properly discharged. However, where a voluntarily admitted patient demands to be discharged, and regardless of his or her condition, the U.S. Supreme Court has determined that the patient must be discharged, and that the failure to discharge the patient is a violation of that patient's constitutional rights. In addition, institutionalized patients must not be confined to in-patient settings where less restrictive settings are available and more appropriate. As a result, nurses must be diligent advocates in the discharge process, and proceed in a manner that is in the patient's best interest, without violating that patient's constitutional rights.

Third-Party Litigation

Recently, state supreme courts have had an opportunity to consider the issue of therapist liability to third parties. Most of the third-party litigation reviewed by state supreme courts involve parents and their children. Typically, a child, in the course of therapy, discloses that he or she has been sexually or physically abused by one or both parents. The allegations are deemed false by the accused parents, and one or both parents sue the therapist for professional negligence. Cases from the Supreme Courts of New Hampshire, Wisconsin, and Pennsylvania indicate that courts may be reluctant but willing to extend a therapist's duty of care to third parties in some instances.

In 1998, the Supreme Court of New Hampshire heard *Hungerford v. Jones.*[37] In that case, Susan L. Jones, a social worker, began treating Laura B. Laura was in her mid-20s and was experiencing nightmares and anxiety attacks. During the course of therapy, Jones convinced Laura that her nightmares and anxiety attacks were indicative of repressed memories of sexual assault and abuse by Laura's father. Jones caused Laura, while in a self-induced trance, to recall five sexual assault instances that were allegedly inflicted by Laura's father. The episodes that Laura recalled began when she was 5 years old and the last episode occurred 2 days prior to Laura's wedding. When Laura's father, Joel Hungerford, learned of the allegations, he authorized his therapist to talk to Jones. Joel Hungerford insisted that the allegations were false.

Jones then directed that Laura discontinue all contact with Joel Hungerford. A few months later, Laura filed criminal charges against her father. Joel Hungerford was indicted for aggravated felonious sexual assault. During the course of Hungerford's criminal trial, Laura's memories were deemed inadmissible because they were scientifically unreliable, and Joel Hungerford was not convicted.

Joel Hungerford then filed this suit against Jones for negligent diagnosis and treatment of his daughter. Jones asked the court to dismiss the case filed against her asserting that she owed Joel Hungerford no duty of care. The trial court then asked the New Hampshire Supreme Court to determine what duty, if any, a mental health provider owed to the father and the alleged sexual perpetrator of an adult patient who discloses the sexual abuse in the course of therapy.

The New Hampshire Supreme Court considered this issue and determined that therapists do have a duty of care to a parent where the therapist or patient takes public action with regard to the alleged sexual abuse perpetrated by the parent. In reaching this conclusion, the New Hampshire Supreme Court observed that a therapist breaches the duty of care to the accused parent when the diagnosis is publicized and results from the use of techniques that are not generally accepted in the mental health community or when the therapist lacks professional qualification. In this case, Jones diagnosed Laura using unproven memory retrieval techniques and attended only one lecture on those memory retrieval techniques.

In 1999, the Wisconsin Supreme Court determined that parents can sue therapists for negligence. The case was *Sawyer v. Midelfort.*[38] In *Sawyer,* Nancy Anneatra was born Nancy Sawyer. Her parents were Thomas and Delores Sawyer. Nancy suffered from a number of psychiatric problems that required hospitalization prior to meeting either of the defendants in this case. Nancy later changed her last name from Sawyer to Anneatra. Nancy met Cecilia Lausted at a women's shelter located in Eau Claire, Wisconsin. Nancy's diary indicated that she already had some memory of being sexually abused by her father prior to meeting Lausted. At the time, Lausted was an unlicensed therapist. She began treating Nancy when Nancy was in her mid-20s, and approximately 13 months after Cecilia started treating Nancy, Thomas and Delores Sawyer learned that Nancy believed that she had been sexually abused by Thomas Sawyer. Nancy confronted her parents about this in the office of Kathryn Bemmann, a physician who was not named as a defendant in this case. Cecilia Lausted was also present. During the meeting, Nancy also accused both of her parents of physically abusing her. Both Sawyers denied Nancy's allegations.

Nancy continued to receive therapy from Cecilia Lausted, but Kathryn Bemmann terminated her treatment of Nancy approximately 2 years after the confrontation with Nancy's parents. Berit Midelfort replaced Kathryn Bemmann as Nancy's psychiatrist. During the course of treatment with Berit Midelfort, Nancy reported that she had been sexually abused by her father, paternal grandfather, uncle, brother, and two priests. Nancy also reported that an aunt and cousins were involved as perpetrators or observers to the sexual assault. Approximately 3 years after the meeting in which Nancy accused her parents of physical abuse and her father of sexual abuse, Nancy filed a lawsuit against her parents. The lawsuit was dismissed not long after it had been filed.

When Nancy was 36, she died from cancer. Her parents did not learn of her death until 6 months later. Once they became aware of Nancy's death, Nancy's mother obtained a court order appointing her as the administrator of Nancy's estate. In that capacity, Delores Sawyer had access to Nancy's medical records.

After reviewing the records, Delores and Thomas Sawyer filed a lawsuit alleging that Cecilia Lausted and Berit Midelfort caused Nancy to develop false memories regarding physical and sexual abuse. In addition, they allege that Lausted was professionally negligent and failed to properly diagnose and treat Nancy, and that she failed to properly handle transference and countertransference issues. In addition, the Sawyers alleged that Berit Midelfort failed to properly supervise Cecilia Lausted.

Originally, the circuit court concluded that this third-party claim failed to state a claim upon which relief could be granted. The court of appeals reversed the rulings of the circuit court, and those reversals were affirmed by the Wisconsin Supreme Court. The Wisconsin Supreme Court concluded that claims by parents were based on the harm suffered by parents as a direct result of the allegations leveled against them. Accordingly, their claims against the defendants could proceed. In reaching this decision, the Wisconsin Supreme Court expressly declined to follow *Hungerford*.

One year after *Sawyer* was decided by the Wisconsin Supreme Court, the Pennsylvania Supreme Court decided *Althaus v. Chon, et al.*[39] In that case, the minor daughter of Richard and Cheryl Althaus began to make allegations of parental sexual abuse while her mother was being treated for skin and breast cancer. At the same time, the daughter's grandmother had been diagnosed with diabetes and pancreatic cancer. The grandmother eventually died from pancreatic cancer.

In the midst of these events, the daughter began experiencing emotional difficulties, and one of her teachers offered her emotional support and assistance in getting the student into a cancer support group. The group was facilitated by a social worker. The daughter developed a rapport with the social worker and began to share the issues with which she had been dealing. The daughter shared with the social worker that her father had inappropriately touched her and that she had flashbacks of her father being in bed and on top of her. The social worker, in compliance with state statute, reported the information to the Children and Youth Services (CYS) office. The CYS office removed the daughter from the Althaus home and physically examined her for signs of sexual abuse. No signs of sexual abuse were uncovered during the course of the physical exam. The daughter was then referred to Judith A. Cohen, a psychiatrist at Western Psychiatric Institute and Clinic's Child and Adolescent Sex Abuse Clinic. The daughter's father was arrested and charged with rape and several other related offenses. The daughter's mother was also arrested and charged with sexual abuse.

During the course of therapy, the daughter's allegations of sexual abuse expanded to include family members, the father's co-workers, and complete strangers. In addition, the events surrounding the alleged abuses became more outrageous. Judith A. Cohen eventually testified that the daughter was unable to distinguish between fact and fiction, and the criminal charges pending against Richard and Cheryl Althaus were dropped.

The family was reunited with the assistance of mental health experts. During the course of reunification the daughter admitted that her sexual abuse allegations were false. The family was reunited, and the parents filed a medical malpractice cause of action against Judith A. Cohen asserting that Cohen negligently diagnosed and treated their daughter, and that her course of treatment potentiated the situation.

The case was presented to a jury who returned a verdict in favor of the parents. The daughter was awarded $58,000 in damages, and the parents were awarded more than $213,000 in damages. Judith A. Cohen appealed that decision contending that she did not owe the parents a duty of care.

The Pennsylvania Supreme Court reviewed the matter and concluded that Judith A. Cohen did not have a duty of care that extended to a patient's parents. They noted that the harm to Richard and Cheryl Althaus occurred prior to Judith A. Cohen's treatment. As a result, the trial court's judgment in favor of the parents was reversed.

In spite of the ultimate decision in *Althaus,* third-party litigation should be a concern for nurses who counsel patients. Currently, most third-party litigation arising from counseling patients involves sexual and/or physical abuse cases in which children allege that they have suffered abuse at the hands of one or both parents. The parents assert that the allegations are untrue, and sue the counselor. The counselor must then prove that her or she was competent to counsel the patient and that methods used to elicit the information are credible and consistent with the standard of care. Failure to use methods that are consistent with the standard of care can indicate that the counselor breached his or her duty to the patient, and that damages to a third party occurred because of that negligence. Although the status of third-party litigation continues to emerge at the state level, it is wise to practice as if third-party litigation will be permitted.

Summary

Nurses counseling patients need to recognize the complexities inherent in the counseling relationship. Failure to use a reasonable degree of care in the exercise of a nurse's responsibility to competently assess, plan, implement, and evaluate the care needed by patients may result in the nurse being liable for the harm that results, and may result in a patient fatally injuring him- or herself or another person.

To minimize these possibilities, nurses need to remember that courts generally impose a duty on health care professionals to warn specific, identifiable individuals whom their patients threaten to harm. This duty to warn, where it exists, does not subject a health care provider to breach of confidentiality causes of action. There are jurisdictions that do not impose a duty to warn, so knowing the rule of law in a given jurisdiction is important.

In addition to imposing liability on a counselor for failure to warn third parties, courts impose liability on health care professionals who engage in sexual activity with their patients. Courts also impose liability on health care professionals and health care facilities that improperly hospitalize patients, fail to protect suicidal patients, improperly administer medication, inadequately supervise patients, and negligently discharge and/or release patients.

Recently, courts have begun to extend the reach of a counselor's liability to third parties. Three state supreme courts have addressed the issue so far. Accordingly, it is unclear whether a majority of jurisdictions will ultimately extend a counselor's liability to third parties. To be safe, in jurisdictions that have not decided the issue, it is prudent to assume that third-party liability will be imposed.

End Notes

1. American Nurses Association (ANA). 2000. *Scope and Standards of Psychiatric-Mental Health Nursing Practice.* Washington, D.C.: American Nurses Association; p. 52.
2. No. 18163-4-III, June 13, 2000.
3. 529 P.2d 334 (Ca. 1976).
4. 403 A.2d 500 (N.J. 1979).
5. 497 F. Supp. 185 (Ne. 1980).
6. 194 Cal. Rptr. 805 (Ca. 1983).
7. No. J-253-96. November 25, 1998.
8. 570 F. Supp. 1333 (Co. 1983) and 751 F. 2d 329 (10th Cir. 1984).
9. 590 So. 2d 446 (Fl. 1991).

10. 416 S.E. 2d 792 (Ga. 1992).
11. 415 A.2d 625 (Md. 1980)
12. No. 97-1208, June 24, 1999.
13. 696 N.E. 793 (Il. 1998).
14. 436 S.W. 2d 753 (Mo. 1968)
15. 366 N.Y.S. 2d 297 (N.Y. 1975).
16. No. 96-662-T. February 24, 1998.
17. 42 U.S.C. 13981
18. 457 U.S. 307 (1982).
19. 238 N.E. 2d 191 (Il. 1968).
20. Medical Protective Company. 1991. As cited in Edenfield B.M. 1991. Psychiatrist's liability to third party victims for patient's acts of violence: The status of the law following *Tarasoff. Psychiatric Malpractice.* Athens, GA: Institute of Continuing Legal Education.
21. 708 S.W. 2d 686 (Mo. 1986).
22. 558 So. 2d 1342 (La. 1990).
23. 859 S.W. 2d 367 (Tx. 1992).
24. No. C97-5580. April 8, 1999.
25. No. 97-L-874. July 26, 1999.
26. 430 U.S. 651 (1977).
27. 506 F. Supp. 915 (Oh. 1980).
28. 946 F. Supp. 96 (Me 1996).
29. 489 So. 2d 800 (Fl. 1986).
30. 369 S.E. 2d 319 (Ga. 1988).
31. 658 A.2d 1286 (N.J. 1995).
32. 679 N.Y.S. 2d 539 (N.Y. 1998).
33. 422 U.S. 563 (1975).
34. No. 84,276. September 30, 1997.
35. 971 P.2d 1169 (Ks. 1999).
36. No. 98-536. June 22, 1999.
37. 722 A. 2d 478 (N.H. 1998).
38. 595 N.W. 2d 423 (Wi. 1999).
39. 756 A. 2d 1166 (Pa. 2000).

The Nurse as Case Manager in a Managed Care Environment 10

Introduction

In many ways, managed care has revolutionized the way that health care services are being delivered. At one time, the cost of providing health care services was escalating exponentially. Now, rising health care costs have slowed, and quality of care concerns have been raised. As a result, managed care has been criticized as an inefficient and cost- rather than patient-focused mechanism through which health care services are delivered. In spite of these criticisms, it is likely that some form of managed care will continue to exist. As inefficient as some may assert that managed care is, it has slowed the escalation in health care costs, and quality of care issues are being addressed. These, and other managed care-related topics, including the work of the Managed Care Working Group convened by the American Nurses Association (ANA), the role of the nurse in managed care environments, the nurse as case manager, contractual issues, and managed care-related case law, including the impact of The Employee Retirement Income Security Act (ERISA) on a patient's ability to pursue health care claims, will be explored in this chapter.

Managed Care Expectations

Managed care describes the array of health care services arrangements that exist between health care providers, payers, and patients. These arrangements provide financial incentives and penalties designed to influence the use of health care services. Originally, managed care was presented to consumers as a mechanism through which coordinated, seamless health care services would be provided. Managed care benefits included waste and redundancy elimination, focus on health promotion and disease prevention, and the effective and efficient management of chronic illness. In addition, provider and payer accountability was anticipated to be heightened, as were investments in patient information systems.

Managed Care Implementation

Because of an overt emphasis on profit making by some managed care organizations, expected benefits have yet to be fully realized. To complicate matters, the widespread move to implementing managed care systems prior to piloting the mechanism has resulted in problems and frustrations that could have been remedied during the pilot process. One issue that continues to plague the system is abuse.

Well-publicized abuses by some managed care organizations continue to highlight the negative aspects of managed care. No case illustrates this point better than *Goodrich v. Aetna U.S. Healthcare of California.*[1] In *Goodrich*, David Goodrich was a deputy district attorney in San Bernadino County, California. He died from a rare form of stomach cancer. His condition was diagnosed in June, 1992. In July, 1992, a surgical oncologist recommended that Mr. Goodrich receive a bone marrow transplant and chemotherapy at a hospital that specialized in cancer treatment. The surgical oncologist was an Aetna-approved provider. However, the hospital to which the oncologist referred Mr. Goodrich for treatment was not an Aetna-approved facility. Aetna did not respond to the surgeon's request for treatment for approximately 4 months. In November, 1992, Aetna denied the request. By that time, Mr. Goodrich was no longer a candidate for a bone marrow transplant.

Approximately 9 months later, liver surgery combined with chemotherapy was recommended. It took Aetna 3 months to respond to this request. Again, Aetna denied the recommended course of treatment. In spite of the denial, Mr. Goodrich had surgery. Later, Aetna paid for most of the surgery, but not Mr. Goodrich's chemotherapy. Approximately 4 months later, it was recommended that Mr. Goodrich undergo another surgery to remove cancerous tissue, and that he have chemotherapy. Six days after submitting the request to Aetna, Mr. Goodrich had the surgery without knowing whether Aetna would cover the interventions. The first day after surgery, Mr. Goodrich's wife, Teresa, received a letter that indicated that Aetna would not cover surgical costs, or the cost of the associated medical care. Mr. Goodrich remained hospitalized after this surgery until he died on March 15, 1995. When he died, Mr. Goodrich had approximately $750,000 in unpaid medical bills. The Goodrich family then sued Aetna U.S. Healthcare of California alleging, among other things, that Aetna U.S. Healthcare of California was responsible for the wrongful death of David Goodrich. A jury heard the evidence and awarded the Goodrich family $747,656 in medical expense compensation, $3.79 million for their wrongful death claim, and $116 million in punitive damages.[2]

Unfortunately, the *Goodrich* case does not appear to be isolated. As a result, some managed care organizations have subjected themselves to jury awards that necessitate them paying hundreds of millions of dollars to injured patients and/or their families. Retrospectively, it would have been less costly for Aetna U.S. Healthcare of California to have responded promptly to the requests concerning Goodrich's treatment and pay his actual medical expenses. Instead, Aetna U.S. Healthcare of California is faced with the prospect of having to pay hundreds of millions of dollars to the Goodrich family.

The Work of the Managed Care Working Group Convened by the ANA

The ANA has issued managed care-related position statements since 1970. More than two decades later, in 1992, the ANA House of Delegates endorsed a report highlighting the potential for managed care to meet the preventive and primary needs of patients, and for nurses to contribute significantly to the health and wellness of managed care patients. However, the performance of some managed care organizations combined with what appeared to be an erosion of nursing's core values led the ANA House of Delegates to adopt comprehensive managed care recommendations: all health plans meet federal standards that require access to an array of providers; health plans be prohibited from discriminating against providers based solely on professional licensure; effective regulatory and oversight authority be created so that national plan standards are enforced; health plans be required to disseminate accurate and understandable information to enrollees including plan policies, outcome performance data, and financial arrangements between plans and participating providers; unrestricted communication between health care providers and patients; and health plans be required to comply with quality of care standards.

Thereafter, in March, 1997, the ANA Board of Directors, led by ANA President Beverly L. Malone, PhD, RN, FAAN, approved the initiation of a managed care project which resulted in the appointment of a group to work on managed care issues,[3] and the formulation, adoption, and publication of *Managed Care: Nursing's Blueprint for Action*.[4] This publication outlined the principles that should characterize any health care delivery system (see sidebar).

In addition to issuing, and disseminating these principles, ANA, Constituent Member Associations (CMAs), specialty nursing groups, other provider associations, and consumer advocacy groups have worked tirelessly to pass state-based managed care legislation designed to protect patients and improve the quality of care delivered by managed care providers. Among the legislative initiatives being debated at the state level are more liberal access to specialists and alternative providers, access to nonphysician providers, access to emergency services, eliminating financial incentives rewarding the delay or denial of care and treatment, banning gag clauses that do not permit a health care provider to discuss all treatment options, hospital stay mandates for procedure specific admissions, other length of stay issues, enactment of mandated benefits like mental health benefits, and the implementation of internal and external grievance procedures that can be accessed without retaliation by consumers and providers. Currently, the most hotly contested legislative issue is insurer liability. So far, only the legislatures in Georgia, Missouri, Oklahoma, New York, and Texas have stripped managed care plans of their immunity from state-based lawsuits.

While incremental reform is occurring at the state level, federal reform is also happening. ANA is actively supporting strong, comprehensive patient protection legislation at the federal level. Comprehensive patient protection legislation has been pursued by ANA (see sidebar) and other specialty organizations for a number of years.

Although the ANA and other professional and consumer advocacy groups work to eliminate the problems associated with managed care, positive aspects of this delivery model have been recognized. Because of managed care, more Americans enjoy access to quality health care services, and the potential for effectively managing care across the life span is greater today than ever before.

The Role of the Nurse in Managed Care Environments

In spite of the troubling aspects of managed care, this health care financing mechanism offers nurses the opportunity to practice in a wide variety of settings and in a wide variety of roles. Nurses continue to practice in traditional settings and roles, but

Patient Protection Legislation Components

Using its grassroots network to deliver nursing message to the U.S. Congress, the ANA asserts that comprehensive patient protection legislation must include, at a minimum:

- Protection for providers who advocate for patients.
- The consumers' access to and an ability to choose among a variety of providers.
- Application to all private insurers.
- Prohibitions against a Health Maintenance Organization's (HMOs) arbitrary interference with the provider's clinical decision making.
- Prohibitions against financial incentives paid for the delay or denial of care and treatment.
- Effective, expedient independent internal and external appeals processes.
- Mechanisms to ensure plan accountability.
- Emergency room, out-of-network, obstetrical/gynecological, and specialist access.
- Guarantees that the managed care network meets the patients' needs.
- Continuity of care.
- Access to needed prescription drugs as well as clinical trials.
- Information about plan quality, exclusions, and service costs.

they are also practicing in nontraditional roles, many of which are the result of the transition to managed care. Nontraditional roles now occupied by registered nurses include, but are not limited to, chief executive officer, chief operating officer, managed care organization owner, case manager, corporate benefits plan liaison, utilization reviewer, and primary care provider.

At no time in nursing's history have the opportunities for nurses been more plentiful. Accordingly, it is imperative that nurses be educationally and experientially prepared to positively contribute to the health care profession. Managed care is the vehicle through which health care services are delivered, so nurses must work to improve the system to ensure that patients receive quality health care services.

The Nurse as Case Manager

Undoubtedly, case managers are in a position to see that patients receive the care they need. Case managers work to see that patients receive health care services that are of the highest quality and delivered in a timely, cost-conscious manner. Case managers provide high-quality, cost-effective health care services in a variety of settings in an effort to enhance a client's quality of life, decrease service fragmentation, and to facilitate the most positive outcome for the patient.

Managed care organizations, ambulatory care clinics, and long-term care facilities, among others, use case managers so that patient progress can be monitored and positive outcomes achieved. In some settings, case managers are considered employees; in others, they are independent contractors. It is important that nurses, and the entity or individual for whom case management services are being rendered, understand the difference. An agreement outlining the case management services that are to be provided is a good place for the employment status of the case manager to be addressed. (See Chapter 6.)

Contractual Issues

Understanding and clarifying the relationship between the parties (the case manager and the entity with whom the case manager is contracting) is critical when it comes to executing an effective case management agreement. In addition to clarifying the relationship between the parties, a comprehensive case management agreement outlines the expectations of each party. So that the expectations are clear, case management contracts should include the following substantive provisions: scope of the agreement, proprietary rights, confidentiality, conflict of interest, duties of the entity with whom the case manager is contracting, duties of the case manager, compensation, indemnification and subrogation, agreement term, renewal and termination, and dispute resolution. Miscellaneous or general provisions should also be included. Issues usually addressed in the miscellaneous or general provisions portion of the case management agreement include legal capacity, severability, modification, approval and notification expectations, force majeure, and choice of law. The concluding portion of all case management agreements is the signature of parties section. These contractual issues were introduced in Chapter 6, and are discussed here in the case management context.

Although the specific provisions of each case management contract will likely be different, it is important for nurses to know that once they sign a contract, they are subjecting themselves to breach of contract causes of action if they fail to comply with the terms of the agreement. Liability for breach can result in the breaching party having to pay monetary damages, but could also result in compelled performance in accordance with the contract. It also subjects the breaching party to potential tort causes of action like interference in economic relationship claims. In addition, where there is reason to believe that the breach occurred in bad faith, the breaching party could be subject to the payment of punitive damages. Accordingly, the execution of a contract is a serious matter and the negotiation of the terms of that contract needs to be treated as such.

Relationship of the Parties

Basically, the difference between an employee and an independent contractor is most striking with the issue of control. In an employer–employee relationship, the employer exercises a maximum amount of control. However, in an independent contractor relationship, control is shared; the entity for whom case management services are being provided articulates their expectations with regard to outcomes, and the independent contractor determines how and when case management services are provided so that those outcomes are achieved.

It is important to understand the employer–independent contractor difference for several reasons. First, an employer–employee relationship connotes a master–servant affiliation in which one party tells the other what to do and how to complete a given assignment. An independent contractor, on the other hand, is not subjected to that kind of relational arrangement. Independent contractor status connotes a relationship in which both parties relate to each other as partner, rather than as superior and subordinate.

Typical independent contractor language in the "Relationship of the Parties" section of case management agreements is:

> Case manager acknowledges that he/she is solely an independent contractor and not an employee of the corporation and is not entitled to any employee rights or benefits (including, but not limited to the accrual of vacation, sick time, health insurance, and retirement benefits). Because of case manager's independent contractor status, no tax withholdings shall be deducted from the compensation provided herein. Case manager acknowledges that he/she is solely responsible for the payment of taxes with respect to the compensation paid to him/her by the corporation.

Scope of Agreement

Case management agreements, as well as agreements executed for other purposes usually begin with a Scope of Agreement section. For case managers, it is in the Scope of Agreement section that providing case management services will be introduced. Scopes will vary. Brief scopes simply state that case management services will be provided. Alternatively, more detailed scopes will delineate each specific service that will be provided under the terms of the case management agreement.

An example of a more detailed Scope of Agreement section is as follows:

> During the term of this Agreement, case manager will provide case management services set forth below. In providing these services, case manager relies on the corporation to complete certain tasks as described herein. It is agreed by the parties that case manager's commitment to provide case management services is contingent upon corporation's timely discharge of its responsibilities under this Agreement.

During the term of this Agreement, case management services shall include:

▌ Conduct case screening;
▌ Identify target populations;
▌ Validate clinical and demographic data;
▌ Administer assessment tools and risk screens;
▌ Identify barriers to availability, accessibility, and affordability of treatment;
▌ Explore motivational and adherence issues;
▌ Review client history and current status;
▌ Identify opportunities for health promotion and illness prevention;
▌ Identify educational needs and readiness to learn;
▌ Evaluate support systems (individual, family, significant other, and community);
▌ Examine patterns of over- and/or underutilization of resources;
▌ Prioritize needs;
▌ Set realistic, measurable, agreed to outcomes;
▌ Select resources needed to achieve outcomes;
▌ Determine treatment options;
▌ Delineate appropriate treatment and care settings;
▌ Ascertain appropriate providers needed to achieve outcomes;
▌ Identify and address gaps in care;
▌ Provide continuity of care;
▌ Advocate for the client to receive needed health care services;
▌ Negotiate and manage financial aspects of care;
▌ Communicate the clients' progress toward desired outcomes;
▌ Coordinate the delivery of services;
▌ Explore optimal, cost-effective options available to the client;
▌ Timely refer clients to the most appropriate providers;
▌ Implement cost-effective interventions;
▌ Ensure compliance with applicable regulations, standards, and legislation;
▌ Secure appropriate community resources;
▌ Provide individual educational opportunities;
▌ Document use of the case management process;
▌ Be accountable for implementing the agreed to treatment plan;
▌ Evaluate the client's progress toward desired outcomes;
▌ Analyze the components of the case management process, highlighting client responses to interventions;
▌ Ensure that the plan of care is realistic and mutually beneficial to all involved; and
▌ Other case management activities consistent with the case manager's scope of practice.

Proprietary Rights

Whereas the Scope of Agreement section outlines what the obligations for each party are in executing the agreement, the Proprietary Rights section states which of the parties owns what tangible and intangible property (including products, documents, information, and other items of value). It may be that the entity with whom the case manager agrees to provide case management services provides office space, equipment, and supplies, as well as health care equipment and supplies. That entity will likely assert that the space, equipment, supplies, as well as other documents and information are owned by the entity, and provided solely for the case manager's use in accordance with the case management agreement. On the other hand, if the case manager uses personal space, equipment, and supplies, the case manager will want to make it clear that the case manager owns those things.

Although this section delineates the ownership of the tangible and intangible property of the parties, it may also grant to the other party the right to use what is owned by the other party. For instance, an entity may grant the case manager the right to use its logo, so long as the case manager restricts its use to executing the services outlined in the case management agreement. Conversely, the case manager may grant the entity with whom the case manager is contracting the right to use the name or logo of the case manager or case management company when marketing case management services.

Typical Proprietary Rights language used in case management agreements is as follows:

> Case manager and/or corporation shall have exclusive ownership and property rights (including all intellectual property rights) in and to all of the services provided under the terms of this Agreement. In addition, case manager and/or corporation shall retain the rights in and title to all case manager and/or corporation content, service or trade marks, and any other intellectual property previously developed by case manager and/or corporation or its affiliates that may be adapted or used by case manager and/or corporation to perform the services under this Agreement, it is understood and agreed by case manager and/or corporation that no rights, patent or otherwise, including but not limited to license to use proprietary software or any subcontractor owned software, are granted to case manager and/or corporation by this Agreement or by the services provided hereunder.
>
> Case manager and/or corporation shall not copy, use, display, distribute, or transfer case manager and/or corporation content, case manager and/or corporation marks, or other intellectual property owned by case manager and/or corporation or any case manager and/or corporation affiliate except as expressly authorized by this Agreement. In addition, case manager and/or corporation shall not reverse engineer, disassemble, or decompile case manager and/or corporation content or other intellectual property owned by case

manager and/or corporation. Notwithstanding the foregoing, case manager and/or corporation agrees that case manager and/or corporation shall be free to use and employ general skills, know-how, and expertise, and to use, disclose, and employ any generalized ideas, concepts, methods, skills, and techniques gained or learned during the duration of this Agreement, so long as case manager and/or corporation does not disclose confidential information.

Case manager and/or corporation shall use its best efforts to protect all case manager and/or corporation content provided under this Agreement, to police the usage thereof, and to ensure that no unauthorized third party uses case manager and/or corporation content provided under this Agreement. Case manager and/or corporation shall not place case manager and/or corporation marks on any content other than case manager and/or corporation content without prior written permission of the other party.

Confidentiality

The case manager's obligation to preserve client confidentiality requires that the case manager balance their commitment to confidentiality with not committing forgery, or altering diagnoses, treatments, medications, or reports. In addition, the commitment to confidentiality must be balanced with the case manager's duty to report statutorily required matters.

For the case manager, confidentiality matters do not stop with the client. There will be confidential information exchanged between the case manager and the entity with whom the case manager is contracting. Because of the exchange of proprietary and confidential information, it is imperative that case management agreements contain a confidentiality provision. Like other provisions, the confidentiality section of an agreement will vary in length. Some confidentiality agreements simply state that confidential, proprietary, and trade secret information will not be disclosed to any third party or used in any manner inconsistent with the case management agreement. Other confidentiality provisions are descriptive, and include an explanation of what does and does not constitute confidential information.

Typical, descriptive Confidentiality language included in case management contracts is as follows:

Case manager acknowledges that he/she may come into possession of confidential and proprietary information and agrees that such information shall not be disclosed to any third person or used in any manner other than as may be required to render the services provided herein. In addition, case manager agrees to keep the terms and conditions of this Agreement confidential.

Confidential information of a party shall include all information, material, and/or data disclosed by one party to the other during the term of this Agreement, and relating to the subject of this Agreement, including all information that a party designates or designated, either orally or in writing, to be of a confidential or proprietary nature, or which one party has reason to believe should be treated as such, including, but not limited to, intellectual property, and all matters relating to finances.

In addition, both parties agree to refrain from disclosing the other party's confidential information to anyone other than its employees, attorneys, accountants, and consultants who have a need to know in order to perform the party's obligations under this Agreement.

Notwithstanding the foregoing, confidential information shall not include information that (1) is or becomes available from public sources through no wrongful act of the other party; (2) is already in the receiving party's possession prior to the date of this Agreement without an obligation of confidentiality, except for information disclosed during discussions related to this Agreement; (3) is rightfully disclosed to the receiving party by a third party with no obligation of confidentiality; and (4) is independently developed by the receiving party, or is required to be disclosed pursuant to any court or regulatory order served on the other party.

Except as may be otherwise agreed to in writing by the parties, the party receiving confidential information from the other party shall:

- Protect and maintain the confidentiality of the disclosing party's confidential information;
- Not sell, transfer, publish, display, disclose, or otherwise make available to others, any confidential information;
- Take all necessary precautions to restrict access to and disclosure of the disclosing party's confidential information by any person or entity, including, without limitation, the non-disclosing party's employees, attorneys, accountants, and consultants who have been provided with confidential information pursuant to this Agreement; and
- Advise the disclosing party immediately in the event that the receiving party learns or has reason to believe that any unauthorized person who has had access to confidential information, or any portion thereof, and will cooperate with the disclosing party in seeking injunctive or other equitable relief in the name of either party against such person.

Each party shall acknowledge that the other party's confidential information contains proprietary information and trade secrets and agrees to maintain the confidential information in a manner using at least as great a degree of care as the manner used to maintain the confidentiality of its own most confidential information. Each party shall acknowledge that the disclosure of any aspect of the other party's confidential information or any information which, at law or equity, ought to remain confidential, will give rise to irreparable injury which is inadequately compensable in damages. Accordingly, each party may seek or obtain injunctive relief against the breach or threatened breach to any of the foregoing undertakings, in addition to any other legal remedies which may be available, and the receiving party hereby consents to the obtaining of such injunctive relief.

Conflict of Interest

Case management agreements will usually require that both parties agree to avoid all conflicts of interest. Where a potential or actual conflict of interest is discovered, case management agreements will likely require that the discovering party immediately notify the other party so that conflict of interest issues can be promptly resolved. For instance, where a managed care organization has a financial interest in a pharmaceutical, medical supply, or other health care services company, and that drug, product, or service is the only authorized drug, product, or service the case manager may use, the managed care company, if a conflict of interest provision is included in the agreement between the organization and the case manager, is contractually obligated to inform the case manager.

Duties of Corporation and Duties of Case Manager

Although the aforementioned provisions are important components of any case management agreement, two of the most important provisions are the Duties of the Corporation and the Duties of the Case Manager sections. It is here that the duties of both parties are outlined. Some agreements limit the duties sections to "any lawful duties necessary to provide case management services." Other contracts provide more detail, and delineate specifically the responsibilities of each party. Although Scope of Agreements outline general responsibilities of the parties, duties address the specific operational responsibilities of each party.

An example of more detailed Duties of Corporation and Duties of Case Manager language is as follows.

Duties of Corporation

Pursuant to this Agreement, the corporation shall:

▪ Authorize case manager to perform case management services outlined herein;
▪ Provide to case manager current, accurate, and complete benefit plan and other reimbursement and/or payment information, including protocols, if any;
▪ Cooperate with case manager in the interpretation of applicable benefit plan, reimbursement, and/or payment information;
▪ Provide case manager with all necessary confidentiality waivers, release of information, and other legal and regulatory documents;
▪ Represent and warrant that plan documents, if any, are sufficient to authorize the case management services as outlined in this Agreement;

- Maintain professional and general liability insurance coverage in the amount of_____ for acts of corporation which shall provide primary coverage for any claims arising from the acts of corporation pursuant to this Agreement;
- Be solely responsible to make benefit determinations, and to communicate those decisions to the beneficiary; and
- Provide an appeals process which may be accessed by case manager, without retaliation.

Duties of Case Manager

Pursuant to this Agreement, case manager shall:

- Upon the receipt and acceptance of a case management referral by corporation, schedule an initial visit with the referred client within _____ hours/business days;
- Review insurance coverage, if any, supplied by corporation and identify the waivers, and other legal and regulatory forms which need to be executed;
- Inform corporation if additional information is needed;
- Obtain pertinent health information from the referred client, as well as the health care providers caring for the referred client, and facilities in which the referred client has received health care services;
- Create a treatment plan, and secure the written consent of the referred client's treating physician, and the referred client;
- Facilitate the referred client's access to health care services;
- Within _____ business days of receiving and accepting each referral, provide to corporation the agreed to treatment plan, signed waivers, and regular status reports, thereafter, which focus on the referred client's progress toward articulated goals;
- Within _____ business days of receiving and accepting each referral, provide to corporation recommendations and expected outcomes where the referred client and treating physician do not agree to the treatment plan;
- Represent and warrant that case manager shall maintain professional liability insurance coverage in the amount of _____, which shall provide primary coverage for any claims arising from acts of case manager pursuant to this Agreement; and
- Comply with all applicable state and federal laws, regulations, and professional codes of ethics.

Compensation

The compensation section identifies what the case manager will be paid for providing case management services that have been described in the Duties of Case Manager section of the case management agreement. Typically, a salary or lump sum total is identified, as well as the increments within which the case manager will receive payment. Some agreements incorporate a late charge to be paid the case manager if payment is not received within an identified time frame. Case managers may also be paid on a per client basis, and if that is the case, the agreement should specifically state the calculation that will be used to determine the amount of the payment due to the case manager. Careful consideration needs to be given to whether or not activities not specifically delineated in the case management agreement will be incorporated in the fee the case manager agreed to accept, or calculated at a separate rate. If the activity falls outside of the fee the case manager will collect, language needs to be added to allow the case manager to be compensated for activities not specifically delineated in the agreement.

The compensation package spelled out in the case management agreement will depend on the needs of the case manager, as well as the corporation with which the case manager is negotiating. It will also depend on whether the case manager will be considered an independent contractor or employee. Where the case manager is considered an employee, compensation will probably include the accrual of vacation, sick, and other paid time off. In addition, life, health, and dental insurance, as well as retirement benefits may be offered. Where the case manager will be retained to work as an independent contractor, these nonmonetary benefits will not be offered. However, profit-sharing, stock options, and other incentives may be included.

Typical Compensation language for the salaried case manager is as follows:

Case manager shall be compensated a total of $_____ for rendering case management services for the duration of this Agreement. Payment shall be in equal monthly installments and case manager shall receive each monthly installment by the last business day of each month. If payment is not received by case manager by the last business day of each month, a $50.00/day late fee will be assessed to corporation.

In addition, case manager shall be reimbursed at the prevailing IRS reimbursement rates for reasonable travel expenses, so long as original documentation is submitted to corporation within the quarter in which the expense was incurred, and is directly related to the delivery of case management services pursuant to this Agreement. Corporation also agrees to reimburse case manager for all expenses, fees, and dues necessary for case manager to provide case management services delineated herein so long as original documentation is provided to corporation within the quarter in which the expense was incurred. Bonuses, annual compensation increases, and payment for attendance at continuing education programs may be negotiated annually. Incentive compensation in the form of bonuses, annual compensation increases, or in the giving of anything of value shall be based on quality outcomes and not on the denial or rationing of health care services.

Indemnification and Subrogation

Agreements between case managers and corporations not only need to address compensation, but also indemnification and subrogation. *Indemnification* occurs where one party agrees to take responsibility for losses that stem from a given transaction. When Indemnification is included in case management agreements, it is a pledge extended from one party to another to hold the other party harmless if any claims arise out of the wrongdoing of the party offering to indemnify the other party. Failure to include an indemnification clause in a case management agreement could result in the case manager being held liable for the wrongdoing of the entity with whom the case manager is contracting. Accordingly, it is imperative for the case manager to include an indemnification clause in every agreement to provide case management services.

Alternatively, *subrogation* describes an ability to substitute one party for another in a cause of action. Subrogation, in effect, allows an individual or entity to sue another person or entity (a nurse employee, for example) to recover money lost because of a negligence or malpractice verdict in favor of the patient-plaintiff. Subrogation has been used by health care facilities to recover losses after facilities are adjudged liable for negligence or malpractice of the nurse. That being the case, it is prudent for case managers to seek the waiver of an entity's rights to subrogation, or to ensure that the right to subrogation exists for both parties. Although entities with whom case managers contract will likely not waive this right, it is helpful to know that the right of subrogation exists for all parties entering into any agreement.

An example of language that comprises Indemnification and Subrogation sections is as follows:

> Corporation agrees to indemnify case manager and hold him/her harmless from and against any and all claims, losses, liabilities, suits, damages, and expenses incurred by case manager, including court costs, and attorney fees, so long as the action of the corporation pursuant to this Agreement, is at issue. Additionally, corporation agrees to refrain from pursuing its' subrogation rights against case manager.

Term, Renewal, and Termination

The term, renewal, and termination clauses in an agreement to provide case management services should identify the date upon which the contract starts, as well as the date upon which the case management agreement expires. Typically, the parties to an agreement will include a clause that permits the agreement to be renewed or extended for a time-limited period where both parties agree, and where neither party elects to terminate the agreement.

In addition to identifying the time frame during which the case management contract will be in effect, the process for terminating case management agreements needs to be articulated, as well as the grounds for terminating the agreement. Where the agreement is terminated for a reason that is enumerated in the agreement, the agreement will be said to have terminated for cause. *For cause* reasons for termination typically include, but are not limited to, the commission of a crime, failure to act in accordance with professional standards of practice, failure to act in accordance with one's fiduciary duties, and acting in a manner that compromises the integrity of the other party. Typically, agreements terminated for cause result in the payment of no or little money to the terminated party. On the other hand, agreements terminated without cause generally result in the terminated party receiving a more significant severance package. Termination without cause simply means that one party wishes to discontinue its association with the other party. Termination can be for no reason, or for a reason not articulated in the for cause section of the agreement. So long as the termination does not occur for discriminatory or other illegal reasons, the termination will be upheld in the civil justice system. Where one party elects to terminate the agreement, whether for cause or without cause, notification must be provided in compliance with the time frames identified in the case management agreement.

Typical Term, Renewal, and Termination provisions are as follows:

This Agreement shall commence on _____, 200_ and shall continue until _____, 200__, unless it is terminated earlier as provided herein. If this Agreement is not terminated by either party prior to ninety (90) before the Agreement's expiration date, this Agreement shall automatically renew each year for successive one year terms.

Case manager may immediately terminate this Agreement "for cause" for: failure of corporation to make timely payment to the case manager; any corporate changes in requirements, protocols, procedures, or requirements which affect case manager's duties; bad faith on the part of the corporation; a finding that the corporation committed Medicare fraud or abuse; and for the corporation's failure to effectively perform any of the provisions set out in this Agreement. Where this Agreement is terminated "for cause" the case manager shall receive the following severance package . . .

Additionally, either party may terminate this Agreement without cause provided that the terminating party provides ninety (90) days written notice to the other party. Where the corporation terminates this Agreement without cause, the case manager shall receive the following severance package . . .

Dispute Resolution

Although most agreements expire or terminate smoothly, some do not. Where agreement termination or expiration fails to occur smoothly, or where disputes arise during the term of the agreement, it will be advantageous to exercise the dispute resolution clause. A *dispute resolution clause* requires that both parties use their best efforts to resolve disputes that may arise, but provides a dispute resolution mechanism when the best efforts of the parties prove futile. Typically, dispute resolution clauses require that the guidelines of the American Arbitration Association be adhered to, and that the arbitrator selected to resolve the dispute be acceptable to both parties.

Typical Dispute Resolution language is as follows:

> Both parties agree to use their best efforts to amicably resolve any disputes under this Agreement without recourse to formal dispute resolution procedures. However, should the parties be unable to resolve a dispute under this Agreement, both parties agree that all disputes arising out of this Agreement shall be settled using arbitration procedures outlined by the rules of the American Arbitration Association. The American Arbitration Association shall appoint an Arbitrator acceptable to both parties within thirty (30) days of being notified by one party that the other party would like to submit a dispute to arbitration. Arbitration proceedings shall take place in (place, city, state) _____, and the courts of the state of _____ shall have jurisdiction for purposes of enforcing arbitration awards. Both parties shall submit to the Arbitrator its proposed resolution of each issue. The Arbitrator shall use his/her best efforts to conclude arbitration within thirty (30) days of his/her appointment as Arbitrator. The decision of the Arbitrator shall not be appealable to any court or other entity and shall be final, non-appealable, and binding on each party. The reasonable cost of Arbitration shall be paid by the non-prevailing party. However, each party is responsible for paying its own attorney fees.

Miscellaneous or General Provisions

The last substantive section of case management agreements is usually referred to as the Miscellaneous or General Provisions section. This portion of the case management agreement clarifies that the agreement being entered into is the only agreement that exists between the parties, and that each party has the legal capacity and authority to enter into the agreement. This section also contains a statement, usually referred to as a severability clause, which states that if any single provision in the agreement is deemed to be invalid for any reason, that the remaining provisions will be unaffected. Severability clauses ensure that uncontested agreement provisions remain in effect, and that services or products which are the subject of the agreement continue to be provided.

Additionally, the Miscellaneous section usually contains a provision that allows the term of the case management agreement to be amended or modified if both parties agree, and asserts that where one party to the agreement needs to obtain the approval of the other party, that the party giving approval will do so reasonably and without delay. This section also includes what is commonly referred to as a *Force Majeure* clause. This clause ensures that where an act of God (such as a natural disaster, war, riot, power failure) prevents one party from fulfilling their responsibility according to the agreement, that the terms of the agreement will be unaffected, and that the party prevented from performance has a reasonable opportunity to complete their performance. Also, the miscellaneous section usually includes a Contact Information section, as well as a Conflict of Laws provision. In the contact information section, both parties are required to list their address, telephone, fax number, and e-mail address, if applicable. This ensures that the information is exchanged in a timely fashion.

The conflict of laws provision seeks to clarify what state's laws will be used if a conflict arises. This provision is important, and should not be ignored, or negotiated away too readily. Sometimes, the outcome can depend on the laws in the state identified in the agreement. Typical Conflict of Laws language in case management agreements will be as follows: "All legal issues arising out of this agreement shall be governed by the laws of the state of _____."

Typical "Miscellaneous" or "General Provisions" include the following:

- Corporation agrees to obtain the permission of case manager prior to using case manager's name in any marketing material.
- This Agreement is the sole Agreement between the parties regarding the subject matter of this Agreement and all earlier Agreements (formal or informal, written or oral), understandings, and covenants, if any, shall be deemed to have merged and integrated herein.
- Each of the parties warrants that it has the legal authority to enter into this Agreement, that there are no legal impediments to its entering into this Agreement, and that all approvals required for its execution of this Agreement have been received.
- In the event that any provision of this Agreement is found by a court to be void or unenforceable, the provision shall be construed to be separable from the other provisions of this Agreement which shall retain full force and effect.
- This Agreement may be amended or modified only by a writing mutually agreed to and signed by both parties.
- Wherever the approval of one party is required of the actions of the other party hereunder, such approval shall not be unreasonably withheld or delayed.
- Neither case manager nor corporation shall be responsible for delays or failure of performance resulting from acts beyond the reasonable control of either party (such as acts of God, riots, acts of war, and epidemics, power failures, earthquakes, or other disasters), provided such delays or failures of performance could not have been prevented by reasonable precautions and could not have been reasonably circumvented by either party through the use of alternative sources, work around plans, or other means. Upon the occurrence of any such event, the contractual dates shall be extended for a period equal to the duration of the force majeure event.

Party Signatures

The final portion of the case management agreement is usually the signature section. This section requires that both parties sign and date the agreement. It is only when the agreement is signed and dated by both parties, that it is deemed fully executed. Having a fully executed agreement indicates that the parties have voluntarily agreed to the terms which will govern their interaction.

Managed Care Case Law

While federal and state legislation is being debated, the judicial branch of the United States is hearing more managed care cases. These cases suggest that managed care providers need to be aware of the acts and omissions which give rise to civil liability. Among the unique, managed care-related issues being decided in U.S. courts are breach of a provider's fiduciary duty to his/her patient,[5] failure on the part of the health care provider to disclose any financial incentives the provider has to recommend that specific treatments be administered or not administered,[6] antitrust violations,[7] fraud,[8] bad faith,[9] and conflict of interest[10] causes of action. Negligence and malpractice causes of action are also being tried against managed care entities and providers. In addition, some managed care cases have focused on the failure to provide complete and proper care,[11] negligent referral,[12] and the negligent hiring, retention, and evaluation of providers.[13]

Not only has the civil justice system been hearing managed care cases, but the criminal justice system has also been deciding managed-care related cases. One of the first criminal, managed care cases was published in the *New York Times*.[14] According to the article, criminal charges were filed against several defendants: a managed care organization, and its agents, and employees. The charges alleged that reckless homicide had been committed by the defendants in connection with the deaths of two women whose Pap smears were incorrectly read by the laboratory that contracted with the managed care organization to provide laboratory services.

Although some managed care cases illustrate the courts' willingness to subject health care professionals and entities to criminal prosecution, there are beginning to be cases filed by health care professionals against licensure boards where the licensure board threatens to impose disciplinary action because of managed care-related decision making. For example, in *John F. Murphy and Blue Cross Blue Shield of Arizona v. Board of Medical Examiners of the State of Arizona*,[15] John F. Murphy, MD, was serving as the medical director at Blue Cross Blue Shield of Arizona when he refused to precertify one physician's request to perform a laparoscopic cholecystectomy on a patient citing that it was medically unnecessary. The medical director offered to have the matter referred to a third-party specialist for review, but the patient and the patient's physician declined the offer. The patient's physician performed the surgery, and after pathology reports substantiated the need for the surgery, Blue Cross Blue Shield of Arizona paid the claim.

Thereafter, the patient's physician filed a complaint with the Arizona Board of Medical Examiners alleging that Dr. Murphy's refusal to precertify the procedure was unprofessional, and that the decision illustrated the doctor's incompetence. The Arizona Board of Medical Examiners commenced an investigation, and subpoenaed Blue Cross Blue Shield of Arizona documents. Dr. Murphy and Blue Cross Blue Shield of Arizona objected, and among other things, claimed that the medical director was not practicing medicine and that the Board of Medicine did not have the right to hear the matter. Dr. Murphy and Blue Cross Blue Shield of Arizona filed a lawsuit asserting that the Board of Medicine could not decide the matter, and asked the court to prevent the Board of Medicine from issuing any decision in the matter concerning John F. Murphy, M.D. The Arizona Court of Appeals determined that the Board of Medicine had the right to regulate the conduct of John F. Murphy, MD, because he rendered medical decisions.

Whereas *John F. Murphy* indicates how licensure boards will handle their practitioners practicing in managed care environments, other cases illustrate the way in which managed care issues are being addressed in courts around the country. Nurses, as well as other health care professionals practicing in managed care environments, need to be aware of these causes of actions, and practice in a way that is consistent with the principles delineated in this emerging area of the law. Four cases: *Linthicum, Gurule, Wilson,* and *Long* are demonstrative and are discussed below.

In *Linthicum v. Nationwide Life*,[16] Jerry Linthicum was hospitalized by his family physician, Dr. James Skinner in September, 1979. A tumor on one of his parathyroid glands was surgically removed. Pathology reports indicated that the tumor was a benign parathyroid adenoma. Following surgery, Jerry saw the doctor monthly, returned to work, gained 25 pounds, and resumed his active lifestyle.

April 1, 1980, Sandra Linthicum, Jerry's wife, obtained medical insurance from her employer. Sandra included coverage for Jerry. Prior to April 1, 1980, Jerry saw the doctor January 16, February 25, and March 18. Blood tests were taken. The blood test taken in March showed that Jerry's blood pressure and calcium level were slightly elevated.

June 12, 1980, Jerry was admitted to the hospital, and on July 11, 1980, surgery was performed and extensive metastatic carcinoma of the parathyroid glands was discovered. Jerry's entire thyroid gland was removed, as well as the parathyroid glands. However, the cancer had spread throughout Jerry's neck and into the chest area. The surgeon who performed the June 12, 1980, surgery, and another physician examined the records and tissue samples from Jerry's 1979 surgery and concluded that the tumor discovered in 1979 had been malignant.

The bills from Jerry's June and July hospitalization were submitted to the insurance plan for payment. On October 20, 1980, a denial of payment letter was sent from the insurance plan to Sandra's employer. The letter stated that the denial was based on the previous existing illness clause, which precludes payment for any charges incurred for an illness for which the insured person received medical care or treatment within 90 days preceding the effective date of the insurance policy.

Jerry was admitted to the hospital again on October 28, 1980. When the admitting clerk processed Jerry's insurance information, she discovered that his previous hospital stay had not been paid. The insurance company was contacted by telephone, and a representative from the insurance company told Sandra that the bill had not been paid because it was considered a previously existing condition, and not covered. This news came as a surprise to Jerry and Sandra; they had not been informed about the decision to deny payment.

Subsequently, Jerry was transferred to another hospital that admitted "charity" patients. From October, 1980, until his death in February, 1982, Jerry remained a charity patient, and was treated on an out-patient and in-patient basis. Prior to his death, Jerry became paralyzed, and his family provided care for him while he was treated at home.

After Jerry died, his wife brought suit for breach of contract and bad faith. A jury awarded his wife $14,951.13 for breach of contract, $150,000.00 for bad faith, and $2 million in punitive damages. The punitive damages award was ultimately appealed to the Arizona Supreme Court. Because there was insufficient evidence of an evil mind on the part of the insurance company, the award of punitive damages was deemed inappropriate.

In *Gurule v. Illinois Mutual Life and Casualty Company*,[17] Ramon Gurule purchased "paycheck replacement" individual disability insurance from Illinois Mutual in 1974. The policy provided disability benefits for a maximum of 5 years. On February 18, 1981, Gurule filed a total disability claim with Illinois Mutual stating that he injured his back and teeth in a January 10, 1981, automobile accident. At that time, Gurule was a self-employed carpet installer earning $1,400 per month.

Gurule sought treatment for his injuries from a dentist and a family practitioner. Gurule was first treated by his family practitioner on February 17. The family practitioner reported that Gurule had a cervical and dorsal sprain and had been continuously disabled since the day of the accident. That disability status was reconfirmed in April 1981. On April 8, 1981, Gurule further injured his back in a second car accident. Illinois Mutual made its first disability payment on April 29, 1981, almost 1 month later under the terms of the policy. The insurance company made a second payment on May 28, 1981.

In June, 1981, Illinois Mutual scheduled an independent medical examination for July 20, 1981. The independent medical examiner was told that the examination was warranted because of a lack of clinical evidence affirming a possible total disability status. The insurance company did not forward to the independent medical examiner its' definition of total disability, nor did it ask the independent medical examiner to provide objective clinical evidence of disability. In addition, the independent medical examiner was not provided with a list of Gurule's job duties.

In July, 1981, Gurule's family practitioner provided Illinois Mutual with additional reports verifying total and continuous disability. Additionally, the insurance company received an electromyogram report indication that Gurule's symptoms were characteristic of right C-8 nerve root irritation.

On July 31, 1981, Illinois Mutual received a report from the independent medical examiner, who concluded that Gurule had a lack of objective physical findings to support a finding that he was totally disabled. Following the receipt of this report, Illinois Mutual terminated Gurule's disability payments. Gurule accepted the decision of the insurance company and returned to work for 1 day in November, 1981. According to his family practitioner, after 1 day of work, Gurule appeared in his office in extreme distress and experiencing pain in both his lumbar and cervical spine. Pain also radiated to his right arm. The family practitioner informed Illinois Mutual that he had instructed Gurule not to return to work and that he disagreed with the actions taken by Illinois Mutual and conclusions reached by the independent medical examiner.

By this time, Gurule had obtained the assistance of legal counsel, who urged Illinois Mutual to reinstate benefits. Instead, Illinois Mutual arranged another independent medical examination. This independent medical examiner concluded that no evidence of permanent impairment was noted, and suggested that Gurule return to work over the next 45 to 60 days. On December 30, 1981, Gurule's attorneys sent Illinois Mutual notes from the orthopedic specialist who examined Gurule at the request of Gurule's family practitioner. The orthopedic specialist suggested that Gurule be hospitalized for physical therapy.

On January 22, 1982, Gurule's attorneys threatened to sue if benefits were not reinstated. The General Counsel for Illinois Mutual agreed to reinstate benefits as a show of good faith. However, on May 3, 1982, in a letter to Gurule's attorneys, Illinois Mutual again terminated Gurule's benefits. Gurule's attorneys filed suit against Illinois Mutual on July 14, 1982. The case was tried in front of a jury that awarded Gurule $25,506.54 for breach of contract. They also awarded $90,000.00 in bad faith damages, and $384,493.46 in punitive damages.

In *Wilson v. Blue Cross of Southern California,*[18] Howard Wilson, Jr. was admitted to College Hospital in Los Angeles. His admitting diagnosis was major depression, drug dependency, and anorexia. His treating physician determined that he needed 3 to 4 weeks of in-patient care.

Ten days after the admission, Blue Cross of Southern California communicated to the hospital that it would not pay for any further hospital care. Howard was immediately discharged from the hospital. The Blue Cross denial of payment occurred despite a clause in the insurance policy stating that benefits for mental and nervous disorders or for pulmonary tuberculosis shall be limited to an aggregate of 30 days during any period of 12 consecutive months.

On March 31, 1983, Howard committed suicide. Afterward, his family filed suit alleging that the involved insurance agencies had tortiously breached the insurance contract with Howard, and that their actions resulted in Howard's wrongful death. A jury heard the case, and returned a verdict that awarded Howard's family $25,506.54 in breach of contract damages, $90,000.00 in bad faith damages, and $384,493.46 in punitive damages. The punitive damage award was later overturned by Arizona Supreme Court. They concluded that the facts of this case did not warrant a punitive damage award because the alleged wrongdoers did not act with conscious disregard for Howard.

In *Long v. Great West Life and Annuity Insurance Company, et al*,[19] the Supreme Court of Wyoming heard a case which involved Larry Long, a state government employee who participated in the employer's health insurance plan. The plan granted the plan administrator with total plan administration control.

In accordance with the terms of the plan, Larry Long's neurologist recommended that Larry have back surgery. The neurologist was a non-network physician, but submitted a preauthorization request. The preauthorization request resulted in a telephone-based utilization review process. The utilization review organization denied the request of the neurologist, and cancelled surgery. Later, Larry learned that the utilization review organization recommended that he undergo a more conservative course of treatment of steroid injections. He saw an anesthesiologist who determined that he could not, in good faith, administer the injections without subjecting Larry to considerable risk. Larry communicated this to the utilization review organization, but authorization to have surgery was denied. Several days later, Larry was examined by a neurosurgeon who described the L4-5 herniation Larry had as "huge" and "impressive." The neurosurgeon characterized alternative treatments as a waste of time and resources, and recommended that surgical intervention be commenced. Finally, approximately 6 weeks later, and after his condition deteriorated, Larry underwent surgery and it was paid at the reduced, unauthorized rate. Approximately 8 months later, Larry filed suit. The case was eventually heard by the Wyoming Supreme Court. In reviewing the matter, the court determined that where an entity inserts itself in the decision-making process, the court will impose a fiduciary relationship on the entity. This case focused on the denial of services made by a utilization review organization, and the court determined that the utilization reviewer was making medical decisions when those decisions amount to the denial of treatment. As a result, the case, which had previously been dismissed, was scheduled for trial. The trial's outcome has not yet been published.

As these cases indicate, health care providers continue to be held accountable for the actions they take regarding patients. In fact, that accountability extends beyond the individual who interacts with the patients. Medical directors and utilization review personnel are also being held accountable. Nurses practicing in these kinds of indirect care/decision-making positions should be aware that they, too, are subject to liability if they fail to act in accordance with the standard of care.

Employee Retirement Income Security Act

Enacted in 1974, the Employee Retirement Income Security Act (ERISA)[20] established uniform federal standards to protect employee pension plans from fraud and mismanagement. Today, ERISA regulates employee pension and benefit plans, including all employer-provided health insurance plans in ways that could not have been anticipated in the mid 1970s. Health insurance plans not regulated by ERISA include those plans offered through federal, state, and local governments, religious institutions, and some educational organizations.[21]

ERISA, via its *preemption clause,* voids all state laws that directly and indirectly regulate employee health plans. However, ERISA allows states to regulate the business of insurance, traditional carriers conducting traditional insurance business, and the terms and conditions of health insurance. The effect is that employers offering employees insurance benefits through self-funded plans are outside the reach of any state action.[22] Consequently, many employers have chosen to self-insure. In June, 1998, it was estimated that more than 122 million Americans were in ERISA-shielded health plans.[23]

In response, a small but growing number of states (Georgia, Missouri, Oklahoma, New York, and Texas) passed legislative initiatives that permit consumers to sue health maintenance organizations in state courts for the quality of care they receive. In addition, courts around the country seem to be restricting ERISA's reach. For example, in *Berger v. Livengrin Foundation,*[24] U.S. District Court for the Eastern District of Pennsylvania determined that where a company's health insurer refused to pay for in-patient alcohol treatment, and required the insured to seek outpatient treatment where she was sexually assaulted by the out-patient treatment counselor, that the insured could proceed with her medical malpractice claim under Pennsylvania state law. The court reasoned that ERISA preempted only quantity of care claims, and not quality of care complaints, and that this patient was not complaining about the quantity of care she received, but rather the propriety in failing to recommend in-patient treatment, and in selecting the health care provider. As a result, the court refused to allow ERISA to shield this insurer from this cause of action.

The issues regarding ERISA are not yet well settled. However, nurses and other health care providers can work to avoid the patient's invoking of an ERISA-based claim by providing that patient with the quantity and quality of care that patient needs.

Summary

Although managed care has successfully slowed the rising cost of health care, quality of care issues need to continue to be addressed. The emerging body of managed care-related case law suggests that there is substantial room for improving the quality of care delivered to managed care patients. Having said this, it is important to recognize that quality of care issues existed in the era the preceding managed care.

Courts continue to hold health care professionals responsible for the quality of care rendered their patients. Managed care cases reviewed by courts around the United States continue to hold those making treatment decisions accountable. Courts are also rewarding health care providers who insist on providing quality health care services. *Self v. Children's Associated Medical Group*[25] is illustrative. In *Self,* Thomas Self, a physician-employee settled a wrongful termination cause of action against Children's Associated Medical Group for $2.5 million. This was on the heels of a $1.75 million jury verdict that did not include punitive damages. Dr. Thomas Self, a pediatrician, charged that he was terminated for spending too much time with patients and for ordering too many tests. The court, in rendering this decision, observed that corporate financial pressures should not be substituted for independent provider decision making.

The court's decision in *Self* should serve as a reminder that health care providers, including nurse case managers, must not let the professional decisions they make be driven by financial pressures. Where a case manager is concerned about his or her ability to make independent professional judgments, that case manager might consider making the "no substitution for professional decision making" principle an explicit provision of case management agreement they execute. Including this and other contractual issues will result in both parties being more clear about the expectations of themselves, and of the other party.

In this chapter, a number of managed care-related issues have been addressed. The contractual components of a case management agreement have been highlighted. In addition, the work of ANA's Managed Care Working Group has been outlined, as well as the role of the nurse in managed care, the nurse as case manager, and managed care-related case law, including the impact of ERISA on a patient's ability to sue managed care organizations.

These topics have been presented to better inform nurses about this relatively new health care financing mechanism known as managed care, and the legal issues that arise in managed care environments. Although the implementation of managed care has not been without problems, it is likely to be the framework within which health care services are provided in the United States for some time. As a result, it is important for nurses and other health care providers to know what their legal responsibilities are, and to practice in a way that is consistent with those responsibilities.

End Notes

1. No. RCV020499 (Super. Ct. of San Bernadino, California, 1999).
2. 99 LWUSA 512.
3. ANA Managed Care Working Group members participating in work group meetings included: Chair: Beverly L. Malone, PhD, RN, FAAN; Reuben Fernandez, MA, RN; Sara McCumber, BS, RN, C; Marilyn Stevenson, MA, RN; Kathleen White, PhD, MS, RN; Jessie M. Colin, MSN, RN; Mary Runyan, RN; Clair Jordan, MSN, RN; Pat Kabele-Toland, MS, RN; Mary Anne McCrea, RN, MS, CNA; Mary Kay Pera, BS, RN; Barbara Lumpkin, RN; Emily McDowell, EdD, RN; Patty Koenig, RN; Anne Powell, MS, RN; Mary Jo Connelly, MS, RN; Judy Collins, MA,

ARNP, CS; Mary Ann Christopher, MSN, RNCS, FAAN; Gery Lamb, PhD, RN, FAAN; Fran Hicks, PhD, RN, FAAN; Carol Ann Romano, PhD, RNC, FAAN; Joan L. Quinn, MS, BSN; and Jennifer Walkowiak, MS, RN.

4. American Nurses Association (ANA). 1998. *Managed care: Nursing's blueprint for action* (MC981). Washington, D.C.: American Nurses Association.

5. *Fox v. HealthNet of California,* No. 219692 Riverside City, (Cal. Sup. Ct. 1993).

6. *Neade v. Portes,* No. 2-97-1099. (Illinois Court of Appeals, March 31, 1999), and *Shea v. Esensten,* No. 99-1388, (U.S. Court of Appeals, 8th Cir. March 31, 2000).

7. Waxman, J.M. 1995. Antitrust and integrated delivery systems: The safety zone. *Health Care Innovations* 5(1): 16–18.

8. *HealthAmerica v. Menton,* 551 So. 2d 235 (Al. 1989); and *Pulvers v. Kaiser Permanente,* 99 Cal.App. 3d 560, 160 Cal. Rptr. 3d 392 (1979).

9. *Hughes v. Blue Cross of Northern California,* 215 Cal. App. 3d 832, 263 Cal. Rptr. 850 (Ct. App. 1989).

10. *T2 Medical Company v. The Federal Trade Commission,* (1994).

11. *Delucia v. St. Lukes Hospital,* No. 98-6446 (U.S.D.C. East. Dist. Penn. May 24, 1999), and *Wickline v. State of California,* 192 Cal. App. 3d 1630, 239 Cal. Rptr. 810 (1986).

12. *Stelmach v. Physicians Multispecialty Group,* No. 53906 (Mo. Ct. App. 1989).

13. *Harrell v. Total Health Care,* No. WD 39809 (Mo. Ct. App. 1989).

14. Kolata, G. 1995. Medical laboratory faces charges in cancer deaths. *New York Times* April 13: A16.

15. 949 P. 2d 530 (Az. 1997).

16. 723 P. 2d 675 (Az. 1986).

17. 734 P.2d 85 (Az. 1987).

18. 222 Cal. App. 3d 660 (Ca. 1990)

19. 957 P.2d 823 (Wy. 1998).

20. 29 U.S.C. § 1001 et seq.

21. Reed, S., and Keepnews, D. 1998. ERISA and health care regulation: Understanding the issues. *Nursing Trends and Issues* 3(10).

22. *Pilot Life v. Dedeaux,* 481 U.S. 41 (1987).

23. *Legislative Network for Nurses.* 1998. June 10: 91.

24. 2000 LWUSA 370 (May 1, 2000).

25. No. 695870 (Cal. Sup. Ct., 1998).

The Nurse as Credentialed Health Care Provider 11

Introduction

Credentialing, when referring to the health care industry, can be used to refer to a mechanism professionals use to maintain competence and to stimulate continued self-improvement or the process health care organizations use to select providers. Readily identifiable credentialing mechanisms include the completion of academic degrees, licensure, and certification. Credentialing mechanisms were established to ensure that an acceptable level of performance is achieved; confer occupational identity; protect the public, organizations, governments, and other stakeholders from substandard practice; and exert organizational control over professionals and services rendered.[1]

This chapter discusses credentialing activities engaged in by the nursing profession; then credentialing activities engaged in by health care organizations are outlined. Following that, the nurse as credentialed health care provider is discussed. Finally, credentialing-related case law are presented.

Credentialing and the Nursing Profession

Nursing, like other professions, engages in a number of credentialing activities: (1) licensure by state governments of individuals who meet predetermined minimum standards, which is mandatory for many occupations and serves to identify the individuals who have permission to practice a licensed profession; (2) accreditation of institutions and educational programs; (3) certification of nurses in a number of specialty areas, which assures the public that the nurse who passed the certifying examination has met the predetermined standards of the certifying body, and that a body of knowledge has been mastered; and (4) recognition by peer reviewed organizations used to attest that an organization conducts its business in accordance with articulated standards, and with integrity and credibility.

Licensure activities were discussed in detail in Chapter 2 of this book. However, it is important to understand that, in the United States, licensure is a matter of state prerogative, and is used to protect the public. Minimum standards must be met to apply for licensure, and a licensing examination must be successfully completed. Individuals who do not meet eligibility requirements and who do not pass the licensing exam are prohibited from practicing nursing. Licensees must meet predetermined standards to maintain licensure. Licensure is a unique credentialing tool in that it is overseen by state governments and is required for individuals to practice nursing.

Accreditation is another credentialing activity engaged in by the nursing profession. Accreditation, unlike licensure, is usually voluntary and does not involve governmental entities. Accreditation is the process by which organizations and/or programs are assessed, evaluated, and given accredited status using predetermined structure, process, and outcome criteria. Accreditation activities seek to improve the quality of services rendered by accredited organizations. Reassessment and re-evaluation are integral components of accreditation activities to ensure continued adherence to accreditation standards.

The American Nurses Credentialing Center (ANCC) seeks to ensure that quality, continuing education offerings are provided to nurses through its international accreditation program. ANCC's accreditation program is based on the *Scope and Standards for Nursing Professional Development* (ANA 2000. Washington, D.C.: American Nurses Publishing). The program is voluntary, peer reviewed, and governed by nine commissioners who are knowledgeable about accreditation, continuing education, adult education, and staff development.

ANCC's Commission on Accreditation accredits approvers and providers of continuing education in nursing. *Approvers* have the capacity and responsibility to review and approve nursing continuing education programs. ANCC approvers include the state nurses associations, specialty nursing organizations, and the federal nursing service. *Providers* are those organizations that may provide ANCC-accredited continuing education programs in nursing. Accredited providers include the state nurses associations, specialty nursing organizations, the federal nursing service, higher education institutions, commercial products companies, health care institutions, and international organizations.

In nursing education, the most familiar accrediting bodies are the American Association of Colleges of Nursing (AACN) and the National League for Nursing (NLN). AACN is an organization composed of deans of baccalaureate and higher schools of nursing; the NLN accredits home health organizations and nursing education programs.[2]

Certification, like accreditation, is a nongovernmental credentialing activity that attests that an individual has met certain predetermined standards specified by a certifying body. Like licensure, certification is testing based. However, unlike licensing examinations, certification examinations are voluntary and seek to identify those individuals who have mastered the body of knowledge. Licensing examinations, on the other hand, seek to identify those who meet minimum standards. Certification assures the public that a certified individual has mastered a body of knowledge in a particular nursing specialty. Certified nurses have the privilege of using the certification mark bestowed by the certifying body, so long as the criteria for recertification are met.

The ANCC offers more certification examinations for nurses than any other certifying body. When the program began in 1974, 691 candidates took examinations in one of three nursing specialties. In 1999, 12,954 candidates took 1 of 32 certification examinations.

Certification examinations offered by the ANCC are objective tests that are psychometrically sound and legally defensible. The examinations are developed by ANCC test development committees composed of representative experts in the specialty practice. The committees define content areas to be covered on an examination, as well as relative emphasis of each content area, and the nature of professional knowledge, abilities, and skills to be measured.

Examination questions are obtained from certified nurses throughout the United States. Test questions undergo a rigorous review and revision process to ensure that each test question is sound. In addition to psychometric and editorial review, each test question is reviewed, critiqued, and rated for accuracy and relevancy by subject matter experts.

Recognition, like certification, is another credentialing activity engaged in by the nursing profession. Recognition, unlike certification, is a credentialing activity used to reward organizations for conducting its business with integrity, credibility, and consistent with recognition standards.

In addition to the accreditation and certification programs offered by the ANCC, a recognition program is also offered. ANCC's recognition program is the Magnet Nursing Services Recognition Program. The program was created to recognize excellence in

- the management, philosophy, and practice of nursing services.
- adherence to national standards for improving the quality of patient care services.
- leadership of the nurse-administrator in supporting professional practice and continued competence of nurses.
- understanding and respecting the cultural and ethnic diversity of patients, their significant others, and health care providers.

Magnet Nursing Services Program goals are to

- identify excellence in the delivery of nursing care to patients.
- promote the quality of health care services in an environment that supports professional nursing practice.
- provide a mechanism for the dissemination of best practices in nursing services.

Forces of Magnetism

- Strong nursing leadership
- Open, interactive, and integrated organizational structure
- Collegial, participative management style of hospital leadership
- Employee-friendly personnel policies and programs implemented with employee input
- Use of professional models of care
- Quality of care was the organization's priority
- Beneficial and constructive quality improvement programs were in place
- Adequate consultation and human and financial resources
- Level of autonomy was such that nurses were able to practice using the entire scope of practice
- Community involvement was ongoing, and the organization was viewed as a model corporate citizen
- Nurses were valued as teachers of patients and of other nurses
- The image of nursing was one that was vital to accomplishing the mission of the organization
- Mutual respect was demonstrated in nurse–physician relationships
- Orientation, in-service, continuing education, formal education, and career development activities were valued, and encouraged by the organization.

American Academy of Nursing (AAN). 1983. *Magnet hospitals: Attraction and retention of professional nurses.* Kansas City, MO: American Academy of Nursing.

ANCC's Magnet Nursing Services Recognition Program was borne out of a 1980 research study conducted by the American Academy of Nursing (AAN).[3] The study sought to identify factors that, in spite of a nursing shortage, attracted and retained nurses to certain health care organizations. More than 165 hospitals across the United States were studied, and 14 factors distinguished 41 hospitals from the rest of the study sample. Those 14 factors eventually became known as the *forces of magnetism* (see sidebar). The identification of these forces of magnetism, as well as the ANA *Scope and Standards for Nurse Administrators* (1996. Washington, D.C.: American Nurses Publishing) was used to create an international recognition program that focuses on the contribution nurses make in health care settings.

In 1994, the University of Washington Medical Center in Seattle, Washington, was the first health care organization, to be awarded Magnet status. In 1998, the program expanded to include long-term care facilities. Two years later, program expansion continued when the Magnet Nursing Services Recognition Program captured the attention of international health care organizations.

Like ANCC's accreditation and certification programs, the Magnet Nursing Services Recognition Program is voluntary and peer reviewed. The ANCC offers these credentialing services to improve nursing practice and promote high-quality health care services.

Credentialing and Health Care Organizations

Traditionally, health care organizations have limited their credentialing activities to physicians. Traditional notions of credentialing persist today. In the March 27, 2000, issue of *Modern Healthcare,* J. Duncan Moore, Jr. defined credentialing as "the granting of hospital staff privileges to physicians based on thorough background checks of their education, qualifications and performance records."[4] This kind of credentialing occurs in three circumstances and is applicable to physicians, as well as other health care professionals: (1) filing an application to practice in a given setting; (2) renewal of an application to practice; and (3) disciplinary proceedings. The credentialing process is rigorous, and decisions regarding the ability of providers to practice in a setting are among the most important decisions made by health care organizations. Not only is the credentialing process rigorous, it is also lengthy. It takes between 90 and 120 days to complete the formal application process. Extensive background data are gathered and presented to the organizations' credentialing committee, the body that recommends to the organizations' governing body whether or not clinical privileges should be awarded. In the past, these committees have been comprised solely of medical staff members. However, as nonphysician providers have needed clinical privileges to care for their patients, health care organizations have had to reconsider physician-only clinical privileges. Today, many organizations have adopted policies that allow nonphysician providers such as dentists, podiatrists, nurse-practitioners, nurse-midwives, and physician assistants an opportunity to obtain clinical privileges. Jan Jones-Schenk, MNA, RN, CNA, past president of the American Nurses Credentialing Center, suggests that credentialing committees "include clinical peers who are best suited to determine eligibility and qualification."[5]

Where clinical privileges are granted to a first-time applicant, provisional status is awarded for a period of between 6 and 12 months. After that period, clinical privileges are typically extended for an additional 6 to 24 months. There are several categories of staff privileges (see sidebar).

Credentialing of Nurses

Nurses have traditionally practiced as employees in health care organizations. Now that advanced practice nurses may bill Medicare for their professional services per-

Staff Privileges Categories

- *Active*—this level of clinical privileges allows the health care provider to admit patients and participate in other hospital programs.
- *Courtesy*—this level of clinical privilege is awarded when a limited number of patients will be admitted and when the health care provider is an active member of another medical staff.
- *Affiliate*—this clinical privilege level is awarded when the health care provider is no longer active, but has a long-standing relationship with the hospital.
- *Outpatient*—this level of clinical privileges is awarded where the health care provider is regularly engaged in the care of patients in outpatient settings or in programs sponsored by or on behalf of the health care organization.
- *Honorary*—this level of clinical privilege is awarded when the health care provider is no longer active, but who has outstanding accomplishments or reputation. Honorary staff privileges are distinguished from affiliate staff privileges in that honorary staff privileges permit the health care professional to continue to admit patients to the organization.
- *House*—this level of clinical privilege allows a health care professional to admit patients within a specialty area with the approval of an active staff member.
- *Allied Health Professional*—this level of clinical privilege permits non-physician health care providers to provide specified patient care services.

formed in all settings, clinical privileges must be awarded if patients are going to be admitted and/or cared for by advanced practice nurses.

When clinical privileges are sought by the advanced practice nurse at any organization, the organization is obligated to thoroughly investigate all aspects of the advanced practice nurses' life. Information will be requested on the applicants' license to practice advanced practice nursing; the status of clinical privileges at any other health care organization; status with the Drug Enforcement Administration (DEA); educational program(s) and clinical experiences; work history; malpractice insurance policy; and the advanced practice nurses' professional liability claims history, including any malpractice payments made, disciplinary action taken, adverse clinical privilege actions taken by health care organizations, and adverse action taken by professional societies. All information will be collected from primary sources, and the applicant must sign a statement attesting that the information provided is accurate and complete.

Disciplinary action information has been more easily collected since the implementation of the Health Care Quality Improvement Act (HCQIA). The HCQIA authorized the establishment of the National Practitioner Data Bank, a clearinghouse designed to collect and release adverse credentialing action taken against health care providers, including nurses. HCQIA also grants health care institutions immunity if satisfactory procedures are followed during the credentialing process.

With regard to the National Practitioner Data Bank, health care organizations are required to file reports when a health care provider's license is restricted, medical malpractice payments are made on behalf of health care providers, clinical privileges are adversely affected for more than 30 days, clinical privileges are surrendered or voluntarily restricted for more than 30 days, and the decision to issue an order for the summary suspension for more than 30 days is based on professional competence or conduct. With the exception of summary suspensions, most actions are reportable to the National Practitioner Data Bank when final action has been taken.

After reports are filed with the National Practitioner Data Bank, reports are available to hospitals and other health care organizations. In addition, hospitals and health care organizations are required to request information from the National Practitioner Data Bank every 2 years, and any time a physician or other licensed health care practitioner applies for medical staff or clinical privileges.[6] Hospitals and health care organizations failing to request data from the National Practitioner Data Bank are presumed to have knowledge of any information in the possession of the data bank.

In addition to the establishment of the National Practitioner Data Bank, the HCQIA provides immunity to health care organizations that incorporate five procedural safeguards in their credentialing process. First, procedural safeguards must include providing a health care provider with a notice stating that a professional review action has been proposed, the reasons for the proposed action, a statement communicating the health care provider's right to a hearing on the proposed action, the time limit (not less than 30 days) within which the health care provider must request a hearing, and a summary of the health care provider's rights during the hearing.[7] Second, where a health care provider requests a hearing within the identified time frame, the health care provider must be given a notice stating the time, date, and place of the hearing, which should not be less than 30 days after the date of the notice, and a list of witnesses expected to testify in connection with the proposed action.[8] Third, HCQIA procedural safeguards require that where a hearing is requested, the hearing must be held before a mutually acceptable arbitrator, before a hearing officer appointed by the entity who is not in direct economic competition with the practitioner, or before a panel of individuals appointed by the health care organization who are not in direct economic competition with the health care provider.[9] Fourth, HCQIA safeguards require that during the hearing, the health care provider has the right to representation by an attorney or other person chosen by the health care provider; have a record made of the proceedings, copies of which may be obtained by the health care provider; call, examine, and cross examine witnesses; present relevant evidence; and submit a written statement at the close of the hearing.[10] Fifth, HCQIA safeguards require that following the hearing, the health care provider has the right to receive written recommendation of the arbitrator, officer, or hearing panel, and receive a copy of the organization's final decision.[11]

Although immunity is extended to health care organizations when HCQIA procedural safeguards are followed, immunity is not extended to civil rights claims and does not prevent a provider from seeking injunctive relief following an adverse credentialing decision. In addition, the HCQIA allows attorneys for health care organizations to seek reimbursement for the cost of defending the suit, including attorney's fees where procedural safeguards were followed and the health care organization substantially prevails in a credentialing-related cause of action.[12]

Credentialing-Related Case Law

Credentialing-related case law involving health care providers has developed to a significant degree because of credentialing decisions that are adverse to a physician seeking to be awarded a credential or clinical privileges. With regard to nurses, a growing body of credentialing-related case law is being developed out of the denial of requests to award clinical privileges to advanced practice nurses. Six cases are illustrative.

First, in *Oltz v. St. Peter's Community Hospital*,[13] Tafford Oltz, a nurse anesthetist provided anesthesia services, via a billing agreement, for St. Peter's Community Hospital in Helena, Montana. After three anesthesiologists complained about the services being provided by Mr. Oltz, the Board of Trustees for St. Peter's Community Hospital decided to enter into an exclusive contract for its anesthesiology services. The contract was awarded to anesthesiologists who already provided anesthesiology services at the hospital. With the contract awarded, the billing agreement under which Mr. Oltz had been practicing was terminated. Following the termination of the billing agreement, anesthesiologists at St. Peter's Community Hospital offered Mr. Oltz a salaried position as an employee, under their supervision. The salary offered to Mr. Oltz was $40,000. Mr. Oltz rejected the offer and sought employment elsewhere. He then sued the hospital and anesthesiologists alleging that the exclusive contract unreasonably restrained competition, and that the anesthesiologists and hospital had conspired against him in executing the exclusive deal. Subsequent proceedings in this case have not been published.

The anesthesiologists settled the case filed against them for $462,000, and a jury awarded Oltz almost $500,000 in damages. The trial judge ordered a new trial finding that the jury award was excessive.[14]

Approximately 1 year after *Oltz, Nurse Midwifery Associates, et al v. Hibbett*[15] was decided by the U.S. Court of Appeals for the Sixth Circuit. Originally, the Sherman Antitrust Act case was filed in the U.S. District Court for the Middle District of Tennessee. The court of appeals heard the case after the trial court judge dismissed all but two claims in favor of the defendant physicians, hospitals, and a physician-owned insurance company. Plaintiffs Susan Sizemore and Victoria Henderson are certified nurse midwives who owned Nurse Midwifery Associates (NMA). Susan Sizemore and Victoria Henderson sought to provide midwifery services in Nashville, Tennessee. Darrell Martin, MD, an obstetrician, agreed to serve as the collaborating physician for NMA. Susan Sizemore and Victoria Henderson sought clinical privileges at three hospitals: Hendersonville Community Hospital, Southern Hills Hospital, and Vanderbilt University Hospital. All three hospitals refused to extend clinical privileges to Susan Sizemore and Victoria Henderson. In the process, several defendant physicians were identified by the plaintiffs as instrumental in keeping the midwives out of the Nashville market. They were Conrad Shackleford, George Andrews, Stephen Melkin, Harry Baer, and B.K. Hibbett.

Not only were Susan Sizemore and Victoria Henderson denied the ability to practice nurse-midwifery in Nashville, Tennessee, Darrell Martin, MD, NMA's collaborating physician, experienced adverse consequences because of his association with NMA. Dr. Martin's professional liability insurance company cancelled his insurance after it determined that Dr. Martin's relationship with NMA increased State Volunteer Mutual Insurance Company, Inc. (SVMIC) underwriting risks to an unacceptable level. As a result, the physician-owned insurance company, SVMIC, was also a defendant in the case.

Susan Sizemore, Victoria Henderson, Darrell Martin, and two of their patients sued the physicians, hospitals, and physician-owned insurance company they thought conspired to restrain competition by denying the midwives' requests for clinical privileges and the physician professional liability insurance. At the District Court level, only two claims survived: the claim of conspiracy between Southern Hills Hospital and Hendersonville Community Hospital, and the conspiracy claim between Vanderbilt University Hospital and B.K. Hibbett.

On appeal, the court added to the claims that the plaintiffs could pursue. Not only could they pursue a conspiracy claim against Southern Hills Hospital and Hendersonville Community Hospital, and a conspiracy claim between Vanderbilt University Hospital and B.K. Hibbett, they could also pursue a conspiracy claim between SVMIC and B.K. Hibbett, and between Stephen Melkin, Harry Baer, and George Andrews, physicians associated with Southern Hills Hospital and who were allegedly instrumental in seeing that clinical privileges were not awarded. Subsequent proceedings in this case have not been published.

Four months after *Nurse Midwifery Associates, Vinod C. Bhan, CRNA v. NME Hospitals, et al*[16] was decided. In *Bhan*, Vinod C. Bhan, a certified registered nurse anesthetist (CRNA) practiced as a nurse anesthetist at Manteca Hospital, a 49-bed hospital in Manteca, California, until the hospital elected not to renew its contract with Associated Anesthesia Services (AAS), an organization that supplied physician and nurse anesthesia providers to the hospital. AAS assigned Bhan and one physician to Manteca Hospital. The hospital notified AAS that it was going to let the AAS contract expire so that it could enter into an exclusive arrangement with physician-only anesthesia providers.

Vinod Bahn alleged that the physician anesthesia providers conspired with the hospital to eliminate him and other potential nurse anesthetists from competing in the local market. He sued the hospital, the hospital administrator, and the physician anesthesia providers with whom the hospital executed a physician-only contract.

The district court granted the request of the defendants to close the case in their favor. On appeal, the court of appeals affirmed the decision of the district court, concluding that Vinod Bahn failed to show that the hospital's physician-only policy substantially restrained competition in a relevant geographic and product market, or that monopolization and attempted monopolization occurred.

Three-and-a-half years after Vinod Bahn's case went to the 9th Circuit Court of Appeals, *BCB Anesthesia Care, Ltd. et al v. The Passavant Memorial Area Hospital Association, et al*[17] was reviewed by the 7th Circuit Court of Appeals. In *BCB*, CRNAs Beverly Werries, Curtis M. Cravens, and Robert Otken owned BCB Anesthesia Care, Ltd., and provided anesthesia services for Passavant Memorial Hospital in Jacksonville, Illinois, the only acute care hospital in that city. The hospital terminated its contract with BCB Anesthesia Care, Ltd., and the nurse-anesthetists sued alleging that the hospital, two staff physicians, and the hospital CEO violated the Sherman Antitrust Act. Specifically, the nurse anesthetists alleged that the hospital's billing practices, staffing decisions, and the decision to terminate their contract violated the Sherman Antitrust Act because the action of the hospital, two staff physicians, and the hospital CEO was a restraint of trade and a boycott.

The nurse-anesthetists alleged that one anesthesiologist, Peter Roodhouse, billed some of BCB's patients and third-party payers for anesthesia service he had not rendered. The anesthetists contended that Roodhouse billed these patients and third-party payers in an attempt to adversely affect BCB. This created a number of double billing problems for BCB. The double billing problems led to one physician, Eric Giebelhausen, calling BCB's billing practices unethical, and that physician urged that the BCB contract be terminated and that Roodhouse provide Passavant's anesthesia services. Roodhouse then scheduled himself to perform the majority of anesthesia services 1 month before the BCB contract was terminated by hospital CEO Clarence Lay. Following the termination of BCB's contract, the hospital increased its anesthesia-related fees. The nurse-anesthetists were given an opportunity to practice as employees, under the supervision of Roodhouse. The nurse anesthetists objected to this proposed arrangement, asserting that the Illinois Nurse Practice Act did not require physician supervision.

At the district court level, the case was dismissed. The nurse anesthetists appealed. The 7th Circuit Court of Appeals affirmed the decision of the district court, asserting that staffing decisions at a single hospital are not anticompetitive, in violation of the Sherman Antitrust Act. In spite of that ruling, the court of appeals concluded that the nurse-anesthetists had met their Sherman Antitrust Act burden of proof associated with showing that the issues before the court had a substantial impact on interstate commerce. Unfortunately, the court of appeals determined that its inquiry did not end with an analysis of the impact of interstate commerce. Rather, the court's inquiry only started with an analysis of the impact on interstate commerce. The court of appeals characterized this case as one that focused on one hospital's staffing pattern and privilege decisions. Looking to *Bhan* for support, the appellate court concluded that hospitals have the unquestioned right to exercise reasonable control over the individuals to whom it grants staff privileges. The court pointed out that the nurse-anesthetists could still practice at Passavant Hospital, and noted that nurse-anesthetists did not suggest that patients were foreclosed from going elsewhere. In reaching its decision, the court of appeals observed the only restraint alleged by the nurse-anesthetists was they could not now practice in the business form they preferred, and that anesthesia-related fees charged by the hospital are higher than they were when BCB was providing the services. Accordingly, the alleged restraints were determined to be not illegal or in violation of the Sherman Antitrust Act.

Approximately 16 months following *BCB, Griffin, Jenkins, and King v. Guadalupe Medical Center, Inc., and Premier Anesthesia, Inc.*[18] was decided by the New Mexico Court of Appeals. Here, CRNAs Joseph Griffin, Phillip Jenkins, and James King provide anesthesia services at Guadalupe Medical Center in Carlsbad, New Mexico. Guadalupe Medical Center required that nurse-anesthetists be under the supervision and direction of a physician. This requirement was more proscriptive than state law required. Dr. Leyba was the physician anesthesiologist who supervised Griffin, Jenkins, and King. Dr. Leyba left Guadalupe Medical Center, and the hospital contracted with Premier Anesthesia, Inc. to provide anesthesia services. The contract with Premier Anesthesia, Inc. required that employment be offered to Griffin, Jenkins, and King, and that the services provided by nurse-anesthetists be supervised by a Premier Anesthesia, Inc. physician.

Griffin, Jenkins, and King refused to be bound by the conditions contained in the hospital's agreement with Premier Anesthesia Services, Inc. They sued the hospital and Premier Anesthesia, Inc., contending that the agreement between the hospital and Premier destroyed the independence of the nurse-anesthetists and illegally restrained competition. At the district court level, the judge determined that New Mexico's antitrust laws were not violated, and that the hospital and Premier Anesthesia Inc. did not engage in any unlawful conduct. The court of appeals agreed.

Sixteen months later, *Minnesota Association of Nurse Anesthetists, et al v. Unity Hospital, et al*[19] was heard by one of Minnesota's District Courts. In this case, 12 CRNAs and the Minnesota Association of Nurse Anesthetists ("Plaintiffs") sued three hospitals, two administrators, anesthesiologists at the three hospitals, their practice group and administrator, anesthesiologists at another hospital and their practice group ("Defendants").

Plaintiffs asserted that Defendants conspired to eliminate the use of CRNAs so that they could maintain their unusually high compensation level, facilitate fraudulent billing, and increase their dominant position in the market place. In so doing, Plaintiffs alleged that federal and state antitrust laws had been violated, as well as the

Minnesota Consumer Fraud Act, the Minnesota Deceptive Trade Practices Act, the Minnesota Whistleblower statute, and civil conspiracy. In addition, Plaintiffs alleged that Defendants interfered with their contractual and prospective business and economic relations, competed unfairly, breached their duty of good faith and fair dealing, and that defendant hospitals wrongfully terminated the nurse-anesthetists. A number of Plaintiffs' claims were dismissed by the district court judge, including the Minnesota Consumer Fraud Act, tortious interference with Plaintiffs' contractual and prospective business and economic relations, unfair competition, breach of good faith and fair dealing, and the wrongful termination of the nurse-anesthetists.

The crux of Plaintiffs' antitrust claim was that their removal as hospital employees resulted in a public injury because the nurse-anesthetists were no longer available to correct double billing practices they believed constituted Medicare fraud. The district court judge concluded that this was not the type of injury antitrust laws were designed to prevent, and as a result, no legally cognizable antitrust injury occurred. In addition, the judge determined that their antitrust claims failed because Plaintiffs did not present evidence that tended to exclude the possibility that Defendants acted independently, or that showed that the hospitals acted against their own self-interest in terminating the nurse-anesthetists as employees. Nor did Plaintiffs present evidence of the Defendants' market power in the relevant market.

Summary

Although some cases filed by advanced practice nurses have been successfully concluded, there are others that have been dismissed or decided in favor of hospitals, practice groups, physicians, and administrators. Despite these mixed results, great strides have been made in the effort to ensure that patients have access to quality, cost-effective services rendered by advanced practice nurses. In 1998, the Health Care Financing Administration (HCFA) began permitting nurse practitioners and clinical nurse specialists to bill for their professional services regardless of practice setting, and in March, 2000, HCFA removed the physician supervision restriction for nurse-anesthetists. To be recognized as an advanced practice nurse, HCFA requires that advanced practice nurses be credentialed. New credentialing requirements for nurse practitioners and clinical nurse specialists became effective on January 1, 2000. Accordingly, credentialing will continue to be an increasingly important aspect of the practice of nursing, especially for advanced practice nurses. Currently, managed care organizations are not providing advanced practice nurses with access to their provider panels, but that might change as the care delivered by advanced practice nurses continues to yield positive, cost-effective results for patients. When opportunities to be added to practice panels present themselves, it will be important for advanced practice nurses to understand the credentialing process, and to present evidence that reflects their competence and that communicates that the advanced practice nurse would be an asset to the organization.

For nurses who are not advanced practice nurses, the focus on continuing competency requires that the credentialing process be understood, and that evidence be gathered that suggests that the nurse is competent to practice in the setting in which the nurse currently works. Some state boards of nursing are beginning to pilot mechanisms to monitor a nurse's continuing competence, and employers may do the same.

For the nursing profession, engaging in all aspects of credentialing is relatively new, but necessary. It is by these credentialing activities that occupational identity is achieved, and the occupations' commitment to public protection is demonstrated.

End Notes

1. American Nurses Association (ANA). 1979. *The Study of Credentialing in Nursing: A New Approach. Volume 1, The Report of the Committee.* Kansas City, MO: American Nurses Association; pp. 22–24. Study Committee Chairperson, Margretta Madden Styles, EdD, RN, FAAN.
2. Barnum, B.S. 1997. Licensure, certification, and accreditation. *Online Journal of Nursing* August: 504. Available from URL: http://www.nursingworld.org/ojin/tpc4_2.htm.
3. American Academy of Nursing. 1983. *Magnet hospitals: Attraction and retention of professional nurses.* Kansas City, MO: American Academy of Nursing.
4. Moore Jr., J.D. 2000. Credentialing in a vacuum. *Modern Healthcare* March 27: 38.
5. Jones-Schenk, J. 1998. The brave new world of advanced practice: Credentialing and privileging. *Applied Nursing Research* 11(3): 99–100.
6. 42 U.S.C. 11135(a).
7. 42 U.S.C. 11112(b)(1).
8. 42 U.S.C. 11112(b)(2)(B).
9. 42 U.S.C. 11112(b)(3).
10. 42 U.S.C 11112 (b)(3)(C).
11. 42 U.S.C. 11112(b)(3)(D).
12. *Smith v. Ricks,* 31 F.3d 1478 (9th Cir. 1994), cert. denied, 115 S.Ct. 1400 (1995).
13. 861 F.2d 1440 (9th Cir. 1988).
14. Ibid, p. 1445.
15. 918 F.2d 605 (6th Cir. 1990).
16. 929 F.2d 1404 (9th Cir. 1991).
17. 36 F.3d 664 (7th Cir, 1994).
18. 933 P.2d 859 (N.M. 1997).
19. 5 F. Supp. 2d 694 (Mn. 1998).

Conclusion: Ethical Components of Nursing Practice 12

Introduction

In the preceding chapters, the legal aspects of nursing practice were explored. Chapter 1 introduced readers to the U.S. legal system, and to the executive, legislative, and judicial branches of government. Chapter 2 focused on the regulatory aspects of nursing practice. Chapters 3 and 4 examined the civil and criminal litigation processes, respectively. Chapters 5 and 6 looked at the legal issues nurses face related to their employment status as employee or independent contractor. Chapters 7, 8, 9, and 10 addressed the legal issues associated with nurses practicing as educators, administrators, counselors, and case managers. Chapter 11 introduced the concept of credentialing and its application to the profession of nursing. In spite of the breadth of legal issues discussed, an important aspect of the regulation of nursing practice has not yet been introduced, and that is the nurse's responsibility to practice ethically.

Although an in-depth analysis of the specific ethical issues faced by nurses is beyond the scope of this book, it is important to acknowledge that the practice of nursing is multidimensional, and that with any clinical or professional practice issue faced by nurses there are both legal and ethical implications. Accordingly, this chapter introduces the ethical components of nursing practice by comparing and contrasting the differences between laws and ethics, the principles delineated in the *Code of Ethics for Nurses,*[1] and some of the ethical issues encountered by nurses practicing as employees, independent contractors, educators, administrators, counselors, case managers, and credentialed health care professionals.

Comparing and Contrasting Laws and Ethics

In the United States, laws are binding rules of conduct that are issued by state legislatures, the U.S. Congress, or courts, and are enforced by an identified authority. These issues were addressed in Chapter 1. Ethics, on the other hand, is an area of philosophy that examines an individual's values, beliefs, and actions. Those values, beliefs, and actions studied are articulated as ethical principles.

Ethical principles are values and belief statements that govern one's choices and actions. Ethical dilemmas occur when an individual encounters a situation in which there are equally unfavorable alternatives. In an effort to work through ethical dilemmas, it is helpful to have a framework to use. That framework involves the identification of ethical theories and concepts, and then their application to the specific dilemma.

Although egoism, social contract, natural law, and principalism may be pointed to as ethical theories, in actuality there are only two major categories of ethical theories: deontology and teleology. *Deontology* attempts to determine what is right or wrong based on one's duty or obligation to act with a primary focus on treating individuals as ends in themselves rather than as means to the ends of others. *Teleology* attempts to determine right or wrong based on the consequences or outcomes of an action. *Utilitarianism* is a teleological theory that judges acts based on whether the action results in the greatest good for the greatest number. According to this teleological theory, ethical acts bring about good, and unethical acts bring about harm.[2]

There is a hierarchy of reasoning in ethics that includes judgments, rules, principles, and theories. This hierarchy proceeds from ethical thinking that is least generalizable (judgments) to that which is most generalizable (theories).

Nurses encountering ethical issues may find it helpful to work through their dilemmas analyzing the situation in light of each of the competing ethical theories. The exercise might provide insight into the perspectives of each of the stakeholders: the nurse, the patient, the patient's loved ones, the health care organization, and other members of the health care team.

Alternatively, resolution to the ethical dilemmas encountered by health care professions might be facilitated as ethical principles involved in the dilemma are identified and discussed. With ethical dilemmas, there are usually one or more of the following four ethical principles is involved: autonomy, justice, beneficence, and nonmaleficence. *Autonomy* is often expressed as respect for autonomy or respect for persons. *Beneficence* is the obligation to do good or be of benefit. *Nonmaleficence* is intentionally and unintentionally doing no harm. *Veracity* is telling the complete truth, and not misleading others.[3] *Respect* for others also recognizes that people have ethnic and cultural values, beliefs, and traditions that must be honored.

Using these ethical theories and principles, nurses can gain understanding about their own position regarding the ethical dilemma encountered in the practice setting, and can better understand the perspectives of other stakeholders. It is this dialogue that might help the stakeholders resolve the perplexing ethical dilemma.

Ethical dilemmas are perplexing because there are sometimes no clearly "right" or "wrong" courses of action. An ethical dilemma exists when (1) no matter what action is taken, some harm results, and/or (2) there are compelling, reasoned arguments for different or opposite courses of action. In contrast, what is right or wrong from a legal perspective is clearly articulated in the laws that either permit or prohibit certain actions. This difference is one of the things that distinguishes ethical issues from legal issues.

For nurses, professional practice actions fall into one of four categories. First, a nurse's action can be both legal and ethical. This occurs when the nurse practices in accordance with the standard of care. Second, the course of action may be legally permissible, but unethical. This may occur when a nurse administers a prescribed medication to a patient who does not need it or to facilitate the death of the patient. Third, the action may be ethical, but illegal, and fourth, the action can be illegal and unethical. Ethical, but illegal actions may include assisting a competent patient to commit suicide where state laws prohibit this kind of conduct. By contrast, illegal and unethical conduct includes a wide range of actions, the most egregious of which is killing a patient.

Chapter 3 identified a number of cases that had been filed because of the alleged legal wrongdoing of nurse employees. These cases examined only at the legal implications of a nurse's action or failure to act. In an effort to ascertain whether or not legal liability has potentially been incurred in a given patient care situation, nurses should ask themselves four questions: Have I assumed a duty to care for this patient? Have I breached the duty I assumed? Has the breach of my duty caused some harm? And, if the breach of my duty has caused some harm, what kind of damage has been done?

With regard to the first question, if the nurse has assumed a duty to care for the patient, the law requires that the nurse act in accordance with the standard of care. Where the nurse has assumed a duty to care for the patient, liability may be imposed if the answer to the next question is "yes." If the nurse has not assumed a duty to care for the patient, then that nurse has incurred no legal liability.

With regard to the question of a breach of duty to the patient, if the nurse fails to act consistently with the standard of care, then that nurse has breached his or her duty to the patient. Legal liability may be imposed if the answer to the next question is "yes." If, on the other hand, the nurse has acted in accordance with the standard of care, then that nurse has not breached his or her duty to the patient, and incurs no legal liability

If the breach of duty to the patient has caused some harm, then legal liability may be imposed if the answer to the next question is also "yes." If the breach of the nurse's duty to the patient has caused no harm, then legal liability will not be incurred.

Finally, with regard to the kind of damage done because of the breach of duty, the nurse is responsible for that harm, if the patient has been harmed in some way.

It is only where the answer to all four questions is "yes" that the law imposes some consequence. In civil matters, the consequences for nurses are calculated in terms of dollars that must be paid to make whole the patient and/or the patient's loved one's; harm is calculated using monetary sanctions and incarceration in the criminal context. Chapter 4 explored the consequences nurses face when they commit crimes. In the context of an administrative hearing before a licensure board, consequences may include the payment of monetary fines and the revocation of a nurse's ability to practice nursing in that jurisdiction.

Once the nurse has determined whether or not a given course of action is legal, he or she should then determine whether or not that same course of action is ethical. Answering the following questions in relation to each of the stakeholders (nurses, the patient, the patient's family, the health care organization, and other members of the health care team) may be enlightening:

- What health issues are involved?
- What ethical issues are involved?
- What ethical theories and principles are implicated?
- What additional information is needed?
- Who will be affected by this decision? What are the values and opinions of the stakeholders involved?
- What ethical theories and principles conflict?
- Has the Code of Ethics for Nurses addressed this issue? And, if a decision should be made, who should make it?

Although this process may narrow the issues that divide the stakeholders, the answers to these questions may not result in identifying an agreed to course of action. The process can, however, work to convene all of the stakeholders so that the varying perspectives can be discussed. Most health care settings today have standing ethics committees that are expressly designed to deal with the ethical issues and conflicts that arise in the health care setting.

This deliberative approach might have helped the nurse to more constructively work through the ethical dilemma that was at issue in *Warthen v. Toms River Community Hospital*.[4] In this case, Corrine Warthen worked at Toms River Community Memorial Hospital as a registered nurse for 11 years until she was terminated for refusing to dialyze a terminally ill patient with multiple problems. Warthen was periodically assigned to dialyze this patient. Twice, during dialysis, the patient went into cardiac arrest and suffered severe internal hemorrhaging. At some point, Corrine Warthen approached her head nurse and asked that she not be assigned to the patient because she had ethical, medical, and philosophical objections to continuing to dialyze the patient contending that the patient was suffering dialysis-induced complications. The head nurse granted Warthen's request and reassigned her to another patient. Weeks later, the head nurse again assigned Corrine Warthen to the patient Warthen previously asked to not be assigned to. Warthen again objected, saying that she thought that she and the head nurse had agreed that Warthen would not be assigned to dialyze this specific patient. Warthen talked to the patient's physician, who told Warthen that the patient's family wanted dialysis performed, and that the patient would not survive without the procedure. Therefore, dialysis would continue. Warthen continued to refuse to dialyze the patient, and the head nurse informed

Warthen that she would be terminated if she did not agree to perform dialysis on the patient. Corrine Warthen did not change her mind, and the hospital terminated her.

Corrine Warthen then filed a wrongful termination cause of action. Warthen contended that her termination was a violation of the public policy exception to the employment at will doctrine, which prohibits employees from being terminated in violation of the public policy of the state. The wrongful termination cause of action, as well as the public policy exception, was described in the section Exception At Will in Chapter 5 (see page 121). Warthen pointed to the American Nurses Association's *Code for Nurses* to justify her refusal to dialyze the terminally ill patient. Warthen cited the provision that states: "The nurse provides services with respect for human dignity and the uniqueness of the client, unrestricted by considerations of social or economic status, personal attributes, or the nature of health problems."[5] Corrine Warthen's contention was that dialyzing this patient compromised the patient's dignity.

Warthen's case was eventually heard by an appellate court in New Jersey where the decision of the trial court to grant summary judgment in favor of the hospital was affirmed. In reaching that decision, the appellate court determined that patients have a fundamental right to expect that health care treatment will not be terminated against their will. Here, there was no indication that the patient or his family wanted treatment to be discontinued. In fact, the patient's family made it clear that they wanted treatment to continue. According to the appellate court, this basic policy mandate outweighed any policy favoring the right of a nurse to refuse to participate in treatments that the nurse believed threatened human dignity. They also observed that Warthen's claim served only Warthen, and that for the court to rule in her favor would leave the public to wonder when and whether they would receive nursing care. This, according to the appellate court, was unacceptable. In the court's concluding remarks, the appellate courted noted that Warthen might have eased her own conscience by refusing to dialyze a terminally ill patient, but that in so doing she neither benefited society at large, the patient, or the patient's family. As a result, the public policy exception was deemed inapplicable, and her termination was upheld.

In light of *Warthen,* it is advisable for nurses to work through these kinds of issues using the problem-solving, decision-making structures that are in place in their facilities. Processing the ethical dilemma Warthen faced through an ethics committee might have resulted in a decision Warthen found acceptable, and may have prevented her termination.

The Code of Ethics for Nurses

The *Code of Ethics for Nurses*[6] (the Code) outlines specific provisions that the nurse should use to guide and evaluate actions. The Code is an example of a set of ethical rules. The Code also informs the nurse and society of the profession's expectations

Code of Ethics for Nurses

1. The nurse, in all professional relationships, practices with compassion and respect for the inherent dignity, worth, and uniqueness of every individual, unrestricted by considerations of social or economic status, personal attributes, or the nature of health problems.
2. The nurse's primary commitment is to the patient, whether an individual, family, group or community.
3. The nurse promotes, advocates for, and strives to protect the health, safety, and rights of the patient.
4. The nurse is responsible and accountable for individual nursing practice and determines the appropriate delegation of tasks consistent with the nurse's obligation to provide optimum patient care.
5. The nurse owes the same duties to self as to others, including the responsibility to preserve integrity and safety, to maintain competence, and to continue personal and professional growth.
6. The nurse participates in establishing, maintaining, and improving health care environments and conditions of employment conducive to the provision of quality health care and consistent with the values of the profession through individual and collective action.
7. The nurse participates in the advancement of the profession through contributions to practice, education, administration, and knowledge development.
8. The nurse collaborates with other health professionals and the public in promoting community, national, and international efforts to meet health needs.
9. The profession of nursing, as represented by associations and their members, is responsible for articulating nursing values, for maintaining the integrity of the profession, and its practice, and for shaping social policy.

Available from URL: http://www.nursingworld.org/ethics/chcode10.htm.

and requirements in ethical matters. Key ideas contained in the Code are respect for human dignity, the patient's right to privacy and confidentiality, patient and public safety, responsibility and accountability for nurses, nursing competence, participation in research, quality patient care, nursing integrity, and collaboration with other health care team members.

Because of *Warthen*, it is important for statements contained in the Code to be interpreted in light of the fundamental rights of patients to avoid the termination of health care services terminated against their will, and in a way that protects society at large. In no case should the *Code of Ethics for Nurses* be used at the expense of a patient's life or contrary to the wishes of the patient's family.

Ethical Issues Confronting Nurses

Regardless of practice setting or employment status, nurses face legal and ethical issues every day. Many issues will have both legal and ethical components.

For example, nurses working as employees have certain legal and ethical obligations to their employers. However, they also have legal and ethical obligations to their patients. A number of those legal responsibilities were discussed in Chapter 5. As in *Warthen,* sometimes those multiple obligations conflict. The consequence of that conflict can be significant for patients, nurses, and employers. To avoid consequences experienced by Corrine Warthen, nurses should ask how their organization addresses ethical issues, and should be prepared to take the ethical issues they face through a process the employer has in place. Typically, that mechanism is an ethics committee. If a health care organization does not have a mechanism in place to deal with ethical issues, the nurse can suggest that a mechanism be created, and then participate in the development of that process.

Nurses working as independent contractors, like nurses who are institutional employees, face a wide array of ethical clinical and professional practice issues. Contractual issues may contribute to some of those ethical dilemmas. Chapter 6 delineated the contractual issues faced by independent contractors, but did not discuss any potential ethical issues. Accordingly, it is important to acknowledge that nurses working as independent contractors will likely face more traditional clinical and professional practice ethical issues, such as whether to embark on one form of treatment or another, or whether to discontinue treatment. They will also face issues associated with whether or not or to whom to make a referral, provide uncompensated care, make patient care decisions that negatively impact the nurse independent contractor's compensation, and make disclosures about patients to third parties. This list of ethical concerns is not exhaustive, but represents an example of the range of ethical questions independent contractors can expect to face.

Like nurse-independent contractors, nurse-educators face unique ethical issues. Chapter 7 identified some of the legal aspects of the nurse educator role, including the legal implications of catalogs of course offerings, accommodating students with disabilities, dismissing students, providing students with a safe environment, warning third parties, structuring clinical experiences, intellectual property issues, and maintaining the privacy of academic records. However, no ethical issues were mentioned. It is in these educational settings that evaluating the student's classroom and clinical performance, accepting students into and dismissing students from the nursing program, and preserving a student's privacy may pose potential ethical dilemmas for nurse-educators, because these situations require the nurse-educator to pass judgment on a student's performance.

For nurses practicing as administrators, Chapter 8 dealt with a wide range of legal issues that impact nurses serving in leadership positions. Several doctrines were outlined, as were potential causes of action. However, these topics were addressed only from a legal perspective. Like nurses practicing in other settings, nurse-administrators encounter numerous ethical dilemmas. Not only do nurse-administrators encounter clinical and professional practice dilemmas, but they also have to deal with corporation-related ethical dilemmas. These corporation-focused ethical dilemmas require that the nurse-administrator balance his or her fiduciary status within the organization with his or her obligation to provide safe care for the patients and a safe work environment for the staff for whom the nurse-administrator is responsible. Allocation of scarce resources is a key problem for nurses-administrators, and ethical principles of distributive justice may apply.

For nurses who counsel patients, there are numerous ethical issues that are encountered. Chapter 9 focused exclusively on the legal issues, including the breach of confidentiality, failure to warn third parties, sexual misconduct, improper hospitalization, failure to protect suicidal patients, improper medication administration, negligent patient supervision, the negligent release and discharge of patients, and third-party litigation, but did not identify any of the related ethical issues. As a result, it is important to recognize that nurses working in counseling situations and with vulnerable populations have an ethical obligation to ensure that the patient is protected from potential harm, and that a therapeutic nurse–patient relationship is maintained at all times.

Nurses practicing as case managers in managed care environments also have ethical obligations to the patients for whom they care. Legal issues that arise in managed care were identified in Chapter 10; however, none of the potential ethical issues were mentioned. Accordingly, nurses practicing as case managers, like nurse-independent contractors and nurse-administrators, face potential ethical dilemmas associated with the contracts they execute, and they will likely face ethical issues that are corporation focused, as well as those that are more clinical in nature. For instance, nurse-case managers will have to recognize their obligation to act in the best interest of the patient despite the impact of that obligation on their personal compensation or that of the health care organization for which the nurse is providing case management services.

Chapter 11, rather than focusing on another nursing role, examined the concept of credentialing. The credentialing process is relatively new to the profession of nursing, and the case law has developed to a large extent around decisions made about whether to grant physicians clinical privileges. However, the chapter noted that an emerging body of law is developing with regard to requests by advanced practice nurses to be granted clinical privileges. The legal issues associated with those requests were discussed in some detail. However, the ethical issues associated with the credentialing process were not identified. Therefore, it is important to recognize that nurses participating in the credentialing process also face a number of ethical issues.

These issues include being completely truthful about one's educational and experiential background, the credentials one asserts that he or she possesses, and disclosing requested information that may be perceived as adverse by the nurse applying for clinical privileges.

Summary

Nurses, regardless of practice setting, have an affirmative responsibility to act in accordance with the standard of care. Failing to meet that standard subjects nurses to legal liability. The first 11 chapters of this book dealt exclusively with those issues.

This chapter acknowledged that practicing in accordance with the standard of care must also be accompanied with a commitment to practice ethically. To ensure that nurses have the introductory information they need to practice ethically, a comparison between laws and ethics was presented, as well as ethical theories and principles nurses can use to work through the ethical dilemmas they encounter. In addition, the principles contained in the *Code of Ethics for Nurses* were listed, legal and ethical decision-making models were identified, and some of the ethical issues faced by nurses practicing as employees, independent contractors, educators, administrators, counselors, case managers, and credentialed health care providers were outlined.

End Notes

1. Available from URL: http://www.nursingworld.org/ethics/chcode10.htm.
2. Guido, G.W. 1997. *Legal issues in nursing.* Stamford, CT: Appleton & Lange; p. 359.
3. Ibid, p. 361.
4. 488 A. 2d 229 (N.J. 1982)
5. American Nurses Association (ANA). 1981. *Code for Nurses.* Kansas City, MO: American Nurses Association, p. 5.
6. ANA. 2001. *Code of ethics for nurses.* Washington, D.C: American Nurses Publishing.

Licensure Guidelines Issued by ANA's House of Delegates A

Alternative approaches to state licensure should meet the following guidelines:

- Interstate practice legislation clearly defines key terms and is precisely drafted to ensure that the primary objective to be accomplished by interstate practice are achieved (i.e., asserting jurisdiction over out-of-state nurses practicing in a state).
- The rulemaking process to implement any interstate practice legislation is clearly spelled out in the legislation and proposed implementation regulations of key provisions are developed simultaneously with any legislation.
- Clear parameters are established related to the confidentiality of any information shared with other states as well as who shall have access to such information.
- The sharing of any information related to disciplinary matters, other than final orders and emergency suspensions is prohibited unless a clear and convincing need exists to protect the public.
- The process for selecting an entity to conduct data collection or provide other services related to implementation of interstate practice is open and competitive.
- Before any immunity from liability is extended to nongovernmental entities, careful scrutiny occurred to ensure that those entities are appropriately accountable for their actions.
- Mechanisms are established to ensure that the process used by any entity collecting data be reconciled with state law and procedures regarding collecting, maintaining, and distributing licensure and disciplinary information.
- The rights of individual nurses to a fair hearing of any disciplinary matter are protected, and no unfair or undue burden, financial or otherwise, is placed on a nurse's exercise of his or her right to a fair hearing.
- Approaches to interstate advanced practice nursing are addressed for consistency in connection with interstate practice for other RNs.
- Mechanisms are in place to ensure that nurses had ready and ongoing access to practice-related information, including current board of nursing policies.

- Mechanisms are in place to ensure that the BON knows who was practicing in its state under authority of a license granted by another state or through an interstate practice agreement.
- The state of predominant practice is the state of licensure; if the nurse is not practicing, the nurse is to be licensed in his or her state of residence.
- Employers are held accountable for ensuring that they use appropriately licensed staff or otherwise authorized to practice under state law.
- Interstate practice is not implemented in a way that allows persons to circumvent or contravene existing public policy as expressed by a state's laws or policies, including laws on the use of strikebreakers and striker replacement or initial and continuing licensure requirements.

With regard to interstate practice issues, this same report directed that the ANA

1. continue to demonstrate a commitment to consumer access to nursing services, recognizing that nursing practice occurs across state lines.
2. request that the NCSBN provide the ANA with evidence that research has been conducted to

   - determine the scope and nature of cross state practice including but not limited to telenursing.
   - describe problems with the current nursing licensure system that result in decreased access to care or threats to public safety.

3. Request that the NCSBN report to the ANA a detailed fiscal and administrative analysis of each alternative licensure model considered by the Multi-State Regulation Task Force to include an estimate of the impact on each state or jurisdictional licensing board and on individual licensed nurses, and a fiscal analysis of the cost and maintenance of the mutual recognition computer system (NURSYS), legal fees, administration costs, and revenue impact.
4. Request that the NCSBN report to the ANA a detailed legal analysis of all questions related to the implementation of mutual recognition agreements between state licensure boards, including but not limited to labor implications, enforceability, confidentiality, Constitutional issues, licensure state, jurisdiction, and effect on state laws other than practice acts.
5. Support the implementation of a national licensure data base with the following criteria:

   - Disciplinary information reflects only final board orders.
   - Data elements to be included are explicit and subjected to public hearing in each jurisdiction.
   - Access, availability, and confidentiality parameters are explicit and subjected to public hearing in each jurisdiction.
   - Safeguards for individual nurse information are implemented, and

■ projected costs for implementation and maintenance are made public prior to implementation.

6. Develop model guidelines for state nursing associations to use if they desire to pursue legislation to allow entry into agreements with another state(s) to facilitate cross state border practice.

American Nurses Association (ANA). 1998. *Summary of Proceedings.* 1998 House of Delegates, June 26–July 1; pp. 59–61.

Advanced Directive: Examples

B

Advanced Directive

of _____

Advance Directive for Health Care

I,_____, being of sound mind and eighteen (18) years of age or older, willfully and voluntarily make known my desire, by my instructions to others through my living will, or by my appointment of a health care proxy, or both, that my life shall not be artificially prolonged under the circumstances set forth below. I thus, do here by declare:

I. Living Will

A. If my attending physician and another physician determine that I am no longer able to make decisions regarding my medical treatment, I direct my attending physician and other health care providers, pursuant to Oklahoma Rights of the Terminally Ill or Persistently Unconscious Act, to withhold or withdraw treatment from me under the circumstances I have indicated below by my initials and signature. I understand that I will be given treatment that is necessary for my comfort or to alleviate my pain.

_____
initials

B. If I have a terminal condition:

1. I direct that life-sustaining treatment shall be withheld or withdrawn if such treatment would only prolong my process of dying, and if my attending physician and another physician determine that I have an incurable

and irreversible condition that even with the administration of life-sustaining treatment will cause my death within six (6) months.

_____
initials

2. I understand that the subject of the artificial administration of nutrition and hydration (food and water) that will only prolong the process of dying from an incurable and irreversible condition is of particular importance. I understand that if I do not sign this paragraph, artificially administered nutrition and hydration will be administered to me. I further understand that if I sign this paragraph, I am authorizing the withholding or withdrawal of artificially administered nutrition (food) and hydration (water).

_____
initials

C. If I am persistently unconscious:

1. I direct that life-sustaining treatment shall be withheld or withdrawn if such treatment would only prolong my process of dying, and if my attending physician and another physician determine that I have an incurable and irreversible condition that even with the administration of life-sustaining treatment will cause my death within six (6) months.

_____
initials

2. I understand that the subject of the artificial administration of nutrition and hydration (food and water) that will only prolong the process of dying from an incurable and irreversible condition is of particular importance. I understand that if I do not sign this paragraph, artificially administered nutrition and hydration will be administered to me. I further understand that if I sign this paragraph, I am authorizing the withholding or withdrawal of artificially administered nutrition (food) and hydration (water).

_____
initials

II. My Appointment of My Health Care Proxy

A. If my attending physician and another physician determine that I am no longer able to make decisions regarding my medical treatment, I direct my attending physician and other health care providers pursuant to the Oklahoma Rights of the Terminally Ill or Persistently Unconscious Act to follow the instructions of_____, whom I appoint as my health care proxy. If_____is unable or unwilling to serve as my health care proxy, I appoint _____, as my alternate health care proxy. My health care proxy is authorized to make whatever medical treatment decisions I could make if I were able, except that decisions regarding life-sustaining treatment can be made by my health care proxy or alternate health care proxy only as I indicate in the following sections:

B. If I have a terminal condition:

1. I authorize my health care proxy to direct that life-sustaining treatment shall be withheld or withdrawn if such treatment would only prolong my process of dying, and if my attending physician and another physician determine that I have an incurable and irreversible condition that even with the administration of life-sustaining treatment will cause my death within six (6) months.

_____
initials

2. I understand that the subject of the artificial administration of nutrition and hydration (food and water) that will only prolong the process of dying from an incurable and irreversible condition is of particular importance. I understand that if I do not sign this paragraph, artificially administered nutrition and hydration will be administered to me. I further understand that if I sign this paragraph, I am authorizing the withholding or withdrawal of artificially administered nutrition (food) and hydration (water).

_____
initials

C. If I am persistently unconscious:

1. I authorize my health care proxy to direct that life-sustaining treatment shall be withheld or withdrawn if such treatment would only prolong my process of dying, and if my attending physician and another physician determine that I have an incurable and irreversible condition that even with the administration of life-sustaining treatment will cause my death within six (6) months.

_____
initials

2. I understand that the subject of the artificial administration of nutrition and hydration (food and water) that will only prolong the process of dying from an incurable and irreversible condition is of particular importance. I understand that if I do not sign this paragraph, artificially administered nutrition and hydration will be administered to me. I further understand that if I sign this paragraph, I am authorizing the withholding or withdrawal of artificially administered nutrition (food) and hydration (water).

_____
initials

III. Conflicting Provision

I understand that if I have completed both a living will and have appointed a health care proxy, and if there is a conflict between my health care proxy's decision and my living will, my living will shall take precedence unless I indicate otherwise.

_____
initials

IV. Other Provisions

A. I understand that if I have been diagnosed as pregnant and that diagnosis is known to my attending physician, this advance directive shall have no force or effect during the course of my pregnancy.

B. In the absence of my ability to give directions regarding the use of life-sustaining procedures, it is my intention that this advance directive shall be honored by my family and physicians as the final expression of my legal right to refuse medical or surgical treatment including, but not limited to, the administration of any life-sustaining procedures, and I accept the consequences of such refusal.

C. This advance directive shall be in effect until it is revoked.

D. I understand that I may revoke this advance directive at any time.

E. I understand and agree that if I have any prior directives, and if I sign this advance directive, my prior directives are revoked.

F. I understand the full importance of this advance directive and am emotionally and mentally competent to make this advance directive.

Signed this _____ day of _____, 20___.

_____
Signature

_____
Address

_____
City,   County   State

This advance directive was signed in my presence:

_____
Witness Signature

_____
Address

_____
City,   County,   State

_____
Witness Signature

_____
Address

_____
City,   County,   State

Actions That Can Result in Sanctions by HCFA C

General

1. Billing for a clinical diagnostic laboratory test, other than on an assignment-related basis. This provision includes tests performed in a physician's office, but does not include tests performed in a rural health clinic.
2. Billing for an intraocular lens inserted during or after cataract surgery for which payment may be made for services in an ambulatory surgical center.
3. Failing to complete a claim form relating to the availability of other health benefit plans, or providing inaccurate information relating to the availability of other health benefit plans on the claim form.
4. Failing to report information concerning ownership, investment, and compensation arrangements.
5. Failing to submit a claim for a beneficiary within 1 year of providing services, or imposing a charge for completing and submitting the standard claims form.

Nonassignment

1. Failing to provide information about a referring physician, including the referring physician's name and unique physician identification number, where payment is sought on an unassigned basis.
2. Failing to provide the diagnosis code or codes after repeatedly being notified by HCFA of the obligations on any request for payment or bill submitted on a nonassigned basis;
3. Furnishing physician services and billing on a nonassigned basis or collecting money in excess of the limiting charge, or failing to make an adjustment or refund to the Medicare beneficiary.
4. Billing for physicians' services on a nonassigned basis for a Medicare beneficiary who is also eligible for Medicaid.

5. Billing or collecting for any services on a nonassigned basis by nonphysician health care providers, including physician assistants, nurse practitioners, clinical nurse specialists, certified registered nurse anesthetists, certified nurse-midwives, clinical social workers, and clinical psychologists.

Durable Medical Equipment Suppliers

1. Charging for covered items (on a rented basis), by suppliers of durable medical equipment, after the rental payments may no longer be made (except for maintenance and servicing).
2. Making unsolicited telephone calls to Medicare beneficiaries by any supplier of durable medical equipment regarding the furnishing of covered equipment or services.
3. Failing to make a refund to Medicare beneficiaries for a covered item for which payment is precluded due to an unsolicited telephone contact by any durable medical equipment supplier.
4. Charging for a covered prosthetic device, orthotic, or prosthetic which is rented, after the rental payment may no longer be made (except for maintenance and service).
5. Making unsolicited telephone contact to Medicare beneficiaries regarding the furnishing of prosthetic devices, orthotics, or prosthetics.
6. Completing the medical necessity section of the certificate of medical necessity or failing to provide the fee schedule amount and the supplier's charge for the medical equipment or supply prior to distributing the certificate to the physician.
7. Failing to make refunds in a timely manner to Medicare beneficiaries where the item or service is denied or determined to not be medically necessary or reasonable.
8. Failing to make refunds to Medicare beneficiaries for items or services billed on an assigned basis if the supplier did not possess a Medicare supplier number, if the item or service is denied in advance, or the item is determined to be not medically necessary or reasonable.

Nonparticipating Physicians

1. Charging a Medicare beneficiary more than the designated charge for radiologist services.
2. Charging a Medicare beneficiary more than the delineated charge for mammography screening.
3. Billing for an assistant at cataract surgery performed on or after March 1, 1987.

4. Failing to accept payment on an assigned basis, by any nonparticipating physician, and failing to refund beneficiaries for services that are not reasonable or medically necessary or are of poor quality.
5. Billing for an elective surgical procedure on a nonassigned basis, whose charge is at least $500.00, and who
   ▪ fails to disclose the charge and coinsurance amounts to the Medicare beneficiary prior to rendering the service; and
   ▪ fails to refund any amount collected for the procedure in excess of the charges recognized and approved by the Medicare program.

Physicians

1. Billing diagnostic tests in excess of the scheduled fee amount.
2. Failing to promptly provide the appropriate diagnosis code or codes upon request by HCFA or a carrier on any request for payment or bill submitted on a nonassigned basis.

Employers

1. Any employer failing to provide an employee's group health insurance coverage information to the Medicare contractor.

Insurers

1. Issuing a Medicare supplemental policy that has not been approved by the state regulatory program or does not meet federal standards.
2. Selling or issuing nonstandard Medicare supplemental policies.
3. Selling a Medicare supplemental policy and who
   ▪ fails to make available the core group of basic benefits as part of its product line; or
   ▪ fails to provide the individual (before the sale of the policy) an outline of coverage describing the benefits provided by the policy.
4. Failing to
   ▪ suspend a Medicare supplemental policy at the policyholder's request (if the policyholder applies for and is determined eligible for Medicaid), or
   ▪ automatically reinstate the policy as of the date the policyholder loses medical assistance eligibility (and the policyholder provides timely notice of losing his or her Medicaid eligibility).
5. Failing to refund or credit as required by the supplemental insurance policy loss ratio requirements.

6. Issuing a Medicare supplemental policy that
   - does not waive any time periods applicable to preexisting conditions, waiting periods, elimination periods, or probationary periods, if the time periods were already satisfied under a preceding Medicare policy, or
   - denies a policy, conditions the issuance, or effectiveness of the policy, or discriminates in the pricing of the policy based on health status or other criteria.
7. Issuing a Medicare supplementary policy that
   - fails to provide medically necessary services to enrollees through the issuer's network of entities;
   - imposes premiums on enrollees in excess of the premiums approved by the state;
   - acts to expel an enrollee for reasons other than nonpayment of premiums;
   - does not provide each enrollee at the time of enrollment with specific information regarding policy restrictions; or
   - fails to obtain a written acknowledgment from the enrollee of receipt of the information.

Available from URL: http://www.hcfa.gov/medicare/fraud/CMP2.HTML.

Glossary D

Accreditation—The process by which organizations and/or programs are assessed, evaluated, and given accredited status using predetermined structure, process, and outcome criteria.

Advanced practice registered nurse—One who meets the statutory definition to be called either a nurse practitioner, clinical nurse specialist, nurse-midwife, or certified registered nurse anesthetist.

Administrative agency—A governmental agency charged with carrying out statutory mandates.

Administrative Procedures Act (APA)—Statutes that delineate the processes administrative agencies must follow.

Admiralty—Pertaining to navigable waters..

Advance directive—Documents that describe how an individual wishes that end-of-life decisions be handled.

Age Discrimination in Employment Act (ADEA)—A federal law that prohibits employers from discriminating against older individuals.

Alternative dispute resolution—Mechanisms used to resolve legal disputes before they are tried in a court of law. Two primary mechanisms are arbitration and mediation. In arbitration, an impartial third-party hears the dispute from the perspective of both parties and renders a decision. The decision is usually binding on both parties. Mediation, on the other hand, uses a third party to assist the parties in resolving the dispute.

Alienage—One's heritage.

American Association of Colleges of Nursing (AACN)—Located in Washington, D.C., this organization is dedicated to advancing the interest of baccalaureate and higher degree programs in nursing.

American Nurses Association (ANA)—The voluntary professional nurses association to which any and every nurse can belong that works to advance the interests of nurses practicing in the United States.

American Nurses Credentialing Center (ANCC)—The nation's foremost credentialing center located in Washington, D.C. The American Nurses Credentialing Center is a separately incorporated, separately governed credentialing organization owned by the American Nurses Association.

Americans with Disabilities Act (ADA)—A federal law that prohibits discrimination against qualified individuals with disabilities.

Answer—The document filed with the court in which a petition or complaint has been filed by the plaintiff.

Antitrust acts—Federal and state statutes designed to protect trade and commerce by prohibiting restraints on trade, price discrimination, price fixing, and monopolization.

Appeal—To seek reversal of a decision of any court.

Approver—An accredited status awarded to eligible organizations that successfully complete the application process by the Commission on Accreditation at the American Nurses Credentialing Center. It allows the organization to approve educational offerings other organizations are offering for continuing education purposes.

Arbitration—One alternative dispute resolution mechanism used to resolve cases prior to trial.

Arraignment—That portion of the criminal litigation system in which an accused individual has the opportunity to plead guilty or not guilty to the crime allegedly committed.

Assault—The fear of being unlawfully touched.

Autonomy—The ability to function independently.

Bad faith—The conscious doing of a wrong or with ill will.

Bail—Money paid or anything of value surrendered to ensure that a specific individual remains within the jurisdiction or appears at a specific court proceeding.

Battery—The unlawful touch of another human being.

Beneficence—The ethical obligation to do good and not harm.

Bill of Rights—The first 10 amendments to the U.S. Constitution that give individuals additional rights.

Board of nursing (BON)—The administrative agency charged with enforcing the practice act for nurses.

Bribery—The payment of money or of anything of value in exchange for certain behavior.

Captain of the ship—A doctrine that used to be applied, especially in operating rooms. It worked to hold physicians accountable for the acts of others because the physician was the identified person in charge of the operating room.

Case manager—A role filled by nurses, as well as other health care professionals, whose responsibility it is to oversee the care and treatment of an individual patient or groups of patients.

Cause of action—A claim or a case filed by a plaintiff.

Certified registered nurse anesthetist (CRNA)—An advanced practice nurse who is authorized to administer anesthesia in accordance with the provisions of applicable nurse practice acts.

Certification—A credentialing activity that identifies individuals who have mastered a body of knowledge. Typically, mastery is assessed using a psychometrically sound, legally defensible, objective examination.

Charitable immunity—A doctrine used to shield charitable organizations like hospitals from liability for its employees' acts of negligence.

Civil Rights Act of 1964—A federal law that seeks to ensure that all Americans are free from discrimination.

Clinical nurse specialist (CNS)—An advanced practice nurse who, in accordance with the requirements of applicable nurse practice acts, practices as an expert clinician and manages patients with complex nursing problems.

Clinical privileges—Permission to practice in a given setting.

Commission on Graduate of Foreign Nursing Schools (CGFNS)—The organization that processes applications from nurses abroad to practice nursing in the United States.

Compact—The agreement that is signed by representatives of member state boards of nursing.

Comparative negligence—A defense to a charge of negligence in which damages are reduced in accordance with the percent of negligence attributed to plaintiff.

Competence—Practicing in accordance with the prevailing standard of care.

Complaint—The document plaintiff files with the applicable court that identifies how the plaintiff was harmed, by whom, and the redress sought.

Compounding a crime—The crime that is committed when a person who has been injured by a felony, agrees with the criminal not to prosecute conditioned on a promise of restitution or other agreement.

Comprehensive Drug Abuse Prevention and Control Act of 1970—Also known as the Controlled Substances Act, this federal law delineates which individuals may prescribe and administer controlled substances.

Comprehensive Omnibus Budget Reconciliation Act of 1986—A federal law that includes the Emergency Medical Treatment and Active Labor Act (EMTALA) enacted to prohibit transferring patients without first stabilizing them and refusing to treat indigent patients in medical emergencies.

Confidentiality—Nondisclosure of information or data.

Congress—The federal legislative body in the United States composed of the House of Representatives and the Senate.

Consolidated Omnibus Budget Reconciliation Act (COBRA)—A federal that addresses at least one health care issue: patient dumping.

Consumer Fraud Act—A statute that prohibits false and misleading information from being given to consumers.

Contributory negligence—A defense that can be asserted by defendants when the plaintiff does or fails to do something to protect themselves from injury. This defense is used in a minority of jurisdictions. The majority of jurisdictions have begun to favor the use of comparative negligence.

Conviction—To be found guilty or to plead guilty of committing a crime.

Copyright—The time-limited privilege granted to an owner of literary and artistic works to publish, reproduce, and sell the works.

Copyright Act of 1996—The federal statute that governs copyrights.

Copyright office—Located in Washington, D.C., it is this office that process and houses all applications and copies of copyrighted material.

Corporate negligence—A doctrine that is used to hold organizations liable for the negligent acts and omissions of its employees.

Credentialing—Mechanisms used to maintain competence and stimulate continued self-improvement, as well as the process organizations use to select providers who will have the ability to care for patients.

Crime—A societal wrong. Consequences include the payment of sanctions, as well as incarceration and execution.

Damages—The harm, in dollars, incurred by the plaintiff because of the wrongdoing of the defendant.

Deceptive Trade Practices Act—A statute that prohibits the less-than-truthful practices on the part of some businesses.

Defendant—The person or entity being sued or tried for an alleged criminal act.

Defraud—To recklessly falsify or misrepresent a material fact on which another relies.

Deontology—An ethical theory that attempts to determine what is right or wrong based on one's duty or obligation to act rather than the action's consequences.

Department of Justice—The governmental entity charged with enforcing the federal laws of the United States, providing legal counsel in federal cases, supervising federal penal institutions, and investigating alleged violations of federal law. The agency is headed by the attorney general.

Department of Labor—The governmental entity charged with enforcing more than 180 federal workplace-related laws, including wage and hour, health and safety, employment and pension, unemployment, and worker's compensation issues.

Deposition—An interview, under oath.

Disciplinary action—Action taken by the state board of nursing to restrict the rights of a licensee to practice within that jurisdiction.

Discovery—The process in civil proceedings in which information is gathered, evidence collected in preparation for trial.

Double jeopardy—A doctrine that prohibits an individual from being tried twice for the same crime.

Duress—Being compelled, forced, threatened, or intimidated.

Egoism—An ethical theory that considers self-interest and self-preservation as the only proper goal of all human actions.

Embezzlement—Taking of personal property that one lawfully possesses but belongs to another with the intent of permanently depriving the other of it.

Emergency Medical Treatment and Active Labor Act (EMTALA)—A federal law that prohibits transferring unstable patients and refusing to treat indigent patients in medical emergencies. Part of the Comprehensive Omnibus Budget Reconciliation Act of 1986.

Emotional distress—Emotional harm that results from the wrongdoing of another.

Employee—An individual hired by another or an entity to perform a specific job.

Employee at will—The status of an employee working without an employment contract.

Employee Retirement Security Income Act (ERISA)—A federal statutory scheme governing the funding, vesting, and administration of pension plans. The act's ability to shield managed care organizations from liability has been the subject of significant managed care litigation.

Endorsement—One of the ways an individual can be authorized to practice nursing within a specific jurisdiction. It requires that the individual hold a current license, that is in good standing, within another jurisdiction.

Equal Employment Opportunity Commission (EEOC)—The governmental entity responsible for enforcing employment-related disputes that involve discrimination.

Equal Pay Act—A federal law that requires that pay be the same among individuals performing the same job.

Equal protection—A 14th Amendment constitutional right that requires that similarly situated people be treated similarly.

Ethical dilemma—A situation that requires that a choice be made between two equally unfavorable alternatives.

Ethical principles—Concepts or ideas that give meaning to one's life and provides a framework for one's decisions and actions.

Ethics—An area of philosophical study in which values, beliefs, and actions are examined.

Evidence—Proof that something did or did not occur.

Excises—Taxes paid for the manufacture, sale, or consumption of commodities or on licenses to practice certain professions or corporate privileges.

Fair Health Information Protection Act of 1994—A federal law that protects the health information of individuals.

Fair Labor Standards Act (FLSA)—A federal law that prohibits the labor of children and requires that certain standards be maintained with regard to minimum wage and maximum work weeks.

False Claims Act—A federal statute that makes it a criminal offense to make or present false claims against the U.S. government.

False imprisonment—The unlawful confinement or restriction of the movements of another person.

False pretenses—Obtaining the property of another because of an untrue statement or act that is calculated to deceive and that results in the victim of the property parting with it.

Family Educational Rights and Privacy Act (FERPA)—A federal statute requiring that student records be kept confidential.

Family Medical Leave Act (FMLA)—A federal law that provides employees with the opportunity to care for family members without compromising their jobs.

Federal law—Statutes passed by Congress and signed into law by the U.S. President.

Federal Privacy Act of 1974—A federal law that protects the privacy of individuals.

Felony—A type of serious crime, the punishment for which can result in incarceration for periods of 1 year or more.

Fidelity—Being faithful or loyal.

Final Agency Order—The document issued by administrative agencies, like boards of nursing, that contain findings of facts and conclusions of law. It represents the ending of an administrative hearing process.

Forgery—Knowingly altering or signing a document as if the signor is someone else, with the intent of defrauding another.

Fraud—Intentional perversion of a material fact relied on by the plaintiff that causes harm.

Fundamental rights—Constitutional rights enjoyed by everyone. If any of these rights are denied to everyone, due process issues arise. If they are denied to some, then equal protection issues arise. Fundamental rights include the right of privacy, as well as the right to vote and travel.

Good standing—The states of an individual's license to practice nursing. It reflects the fact that there are no restrictions placed on the licensee.

Grand jury—The body of citizens, the number of whom varies from state to state, that determines whether probable cause exists to indict a specific individual or entity with the commission of a crime.

Grandfather clause—An exception to a restriction contained in a new law or regulation that permits those who do not possess the requisites delineated in the new statutory scheme to continue to work.

Harassment—Words, gestures, and other actions that annoy, alarm, and abuse another person.

Health Care Financing Administration (HCFA)—The governmental agency charged with overseeing the Medicare, Medicaid, and state-based children's health programs.

Health care proxy—The individual a competent person identifies as the primary health care decision maker when the currently competent person is no longer so.

Health Care Quality Improvement Act (HCQIA)—The federal statutory scheme that resulted in the creation of the National Practitioners' Data Bank.

Health Insurance Portability and Accountability Act (HIPPA)—A federal law that requires that the health-related records of individuals be secure and kept private.

Hearing—The setting in which formal administrative proceedings occur.

Immigration Reform and Control Act—A federal law that governs naturalization and immigration in the United States.

Immunity—Being protected from prosecution.

Indemnify—To restore the victim of a loss by payment or replacement.

Independent contractor—The status of a business relationship that is governed by a contract. Independent contractors control the means by which projects are completed.

Indictment—Being accused of committing a crime. It is an accusation that is reduced to a writing presented by a grand jury charging that a specific individual has done or failed to do something required by criminal law.

Insanity—Denotes a degree of mental illness that negates an individual's ability to be legally responsible for his or her actions and any crimes occurring as a result.

Intellectual property—Any product of the human intellect that is embodied in the goods and services a company offers and by which the company is known. Patents, trademarks, and copyrights are examples of intellectual property.

Intent—Purposeful determination.

Intentional indifference—Purposeful disregard.

Interrogatories—The document that is exchanged between parties to civil litigation that requires the other party to prepare written responses, under oath.

Interstate commerce—A constitutional principle that requires that individuals have the freedom of movement within and between states.

Judiciary—The branch of government that oversees the civil and criminal litigation processes in the United States.

Jury—Individuals from the community selected to determine whether an individual or entity committed the offense for which that individual or entity is accused.

Just cause—Based on reasonable grounds. With licenses, it implies that charges be made and notice of hearing be given to the licensee before action is taken.

Justice—An ethical principle that signifies an obligation to be fair to all people.

Kickback—Receiving anything of value to induce future purchases.

Larceny—The taking and carrying away of another's personal property with the intent of permanently depriving that individual of the property.

Last clear chance doctrine—A defense that can be asserted by defendants where the plaintiff had the last chance to avoid the consequences for which they seek compensation through the civil justice system.

Laws—Binding rules of conduct issued by state legislatures, the U.S. Congress, courts, and regulatory agencies, and that are enforced by an identified authority.

License—That document, writing, or other evidence that communicates to others that the identified individual is authorized to engage in an activity or profession.

Licensee—The holder of a license.

Licensed practical/vocational nurse (LPN/VPN)—An individual who has completed a 1-year educational program at a vocational institution, and who practices under the supervision of a registered nurse, physician, or dentist.

Limited liability company (LLC)—A type of corporation that shields an individual's personal property from being seized in litigation.

Litigation—All aspects of the legal process.

Loss of consortium—Traditionally, the loss of the sexual relationship between spouses. The doctrine has been expanded to include losses of companionship enjoyed by parents, children, and others.

Magnet Nursing Services Recognition Program—An international program of the American Nurses Credentialing Center in which excellent health care organizations are recognized.

Managed care—Primarily a financing mechanism, it the predominant system through which health care services are delivered in the United States.

Manslaughter—Unlawful killing of another human being without malice or premeditation.

Maritime—Like admiralty, pertaining to navigable waters.

Mayhem—The crime that is committed when someone is permanently disfigured or otherwise permanently rendered less able to fight offensively or defensively.

Medical Records Confidentiality Act of 1995—A federal law that requires that an individual's medical record information be kept private, and not be shared with third parties unless the disclosure is authorized by the individual.

Misdemeanor—A less serious criminal offense. Consequences can include the payment of fines, monetary penalties, community service, and incarceration for periods of less than 1 year.

Multistate licensure—A concept that seeks to provide nurses with the ability to practice across state lines without having to have a license issued in each jurisdiction.

Murder—The unlawful killing of another human being with malice aforethought.

Mutual recognition—The multistate licensure model proposed by the National Council of State Boards of Nursing.

National Collegiate Licensure Exam (NCLEX)—The licensure exam administered by state boards of nursing, the passage of which permits an individual to practice in that jurisdiction.

National Council of State Boards of Nursing (NCSBN)—The national organization to which state boards of nursing are members.

National Labor Relations Act (NLRA)—A comprehensive federal law regulates the relationship between employers and employees.

National Labor Relations Board (NLRB)—The independent administrative agency created by the National Labor Relations Act. Its purpose includes remedying unfair labor practices, and conducting secret ballot elections among employees in collective bargaining units to determine whether or not the employees wish to be represented by a labor union.

National League for Nursing (NLN)—A national nursing organization located in New York that is dedicated to advancing the quality of nursing education.

National origin—The country in which a person is born, or the country from which a person's ancestors came.

National Practitioner Data Bank—A clearinghouse that collects adverse information about health care providers.

Natural law theory—An ethical theory that suggests that actions become morally or ethically right when they are in accord with natural law. The theory can be theistic or atheistic.

Naturalization—The process of becoming a citizen of the United States.

Negligence—Failing to act as a reasonably prudent individual in the same or similar circumstances.

Nonmaleficence—The requirement that health care providers do no harm to patients either intentionally or unintentionally.

Nurse-midwife—An advanced practice nurse who care for mothers during the pregnancy and delivery processes.

Nurse practice act (NPA)—The state statutory scheme that delineates what nurses are authorized and not authorized to do.

Nurse practitioner—Advanced practice nurses who provide primary and ambulatory care services.

Obligationism—An ethical theory that attempts to resolve ethical dilemmas by balancing distributive justice with beneficence. Distributive justice means doing the greatest good for the greatest number of people.

Occupational Safety and Health Act (OHSA)—A federal law that requires employers to meet safety and health standards. The act created the Occupational Safety and Health Administration, which is charged with enforcing the Occupational Safety and Health Act.

Open Meetings Act—A state and federal statute that requires that administrative agency meetings be open to the public.

Open Records Act—A state and federal statute that requires that administrative agency records be open to the public.

Patent—A time-limited intellectual property right granted to an inventor, conveying the inventor the exclusive right to make, use, and sell the invention.

Patent Act of 1994—The federal statute that governs the issuance of patents.

Paternalism—An ethical theory at work when others make decisions on or behalf of an individual.

Patient Self-Determination Act—A federal law that requires that individuals be afforded the opportunity to make end of life decisions for themselves.

Peer review—The process of having one's colleagues involved in the evaluation process.

Perjury—Making false statements under oath.

Pew Health Professions Commission—An organization that seeks to improve the health care system in the United States.

Plaintiff—An individual or entity filing a lawsuit.

Plea bargain—The process that results in an accused individual pleading guilty to less serious crime in return for a lighter sentence. These agreements are subject to court approval.

Pretrial conference—The meeting between opposing counsel and the judge before trial in which the issues are narrowed, and other stipulations are made.

Principalism—An ethical theory that seeks to resolve ethical dilemmas using more than one ethical theory.

Probable cause—Reasonable cause or having reasonably trustworthy information.

Procedural due process—A 14th Amendment constitutional guarantee that individuals will have access to fair procedures. This includes giving individuals notice and the opportunity to be heard in judicial proceedings.

Provider—An individual or entity offering continuing education opportunities that has been subjected to peer review, and an external evaluation, and that has successfully completed that process.

Qui tam action—A legal claim brought by someone, a relator, who has first-hand information about an organization's violation of the law. The relator sues the organization on behalf of the relator and the United States.

Rape—Nonconsensual sexual intercourse.

Reasonable accommodation—Modifications employers must make for employees who are disabled in order to comply with the Americans with Disabilities Act.

Reasonable care—That degree of care an ordinarily prudent person would exercise in the same or similar circumstances.

Reasonable doubt—Doubt that causes prudent individuals to hesitate before acting in matters of importance to them.

Reasonably foreseeable—A consequence that could have been anticipated by an ordinarily prudent individual.

Rebuttable presumption—Results in something being considered true until contrary evidence is presented.

Registered nurse—An individual who cares for and treats human responses to actual or potential health problems, and who is authorized to practice nursing within a specified scope of practice by applicable state nurse practice acts.

Regulation—A rule or order issued by a governmental agency to carry out the intent of the law that agency is charged with overseeing.

Reinstatement—A request made by a license holder to have their license activated so that they may practice in accordance with applicable state laws.

Release—A document signed by the parties in civil litigation that states that no further claims will be pursued.

Requests for admission—A discovery document that seeks to narrow the issues to be tried. Typically, one party is requested to agree or disagree with a series of statements made by the other party.

Requests for production—A discovery document that requires one party to turn over specifically requested tangible evidence.

Res ipsa loquitur—A doctrine that shifts the burden of proof from plaintiff to defendants. It infers that the alleged wrongdoing would not have occurred in the absence of negligence.

Respondeat superior—A doctrine that works to hold employers liable for the acts of employees.

Right to counsel—A 6th and 14th Amendment constitutional right of a criminal defendant to have an attorney. If the defendant is unable to afford an attorney, a court-appointed attorney will be assigned.

Robbery—Taking by force another's personal property from his or her person or presence.

Rule—A standard, guide, or regulation.

Rulemaking—An activity engaged in by administrative agencies whereby standards, guidelines, or regulations are established.

Scope of practice—The breadth within which one must practice.

Self-determination—The ability to determine for oneself how end-of-life issues will be handled.

Self-incrimination—Being a witness against oneself. The 5th amendment of the U.S. Constitution prohibits an individual from being required involuntarily to be a witness against him- or herself.

Settlement—An agreement reached by parties in civil litigation that resolves the dispute. It may involve all parties, or some of the parties.

Severability—A doctrine that permits the striking of one provision of a contract without invalidating the entire contract.

Sherman Antitrust Act—The federal statutory scheme designed to protect trade and commerce.

Social contract theory—An ethical theory that espouses the belief that income, wealth, liberty, opportunity, and self-respect must be distributed equally.

Solicitation—Encouraging, enticing, or inducing another to commit a crime.

Statutory rape—Sexual intercourse with anyone under the age of consent. The age of consent varies from state to state, but may be either 16, 17, or 18 years of age.

Strict liability—A concept used in torts and product liability causes of action. It results in a manufacturer being liable for any and all defective or hazardous products.

Subornation of perjury—Encouraging, enticing, or inducing another to make false statements under oath.

Subpoena—A document that commands an individual to appear at a certain time and place so that testimony in a legal matter can be given.

Subpoena duces teum—A document that commands someone to produce something tangible, for example, books, records, or pictures, at trial.

Subrogation—The substitution of one party in the place of another.

Substantive due process—The constitutional guarantee that no person be arbitrarily deprived of life, liberty, or property.

Surety bond—An obligation of a guarantor assumed for a third party to pay a second party upon default by the third party.

Suspension—A temporary cutting off of one's ability to practice one's profession.

Taxes—Money paid for the support of the government.

Telehealth—Using electronic means to provide health care services between health care provider and patient.

Teleology—An ethical theory that is used to determine right or wrong based on the consequences of an action.

Tort—A civil wrong.

Trademark—An intellectual property right to exclusively use authentic, distinctive marks.

Trial—The judicial forum in which disputes between parties are addressed.

U.S. Constitution—The document that contains the fundamental and foundational laws of the United States.

U.S. Patent and Trademark Office—Located in Arlington, Virginia, it is this office that patent and trademark applications are processed.

U.S. Supreme Court—It is the court of last resort. The nine Justices who sit on the U.S. Supreme Court are given lifetime appointments by the U.S. President.

Undue influence—Improperly persuading another to do or not do something they would not have done otherwise.

Uniform Health Care Information Act of 1988—A federal law that governs how health information is to be handled.

Utilitarianism—A teleological theory that judges acts based on their usefulness. Useful acts bring about good, and useless acts bring about harm.

Veracity—Telling the complete truth.

Verdict—The formal decision made by a jury.

Vicarious liability—A doctrine that works to hold organizations responsible for the acts of their employees.

Willful misconduct—Failure to exercise ordinary care to prevent injury to a person who is known or should have reasonably been known to be in the zone of danger.

Workplace Violence Prevention Act—A federal law designed to prevent violence in U.S. work settings.

Acronyms E

AACN	American Association of Colleges of Nursing
AAN	American Academy of Nursing
ABG	arterial blood gas
ADA	Americans with Disabilities Act
ADEA	Age Discrimination in Employment Act
ANA	American Nurses Association
ANCC	American Nurses Credentialing Center
APA	Administrative Procedures Act
APRN	advanced practice registered nurse
BFOQ	bona fide occupational qualification
BON	board of nursing
BVNE	Board of Vocational Nurse Examiners
CDC	Centers for Disease Control and Prevention
CE	continuing education
CGFNS	Commission on Graduates of Foreign Nursing Schools
CMA	Constituent Member Associations
CMV	cytomegalovirus
CNS	clinical nurse specialist
COBRA	Consolidated Omnibus Budget Reconciliation Act

COPD	chronic obstructive pulmonary disease
CPR	cardiopulmonary resuscitation
CRNA	certified registered nurse anesthetist
CYS	Children and Youth Services
DEA	Drug Enforcement Agency
DRG	diagnosis related group
EKG	electrocardiogram
EMTALA	Emergency Medical Treatment and Active Labor Act
EEOC	Equal Employment Opportunity Commission
EPINet	Exposure Prevention Information Network
ERISA	Employee Retirement Income Security Act
FERPA	Family Educational Rights and Privacy Act
FLSA	Fair Labor Standards Act
FMLA	Family and Medical Leave Act
HCFA	Health Care Financing Administration
HCQIA	Health Care Quality Improvement Act
HDCT	high-dose chemotherapy treatment
HIPPA	Health Insurance Portability and Accountability Act
IRS	Internal Revenue Service
LPN/LVN	licensed practical/vocational nurse
MPA	Model Practice Acts
NCLEX	National Council Licensure Exam
NCSBN	National Council of State Boards of Nursing
NLN	National League for Nursing
NLRA	National Labor Relations Act
NLRB	National Labor Relations Board
NM	nurse-midwife
NP	nurse practitioner
NPA	Nurse Practice Act

NURSYS	mutual recognition computer system
OSHA	Occupational Safety and Health Act
OWBA	Older Workers' Benefit Protection Act
PAR	patient accountability record
RN	registered nurse
SNA	state nurses associations

Index

See also Table of Cases, which lists the cases discussed in the book in each chapter in the order of their discussion, starting on page *xv*.

Death and dying:
    living will, 59, 269–273
    murder, 105, 195–196, 198
    suicide, 201–203
    wrongful death, 75–76
Defendant. *See* Nurse as defendant in civil
    litigation
Delaware, 115, 143
Disabilities, 132–135, 164–165
Disciplinary process, 23–27, 37–40, 41
Discrimination, 131–136, 142–144, 182–185
District of Columbia, 14, 115, 140, 143
    Barbara Woods v. *D.C. Nurses' Examining
      Board*, 35–36
    District of Columbia v. *Jane Doe et al*, 167
    Nurse Practice Act (NPA), 11
Documentation:
    cases in civil litigation, 64–66
    of isolation and restraints, 107
Drug violations, 113–115, 153, 246
Dual persona doctrine, 127–128
Due process, 2, 35, 96
    in administrative procedures act (APA), 35
    fifth amendment due process rights, 96
    fourteenth amendment rights, 96
    procedural due process, 96
    substantive due process, 96

E
Education, 11, 19, 21–22, 31, 47–49, 163–174
    See also Continuing competency; Nurse
      practicing as educator
Emergency Medical Treatment and Active
    Labor Act (EMTALA), 7
Emotional distress claims, 78–79
Employee, nurse practicing as, 119–148
    See also Nurse as employee
Endorsement. *See* Licensure
Ethical components of nursing practice, 255–263
    autonomy, 256
    beneficence, 256
    Code of Ethics for Nurses, 255, 259–261, 262
    comparing and contrasting laws and ethics,
      255–259
    confidentiality, 47–49, 224–226
    ethical dilemmas, 256–257
    ethical issues confronting nurses, 261–263
    ethical principles, 256
    nonmaleficence, 256

    nurse professional practice legal/ethical
      actions, 257
    respect for others, 256
    veracity, 256
    Warthen v. *Toms River Community Hospital*,
      258–259, 260, 261
    See also Confidentiality

F
Fair Health Information Protection Act of 1994, 46
False imprisonment, 77–78, 107
Federal law, 3–4, 5
    circuit courts, 4, 5
    federal court system, 4, 5
    protecting employees, 131–140
    pursuing health-related claims, 7, 8
    U.S. Constitution, 3, 4, 5
Federal Privacy Act of 1974, 46
Felonies, 104
Florida, 115, 140, 143, 145, 185
    independent contractor cases, 159
    John v. *Department of Professional Regulation*,
      19
    Kirkland v. *State Department of Health*, 205
    O'Connor v. *Donaldson*, 207
Foreign nurses, application for licensure, 19
Fraud and abuse, 108–112, 117, 189–190

G
Georgia, 14, 47, 114, 140, 143, 217, 238
    Ahrens v. *Katz*, 65–66
    Brooks v. *Coliseum Park Hospital, Inc.*, 205
    computer invasion of privacy, 47
    Deese v. *Carol City County Hospital*, 68
Good Samaritan Acts, 80
Governmental immunity, 141, 176–177
Guam, 11, 14, 114

H
Hawaii, 42, 115, 123, 131, 140, 143
Health Care Financing Administration (HCFA):
    actions that can result in sanction by, 275–278
    advanced practice nurses and, 252
    health care fraud, 108–112
    site of care, 42
Health care professional, defined, 14
    See also Nurse as credentialed health care
      provider; Nurse as regulated health care
      professional

Health Care Quality Improvement Act
(HCQIA), 247
Health Insurance Portability and
Accountability Act (HIPAA), 47, 188–
189, 194

I

Idaho, 42, 115, 143
  Brooks v. *Logan,* 168
  Sparks v. *St. Lukes Regional Medical Center,*
    68–69
  Tuma v. *Board of Nursing of the State of Idaho,*
    38
Illinois, 19, 115, 123, 131, 140, 143
  Alvis v. *Henderson,* 57–58
  Chiricosta v. *Winthrop-Breon, et al,* 69
  Court of Appeals, 19–20
  John v. *Department of Professional Regulation,*
    19
  Northern Trust Co. v. *Louis A. Weiss Memorial*
    Hospital, 69
Immunity, 140–141, 176–177
Independent contractors, 119, 122–123, 149–
  162
  See also Nurse as independent contractor
Indiana, 105, 115, 143
Insanity defense, 98
Intellectual property issues, 21, 169–71
Intent, levels of, 98
Intentional indifference, claims of, 79
Iowa, 20, 42, 115, 140, 143

J

Juries, 89–91

K

Kansas, 115, 143
  Hesler v. *Osawatomie,* 207–208
  State v. *Lora,* 112
Kennedy, Edward, 139
Kentucky, 42, 47, 115, 143, 185
  NKC Hospitals, Inc. v.*Anthony,* 67–68

L

Larceny, 107
Last clear chance doctrine, 81
Legal cases discussed in book, xv–xxi
Liability, 15, 98, 180
Libel, 77
Licensed nurse, 21

Licensed Practical/Vocational Nurse (LPN/
  LVN):
  definition and description in NPA, 14
  protection of term, title and abbreviations,
    21
Licensed professional nurse, 21
License/licensure, 14–15
  ANA guidelines concerning mutual recog-
    nition, 42–43, 265–267
  BONs and, 12, 18–21, 27–28, 41–42
  eligibility criteria for application to licen-
    sure, 19
  by endorsement, 18, 19
  initial licensure requirements, 18–20
  licensees, 15, 20–21
  multistate licensure trends, 40–43
  mutual recognition, 40–42
  national licensure examination, 18, 19–20
  rapid endorsement provision, 42
  reinstatement and renewal, 20
  suspension or revocation, 27
  See also Nurse as regulated health care
    professional
Living wills, 59, 269–273
Loss of chance doctrine, 79–80
Loss of consortium, 78, 125
Louisiana, 14, 20, 115, 143
  Aron D. Hemphill v. *Louisiana State Board of*
    Nursing, 6
  Daniel v. *St. Francis Cabrini Hospital of*
    Alexandria, 56
  Gordon v. *Willis Knighton Medical Center,*
    61–62
  Kimball v. *St. Paul Ins. Co.,* 56
  McClain v. *Glenwood Regional Medical*
    Center, 69
  Odom v. *State Department of Health and*
    Hospital, 62
  Parker v. *Southwest Louisiana Hospital Asso-*
    ciation, 70–71
  Pellerin v. *Humedicenters, Inc.,* 62
  Samuels v. *Southern Baptist Hospital, et al,*
    112–113
  Vallery v. *Southern Baptist Hospital,* 125

M

Magnet Nursing Services Recognition Program,
  138, 243, 244–245
Maine, 115, 140, 143
Malpractice, 7, 74

Malpractice insurance, 38
Managed care, 108, 215–240, xi-xii
   See also Nurse as case manager
Mandatory overtime, 49, 123, 144
Manslaughter, 105–106
Maryland, 20, 42, 114, 115, 140, 143
   Barbara Woods v. *D. C. Nurses' Examining
      Board,* 35–36
   gender discrimination/parental leave case,
      138
   President and Directors of Georgetown College
      v. *Hughes,* 176
Massachusetts, 115, 140, 145, 186
   Dana-Farber Cancer Institute and scope of
      practice case, 49
   Darian v. *University of Massachusetts,* 165
Medicaid, 108, 159, 189
Medical Records Confidentiality Act of 1995,
   46
Medicare, 108–109, 117, 150, 159, 187, 189
Mental illness, 98, 200–203
   See also Nurse as counselor
Michigan, 115, 140, 143
   Boretti v. *Wiscomb,* 64
   Hyde v. *University of Michigan Board of
      Regents,* 177
   Warren v. *Caro Community Hospital,* 142
Minnesota, 115, 140, 143, 185
   Mercil v. *Mathers,* 56
Miranda warning, 97, 99–100, 102
Misdemeanors, 104
Mississippi, 30, 42, 114, 115, 143
   Coleman v. *Rice,* 180
   Hogan v. *Mississippi Board of Nursing,* 30
   Jones v. *Baptist Memorial Hospital-Golden,* 177
   Mississippi University for Women v. *Hogan,* 2
Missouri, 115, 140, 143, 217, 238
   Downey v. *Mitchell,* 56
   Honey v. *Barnes Hospital, et al,* 201
   independent contractor case, 159
   Kirk v. *Mercy Hospital Tri-County,* 121–122
Model practice acts (MPAs), 11, 33–34, x
   on board composition, powers and respon-
      sibilities, 16–18
   on title, term, and abbreviation protection, 21
Modern Healthcare, 107, 117, 139, 245
Montana, 20, 45, 115, 143
   Blythe v. *Radiometer American Inc.,
      Community Medical Center, and Michael
      Biggins,* 125

Moore, J. Duncan, Jr., 245
MPAs. *See* Model practice acts
Murder, 105, 195–196, 198
Mutual recognition, 42–43, 265–267

N
Narcotics violations, 113–115
National Council Licensure Exam (NCLEX), 19
National Council of State Boards of Nursing
   (NCSBN):
   board composition, powers and responsi-
      bilities, 16, 17–18
   chemical dependence issues, 29
   continued competency position, 47
   evaluative criteria used by, 41
   licensee responsibilities, 20
   Model Practice Acts (MPAs), 11, 33–34
   on multistate licensure, 40–42
   NPA violations recommendations, 22, 26
   reporting obligations, 28
   requirements for APRNs, 13, 14
   severability clause, 32
National League for Nursing (NLN), 242
Nebraska, 42, 115, 140, 143
   Hazel Scott v. *The Board of Nursing of the
      State of Nebraska,* 21
   Miles v. *Box Butte County,* 63
   Scott, Hazel v. *The Board of Nursing of
      Nebraska,* 21
   Skar v. *City of Lincoln,* 81, 82–83
Needlestick Safety and Prevention Act, 139–140
Needlesticks and sharps injuries, 124–128
Negligence, 7, 38, 54–73, 92, 204–208
   assessment failures, 57–59
   breach, 68–69
   causation, 71
   contributory and comparative, 81–83
   corporate, 177–179
   damages, 72–73
   defamation, 76–77
   discharge and release, 206–208
   duty, 54–57
   implementation failures, 61
   malpractice, 74–75
   negligent hiring, 182–184
   NPAs and, 69–70
   patient supervision, 204–206
   planning failures, 59–60
   practice standards, 70
   wrongful birth and death, 74–76

Nurse as defendant in civil litigation (*continued*)

Mathias v. *St. Catherine's Hospital, Inc.*, 56

McClain v. *Glenwood Regional Medical Center*, 69

McMullen v. *Ohio State University Hospitals*, 71–72

Mercil v. *Mather*, 56

Meuser v. *Rocky Mountain Hospital*, 77

Miles v. *Box Butte County*, 63

negligence, 54–73, 92

negligence per se, 73

negligent emotional distress, 78

NKC Hospitals, Inc. v. *Anthony*, 67–68

Northern Trust Co. v. *Louis A. Weiss Memorial Hospital*, 69

nurse-patient relationship, 55

Nurse Practice Acts (NPAs), 69–70

Odom v. *State Department of Health and Hospital*, 62

opening statements, 89

Parker v. *Southwest Louisiana Hospital Association*, 70–71

patient advocate case, 67–68

patient privacy case, 66–67

Pellerin v. *Humedicenters, Inc.*, 62

plaintiff files petition/complaint, 84

plaintiff's case, 90

planning-related failures, 57, 59–60

policies, procedures, protocols, and pathways, 70–71

Porter v. *Lima Memorial Hospital*, 55–56

pre-trial conference, 88–89

professional negligence and causation, 71–72

professional practice standards, 70

reasonable care, 57

requests for admission, 87, 88

requests for production, 86–87

respectable minority exception, 80

Reynolds v. *Swigert*, 75–76

Sandejar v. *Alice Physicians and Surgeons Hospital*, 81–82

scope of practice, 69–70

Scribner v. *Hillcrest Medical Center*, 64–65

self-determination, 59, 269–273

Skar v. *City of Lincoln*, 81, 82–83

Smith v. *Cote*, 75

Sparks v. *St. Lukes Regional Medical Center*, 68–69

statute of limitations, 83–84

timely communication of patient findings, 60–61

trial, 89–91

Vassey v. *Burch*, 57

verdict, 91

Vidana v. *Garfield Medical Center*, 60

witnesses, 90

wrongful birth, 74–75

wrongful death, 75–76

Nurse as educator, 163–174

Brooks v. *Logan*, 168

Carter v. *Anderson Memorial Hospital*, 168–169

catalogs, 163–164

clinical experiences, 168–169

Copyright Act of 1976, 170–171

Darian v. *University of Massachusetts*, 165

dismissing students, 166–167

District of Columbia v. *Jane Doe et al*, 167

Falvo v. *Owasso Independent School District, No. I-011, et al*, 172, 173

Family Educational Rights and Privacy Act (FERPA), 172–173

Gasper v. *Bruton*, 168

intellectual property issues, 169–171

Lidecker v. *Kendall College*, 163, 164

Morin v. *Cleveland Metropolitan General Hospital School of Nursing*, 166

Patent Act of 1994, 169

privacy of academic records, 172–173

providing students a safe environment, 167

School of Nursing, et al v. *Joy Ann Babb*, 163, 164

students with disabilities, 164–165

trademark and service mark, 170

University of Texas Health Science Center at Houston, 163, 164

warning third parties, 168

Nurse as employee, 119–148

abandonment, 119–121, 123

Age Discrimination in Employment Act (ADEA), 131–132

Americans with Disabilities Act (ADA), 132–135

ANA Principles for Nurse Staffing, 130

Bivens v. *State of Oklahoma*, 141

Blythe v. *Radiometer America Inc., Community Medical Center, and Michael Biggins*, 125

bona fide occupational qualification (BFOQ), 135

State nurses associations (SNAs), 42, 43, 140
Statute of limitations, 83–84
Suicidal behavior, 201–203

T
Telehealth, 43–46
Tennessee, 115, 140, 143
    Special Worker's Compensation Appeals
      Panel of the Tennessee Supreme Court,
      126
    Stout v. *Johnston City Medical Center Hospital,*
      126
Texas, 14, 28, 42, 115, 131, 140, 143, 217, 238
    Bigtown Nursing Home v. *Newman,* 78
    Board of Vocational Nurse Examiners
      (BVNE), 131
    Hatley v. *Kassen,* 202–203
    Lunsford v. *Board of Examiners,* 54–55
    Page v. *Goodman-Wade Enterprises, Inc.,*
      186–187
    peer review in NPA, 28–29
    Sandejar v. *Alice Physicians and Surgeons
      Hospital,* 81–82
    Texas Board of Nursing Examiners, 28
    Texas Nurse Practice Act, 186
    Texas Peer Assistance Program for Nurses,
      28, 29
    *University of Texas Health Science Center at
      Houston,* 163, 164
    whistleblower protection, 185, 186
Title VII of the Civil Rights Act 1964, 135, 142
Trial, 89–91, 102–103
Trial courts, 7

U
Uniform Health-Care Information Act of 1988,
    46
Unprofessional conduct, defined, 38
U.S. Constitution:
    Article 1: Congressional Powers, 3
    Article 2: Presidential Powers, 3, 4
    Article 3: U.S. Supreme Court Powers, 3, 4,
      5
    Bill of Rights, 1
U.S. Department of Labor, 137

U.S. legal system, 1–9
    Bill of Rights, 1
    circuit courts, 4, 5
    equal protection, 2
    federal court system, 4, 5
    federal law, 3–4, 5
    procedural due process rights, 2
    pursuing health-care related claims, 7, 8
    state law, 6–7
    substantive due process, 2
    U.S. Constitution, 1–4, 5
U.S. Supreme Court:
    Miranda v. *Arizona,* 100
    pathways to, 7, 8
    Roberts v. *Galen of Virginia, Inc.,* 7
Utah, 42, 115, 140, 143, 185

V
Vermont, 115, 143
Violations and penalties, detailed in an NPA,
    22–23, 28
    case management agreement, 221–222
Violence *See* Assault and battery; Murder;
    Suicide; Workplace violence
Virginia, 12, 115, 143
    Roberts v. *Galen of Virginia, Inc.,* 7
Virgin Islands, 11, 115
Vocational nurse, 21

W
Washington, 20, 42, 114, 115, 140, 143, 185
    Lewis v. *Long View School District No. 122,*
      203
Washington, D.C. *See* District of Columbia
West Virginia, 14, 20, 115, 131, 140, 143
Whistleblower protection, 7, 49, 130–131,
    185–186
Whistleblower Protection Act, 185
Wisconsin, 42, 115, 140, 143
    Sawyer v. *Midelfort,* 209–210
Workplace violence, 144–145
Wrongful birth, 74–75
Wrongful death, 75–76, 196
Wyoming, 115
    Slagle v. *Wyoming State Board of Nursing,* 40